Black Heritage Sites
THE NORTH

Also by Nancy C. Curtis, Ph.D.

**Black Heritage Sites:
The South**

Black Heritage Sites

The North

Nancy C. Curtis, Ph.D.

The New Press / New York

Library of Congress Cataloging-in-Publication Data

Curtis, Nancy C.
    Black Heritage Sites: The North / Nancy C. Curtis.
        p.   cm.
  Includes index.
    1. Historic sites—United States—Directories.
  2. Afro-Americans—History. I. Title.
E159.C65   1996
973.0496073—dc20   95-5788

Published in the United States by The New Press, New York
Distributed by W. W. Norton, New York

The New Press was established in 1990 as a not-for-profit alternative
to the large, commercial publishing houses currently dominating
the book publishing industry. The New Press operates in the public
interest rather than for private gain, and is committed to publishing,
in innovative ways, works of educational, cultural, and community
value that might not be considered sufficiently profitable.

Printed in the United States of America

9 8 7 6 5 4 3 2 1

Contents

The States 21

Preface

My father's mother, Martha Chevis, was born before the Civil War in rural, nineteenth-century Kentucky. Martha, who probably was born in slavery, lived in Bourbon County, Kentucky. My father, who died when I was twelve years old, never talked about his childhood, his mother, or his other ancestors. His reluctance to talk about his family history was typical of all of the adults whom I knew when I was growing up—my adult relatives and my parents' friends never talked in my presence about their family heritage, their childhood experiences, or their genealogy.

In home and at church we learned about outstanding Black Americans—Carter G. Woodson, Marian Anderson, George Washington Carver, Mary McLeod Bethune, Paul Robeson, A. Philip Randolph—and we took pride in their achievements. In contrast, personal family histories were shrouded in secrecy. The adults I knew believed that stories about the past dredged up harsh memories of slavery and the decades that followed—the hard times, the racial hatreds, the lynchings and other outrages against individuals, the shame, and the bitter experiences that they believed were best forgotten. They wanted to shield the young from these hard memories because they felt the burden of those memories should not be carried forth as impedimenta into the future. They wanted to provide us with a fresh slate because they were optimistic that the future would be better.

When Alex Haley published *Roots* and thousands of families saw the video drama that followed, our family watched, too. Haley's story stirred old memories and impelled the asking anew of old questions. Families that previously had been silent about their heritage began to talk about the subject. As my mother told the stories that started with my great-grandmothers, the panorama of my family history began to unfold. Years later I traveled to Kentucky, where I first gleaned bits of information about my father's family. I spoke with a Black woman, Mrs. Mary Reeves, who had seen "Aunt Martha," as she called my grandmother, through the eyes of a small child. My grandmother was tall and slender, she said; her brown skin was touched with a reddish hue, and she had a friendly smile as she spoke to children who passed by each morning on their way to school. They always saw her standing on her porch, early, hanging up items she had laundered and ironed for white families in her town.

From a visit to the Bourbon County Courthouse, I gathered a little more information. By the time she was twenty-three, or even before, Martha was married. At twenty-three she could not read or write. Although her parents were born in Kentucky, both of her maternal grandparents (my great-great-grandparents) were born in Virginia. Her paternal grandmother was born in Virginia, and her paternal grandfather (my great-great- grandfather) was born in Africa.

After traveling west across the rolling green hills of the Western Kentucky Parkway, I sat in the Todd County Courthouse and began to learn about my maternal great-grandmothers, Ann and Alice, who were born in slavery. I found Alice's name in a large will book in the courthouse. She was regarded as property to be transferred as her owner wished. When she was a young child, her master had willed her to be a servant to his young daughter. Fortunately for Alice, the Civil War ended four years after the will was written. Although she later experienced other sorrows, she and other African Americans no longer were forced to serve as slaves.

After learning about Alice, I began to hunger for some visible evidence of my ancestors' existence. I wanted to see some of the places they had lived or at least places that resembled those they had known. Ann and Alice had remained in southwestern Kentucky after emancipation. Their children, along with other African Americans, owned and tilled rich farmland in Todd County. Decades ago the farms were sold. When I visited the family's former land for the first time in 1988, only one of the family houses, built around 1916, remained. The schoolhouse where my grandfather and his brother-in-law taught part-time was no longer standing. Their original church was demolished long ago and replaced by a more modern building. My grandfather sold his farm and moved his family from their rural Todd County farm to Hopkinsville, Kentucky, when my mother was entering third grade—my grandparents believed their children could get a better education in the city. Although my grandfather died before I was born, I visited my grandparents' house in Hopkinsville at the ages of four and six and never forgot how the house looked. The gray, frame, two-story house was located midway up a sloping hill. The long, wide, gracious porch had a comfortable swing. On one visit my brother and I sat on the porch floor cradling a quartet of wiggling puppies in our laps. Grandma's house had cool rooms with muted light and a wide lawn in back punctuated with grapevines and a tall walnut tree. One day when we were standing under the tree, a walnut fell on my brother's head, sending us into endless gales of laughter. There were chickens, too, that we very often fed handfuls of grain.

In 1988 I returned to Hopkinsville with a camera, seeking to record the bit of history that I remembered so well, but my grandmother's house had been torn down. No family member had a photograph of the house. The feeling of loss led me to wonder again what kinds of houses my great-grandparents had lived in before emancipation and after freedom. How did other Black families live in slavery? Did examples of their houses still stand? What did their schools, their churches, and the stores where they bought goods look like? The search for my family tree had opened up a flood of wishing and wanting for some visual record, something to show me some of the things that I had learned in words. The work of this book had begun.

The search for structures associated with Black history began with the mailing of more than five hundred letters to national, state, and local historical associations and museums in the United States, to every historically Black college in the country that I could identify, to Black history departments in colleges nationwide, and to other historic sites across the coun-

try. The search, designed to be as comprehensive as possible, included a review of manuscripts, books, and articles about Black history and about historic sites in America. The questionnaires began to return, many with references to additional sites or to other knowledgeable individuals. The highlight of the search, however, came with my own personal visits to towns throughout Michigan, Indiana, Kentucky, Ohio, California, Oklahoma, Tennessee, Louisiana, Mississippi, Alabama, Georgia, South Carolina, North Carolina, Virginia, and Canada—to see and photograph many of the sites for myself. Seeing the history was a moving experience, as those who take the journey will learn for themselves; it gave a connection with the past that could have been obtained in no other way.

As the manuscript took shape, it included homes, schools and colleges, churches, commercial buildings, cemeteries, and monuments. By publication time almost half of the sites had to be deleted—some because too little information was available, others because of space limitations. Those that remained provided a comprehensive view of a wide range of Black American structures built primarily from the last half of the nineteenth century through the first half of the twentieth century. They included some surprises—I learned for the first time about the iron furnaces where Black slaves labored in Pennsylvania and about the religious campgrounds in North Carolina where Black families had gone after harvest time each year for more than one hundred years. With the exception of some museums, most of the structures included are at least fifty years old. Some buildings were associated with famous African Americans; others belonged to people whose names may be forgotten but who struggled, fought, sacrificed, protested, and marched to attain freedom and advance or who simply lived their lives in dignity, providing as best they could for their children and the well-being of their communities. This book honors the humble as well as the famous.

Tragically, many buildings from the Black heritage already have been lost. As the project was ending, I spent months making personal telephone calls to many of the sites. The calls garnered unexpected information about the status of Black historic sites across the country. While some of the sites have been restored and are well-maintained and cared for, in too many instances sites have been lost to neglect, abandonment, vandalism, or demolition by urban renewal projects, many of which had no direct benefit to Black communities. Urban renewal projects often demolished close-knit neighborhoods to make way for gleaming new office buildings or to make space for highways that cut through Black communities to rush white commuters home to the suburbs. After wholesale demolition, which was promulgated as eliminating slums, Black residents often were crowded into high-density housing that confined large numbers of minorities to one geographic area of town. Black historic sites were demolished to provide land for shopping centers, for expansion of predominantly white college campuses, or simply to provide parking space for downtown buildings. As I made calls across the country, I listened to people who grieved about the loss of their historic sites and who felt they had no choice in the taking of their buildings. To be fair, it should be stated that many other sites were lost because Black people themselves, enchanted by the new vistas opened up by desegregation, left the old parts of town as fast as they could and never looked back. Unfortunately, as they moved away to newer parts of town and to the suburbs, many interesting older buildings, even some designated as historic, fell vacant and were destroyed. In the mid-1990s some of the most precious of historic sites, the irreplaceable Black colleges and universities, were on the verge of closing for lack of financial support.

Counterbalancing the losses, however, were shining examples of communities working diligently to preserve and restore their historic buildings. The task, never easy and rarely inexpensive, was accomplished in several ways, and it can be accomplished in other communities if citizens work together. Many routes are available to historic preservation. For example, volunteer groups can write grants or sponsor fund-raising events for restoring one-by-one the historic buildings in their communities. Fraternities and sororities can adopt a local historic site, working with senior citizens and other groups to rejuvenate it. Architects and historians can ensure that restoration is done in

harmony with the historic era in which the structures were built. School classes, or even an entire school, may wish to adopt a site, clearing overgrown brush and creating historically harmonious gardens. Community groups can purchase informative plaques for sites in towns where few signposts exist to guide visitors and tell the history of the structures. The homeless people who advertise that they will work for food may be willing to clean up the sites, help with painting and carpentry tasks, and perform interior decorating jobs for food and a modest wage. Some historic sites have been abandoned but are structurally sound. If they could be cleaned up and made habitable according to local codes and insurance regulations, a responsible couple in need of shelter might be happy to live in the house, to help to rehabilitate it, and to show the house to visitors two or three days a week in exchange for low rent. Donations from visitors could assist with upkeep of the houses. Articles in local papers can draw visitors to the houses and attract possible donors who wish to see these areas make a comeback.

In many cases old schoolhouses, closed after 1954 desegregation laws were passed, could be turned into community centers and filled with interesting activities for youth and the elderly. Where organizations already exist to provide programs for youth, they may be willing to lease the houses as extension sites. There are several examples in this book of former schools that have been transformed into community centers or into office space for multiracial community programs—read about the Booker T. Washington School in Rushville, Indiana; the Pleasant Plains Rosenwald School in Ahoskie, North Carolina; the McCray School in Burlington, North Carolina; the East End School in Harveysburg, Ohio; the Sumner School in Washington, D.C.; the Ferry Street School in Niles, Michigan; and the Limerick Historic District's Central Colored School in Louisville, Kentucky. Communities also have restored buildings and have sold or rented them to caring organizations. For example, read about the Jewell Building in Omaha, Nebraska; Fisk Chapel of the African Methodist Episcopal Bethel Church in Fair Haven, New Jersey, now a community center; the African Meeting House in Boston, now a museum; the early Frederick Douglass Home in Washington, D.C., now the home of the Caring Institute; the Whitelaw Hotel in Washington, D.C.; the Dunbar (Somerville) Hotel in Los Angeles, California; the Orchard Street United Methodist Church, restored as a museum and now home of the Baltimore, Maryland, Urban League; and the Avalon Hotel in Rochester, Minnesota, now the Hamilton Music Company. This book describes other examples of sites that have been restored. Each new historic site does not detract from the others but adds to the attractiveness of the entire area. Families that take the time to travel to see a historic site probably would enjoy the trip even more if they could see several sites in the same area.

This introduction closes with a caveat or caution—in the mid- to late 1990s, social conditions have changed in a way that has made many homeowners and renters more cautious about strangers who appear to be inspecting or photographing their property. In the early 1990s I spent months visiting sites, almost always in the oldest sections of cities and towns, and, with few exceptions, was met with friendliness. Today, a few

years later, visitors need to be cautious and careful not to trespass on private property, to keep a respectful distance from private homes, and to explain their interest if people ask why their property is being inspected. I remember being amazed when two young ladies walked onto the porch of a private home across from Dr. Martin Luther King Jr.'s birthplace in Atlanta, Georgia, and peered at length into the living room window. Such behavior could create a very stressful conflict today. If the text notes that a site is private and the interior is not accessible to the public, drive or walk by *but do not go onto the property unless invited to do so*. If visitors are respectful, most tenants will appreciate the public's recognition of the value of their property.

If our Black historic sites (and they belong to all Americans) are not saved, a precious part of our history will be lost to future generations. This book will have served its purpose if it encourages armchair travelers as well as travelers who actually visit the sites to appreciate and treasure this part of our country's heritage and to renew their connections with this history that we share.

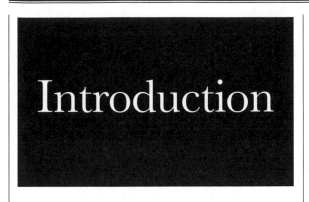

Introduction

In 1619 sixteen Africans who had been captured from a Spanish ship were brought to Virginia on a Dutch warship. The Africans, the first of their race recorded in the English colonies, may have been brought in as indentured servants rather than as slaves to be bound for a lifetime. Their arrival in Jamestown set in motion a series of events that would result in centuries of bondage for an estimated 11 million sons and daughters wrested from the African homeland.

Although some scholars date African American history from that fateful arrival in the colonies, those who arrived on Virginia's shores in 1619 were not the first Africans to come to the Americas. Ivan Van Sertima, professor at Rutgers University, has provided evidence that large African sculptures and pyramids in Mexico and Central America show the influence of African civilizations long before the seventeenth century. The huge African sculptures, called the Olmec Heads, show African influences in the Americas as early as c800 to c400 B.C.E.[1] Ancient statues with African features still stand at La Vanta, Mexico. In addition to the facial features, the sculptures show cultural items—tattoos, earrings, and helmets—associated with Africa. Van Sertima, in his book *They Came before Columbus*, gives additional evidence of contact between Africa and the New World long before Columbus ``discovered'' America.

Other Africans visited the Americas long before the arrival of the Jamestown sixteen. They came as skilled sailors, soldiers, and servants who accompanied Spanish explorers. One of the early explorers, Estevan de Dorantes (Estevanico), was the first African known to have entered the land that is now the United States of America. He was born near the Moroccan coast of Africa. The conquistador Andres Dorantes de Carranca purchased Estevanico to be his servant, and in 1527 the two men traveled together in a six-hundred-person expedition to the Americas. After facing hurricanes, disease, and attacks by Indians in Florida, Estevanico and four other men spent six years as captives of the Indians.

The arrival of the African men and women in Jamestown represented the beginning, in the colonies, of a way of life that would become associated with the wholesale buying and selling of human beings for use as slaves. The Africans who were brought to the colonies in 1619 and those who came later on slave ships did not arrive devoid of a cultural heritage. They came from a continent immense in size, many from civilizations that had excelled in literature, sciences, the arts, and agriculture. Africans had worked as skilled teachers, artisans, oral historians of their tribes, miners, ironworkers, and agronomists. The men and women brought to America in chains came primarily from West African communities that for centuries had evolved stable traditions and patterns of kinship. They had developed religious, political, and legal systems complex and sophisticated enough to maintain order and viability amid the vicissitudes of daily life. Their continent was one of the world's most bountiful in agricultural and mineral resources.

The advent of the slave trade disrupted the natural growth and evolution of African societies. The European interlopers with their superior weapons, trickery, and deceit seized power and then carved up the continent for themselves. With the collusion of some African leaders, themselves consumed by greed, the Europeans drained the country of both material and human resources.

The Atlantic slave trade that began on a small scale grew in scope following the events that brought the first Africans to Jamestown. The same slave trade also initiated a centuries-long quest for freedom that started with rebellions on the slave ships and moved in an unending line to the slave rebellions of Gabriel Prosser, Nat Turner, and Denmark Vesey; to the search for freedom through the deep woods, guided by the shining North Star; through the escape by plunging into the swamps of Florida where the Seminoles lived and fighting with them in the Seminole Wars; to the search for freedom through fighting in the War for Independence, the War of 1812, and the Civil War; to the marches and demonstrations of the twentieth-century civil rights movements—all part of a protracted, determined, and magnificent intent to escape from bondage and to be treated with dignity as human beings. The quest of the Africans eventually impelled the country to redefine the meaning and scope of natural and national laws, rights, and privileges, and it illuminated the meaning of humanity, human worth, and freedom throughout the world.

Wherever circumstances permitted, and in spite of powerful barriers, African Americans established themselves as leaders and active participants in this struggle. The tangible symbols of their fight for freedom are the sites and structures described in this book. Many African Americans who sought freedom and equality from the seventeenth through the early twentieth centuries stayed in or near the underground railroad structures described here. Others lived in the slave cabins, shotgun houses, cottages, and spacious dwellings shown in these pages. They bought and sold goods and developed professional practices in commercial buildings ranging from small, frame buildings to substantial, multistory structures.

After emancipation their children attended school in churches, in one-room schoolhouses, in the Rosenwald schools that replaced the crowded and dilapidated old schoolhouses, and in some larger schools that, though segregated, were architecturally distinguished. Using their own resources and assisted by the American Missionary Association and philanthropists, African Americans developed a system of quality colleges unmatched in number by any other ethnic minority group in America. Fisk University, Howard University, Hampton University, Morehouse College, Spelman College, and Tuskegee University are but a few of the distinguished institutions of higher education that enrolled many of the nation's future leaders.

From the Revolutionary War period on, the African Americans established their own churches. There the congregations met not only their spiritual

needs but also the needs of the community by sheltering fugitive slaves, by helping newcomers to communities, and, later, through leading demonstrations and boycotts that led to enfranchisement and the right to participate in decision-making processes.

Scope and Organization

Black Heritage Sites: An African American Odyssey and Finder's Guide describes a wide variety of historic African American sites. Some are in fine condition; others show signs of neglect. Many sites are in the oldest parts of town or in rural areas, to be found most easily with maps or by telephone calls to local chambers of commerce or city halls. Some sites are designated as state or national historic sites and have regular visiting hours; others are private and may be viewed from the exterior only. While exterior viewing may not be as satisfying as interior tours, the exteriors, even when they are in less-than-ideal condition, still radiate a sense of history and place and resonate with the lives of their former inhabitants.

This book is divided into five regions: South, Northeast, Midwest, Southwest, and West and Noncontiguous States. A few sites in Canada are included as special features following the Detroit, Michigan, sites because they are a short trip from Detroit and because the hospitality of many Canadians created an inviting setting for establishing the northernmost terminus of the underground railroad. Many fugitives settled there in peace, and many of their descendants still live in Canada today.

Each section of this book is introduced with a brief description of the states in that region and highlights of the types of structures a visitor might see—churches, schools, dwellings, commercial buildings, battlefields, cemeteries, and monuments. By using the table of contents, visitors can explore by geographic region or, by using the index, by type of structure or by theme. For example, one family, heading south for a family reunion, may wish to explore all of the Black heritage sites in the reunion area. Another group may wish to explore sites in several states associated with the Civil Rights Movement of the 1950s and 1960s. Another family may wish to drive through several states, visiting the homes or birthplaces of famous Black leaders. Groups may organize to travel anew over old underground railroad routes that wind through several states. Teachers may take their students on a tour of historic African American schoolhouses. The index will prove helpful to families or schools that are arranging geographical or theme tours.

Certain conventions are used throughout this book. For example, headings for sites of national significance are followed by an asterisk (*). These sites are important because of their association with a nationally known leader or because of their association with a civil rights, educational, or social movement of national significance. Other sites are highlighted with an asterisk because the structure at the site is architecturally unique and shows an important aspect of African American life. Over time the names of some sites have changed. The site name given is the name with historical significance to the African American heritage. Sites that would be of interest to children are indicated by 🎎 following the visiting-hours information.

In addition, shortened forms of print and computer sources are given after sites; more complete bibliographic citations are in a list of works consulted at the end of each state. Site sources include books, journals, newspaper articles, site brochures and fliers, research manuscripts, dissertations, and information compiled from more than 500 questionnaires and 700 telephone calls and numerous personal visits.

Two sources frequently used were the National Register of Historic Places Inventory Nomination Form (NRHPINF) and the National Register of Historic Places Registration Form (NRHPRF). Although these forms were widely used, consistent attempts were made to update the information through telephone calls and through written information from other sources. The National Register forms, compiled by different individuals or groups, describe the location, architectural style and date of construction, historical significance, and bibliographic references for thousands of individual sites. The NRH-PRF certifies that the property has been accepted in the National Register. In the 1970s information was compiled and published in summary form in a book

titled *The National Register of Historic Places*. However, the information became too voluminous to be published as a whole in book form; therefore, the entire listing currently is accessible through computer listings through the National Register Information System or by accessing the individual nomination or registration forms. Site listings may be obtained for a copying fee from the individual states. Limitations of staff time in the state offices may determine the staff's ability to respond.

The National Register forms are used by various individuals or groups to obtain information about houses, schools, commercial buildings, battle sites, and other places of historical significance in the fifty United States as well as in American Samoa, the Federated States of Micronesia, Guam, the Republic of the Marshall Islands, the Commonwealth of the Northern Mariana Islands, the Republic of Palau, the Commonwealth of Puerto Rico, and the Virgin Islands. A list of the State Historic Preservation Officers may be obtained from the Department of the Interior, National Park Service, Preservation Assistance Division, Grants Administration Branch, P.O. Box 37127, Washington, DC 20013-7127.

Visiting hours and fees were verified by telephone calls; however, such information may change from the time of this printing. The information included in this book is the best and the latest that I could gather before publication, but I strongly recommend that visitors call each site in advance to obtain the latest visiting information.

Acknowledgments

This book could not have been written without the help of countless individuals who were generous in sharing valuable information. Members of state, county, and city historic associations, individual site administrators, librarians, church officers, business leaders, and community residents responded with information about sites and geographic locations. Many guided me to other individuals who had valuable information. State historic preservation officers were generous in taking the time to send written information, and when I prepared to visit and photograph sites, they answered my questions about travel conditions in their states and helped me select the sites that would be most visually interesting to photograph.

Hundreds of individuals spoke with me by telephone, providing updated visiting information and, equally important, providing personal viewpoints and historical data about the sites that could have been obtained in no other way.

Several skilled editors—Bonnie Smothers, Robert Cunningham, and Joan Grygel—made the book a better one in several ways. They gave helpful suggestions about including or deleting individual sites according to their significance in Black history, uniqueness of architecture, or accessibility. The extensive pruning was difficult at times because many interesting sites had to be left out, but the deletions made the work more consistent in quality and focus. The editors clarified sentences and paragraphs, checked for consistency, and improved the flow of the words. I am grateful for their considerable help in these areas. Material gathered from many sources showed occa-sional inconsistencies in dates, in spelling of names, or in other factual information. The editors and I searched for such inconsistencies, but responsibility is my own if any inadvertently were overlooked.

The preparing of this work took longer than expected due to the need to gather additional data to round out the description of certain sites and the need to make personal contacts to verify and update information. I am grateful to my mother, Dorothy A. Curtis, and to my brother, George Russell Curtis, and his wife, Betty, for their unfailing assistance and encouragement through these years of compiling information, writing the text, and verifying information. They never wavered in their belief that this specific story about Black historic sites needed to be told; their assurances sustained me every step of the way.

Note

1.   Ivan Van Sertima, *They Came Before Columbus, The African Presence in Ancient America* (New York: Random House, 1976).

The Northeast

The experiences of African Americans in the South and their experiences in the Northeast had both parallels and differences. First, slavery and segregation were legal and were practiced in both regions. Although far more extensive and damaging in its effect in the South, slavery also enriched sea captains and slave traders in the Northeast and produced labor for the region's citizens.

A second parallel involved the existence of mitigating circumstances in both regions. In the South these were created primarily by differences in the character of individual slave owners and by the existence of some individuals who did not favor the cruel practices of slavery. In the North the institution of slavery was weakened by strong abolitionist and antislavery networks that included a secret underground railroad system.

A third parallel was that Black Americans made gains in both regions. Although conditions that were severe enough to break the will of some slaves existed in both the Northeast and the South, significant numbers of African Americans seized whatever opportunities they could find and rose to great achievements in education, religion, the arts, political affairs, and business. From the tests of adversity leaders arose to show ways out of the labyrinth of racism. Perhaps unexpectedly for those who created the racist laws and initiated the acts of hatred, destruction, and killing, such acts often had the effect of strengthening the will and determination of African Americans to overcome and to achieve in a way that brings to mind the Latin phrase *Virescit vulnere virtus* (wounds can increase courage). These ideas are explored in this introduction to the Northeast.

Slavery and Segregation in the Northeast

In the Northeastern states—Connecticut, Delaware, Maine, Massachusetts, New Hampshire, New Jersey, New York, Pennsylvania, Rhode Island, and Vermont—slavery and racial segregation were practiced beginning in the colonial period. This is surprising to many who regard slavery as a Southern phenomenon and who learned in school that the colonies were founded on principles of personal liberties. In the mindset of the colonial era, however, liberties were seen as encompassing white people, not Indians or Africans, and most colonists were untroubled by the contradiction of fighting for liberty for themselves while denying it to others. Thus, slavery did develop and spread in the Northeast. It was not as widespread as in the South because the land and growing conditions were not suitable for developing vast, labor-intensive rice, cotton, and tobacco plantations. Still, slaves were brought in, even in colonial days, to work the land and to labor as house servants.

On the Atlantic seacoast many sea captains earned their fortunes from profits gained in the slave trade. In Massachusetts eighteenth-century seaport towns prospered as ships carried timber and salt fish to the Caribbean and traded them for molasses and sugar. Returning with the molasses, they had it distilled into rum, took the product to West Africa, and traded it for slaves. In this triangle of trade, slaves then were taken to the Caribbean and South America to be sold, and more molasses and sugar were taken on board. Profits made from each point of trade were used to build many fine homes along the Massachusetts shores.

Sea captains in Maine and Rhode Island also joined the slave trade. Even though, according to provisions of the Missouri Compromise of 1820, Maine had joined the Union as a free state, slavery still benefited the state's economy. Maine's large forests provided lumber for building ships that were used for shipping cotton and other goods. The miles of inlets and coves provided convenient harbors for the cargo of human beings that the sea captains brought back to Maine on their return trips.

Such joint commercial ventures produced a sympathy for the South and for the institution of slavery, and many families in the Northeast purchased slaves for their own use. In New York both the Dutch and the English imported slaves from the West Indies and from Africa. The Dutch, who first brought slaves into New York in 1616 for agricultural labor, at first treated the Africans more like indentured servants than as chattels. Over the years, however, the form of slavery changed much as it had in the South, and the process of dehumanization began. Slave owners began to regard slaves as nothing more than property that could be bought and sold just as household goods or farm animals were bought, sold, and willed to others. In New York the importation of slaves increased until by 1698 there were more than 2,000 slaves in the New York Colony. By 1746 there were more than 9,000 adult slaves in the state.

In 1991, remains of enslaved and free Africans from the eighteenth century were uncovered in lower Manhattan. Opened in 1993, The Office of Public Education and Interpretation of the African Burial Ground (OPEI) can be reached at (212) 432-5707.

In many ways slavery was as cruel in the Northeast as it was in the South. To increase control over the slaves, the New York Assembly passed a law in 1702 that forbade trading with slaves and that forbade slaves from assembling or carrying arms. In spite of the closer supervision, however, there was a slave uprising in New York City in 1712; it was not the last such conflict to occur in the state. In the Northeast slaves reacted as they had in the South—by trying to escape. In New York and Pennsylvania newspaper ads offered rewards for the return of runaway slaves. Between 1690 and 1730 Connecticut set up a series of laws to control and "protect" African Americans. Slaves who did not carry with them a pass from their masters were considered runaways. For stealing, a slave could receive up to thirty "strips" or lashes.

Although Maine never had a large Black population, slavery was as heartless there as it was in any other region. Families were separated in slave auctions with little thought to the anguish felt by family members. In an 1875 book, author Edward Bourne called slavery "the great sin of the South."[1] He described a house that once stood in York, Maine, and was used as a slave factory. Entire Black families were impris-

oned for sale at the house, and buyers went there to purchase slaves. Bourne also noted that in the town of Wells, Maine, families were able to purchase slaves from the many small vessels that for almost a century traveled back and forth in the West India trade. He described the agony of a sale in which a mother and daughter were separated:

> Phillis had a little daughter of the age of five years, to whom she was bound by all the ties which take hold of a mother's heart. But a distinguished Revolutionary officer, with the same heartlessness which we have been wont to attribute to those engaged in the slave trade, took this little child from its mother, and, as he would any article of produce, carried her to Saco, and there sold her. The agony of the poor mother in this cruel separation, was said to be indescribable. Yet there were no relentings and no remorse on the part of the trader, which led to any attempt to rescind the unholy contract. It did not seem that our own townsmen had any more doubt, in the judgment of conscience, as to the legitimacy of this traffic; and that a negro was a mere chattel, subject to be bought and sold at the will of the master, than they had that the right of sale in the owner, was a condition or incident of any other property.[2]

The cruelty that could be displayed by slave owners, even in the Northeast, also was exemplified in the home of Colonel John Ashley and his wife, Hannah, in Ashley Falls, Massachusetts. When Hannah Ashley tried to burn a slave girl with a red-hot household implement, the slave girl's sister, Elizabeth, jumped between and took the searing burn instead. Elizabeth steadfastly refused to return to the house even though the Ashleys pleaded with her, and she eventually won her freedom through the Massachusetts state courts.

In New York, a Black man named Austin Steward also was treated cruelly by his master, a man who had brought him from Virginia to New York. Steward, who later wrote a book, *Twenty-Two Years a Slave and Forty Years a Free Man,* stated that it was as hard to have been beaten on the head with a piece of iron in New York as it was to have been beaten this way in Virginia.[3]

Even those slaves in the Northeast who lived in the master's home often lived in terrible conditions. As a child, Sojourner Truth, who later would become a famous spokesperson against social injustice, lived in a cold, damp basement in her master's house in Hurley, New York, sharing her living space with insects and rats.

Opposition to Slavery

Some opposition to slavery existed in the South, although it never was as open as it was in the Northeast. Protest in the Northeast consisted primarily of individual actions and of the strength of the abolitionist and antislavery movements in that region. Abolitionists worked to repeal laws that reinforced slavery, and they supported antislavery candidates. White and Black abolitionists established and maintained an underground railroad, a secret network of men and women who helped fugitive slaves to escape.

It was to the Northeast states that large numbers of slaves sought to escape. Although slavery existed in Maine, the underground railroad was there also. Surrounded on three sides by Canada and on the fourth side by the Atlantic Ocean, Maine provided a desirable route for runaway slaves who fled through Portland, Brunswick, Vassalboro, and China Lake before moving on to Canada. Sometimes boats transported them. A modest number remained in Maine, where they joined the relatively small population of slaves and free people already there.

In New York and Massachusetts several groups, including the Quakers and other religious sects, strongly opposed slavery. In their monthly meetings the Quakers spoke out against slavery, and they were prepared to disown individuals who would not set their slaves free. In New Bedford, Massachusetts, the Quakers worked to make the city hospitable to fugitive slaves and to free Black citizens. They were determined to see that no fugitive slave seeking refuge in New Bedford would be captured and returned to slavery. New Bedford created such a positive atmosphere that when Frederick Douglass arrived in that city, he was surprised to see that laboring Black people there lived better than many slave owners had in his native

Maryland. He was surprised at the confident serenity of the Black men as they worked on the New Bedford docks. Douglass said:

> . . . almost every body seemed to be at work, but noiselessly so, compared with what I had been accustomed to in Baltimore. There were no loud songs heard from those engaged in loading and unloading ships. I heard no deep oaths or horrid curses on the laborer. I saw no whipping of men; but all seemed to go smoothly on. Every man appeared to understand his work, and went at it with a sober, yet cheerful earnestness, which betokened the deep interest which he felt in what he was doing, as well as a sense of his own dignity as a man.[4]

Both Black and white citizens worked against slavery in other areas of the Northeast. In Boston activists included African American leaders Lewis and Harriet Hayden and white abolitionist William Lloyd Garrison, one of the founders of the New England Anti-Slavery Society. The Farwell Mansion in Boston (now the property of the League of Women for Community Service) and the Dillaway-Thomas House in Roxbury, Massachusetts, were stops on the underground railroad. In New York, prominent abolitionists included Frederick Douglass, John Brown, Susan B. Anthony, and William Seward. Harriet Beecher Stowe, who lived in Hartford, Connecticut, wrote *Uncle Tom's Cabin*, one of the most effective books of the day in arousing sentiment against slavery. In Canterbury, Connecticut, Prudence Crandall showed uncommon courage in opening her school to Black students in the face of threats and actual violence directed her way.

Segregation and Achievement

Emancipation of slaves took place far earlier in the Northeast states than in the South. By 1799 New York had provided for the abolition of slavery by specifying gradual manumissions. By 1817 Governor John Jay of New York signed a law specifying that every slave born before July 4, 1799, was to be freed on July 4, 1827. Every child born after passage of the law was to be freed by age twenty-one. The importation of slaves also was prohibited. In 1827 all who still were slaves in New York were freed.

In Connecticut, which became the fifth state in 1788, most citizens opposed slavery. However, one impetus to abolishing slavery in Connecticut came not from philanthropic feelings but from self-interest. As more slaves began to acquire skills, white artisans began to lose their jobs to the unpaid Black workers. Fearful of losing more jobs, the white workers spoke out against slavery and against the importation of more slaves into Connecticut. A state law was passed providing that children of slaves who were born after March 1, 1784, were to be free by age twenty-five. In 1797 the age was changed to twenty-one years. By 1790 there were 2,759 slaves and 2,801 free blacks in the state. In 1848 all slavery was abolished in Connecticut.

With the abolition of slavery in the Northeast, Black citizens still lacked peace of mind. Fugitive slaves who escaped to the region feared being captured by slave traders to be returned to slavery in the South, and unscrupulous slave traders kidnapped free Black men and women to sell in the South. All of the United States was subject to the 1850 Fugitive Slave Law that allowed slave owners to enter Northern states to seize runaway slaves and that provided penalties for obstructing capture. Although American law had abolished the importing of slaves into the country in 1807, slave traders used stealth to get around this rule, and many continued to illegally import slaves.

As a further affront to free Black families, many white men and women wanted to send free Black people out of the country. The American Colonization Society was founded in Washington, D.C., in 1817 with this intent, and by 1829 the Society had a branch in New York. Most African Americans reacted negatively to the idea of emigration; having worked to build the country, they now considered it their home and its rewards their due. Some did, however, accept the idea of moving to Canada where slavery was abolished in 1833.

African Americans in the Northeast faced oppression and segregation in jobs, schools, and voting. In Maine, African Americans saw Irish immigrants take over their waterfront jobs; furthermore, with dwin-

dling opportunities to work in Maine's shipping or lumber industries, many young Black people moved away from the state. In New York much anti-Black sentiment came from immigrants who felt an economic threat from Black workers and who resented being drafted to fight in the Civil War. The War was being fought, these immigrants claimed, to protect the rights of slaves and other Black people who might later compete with them for work. Enraged, they rioted, pouring violently through the streets of New York City, burning property, and lynching as they went. Some African Americans found a safe haven in the Weeksville section of Brooklyn, where they took up arms to protect themselves and their property.

In Boston, William Nell and other African American leaders protested state laws that forbade Black seamen to leave their ships when in Massachusetts ports. They also worked hard to end segregation in Boston's public schools. Schools were segregated, too, in Delaware, which in December 1787 became the first slave state in the union. Delaware's public school system, established as early as 1829, excluded African American children. Black children had to wait until 1907 to become part of a statewide compulsory education system, and they attended segregated schools until 1954.

Although most white citizens in Delaware supported the Union during the Civil War, they continued segregation after the war ended. Delaware instituted poll taxes in 1873, keeping impoverished Black citizens from voting. By 1897, when more African Americans could afford to pay the tax, a literacy test was substituted to bar them again from voting.

Both the South and the Northeast provided some opportunities for African Americans before and after emancipation. In the South such opportunities were more limited, but even segregation provided some niches where a few Black people could become wealthy by serving the Black community. Where slaves in the South had been allowed to preach, often they later provided a strong pattern of leadership in their communities that reached over generations. Some counties in the South encouraged the building of family strength by discouraging slave sales that separated families. In some instances, even though based on unequal status, a bond of affection existed between some slaves and their masters, and the white people helped the freedmen get a start after emancipation. Overwhelmingly, though, in the South, most slaves and freed people who rose to prominence did so through their own quiet diligence and determination.

In contrast, the Northeast states, even though prejudice existed, provided far more opportunities for advancement; this is why the escape route for slaves so often led to the Northeast. Here a person could keep the fruits of his or her labor. If conditions were not satisfactory, he or she could change jobs or move to a different state. Educational opportunities were superior. Savings could be kept to build for one's own future. For these reasons, many Black people in the Northeast rose to prominence, not only in the civil rights arenas but also in a variety of other fields. Lemuel Haynes, for example, preached to a white congregation. Paul Cuffe became wealthy through seafaring activities. In New Bedford, Massachusetts, and other seacoast areas, many African Americans sailed on whaling ships. In New York, Black artists, musicians, actors, and writers flourished during the Harlem Renaissance period, helped by the cultural opportunities that were available to them and that nourished and appreciated their talents. Some who had begun a pattern of achievement were born in the South but migrated to the Northeast and remained there.

Although the Northeast states were caught up in slavery and segregation just as the South was, slave labor was not needed as much, abolitionists spoke out more, and slavery ended earlier there. Furthermore, opportunities for achievement were greater for African Americans in the Northeast. At an earlier date some Black children attended school with white children. Black men, themselves both slave and free, fought for freedom beside white soldiers. One can only speculate what the contributions of these talented men and women would have been if their energies had not been constantly directed at eradicating social injustice. How much more might they have achieved?

Notes

1. Edward E. Bourne, *The History of Wells and Kennebunk from the Earliest Settlement to the Year 1820, at Which Time Kennebunk Was Set Off and Incorporated.* (Portland, Maine: B. Thurston, 1875), 406.
2. Bourne, 407.
3. Helene C. Phelan, *And Why Not Every Man? An Account of Slavery, the Underground Railroad, and the Road to Freedom in New York's Southern Tier* (Interlaken, N.Y.: Heart of the Lakes, 1987), 27.
4. Frederick Douglass, *Narrative of the Life of Frederick Douglass, an American Slave, Written by Himself* (New York: Penguin, 1968), 115–16.

Works Consulted

The Academic American Encyclopedia. Danbury, Conn.: Grolier, 1993. [electronic version]

And Why Not Every Man? An Account of Slavery, the Underground Railroad, and the Road to Freedom in New York's Southern Tier. Helene C. Phelan. Interlaken, N.Y.: Heart of the Lakes, 1987.

"The Black Population of Maine, 1764–1900." Randolph Stakeman. *The New England Journal of Black Studies* 8 (1989): 17–35.

The History of Wells and Kennebunk from the Earliest Settlement to the Year 1820, at Which Time Kennebunk Was Set Off and Incorporated. Edward E. Bourne. Portland, Maine: B. Thurston, 1875.

National Register of Historic Places. Washington, D.C.: National Park Service, 1976.

The Underground Railroad in Connecticut. American Bicentennial Commission of Connecticut. Hartford, Conn.: Connecticut Historical Commission, 1976.

The Underground Railroad in New England. Richard R. Kuns and John Sabino, eds. Boston: American Revolution Bicentennial Administration, Region I, with Boston 200, the Bicentennial and Historical Commissions of the Six New England States, and the Underground Railroad Task Force, 1976.

The Midwest

The settling of the Midwest in the late eighteenth and the nineteenth centuries provided new opportunities and challenges for African Americans. The new territories that would become Illinois, Indiana, Iowa, Kansas, Michigan, Minnesota, Missouri, Nebraska, North Dakota, Ohio, South Dakota, and Wisconsin were attractive to white settlers because of the vast amount of land available for development. Some pioneers had heard, too, of riches to be gained from the fur trade and other commercial activities. The region was attractive to Black men and women because states in the Midwest entered the Union as free states, many of which became important underground railroad routes leading north.

Most of the Southern and Northeastern states were settled in the 1600s. The Midwest, however, was settled much later. After explorers and trappers spread word about vast wilderness regions to the west, bold and hardy men and women began moving west to seek land for themselves or to establish commercial ventures. Thriving towns grew where rivers or overland routes made possible easy transportation of goods. Of the Midwestern states, only Michigan (1668) was settled as early as the 1600s, and Nebraska (1823) and South Dakota (1859) were the last states in this region to be developed by white Americans. As the number of white settlers grew, conflicts over the land became increasingly bitter; taking of the land eventually would lead to the conquest of Native Americans and their removal from desirable land.

African Americans were an important part of the development of the Midwest, yet they often faced deliberately imposed restrictions that were designed to keep them in a subordinate position in society. Although the Revolutionary War had been fought over the issue of freedom and the right to make decisions, the liberties that white men and women sought for themselves were not extended to African Americans and Native Americans. Through the first decades of the eighteenth century, slavery still existed in the South and was a hotly debated issue in other regions of the United States. These debates led to the passage of important legislation that affected African Americans, including the Northwest Ordinance of 1787, the Fugitive Slave Laws of 1793 and 1850, an 1808 law that banned the further importing of slaves into the United States, the Missouri Compromise of 1820–1821, and the Kansas-Nebraska Act of 1854. These laws and their effect on African Americans in the Midwest are discussed in the following sections.

The Northwest Ordinance and Slavery

As the Midwest region developed, citizens throughout the United States debated the issue of slavery in the new territory. Abolitionists saw the issue as a moral one; they claimed that it was wrong to force human beings to work under inhumane conditions for the benefit of others. There were others, too, who opposed slavery, but their opposition was due more to self-interest because they believed that slaves provided competition for white workers who had to be paid wages. Another group, the emigrationists, were not opposed to emancipation, but felt that Black people, once freed, should be shipped out of the United States to colonies in Haiti, South America, or Africa. A fourth group opposed slavery in order to exclude Black Americans from the developing Midwest, which then would be settled by whites only. These ideas formed a complex web of motivations at the time Congress was writing the specifications of the Northwest Ordinance.

In July 1787 the Continental Congress adopted the Northwest Ordinance that established the Northwest Territory, land west of Pennsylvania between the Ohio and the Mississippi Rivers. The territory, called the Old Northwest, later became the states of Ohio, Indiana, Illinois, Michigan, Wisconsin, and part of

Minnesota. One aspect of the ordinance—the prohibition of slavery in the Northwest Territory—made the region especially attractive to slaves who were escaping from bondage in the South. Ohio, the first state in the Northwest Territory to be admitted to the Union (1803), was situated across the river from Kentucky, a slave state. As a free state, Ohio became an attractive escape route from Kentucky and became an important link on the underground railroad. The same was true of Indiana, Illinois, Michigan, and parts of Wisconsin. The underground railroad system, a network of houses, barns, and churches where escaping slaves received food, clothing, and shelter, was extensive and effective in the Midwest.

The Prohibition Against Importing Slaves into the United States

In 1808 Congress passed a law banning the further importation of slaves into the United States. Once this legislation was passed, slave owners who wished to increase their number of slaves could do so only by purchasing them, acquiring them through inheritance, or relying on births to slaves they already owned. Slave owners found ways, however, to circumvent the law that would have decreased the number of new slaves available for purchase. Some sea captains continued to import slaves, sailing silently into numerous hidden coves and harbors. Between 1808 and 1860 they illegally imported 250,000 slaves into the United States. Many slave owners stooped to the level of slave breeding, a procedure they regarded as no more immoral than the breeding of livestock. Other white men went on raids into Northern cities where they captured fugitives or even kidnapped free Black men, women, and children and sold them into slavery in the South.

Although members of Congress had banned the importing of slaves into the United States in 1808, they were not necessarily in favor of abolishing slavery. In fact, in response to pressure from the South, they passed laws that made it easier for slave owners to capture slaves who had fled to the North and the Midwest.

The Fugitive Slave Laws

In 1793 Congress had tried to appease slave owners who were furious about losing their runaway slaves by passing the Fugitive Slave Law, making it easier for states to cooperate in the return of escaped slaves. Slave owners were disappointed, however, because the law was not very effective. Northern states already had begun to abolish slavery, and the Northwest Ordinance prohibited slavery in the region that it regulated. Anti-slavery sentiment was so strong in many towns in the North and the Midwest that many citizens ignored the Fugitive Slave Law and continued to support the underground railroad.

Fearing further loss of their capital—the slaves who were fleeing on foot, by horse-drawn wagon, and by boat—slave owners again angrily demanded assistance from Congress. In response, Congress passed the Fugitive Slave Law of 1850, adding provisions that strengthened the previous law. The new legislation created fear and even panic among groups of free Black people. For example, at the St. Matthews Episcopal Church in Detroit, Michigan, so many church members fled to Canada after passage of the Fugitive Slave Law that remaining members were not able to pay the debt on their new church. An African American was not allowed to testify in court if kidnapped and wrongly identified as an escaped slave. Federal commissioners who returned a person to slavery were rewarded with $10, a welcome incentive at that time. Any person who refused to cooperate with authorities in capturing a slave was punished with a fine or a jail sentence.

In spite of the new danger, many citizens, Black and white, angrily refused to cooperate with the law and even defied its provisions. For example, the African American congregation at Detroit's Second Baptist Church operated an underground railroad station in the basement of their church. At the Quinn Chapel African Methodist Episcopal Church in Chicago, members of the congregation and their friends responded to the Fugitive Slave Law by defiantly vowing to protect each other. Although more than fifty members were former slaves, they boldly vowed to defend themselves at all costs. There was no sure security, however, until Congress repealed the

Fugitive Slave Acts in June 1864 and until the Union won the Civil War the following year.

The Missouri Compromise

Between the passage of the first and second Fugitive Slave Acts, the Missouri Compromise of 1820–1821 was enacted. Its purpose was to try to resolve disputes between the slave states and the free states. The area called Missouri Territory had applied to join the Union in 1818, and slave-owning citizens wanted Missouri to be a slave state. They were opposed, however, by Northerners who wanted new states joining the Union to be free states. After extensive debates in Congress and after a futile attempt to add a provision to the Missouri statehood bill that would gradually eliminate slavery in the state, Congress adjourned without passing the statehood bill.

In 1819 Alabama was admitted to the Union as a slave state, balancing representation of slave and free states in the Senate, but when Maine next applied for admission to the Union, the question of Missouri's status arose again. Henry Clay, Speaker of the House, promoted a plan in which Missouri would be admitted as a slave state and Maine as a free state, and no *additional* slave states would be created west of the Mississippi River and north of the southern boundary line of Missouri. This measure, called the Missouri Compromise, remained in existence until 1854, when it was repealed by the Kansas-Nebraska Act. Although the compromise provided a way to determine whether new states would enter the Union as slave or free states, the compromise did not solve the problem of slavery in the country.

The Kansas-Nebraska Act

In 1854, the Missouri Compromise was repealed by passage of the Kansas-Nebraska Act. This legislation divided land into two territories, Kansas and Nebraska, and specified that settlers in the border states could decide by popular vote whether each state would be a slave state or a free state. The new bill enraged opponents of slavery and deepened the split between North and South. During this period the Republican Party was founded by opponents of the bill. The test of the effectiveness of the new legislation came, however, when Kansas was opened to settlement in 1854 under the terms of the Kansas-Nebraska Act. The issue of establishing Kansas as a slave or a free state captured national interest; proslavery and antislavery groups from other parts of the country moved to Kansas to live and to fight for their side's position. For example, John Brown, a fiery white abolitionist, came to Kansas to join the fight. In 1856 he led a group of men in a battle against proslavery activists at Osawatomie. Instead of having the question of slavery in the state decided by vote, Kansas erupted instead into brutal and bloody battles and massacres over the issue. Each side formed its own government in the battle for supremacy, and the warring region became known as "Bleeding Kansas." At one point, troops had to be called out to help restore order. Although Kansas finally entered the Union as a free state, raids continued along the Missouri-Kansas border throughout the Civil War years.

Equality in the Midwest

In the twentieth century Kansas again entered the national limelight when a Black child, Linda Brown, sought to attend the all-white Sumner Elementary School in Topeka. Her case, *Brown v. Topeka Board of Education,* reached the U.S. Supreme Court where, in May 1954, the Supreme Court declared segregation in public schools to be unconstitutional.

In spite of barriers, there were bright instances where individuals and groups championed the cause of equality in the Midwest. Oberlin College, established in 1833 in Oberlin, Ohio, became the first college in the United States to establish a policy of nondiscrimination in admissions. Central State University and Wilberforce University, both in Wilberforce, Ohio, were among the first colleges in America operated by African Americans. In the military arena Black soldiers won respect for their performance at a number of forts in the Midwest.

Midwest Achievers

In addition to the achievements of the colleges and the African American soldiers as a group, several African Americans in the Midwest were recognized as individuals for their efforts or their achievements. One was Dred Scott, a man who sought his freedom on the basis of having lived in free territory in Illinois and at Fort Snelling, Minnesota, before being taken by his master back into slave territory in Missouri. Although he ultimately lost his legal case, his courage in carrying his plea to the courts strengthened the resolve of abolitionists to continue their work.

Other achievers from the Midwest include Paul Laurence Dunbar, poet; Congressman John Mercer Langston; Colonel Charles Young, the third Black person to graduate from West Point and the highest ranking Black military officer in World War I; Robert S. Abbott, founder of the *Chicago Daily Defender;* Jean Baptiste Point du Sable, Chicago's first settler; Dr. Daniel Hale Williams, a pioneer in heart surgery; Ida B. Wells Barnett of Chicago, a courageous fighter against racism and a researcher of the circumstances surrounding lynchings; Madame C. J. Walker, a millionaire and founder of a hair care and beauty products empire; and Alexander Clark, a civil rights leader in programs based in several states and Consul General to Liberia.

Of the individual African American achievers, one man's achievement was remarkable, even though he later was largely forgotten. The man was York, and he was the only African American member of the famed Lewis and Clark Expedition.

Work Consulted

The Academic American Encyclopedia. Danbury, Conn.: Grolier, 1993. [electronic version]

The West and Non-contiguous States

African Americans in the Western States

African Americans who arrived in the West before the twentieth century worked as explorers, traders, miners and homesteaders, servants, and laborers. Many became entrepreneurs by opening small businesses of their own. As the great railroads opened up the West, Black Americans laid miles of tracks and traveled on those tracks as porters on the trains. Families and individuals were attracted to the western territories by fertile land, by the rich fur trade, by the possibility of gaining wealth in the mines, and by the chance to start life anew in an undeveloped region that seemed to promise a greater degree of freedom. They moved to sparsely settled terrain in the western states—California, Colorado, Idaho, Montana, Nevada, Oregon, Utah, Washington, and Wyoming—because they believed there would be less discrimination there and more freedom than they had previously known. The U.S. Army, too, introduced African Americans to the West, assigning them in the late 1800s to bases in Montana, Washington, Wyoming, and Idaho. Black Americans could be found in every western state.

California's early population included many Black families; 18 percent of California's population in 1790 included people of African descent. Their history often was intertwined with the history of Mexico. Black men and women lived in Mexico when Mexico gained independence from Spain in 1821, and they were present a year later when California became a province of Mexico. Of the forty-four founding families of Los Angeles, twenty-six were of Black heritage, and most had come from the town of Rosario, in Mexico. The last Mexican governor of California, Pio Pico, was a man of mixed African heritage. A landowner and businessman, he owned Pico House, one of the major hotels in Los Angeles. Today visitors can see houses associated with Governor Pico in the old town called El Pueblo de Los Angeles in the city of Los Angeles, and in Whittier and Oceanside, California.

African American Explorers of the West

In the nineteenth century some African Americans traveled through the West as explorers. James Beckwourth, born in 1798, was a Black man who became legendary as an explorer, Army scout, trapper, and mountaineer. Said to have been a member by invitation of an Indian tribe, Beckwourth also spent time in solitary pursuits. He made a lasting contribution to California's development when he discovered an important mountain pass that began a few miles northwest of present-day Reno, Nevada, and led through the Sierra Nevadas to the goldfields of California. In 1851 Beckwourth opened a wagon road into Marysville, California, and the mining region. Serving as a guide, he led visitors through the pass, stopping at his own trading post where the travelers rested and purchased provisions. The pass that he discovered is called the Beckwourth Pass today, and the town of Beckwourth, California, is named for him.

When General John Frémont explored the far west in 1842–1844, Black men were in his expedition, including Mifflin W. Gibbs, a man who later established California's first Black-owned newspaper and became America's first Black judge. Fremont, in 1845, encouraged Californians to revolt against rule by Mexico, and African Americans were present when California was transferred to the United States in 1848 by the Treaty of Guadalupe Hidalgo. Black families had a personal interest in the outcome when Californians and other Americans debated the state's role with respect to slavery, and they were pleased when in 1850 California became the thirty-first state in the union as a free state. The process of Americanization then began in the land that once had been a sparsely settled province of Mexico.

In addition to Fremont's expedition, another important expedition in the West included a Black man. His name was York, and he was a slave. York was among the courageous men who were a part of the Lewis and Clark Expedition. Between 1804 and 1806 they explored the territory between the Missouri River and the Pacific Ocean, crossing wilderness land, most of which had been traversed only by Native Americans. York and the other men crossed the regions of Idaho now called the Nez Percé National Historical Park and the Weippe Prairie. They crossed this land weary and famished, then received desperately needed help from the Nez Percé Indians who provided them with camas roots and dried fish. After bouts of sickness and a period of restorative rest, the men constructed canoes for the final part of their trip to the Pacific Ocean. The men also stopped in Oregon where they built a camp and spent the winter. The Fort Clatsop National Memorial in Astoria, Oregon, has information about the expedition.

Western African American Settlers, Entrepreneurs, and Soldiers

In addition to the explorers, there were the African Americans who came west with wagon trains. George Washington (1817–1895), a Black man who possessed many skills useful for homesteading, traveled to Oregon Territory with a group of families in a wagon train. In 1872 he founded the town that would become Centralia, Washington. The people of Centralia honored and respected him, and a park in Centralia bears his name today.

In 1844 another African American, George Washington Bush, brought his own family and seven white companions to the Puget Sound area, where they became the first settlers in the region. Bush previously had prospered in Missouri, but a law prevented free Black people from settling there. After the group arrived in Oregon, Bush encountered racially restrictive laws again and moved on to Washington

Territory. He established a farm there in the Tumwater area. His name is among those inscribed on a monument there.

William and Sarah Grose were early Black entrepreneurs in Seattle, Washington. They arrived in Seattle in 1860 and began operating a ranch and a hotel there. The house that they built for themselves in 1890 is a rare existing example of the early homes that once were associated with Seattle's Black community.

Richard Allen was another entrepreneur in the early West. He came to the small colony of San Diego around 1847 and with another African American opened a grog shop called the San Diego House (the structure is now a small retail shop in San Diego's Old Town). In Sonora, California, William and Mary Sugg were African Americans who operated a small, private hotel that they built themselves in 1850.

Moses Rodgers, a man who was born a slave, was one of the most successful of the early African American entrepreneurs in the West. After he joined the rush to the California mining country that started in 1849, he became skilled as a mining engineer, acquired a number of mines, and was first to successfully drill for gas in Stockton, California.

Mining opportunities attracted Black families to several other Western states. They found rich lodes in Idaho, Montana, Washington, and Wyoming. Some moved to the mining boom town of South Pass City, Wyoming, which, between 1840 and 1867, was the halfway point on the Oregon-California Trail.

Idaho's mines also attracted a number of African Americans in the nineteenth century. Idaho became the forty-third state in 1890, and although African Americans never made up more than one percent of Idaho's population, they lived there as miners, explorers, trappers, homesteaders, ranchers, and soldiers. Black women, because of lack of other opportunities, usually were domestic workers. By 1870, approximately twenty African Americans lived in Boise, which was Idaho's largest city and the center of mining and ranching activities. By 1900, almost half of Idaho's Black population of 293 individuals lived in Boise or Pocatello. They found work as servants, waiters, laundry workers, hotel workers, and barbers. They also established several small businesses.

Many African Americans came west for the first time as soldiers. African American units called the Buffalo Soldiers served at a number of posts that are accessible to visitors today. The Twenty-fifth Infantry, an all-Black unit from Missoula, Montana, came to Idaho in 1892 to crush labor unrest in the Coeur d'Alene mining region. The Twenty-fourth Infantry, another Black regiment, arrived seven years later with a mandate to arrest striking miners.

From Jim Crow to the Thrust for Equality in the West

As the American West developed, settlers brought their existing ideas about race and status with them. Although many white newcomers approved of slavery and segregation, California did remain in the Union during the Civil War. The segregationist side prevailed, however, when the legislature passed noxious "Black laws" that condoned open discrimination against African Americans.

All Westerners were touched by prevailing state and federal laws, especially those laws enacted when the Civil War ended and during the period of Reconstruction. In the late 1860s and early 1870s many former slaves in the South were destitute and unprotected. The Federal government passed new laws to protect them and created in this way an atmosphere of hope for all African Americans. The Fourteenth Amendment to the Constitution of the United States, ratified in 1868, ensured that former slaves were recognized as citizens and restrained state governments from abridging the rights of former slaves. The amendment insured, in law if not in practice, due process and equal protection of the laws.

The Fifteenth Amendment, passed in 1870, made it illegal for federal or state governments to deprive anyone of the right to vote because of race, color, or previous condition as a slave. Civil rights acts passed in 1871 and 1875 outlawed the use of force, intimidation, or threat to deprive any citizen of the equal protection of the law. The new law gave each citizen the right to use public accommodations, and it forbade discrimination in public conveyances, amusement places, and inns.

By the 1880s, however, the forward thrust of the Radical Reconstruction Period was weakening. Many abolitionists felt that their work was done and were annoyed that Black people were still protesting after emancipation. Many Northerners were in no mood to press for equal rights, especially as African Americans began to move north, competing with white workers for jobs. In the South and elsewhere, the new civil rights laws were widely disregarded. The poll tax, the grandfather clause, and terrorism were used to deny voting rights. Reconstruction ended in 1876 following the inauguration of President Rutherford B. Hayes. Federal troops that had provided a measure of protection for freed people were withdrawn from the South. Jim Crow practices replaced the troops' protection (Jim Crow was a pre-Civil War minstrel show character), and the new divisive laws began to replace the period of just laws. Southern state legislatures repeatedly passed legislation designed to restrict the rights of former slaves, providing a good reason for Black families to make a decision to migrate west. Unfortunately, before the nineteenth century ended, racist state and federal laws would restrict their freedom in the West, too.

In the last decades of the nineteenth century, Congress and the courts seemed to be in no mood to protect the rights of Black Americans. In 1883 the Supreme Court declared the Civil Rights Act of 1875 to be unconstitutional. The new decision specified that unless a state law or action had taken place, federal law had no power to regulate private wrongs or to regulate the conduct and transactions of individual citizens. In the 1896 *Plessy* v. *Ferguson* decision, the Supreme Court upheld the "separate but equal" principle based on a Louisiana statute that separated railroad passengers on the basis of race, thus providing a legal precedent for segregation that lasted until the 1950s. *Plessy* v. *Ferguson* encouraged the spread of segregation, affecting those who had moved their hopes and dreams to the West.

In the nineteenth and early twentieth centuries, Black Americans in the West fought hard for their rights. The thrust for equality was evident in Idaho and California. In 1870, Black Idaho pioneer John West repeatedly tested his right to vote in Boise, only to be turned away from the polls each time. The city of Boise even segregated in the afterlife—the Rose Hill Cemetery there had segregated sites for Chinese and Black burials. Many Black families came to Idaho in the early twentieth century because the state had a major Union Pacific Railroad terminal, and they found work as porters and railroad-yard workers. Beginning in the 1920s, however, Boise's Black families increasingly were confined to a neighborhood south of the railroad tracks. There was a resurgence of Ku Klux Klan activities in Boise and Pocatello, the Idaho towns with the largest Black populations. In 1923, 150 Klansmen in white hooded robes marched through the downtown area of Pocatello and lit a cross on a nearby hillside. In response to growing hostile incidents, Boise's Black community established a chapter of the National Association for the Advancement of Colored People.

In the late 1800s Black workers met prejudice in Idaho's mining camps. Barriers were set up to keep them out, or they were directed to the dirtiest and most menial jobs. Boise County passed a law in 1863 to prevent Black and Chinese people from prospecting. In 1865 the Territorial Legislature introduced a bill to bar African Americans from Idaho. In spite of the barriers, in the 1860s and 1870s Black miners continued to work in mining camps throughout Idaho.

The same discriminatory laws were found throughout the West. A Black man, Frederick Coleman, first discovered gold in San Diego County, California, in 1869. Soon other Black men arrived to stake their claims. The 1850 California census listed 962 Black residents; by 1860 there were 4,086. The possibility of gaining easy wealth also attracted white miners, and many of them protested strongly against working beside Black men in the mines. Delegates to California's 1849 state constitutional convention debated about excluding Black migrants from the state. Although the resolution was rejected, they passed laws barring African Americans from voting and from serving in the militia. Additional legislation specified that Black Americans in California could not testify in court, even if they had been cheated or assaulted by a white person. This encouraged white miners to grab land from Black miners, who were helpless to protest under the law.

Restrictive laws touched all areas of life, reaching even those who had felt secure in California. African Americans felt a stinging betrayal when, in 1852, California passed its own version of the fugitive slave law, allowing slave owners to come into the state to recapture runaway slaves.

By 1855 Black Californians had organized to fight for their rights. They held their own conventions in 1855, 1866, and 1867, and developed plans to defeat the Black laws. Mifflin Gibbs, the Black man who had been a part of John Frémont's expedition, repeatedly traveled to the capital to lobby against the Black laws.

As the new century began, Black Americans were still struggling to improve their economic and social conditions and to eliminate segregation and unjust laws. In California one group decided that the solution was to establish their own all-Black town, a haven where they would not have to endure insults and where they could be independent. In 1908, Colonel Allen Allensworth, a man who was born in slavery, left Los Angeles and, with others, established the town of Allensworth, California. The town thrived for a period but failed when developers broke their promise to provide an adequate water supply. Today, Allensworth exists as a state park visited by approximately 3,000 persons each year.

The African American Community in Los Angeles

Although Colonel Allensworth decided to leave Los Angeles, others remained there, and the Black community increased dramatically in size between 1890 and the 1920s. Biddy Mason, a remarkable Black woman who was treated as a slave in a free state, became one of the community leaders. With the help of friends, she gained her freedom in a California court. Over a period of time she purchased real estate, helped to establish a church, and became a spiritual and economic leader in the community.

As the twentieth century began, the African American community in Los Angeles established associations designed to promote racial unity, education, and justice. Membership grew in the Forum, the Sojourner Truth Club, and the National Association for the Advancement of Colored People. Community newspapers emerged, providing a voice for community concerns. When white-owned hotels shunned Black visitors, a Black man, Dr. John Alexander Somerville, built the elegant Somerville Hotel (later called the Dunbar).

The city of Los Angeles shaped the adolescence of Ralph Bunche. Between 1919 and 1927 Bunche spent his teen years in a house on East Fortieth Street in Los Angeles. Dr. Bunche later became the first Black person to serve as Undersecretary to the United Nations and the first African American to receive the Nobel Peace Prize. One of his greatest accomplishments was to help establish peace in the Middle East by negotiating the 1949 armistice agreement between Egypt and Israel.

In Los Angeles as in other Black communities in the West, the years preceding the Great Depression and the years of the Depression brought contrasts in the welfare of African Americans. Those who were financially successful lived in elegant homes; they established business districts with stores, clubs, and offices for professionals. The Golden State Mutual Life Insurance Company, organized in 1924, became one of the largest African American-owned businesses of its kind in the country.

Black movie stars, such as Louise Beavers, Hattie McDaniel, and Butterfly McQueen, were among the successful in Los Angeles. Although they usually had to portray stereotyped roles, they managed to live personal lives of dignity and elegance.

The Oakland, California, African American Community

In Oakland, California, the Black community increased by hundreds of individuals after the 1906 San Francisco earthquake. Shipbuilding and wartime industries also brought more African Americans to that city. Since it was the western terminus of the Southern Pacific Railroad, many Black porters and railroad workers lived in West Oakland. Several organizations—the National Association for the Advancement of Colored People, the Afro-American League, the Brotherhood of Sleeping Car Porters, and the United Negro Improvement Association (UNIA)—were established in response to restrictions placed on the Black community. Members of the Oakland chapter of the UNIA worked hard to promote the organization's goals of Black pride, pride in Africa, and economic solidarity. Unfortunately, UNIA founder Marcus Garvey was convicted (some say wrongly) of using the mail to defraud investors. Although there was little evidence to support the allegation (a single empty postmarked envelope), Garvey was deported from the United States in 1927. The California chapter remained active for a period, continuing to operate from Liberty Hall on Eighth Street. By the mid 1930s, however, the Oakland Branch of Father Divine's Peace Mission was operating out of Liberty Hall.

The Noncontiguous States: Hawaii and Alaska

The noncontiguous states of Hawaii and Alaska are quite a distance from the western states previously described, but African Americans played a role, too, in the newest of the United States.

Pearl Harbor

Black sailors were on duty in Hawaii when the Japanese bombed Pearl Harbor on December 7, 1941. More than seventy-five naval vessels were based in Pearl Harbor, on Oahu Island, when two waves of Japanese planes struck in a surprise attack, raining destruction on the U.S. Pacific Fleet. Dive bombers, torpedo planes, and fighters hit eighteen ships, destroying more than 200 aircraft and killing more than 2,000 Americans. In those terrifying moments a Black seaman, Doris Miller, became a hero. His assignment in the segregated Navy was as a Messman Second Class on the USS West Virginia; like other Black seamen, he had a menial job—to serve food to white seamen and clear away their dirty dishes. In the surprise attack, Miller was called on to help carry his mortally wounded captain to safety. After doing so he returned to fire a vacated machine gun. Although he had received only minimal classroom training in use of a machine gun, he became a hero by shooting down at least two, and possibly six, Japanese Zeros. The Navy refused to recognize Miller's courage until pressured to do so by newspaper campaigns, the insistence of civil rights organizations, and direct orders from President Franklin Delano Roosevelt. Eventually he was decorated with the Navy Cross.

Alaska

African Americans were present in small numbers in Alaska as early as the 1860s. They came to Alaska in the nineteenth century as seamen and miners. Small numbers served in the U.S. Army unit assigned to maintain order after the 1867 purchase of Alaska from Russia. In 1868, at the U.S. Army base in Sitka, Alaska, six Black individuals were recorded in the population of 391 individuals.

Black men also served on whaling vessels before the turn of the century. They worked in the Klondike gold fields in the 1890s. Although some remained in Alaska after the gold rush, only 168 were recorded in the 1900 census of Alaska. Growth of the African American population remained modest in Alaska until the 1940s through the 1960s. Many came to Alaska during World War II to work on the construction of Elmendorf Air Force Base and Fort Richardson Army Base in Anchorage, Alaska. They liked the relative openness and friendliness of the Alaskan people and, impressed by the many work opportunities, many remained. The situation was ideal for those who had construction skills, who were willing to work as laborers, or who had the entrepreneurial skills to start small businesses.

Living conditions were spartan for everyone. In the early 1950s Anchorage, the largest city in Alaska, had only one main street that was paved, and there was no public transportation system in the city. In the late 1950s and early 1960s African Americans often lived in or constructed small dwellings in the Eastchester Flats and Fairview areas. Two of these modest structures are identified for this volume as typical of the era.

African Americans have been recognized only in the past few years for their heroic work in helping to construct the Alaska-Canada Highway (known as the ALCAN) under the most grueling conditions. During World War II, Black troops were assigned to help build the supply road that connected Alaska's military posts with the midcontinental United States. The 3,695 African American soldiers from the Ninety-third, Ninety-fifth, and Ninety-seventh regiments of the U.S. Army Corps of Engineers composed about one third of the military force that, with civilians, constructed the 1,500 miles of the Alaska-Canada Military Highway. When completed in 1942, the highway extended from Dawson Creek, British Columbia, to Delta Junction, Alaska.

Works Consulted

The Academic American Encyclopedia. Danbury, Conn.: Grolier, 1993. [electronic version]

"Battling the Elements on the Alcan Highway." In *African Americans Voices of Triumph, Perseverance.* Alexandria, Va.: Time-Life, 1993, 160.

"Black Angelenos: The Afro-American in Los Angeles, 1850–1950." Lonnie Bunch. Los Angeles: California Afro-American Museum, Mar. 6, 1989. [manuscript]

Black on a Background of White: A Chronicle of Afro-Americans' Involvement in America's Last Frontier, Alaska. Everett Louis Overstreet. Anchorage, Alaska: Alaska Black Caucus, 1988.

The Black West: A Documentary and Pictorial History. Rev. ed. William Loren Katz. New York: Anchor/Doubleday, 1973.

"A Guide to Black History in Los Angeles." Emily Gibson. *Los Angeles Herald Examiner,* Jan. 30, 1987.

Historical and Cultural Atlas of African Americans. Molefi K. Asante and Mark T. Mattson. New York: Macmillan Publishing Company, 1992, 183.

The History of the East Bay Afro-American Community 1852–Present. Los Angeles: California Afro-American Museum, 1990. [brochure]

Idaho's Ethnic Heritage Historical Overviews. Laurie Mercier and Carole Simon-Smolinski, project codirectors and eds. Boise, Idaho: Idaho Ethnic Heritage Project; cosponsored by Idaho Centennial Commission; National Park Service, U.S. Department of the Interior; and Idaho Historical Society, Mar. 1990. [Files of the Idaho Historical Society, Boise, Idaho]

"Soldiers in the Shadows." In *African Americans Voices of Triumph, Perseverance.* Alexandria, Va.: Time-Life, 1993, 127, 128.

Black Heritage Sites
THE NORTH

Alaska

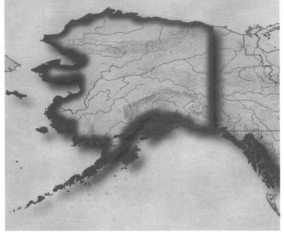

Anchorage

ABC Real Estate

This small cottage was the home for many years of the ABC Real Estate in Anchorage, Alaska. The owner was a Black man named Joseph Jackson who came to Alaska in 1951. He was inspired by a friend's stories of generous paychecks in Alaska. His friend marveled about the economic opportunities available in the far north.

Carpenters were needed for many construction projects in Alaska, and Jackson, who had experience in carpentry, decided to spend about four months working in Anchorage.

When Jackson arrived, there was no housing available for him. He commented later that "Blacks as well as whites were charging $30 a day, with six in a room with double- and triple-bunk beds."[1] Jackson rented a lot made up of twelve feet of space for $25 a month. He and three other carpenters living on the lot cooked their meals in a tent out in the yard. They received the privilege of bathing once a week in the landowner's house.

Joseph Jackson later established his own business, the ABC Real Estate, operating the business out of this cottage on Fifteenth Street for the rest of his life.

ADDRESS: E. Fifteenth Street, one-half block east of Ingra, Anchorage

VISITING HOURS: Private, visitors may drive by

SOURCE: Interview with Joseph Jackson conducted by the author and reported in *Alaska Blacks Salute the Bicentennial.*

Mahala Ashley Dickerson Law Office

This remodeled home on East Fifteenth Avenue has served from 1960 to the present as the original unit of the law office of Alaska pioneer Mahala Ashley Dickerson. Dickerson graduated with honors from Fisk University in 1935 with a major in sociology. She married Henry Dickerson, and they became parents of triplet sons. By the time her sons were six years old and ready to enter first grade, she was able to realize her dream of entering the Howard University Law School. She graduated *cum laude* in 1948.

In 1948 Dickerson became the first African American female admitted to the Alabama bar. A year later she opened the first African American law office in Montgomery, Alabama. One of her accomplishments in Alabama was to rescue a Black family held in peonage by the tenant farmer system. That hiring method insured that Black families would always remain in debt and legally in bondage. Although she was able to help that particular family, she herself met discrimination in her work. When she first began practicing in Montgomery, an Alabama police officer directed her to move from the lawyer's section of the courtroom to the "colored" section. When she explained that she was an attorney, he told her that she would still have to move. Later there was an apology; forty-six years later, in July 1994, Dickerson was invited to be the keynote speaker at the annual meeting of the Alabama Bar Association.

As a young attorney, Dickerson also practiced in Indiana until 1958. Then she fulfilled a dream that brought her and her young sons to Alaska. Although there were other Black people in Anchorage, the African American population was small. At the time many Alaskans were taking advantage of the opportunity to obtain land by homesteading, and Dickerson filed her claim, too. Between 1960 and 1964 she braved rough unpaved roads, Alaskan mosquitoes, and primitive living conditions to homestead 160 prime wilderness acres on a lake in Wasilla, Alaska.

Attorney Dickerson was the first African American admitted to the Alaska bar. She purchased a building in 1960 and remodeled it to serve as her law office. Most of her early clients were white citizens who brought her a variety of general legal problems. As Anchorage's Black population grew, racism also developed, and more and more of her cases involved civil rights and gender problems. As her law practice enlarged, she built a larger office on the same lot in back of the small building. She also built a law office on her land in Wasilla.

In 1982–1983 Dickerson was elected the first Black president of the National Association of Women Lawyers. In 1982 she received the Freedom Award of the National Association for the Advancement of Colored People. In 1994 she received an honorary LLD degree from the University of Alaska.

Attorney Dickerson has quietly supported many philanthropic causes. Al-Acres, a charitable association that she founded, has given scholarships and awards to young Black students. Her autobiography, *Delayed Justice for Sale,* emphasizes that Black people in America may receive justice, but that justice is often delayed and obtained at great price. When she was a child, Dickerson says, Black children looked longingly at the municipal swimming pool in Montgomery but were not allowed to use it. When integration came to Montgomery, white citizens transformed the swimming pool into a flower bed to avoid integration so Black children could not swim there. As a result, Dickerson did not learn to swim until she was thirty-six years old. Today she has a large, beautiful swimming pool in her Wasilla home as well as a lake outside the house, and she is able to

swim every day, illustrating the theme of her autobiography that African Americans often receive delayed justice, but at a price.

DATE ESTABLISHED: House, 1948; law office, 1960

ADDRESS: 1550 E. Fifteenth Street Avenue, Anchorage

TELEPHONE: (907) 276-7454

VISITING HOURS: Private, visitors may walk or drive by

SOURCES: Telephone conversation July 2, 1994, Attorney M. A. Dickerson. "Alaska Blacks Salute the Bicentennial."

Dawson Creek, B.C. to Fairbanks

Alaska Highway

During World War II, African American soldiers played a significant role in building the Alaska section of the Alaska-Canada Military Highway. In 1942 the U.S. Army, believing Alaskan territory to be under the threat of an invasion by Japan, prepared to construct a highway that would connect military posts in Alaska with those in the continental United States. The 1,523-mile highway from Dawson Creek, British Columbia, to Fairbanks, Alaska, would provide a route for trucks to bring army personnel and supplies to Alaska. Although the army recruited civilians for the grueling task, men in the all-Black Ninety-third, Ninety-fifth, and Ninety-seventh regiments of the U.S. Army Corps of Engineers were sent to Alaska to work south from Alaska to the Canadian border. There they would meet white troops who were working north from Canada. The 3,695 Black soldiers made up almost one third of the work force on the highway.

Racism prevailed in the army assignments. To prevent the Black soldiers from mixing with Native Alaskans, the army sent the African Americans to the most remote and primitive sections of the route, where they endured bitterly cold weather and had poor equipment, little fresh food, and no indoor facilities. White soldiers, in contrast, were housed in heated barracks. The Black men saw few people other than the men in their own regiments. Working conditions were grueling; the weather at times reached 70 degrees below zero. The men did construction work in the ice and snow by day and slept in tents by night. When the spring thaws came, they had to slosh through mud and dodge stinging hordes of mosquitoes.

Many of the Black men were from the South. For some, this was their first job in which they received pay equal to that of white workers. In spite of hardships and racial discrimination, their morale remained high, and they finished their assignments with distinction.

In 1946 the Canadian section of the military supply route was turned over to Canada. The entire Alaska-Canada Highway was opened to the public in the following year, and it soon became known as a spectacularly scenic highway for travelers in the far north. Although the Black soldiers' role was almost forgotten over the years, recognition came fifty years after the work was completed. The veterans celebrated the fiftieth anniversary of the highway's completion with a reunion in Tallahassee, Florida. In Alaska, an Alaskan writer named Lael Morgan gathered photographs and stories about their role; this collection became part of a 1992 fiftieth anniversary exhibit at the Anchorage Museum of History and Art.

DATE CONSTRUCTED: Completed 1942

ADDRESS: AK 2 from Fairbanks to the Alaska-Canada border

SOURCES: "Unsung Heroes." "Battling the Elements on the Alcan Highway."

Works Consulted

Alaska Blacks Salute the Bicentennial. Nancy C. Curtis, Ph.D. Anchorage: Leake Temple A.M.E. Zion Church and Great Land Visuals, 1976. [commemorative magazine]

"Battling the Elements on the Alcan Highway." In *African Americans: Voices of Triumph.* Vol. 1, *Perseverance,* 160–1. Alexandria, Va: Time-Life, 1993.

"Unsung Heroes." Lael Morgan. *We Alaskans: The Anchorage Daily News Magazine* (9 Aug. 1992).

California

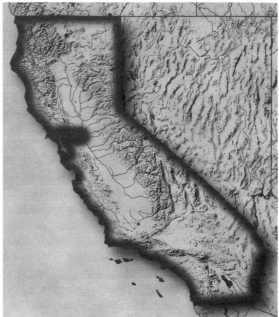

Allensworth (Earlimart Vicinity)*

Colonel Allensworth State Historic Park

Although Allen Allensworth was born a slave in Louisville, Kentucky, in 1842, he dreamed of freedom from an early age. In 1854, when he was twelve years old, his owner sold him to a slavemaster in New Orleans. There he learned to ride horses and gained enough skill to become a jockey. As a youth he ran away several times but was captured and was returned to slavery each time.

When the Civil War started, Allensworth, who was twenty years old, ran away again, escaping to Union Army lines where he helped tend injured soldiers. He already knew how to read and write, and he taught these skills to some of the soldiers.

After the war Allensworth worked at first as a teacher and restaurateur. Later he served as pastor of a Baptist church in Louisville, Kentucky. He then decided to join the military again and in 1866 was appointed chaplain of the all-Black Twenty-fourth Infantry—the first African American to serve as a military chaplain. In 1906 he retired from the Army as a lieutenant colonel—the highest-ranking chaplain and Black officer of his time.

Allensworth, his wife Josephine, and their two daughters, Nellie and Eva, moved to Los Angeles in 1906. He and other African Americans began planning a community where they could be independent and self-governing. They selected a promising site in Tulare County, halfway between San Francisco and Los Angeles. The fertile land was near a railway depot, and the land developer who sold them the acreage made a promise that water would always be plentiful. In 1908 the pioneers began to move into the new town of Allensworth. Soon they developed farms and built homes, a school, a church, a library, and a post office. In 1914, when Colonel Allensworth was on the way to Monrovia, California, to publicize the town, he was fatally struck by a motorcycle. He was buried with honors in a Los Angeles cemetery.

Misfortune began for the town of Allensworth about this time. The land developing company that had promised a good supply of water failed to keep its promise and siphoned off water to white-owned farms in surrounding areas. As a result, the population of Allensworth rapidly dwindled from a peak of 300 to 160. The Depression years brought additional hardships, and many families left the town during World War II. Its abandoned structures began to deteriorate.

Years later, however, the town was restored through the efforts of Cornelius Ed Pope, a Black man who worked at drafting for the state department of parks and recreation. Pope had lived in Allens-worth as a child. Learning in 1969 that remaining structures in Allensworth were soon to be razed by bulldozers, he initiated successful efforts to turn the town into a state park. Restoration began in 1976, and many buildings were rebuilt to the way they looked when the town was founded.

The Visitors Center has exhibits and a film. With advance arrangements visitors can see the interiors of several buildings, including Hindsman Home, a schoolhouse, a church, a library, a hotel, a general store, Smith Home, and a drugstore.

DATE ESTABLISHED:	1908
ADDRESS:	CA 43, 8 miles west of Earlimart
TELEPHONE:	(805) 849-3433
VISITING HOURS:	Visitors Center, daily 8–3; park, 24 hours; guided tour of interiors of several buildings, by appointment; closed Thanksgiving, Christmas, New Year's Day 👫
FEES:	Vehicles, $3/day; overnight camping, $8
SOURCES:	Personal visit, July 1992. Telephone conversation June 30, 1994, Phillip Hall, park ranger. Robert Leiterman, park ranger. NRHPINF. Manuel Bergado, chief ranger, Historic Sites. Brochure from State of California, Department of Parks and Recreation. *National Register of Historic Places*, 77. *California Weekly Explorer.*

Beckwourth

James Beckwourth Cabin

James P. Beckwourth—trapper, explorer, scout, and trader—became such a legend for his life of adventure as a mountaineer that a city, valley, and mountain have been named for him. He was born in Virginia in 1798, the third of thirteen children. His mother was

Black, a slave in his white father's household. As a youth, Beckwourth was sent to school in St. Louis for four years. Then he was apprenticed to a blacksmith in St. Louis but ran away at eighteen to a life of adventure. He learned to hunt and to use guns, Bowie knives, and tomahawks. He became a fur trader at the age of twenty-five with the Ashley Rocky Mountain Fur Company and the American Fur Company.

Beckwourth, who communicated well with Indians, was adopted by the Crow Nation. He lived among them for six years, learning their ways and earning their respect. He was said to have been a warrior and a chieftain. Beckwourth left the Indian tribe in 1837, moving on to establish trading posts (see the listing for the El Pueblo Museum in Pueblo, Colorado) and to serve as an army scout in 1842 during the Third Seminole War. He then moved to California, to a life of travel, trapping, and prospecting for gold.

In 1850 Beckwourth discovered an important northern pass a few miles northwest of present-day Reno, Nevada, that led through the Sierra Nevadas to the gold fields of California. Before his discovery, travelers crossing in wagon trains had to take the wagons apart and hoist them up over high mountain cliffs. Beckwourth was able to open a wagon road into Marysville and the mining region. He led the first wagon train of settlers through the pass he had discovered, and thousands of travelers later traversed the Beckwourth Pass to California.

In 1852 Beckwourth built a home and trading post where westward traveling migrants could stop for food and fresh horses. He died in 1866, but the mountain pass he discovered, the mountain peak and valley, and the town nearby still bear his name. His log cabin in California stands today, much as it was when first built, near the Plumas County hamlet that bears his name.

DATE BUILT:	1852
ADDRESS:	Pass, CA 70, the Feather River Highway, east of the junction with US 395, several miles north of Lake Tahoe; cabin, Rocky Point Road, south of CA 70, 1 1/2 miles east of Chilcoot, between the towns of Beckwourth and Portola (from Beckwourth travel west on CA 70, go past Grizzly Road and turn left on Rocky Point Road; from Portola travel east on CA 70 to Rocky Point Road, turn right onto Rocky Point Road)

VISITING HOURS:	Private, visitors may drive by
SOURCES:	Manuel Bergado, chief ranger. *The Black West.* "A History of Black Americans in California," 72, 90–91. "State Park Units with Black Culture Influence." *A Salute to Black Pioneers.*

Los Angeles

Ralph Bunche House

The Ralph Bunche House is a frame structure in South Central Los Angeles. Dr. Bunche lived in this house from 1919 to 1927. He was born in 1904 in Detroit, Michigan, but both parents died before he was twelve, and he went to live in Los Angeles with his maternal grandmother.

An outstanding student, Bunche attended John Adams Junior High and Jefferson High School. He then enrolled at the University of California at Los Angeles, where he was elected to Phi Beta Kappa. He graduated *summa cum laude*.

Bunche earned his Ph.D. degree from Harvard University in 1934 and started on a brilliant career. He received wide recognition for his work at the United Nations, where he became the highest ranking Black person in the United Nations Secretariat. He was the first Black recipient of the Nobel Peace Prize, which was given for his peacekeeping efforts for the United Nations.

The Dunbar Economic Development Corporation is working with a private corporation to restore the home to its original appearance. The site is marked with a city cultural heritage plaque (see the New York section for additional information on Dr. Bunche).

DATE OF SIGNIFICANCE:	Bunche residence, 1919–1927
ADDRESS:	1221 E. Fortieth Place, South Central Los Angeles
VISITING HOURS:	Private and vacant, visitors may drive by
SOURCES:	NRHPINF. Telephone conversation June 30, 1994, Louise Parsons, A. C. Billbrew Library, Los Angeles. Telephone conversation June 30, 1994, Reginald Chapple, project director, Dunbar Economic Development Corporation. "A Guide to Black History in Los Angeles."

California Afro-American Museum*

The California Afro-American Museum collects, preserves, and displays artifacts that document the African American experience in America. It is housed in a spacious, contemporary, glass-and- brick facility. Three interior galleries provide display space for changing art and history exhibits. Additional facilities include a research library with 50,000 books, archives, a meeting hall, a theater, and a gift shop.

The museum engages in research, produces publications on Afro-American artists and achievers, and presents multimedia presentations, lectures, and a cultural exchange of talented Black artists.

DATE ESTABLISHED:	Building, 1984; museum, 1977
ADDRESS:	600 State Drive, Exposition Park, Los Angeles
TELEPHONE:	(213) 744-7432
VISITING HOURS:	Tues.–Sun. 10–5; closed New Year's Day, Thanksgiving, Christmas ♟♟
FEES:	None
SOURCES:	Jayne Sinegal, library director, California Afro-American Museum. Telephone call to site, June 30, 1994. Aurelia Brooks, C.E.O., California Afro-American Museum Foundation. *California Afro-American Museum.* "A Guide to Black History in Los Angeles." *Museums of Southern California*, 2–3.

The Dunbar Hotel

Dr. John Alexander Somerville was born in Jamaica, the son of an Episcopalian priest. He came to California in 1902 and, as an African American, was unable to find lodging at local hotels because of racial prejudice. Undaunted, he prepared for his career by working his way through college. In 1907 he became the first Black graduate of the University of Southern California's School of Dentistry. His wife, Dr. Vada Somerville, graduated from the University of Southern California School of Dentistry in 1918.

Somerville, who once had been refused rooms in hotels, opened his own hotel in 1928. An elegant building in the Spanish hacienda style, the Somerville was built entirely by Black contractors, laborers, and craftspeople; it was financed by Black community members. The four-story, 100-room hotel in its opening year hosted the first national West Coast convention of the National Association for the Advancement of Colored People.

Lucius Lomas, another prominent Black community leader, purchased the hotel in the early 1930s and renamed it the Dunbar Hotel. It became a center for cultural, business, and social activities and hosted many prominent visitors: W. E. B. Du Bois, Thurgood Marshall, Paul Robeson, Marian Anderson, A. Philip Randolph, James Weldon Johnson, Josephine Baker, Adam Clayton Powell, Langston Hughes, Duke Ellington, Count Basie, Louis Armstrong, Joe Louis, Redd Foxx, Sammy Davis Jr., Roland Hayes, and Bill Robinson.

DATE BUILT:	1928
ADDRESS:	4225 S. Central Avenue, Los Angeles
TELEPHONE:	(213) 234-7882
VISITING HOURS:	Tours by appointment, Mon.–Fri.
SOURCES:	NRHPINF. Telephone conversation June 30, 1994, Mr. Reginald Chapple, project director, Dunbar Economic Development Corporation. "Return of the Dunbar."

El Pueblo de Los Angeles State Historic Park

The original settlers of El Pueblo de Los Angeles came primarily from the city of Rosario in Mexico, where two-thirds of the people were of Black or mixed ancestry. Among those from Rosario who settled in the new community, 50 percent were said to be Black or mixed Black heritage. They created the foundation of the city that is now Los Angeles.

The original settlement, the birthplace of Los Angeles, is now part of a state historic park operated by the city. Although the original houses are gone, more than twenty historical buildings from the colonial period still remain. These include the facade of the Pico House, a hotel built by Pio Pico, a man of mixed Black heritage; he was the last Mexican governor of California.

Eleven buildings are open to the public and four have been restored as museums. The names of the settlers are recorded on a bronze plaque erected in

1981 to honor the city's founders. Tours start from the Visitors Center in the Sepulveda House. Pico House may be viewed from the outside, but has not yet been restored for public viewing of the interior.

ADDRESS: Park, 845 N. Alameda Street; Visitors Center, 622 N. Main; Pico House, 424–436 N. Main Street, Los Angeles

TELEPHONE: (213) 628-1274 or (213) 628-7170

VISITING HOURS: Park, daily 10–8; museums, Tues.–Sat. 10–3; guided walking tours, Tues.–Sat. 10, 11, 12, and 1 except on Thanksgiving Day and Christmas 👫

FEES: None

SOURCES: Telephone call to site, June 30, 1994. Manuel Bergado, chief ranger. "A Guide to Black History in Los Angeles." *Museums of Southern California*, 10–13. "10 Benchmarks and Landmarks." State Park Units with Black Culture Influence. *Black Angelenos.*

Los Angeles Children's Museum

The Ethnic Los Angeles exhibit at the Los Angeles Children's Museum provides a series of innovative learning environments about cultures of ethnic groups in Los Angeles. One exhibit, *From Africa to Los Angeles,* provides a short journey through some of the sights, sounds, tastes, and textures of African American culture from the marketplaces and pyramids of the African continent to the homes and businesses of present-day Los Angeles.

DATE ESTABLISHED: 1979

ADDRESS: 310 N. Main Street, Los Angeles

TELEPHONE: (213) 687-8801 or (213) 687-8800

VISITING HOURS: During school year, Sat.–Sun. 10–5; summer, Sat.–Sun. 10–5, Tues.–Fri. 11:30–5; closed Thanksgiving, Christmas, Easter, July 4 👫

FEES: Adults and children over 3, $5; children under 3 years, free

SOURCES: Candace Barrett, assistant director of exhibits and programs, Los Angeles Children's Museum. Telephone conversation June 26, 1994, Prima Devera, reservations and box office, Los Angeles Children's Museum.

Biddy Mason Tableau and Timeline

Biddy Mason, pioneer, midwife, and philanthropist, is honored by an exhibit at the Broadway Spring Center. The mixed-use building is built on the homestead site purchased by Biddy Mason in 1866. Elevator doors at the lobby level open to a tableau of Mason on the front porch of another Black pioneer family. Outside, a striking 8-foot-by-81-foot timeline on a wall traces her life and history.

Biddy Mason, known affectionately as Grandma Mason, was admired throughout Los Angeles for her skill as a midwife and her willingness to help others. She was born in slavery in Hancock, Georgia, and was sold about 1836 to Robert Marion Smith, a convert to Mormonism, who took Biddy and her three daughters west with a Mississippi company of Mormons in 1848. They started out in wet, muddy weather. Biddy traveled on foot, herding the livestock behind the wagon train across Missouri and Nebraska into Utah.

When Smith left for California about 1851, taking Biddy and her children with him, he was in violation of California laws since California was a free state. Although Biddy befriended some free Black people living in San Bernardino, she continued to serve her owner as a slave.

In 1856 Smith planned to move to Texas and to take Biddy, her daughters, and other slaves south with him. Although he told Biddy that she would be free in Texas, she knew that was not true. Biddy's friends alerted authorities that the African Americans were being returned to slavery. A group that included the local sheriff rushed to Smith's camp in the Santa Monica mountains and rescued fourteen slaves, including Biddy and her daughters and some other relatives. A ruling from the United States District Court emancipated the group that Smith had held in slavery. The Black community in Los Angeles, which had financed the legal proceedings, rejoiced.

People in the Los Angeles area—both wealthy and poor families—called on Mason's help as a midwife. Soon she was able to purchase lots and to build a family homestead at 331 South Spring Street between Third and Fourth Streets. Although Mason became wealthy from real estate investments, she never forgot to return the assistance others had given her. When devastating floods of the 1880s destroyed homes, she opened an account in a grocery store to provide food for homeless people of all races. Los Angeles mourned when Mason died on January 15, 1891.

DATE ESTABLISHED:	1989
ADDRESS:	Broadway Spring Center, 333 S. Spring Street, Los Angeles
TELEPHONE:	(213) 626-2099
VISITING HOURS:	Dawn–dusk
SOURCES:	Telephone call June 26, 1994, to site. *The Story of the Negro Pioneer.* "Grandma Mason Remembered." *Biddy Mason's Place: A Midwife's Homestead, The Power of Place.* "A History of Black Americans in California," 86. *Los Angeles County Historical Directory.*

Museum of African American Art

Museum displays include sculpture from Africa as well as works by contemporary Black artists. In June 1994 the museum had just reopened, having recovered from earthquake damage to the structure. The gallery reopened with an exhibit, *Aninkra Quilt*, featuring the watercolors and monoprints of nationally known but locally based African American artist Varnette Honeywood. In addition to the changing exhibits, the museum has a gift shop gallery offering prints, books, cards, jewelry, figurines, dolls, and African imports.

DATE ESTABLISHED:	Museum, 1975; at this site, 1979
ADDRESS:	4005 Crenshaw Boulevard, Third Floor, Los Angeles
TELEPHONE:	(213) 294-7071
VISITING HOURS:	Wed.–Sat. 11–6, Sun. noon–5
FEES:	None
SOURCES:	Telephone conversation June 26, 1994, Dolores Orduna, gift shop manager, Museum of African American Art. "A Guide to Black History in Los Angeles."

West Adams Historic District

The West Adams Historic District includes several homes, a historic African American business, and churches, all of which are significant to the city's African American history. The district includes the Golden State Mutual Life Insurance Company, the Louise Beavers residence, Hattie McDaniel's residence, and Butterfly McQueen's home.

Land developers laid out tracts and neighborhoods for this community in the late 1890s. They built large, luxurious homes for the rich and famous. In the late 1940s the first Black couple moved into the area, and other families soon followed. White families began to move out of the community, but they returned in the 1970s when they were attracted again by the beautiful old homes.

GOLDEN STATE MUTUAL LIFE INSURANCE COMPANY, at 1999 West Adams Boulevard, is one of America's largest Black-owned insurance companies. Founder William Nickerson Jr. migrated from Texas to California in 1921, seeking personal and economic opportunity. Instead, he found that the 16,000 Black residents of Los Angeles were considered such poor risks by insurance companies that they were charged high premium rates or were denied insurance coverage altogether.

Two other men, Norman O. Houston, an insurance agent from northern California, and George A. Beavers, a Los Angeles business owner and church leader, shared Nickerson's dissatisfaction. In 1924 the three men began organizing a company that would meet the insurance needs of the Black community.

Nickerson purchased a set of law books and taught himself California's insurance codes. The men then secured in advance 500 paid applications for the company they planned to develop. They were successful in raising the needed funds, and in 1925 they received a license to operate as the Golden State Guarantee Fund Insurance Company of Los Angeles.

The fledgling company started its physical existence in a 12-foot-by-14-foot second-story room at 1435 Central Avenue. The business was successful, and within seventy-nine days it was moved to new storefront offices at 3512 Central. Although many businesses collapsed during the Great Depression, Golden State continued to expand.

Nickerson died in 1945. Cofounder Houston was elected president and continued the company's growth. In 1949 Golden State dedicated the present elegant home-office building. Paul Williams, a noted Black architect, designed the five-story, art deco building located in the heart of the upwardly mobile Black community.

By 1984 Golden State Mutual ranked among the fifty largest mutual insurance companies in the nation. Today it promotes an appreciation for the African American cultural heritage by providing a showcase of California's Black pioneers and America's Black artists. The display, located at the home office, includes murals depicting the contributions of Black individuals and families to California's growth and development. The following additional historic West Adams buildings are associated with African Americans:

The LOUISE BEAVERS RESIDENCE at 2219 South Hobart Boulevard belonged to an African American actress who was born in Cincinnati, Ohio, in 1902. Beavers began her career as a film actress in the 1920s. As with other Black actresses through the 1950s, she was typically cast by Hollywood in the role of a maid. She played in such films as *Imitation of Life* (1934) and *Mr. Blanding Builds His Dream House* (1948). She followed another actress, Ethel Waters, in portraying the maid Beulah in the 1950s television series called *Beulah*. Louise Beavers died in 1962.

The HATTIE MCDANIEL RESIDENCE at 2203 South Harvard Boulevard belonged to a Black radio and film actress. McDaniel was born in 1893 (one account gives 1898) in Wichita, Kansas, the thirteenth child of a Baptist preacher and his wife. McDaniel attended public schools in Denver, Colorado, and began her professional career at the age of sixteen or seventeen, singing in tent shows and radio programs. In the 1920s she began touring different states in vaudeville shows. In 1933 she began working on radio shows including the *Amos 'N' Andy Show* and the *Eddie Cantor Show*, and she began acting in films. McDaniel appeared in more than seventy films. Although Hollywood usually assigned the talented actress the stereotyped roles of a maid, McDaniel managed to add to her characterizations an element of assertiveness toward her white employers. The first African American to win an Academy Award, McDaniel was awarded an Oscar in 1946 for her portrayal of

Scarlett O'Hara's maid in *Gone with the Wind*. McDaniel died in 1952.

The BUTTERFLY MCQUEEN HOME, 2215 South Harvard Boulevard, was the residence of another well-known Black actress. Thelma (Butterfly) McQueen was born in Tampa, Florida, in 1911. Her father was a stevedore and her mother was a domestic worker. In 1935 McQueen moved to Harlem to pursue an acting career; there she joined an acting troupe, Jones's Negro Youth Group. Two years later McQueen made her Broadway debut in the George Abbott musical *Brown Sugar*. Although acclaimed for her acting talent on the stage, in films McQueen usually was limited to portraying the role of a domestic worker. She was chosen, for example, to play the role of the maid Prissy in *Gone with the Wind*. Acting assignments were scarce in the late 1940s for McQueen. She produced a one-women concert in 1951 at Carnegie Hall, but it was not a financial success. A succession of jobs followed, including waiting tables in Harlem in the 1960s. In 1975 McQueen received a B.A. degree from City College of New York; in the same year she was inducted into the Black Filmmakers Hall of Fame.

DATE OF SIGNIFICANCE:	Historic district, 1940s; Golden State Mutual Life Insurance Company, 1925; company's art collection, 1949
ADDRESS:	Historic district, S. Figueroa Street, west to Crenshaw Boulevard, and south from Venice Boulevard to Jefferson Boulevard; Golden State Mutual Life Insurance Company, 1999 W. Adams Boulevard, Los Angeles
TELEPHONE:	Golden State Mutual Life Insurance Company, (213) 731-1131
VISITING HOURS:	Movie stars' homes, private, visitors may drive by; Golden State Mutual Life Insurance Company, Mon.–Fri. 9–4:45; closed Sat., Sun., most holidays ⛓
FEES:	Art exhibit, free
SOURCES:	Maria Rosario Jackson, Golden State Mutual Company. "A Guide to Black History in Los Angeles." *Los Angeles County Historical Directory. The African American Encyclopedia*, 141, 1007–8, 1015–16.

Oakland

Liberty Hall

Liberty Hall in Oakland is associated with two historic African American groups: the United Negro Improvement Association and Father Divine's Peace Mission. Marcus Garvey (1887–1940) founded the Universal Negro Improvement Association in Jamaica in 1914. He came to New York and organized a branch of the association in Harlem in 1916. With the slogan, "Up You Mighty Race, You Can Accomplish What You Will," and with an emphasis on Black pride, Black nationalism, and Black economic and political power, the organization inspired African Americans in many cities.

Garvey's movement became one of the largest mass movements of Black people in the United States. In addition to emphasizing independence in America, Garvey also revived earlier attempts to send millions of Black people back to Africa. Although the latter objective was not accomplished, Garvey sowed the seeds for independence movements in the Caribbean region and Africa and for the civil rights movements in the United States.

The Oakland, California, branch, Local 188 of the United Negro Improvement Association, was chartered in 1920. Five years later the association bought the old Western Market Building on Eighth Street and renamed it Liberty Hall. A series of setbacks began soon afterward. Marcus Garvey was deported to Jamaica in 1927. Although the charges against him were questionable, the loss of the leader severely hurt the movement. The nation was entering a financial depression, and UNIA activities began a long decline after a fire severely damaged the building in 1931.

Liberty Hall began to house another organization, the main Oakland branch of Father Divine's Peace Mission. Father Divine, an African American evangelical preacher (about 1877 to 1965), was born in poverty in the South as George Baker. He began his ministry in that region. Moving to New York one year before the arrival of Marcus Garvey, George Baker acquired property in 1919 in the all-white suburb of Sayville, Long Island. There he assumed the name Father Divine and began his Peace Mission, operating a communal household during the Depression that provided free weekly banquets for all who wanted to come. He spoke out against stealing, gambling, smoking, use of liquor, evading debts, and racial prejudice of any kind. By 1926 the Peace Mission was an interracial movement.

By 1936 the Peace Mission had grown and had twenty-eight branches in California. The branch on Eighth Street was one of six in Oakland. During the Depression era the Peace Mission prepared banquets, charging only pennies per person. The facilities also included a dormitory and furniture repair shop. Although the Peace Mission movement began to decline after the start of World War II, this branch was listed in the telephone directory until 1965.

The people of Oakland have become aware of the history of Liberty Hall. Today the restored building is in use again in the old tradition of serving the community. The Jubilee West organization, which has administrative offices and a community center at 1485 Eighth Street, sponsors several programs in a youth center at this address, a thrift shop, and other services in the community. The organization's activities include a job program, a housing program, and an emergency program that distributes goods and services.

DATE BUILT:	1877; first used for the African American community, c1925
ADDRESS:	1483–1485 Eighth Street, Oakland
TELEPHONE:	Jubilee West organization, (510) 839-6776
VISITING HOURS:	Jubilee West organization, Mon.–Fri. 9–5 by appointment
SOURCES:	NRHPRF. Telephone conversation June 30, 1994, Bill Sturm, librarian, Oakland History Room. *International Library of Negro Life and History.*

Oceanside

Santa Margarita Ranch House

The Santa Margarita Ranch House was another home of Pio Pico, California's last Mexican governor (see the listings for Pico House in Los Angeles and for Pio Pico State Historic Park in Whittier, California). The adobe structure was built in the early nineteenth century. It is a one-story residence with a veranda that encircles the house and a central patio. The original small structure was enlarged to include twenty-three rooms. The original winery was converted to a chapel and the bunkhouse to a museum. The Spanish colonial building was later sold and developed as a cattle ranch. Since 1942 it has been used as a part of a U.S. Marine base.

DATE BUILT: Main house, c1827
ADDRESS: Off Vandergrift Boulevard and Basilone Road, Camp Pendleton, Oceanside
TELEPHONE: History office, Camp Pendleton, (619) 725-5758
VISITING HOURS: Private residence, tour times vary
SOURCES: Telephone call June 29, 1994, Camp Pendleton History Office. *National Register of Historic Places*, 70.

San Diego

Richard Freeman House

Richard Freeman was born in the eastern United States. Joining the small African American colony at San Diego about 1847, he bought an adobe building. With another African American, Allen Light, Freeman operated a grog shop, known as the San Diego House, for four years.

San Diego House represents an example of early African American entrepreneurship in San Diego. The state park system plans to reconstruct the nineteenth-century adobe building as part of the Old Town in San Diego State Historic Park. The old grog shop is used now as a retail shop, Casa de Wrightington. The shop has retained its historic appearance outside but not inside, where it has been remodeled as a store. The staff members inside have no information on Richard Freeman; please do not disrupt their activities with inquiries. Visitors may enjoy seeing its exterior and surroundings in the Old Town.

DATE BUILT: 1800s
ADDRESS: San Diego House, Old Town in San Diego State Historic Park, 4002 Wallace Street; Casa de Wrightington, 2783 San Diego Avenue, San Diego
TELEPHONE: (619) 220-5422
VISITING HOURS: Casa de Wrightington, daily 8–6
SOURCES: Manuel Bergado, chief ranger, Historic Sites. Telephone conversation June 26, 1994, Tom Cline, ranger supervisor. "A History of Black Americans in California," 59.

Sonora

Sugg House

Both William and Mary Sugg were born in slavery, but each came separately to Tuolumne County. William Sugg was born in 1828 at Raleigh, North Carolina. He reached California by wagon train before 1852, working as a muleteer and bullwhacker on the journey. His traveling companions settled in the Merced area. Sugg obtained his freedom and began working in the harness business.

Mary Sugg was born in Johnson City, Missouri. She came west to California in 1851 in an eventful trip during which her group suffered a cholera outbreak and had encounters with hostile Indian groups.

William and Mary eventually came to Tuolumne County, an area where hundreds of Black people already lived. They first met at a social function and later moved to Sonora, where they married in 1855.

William Sugg began building this house on Theall Street in 1857. He and friends mixed mud and shaped it into the adobe that forms the interior walls of the home. The rooms were arranged one behind the other—a front room, a middle room, a rear living/dining room, and a 14-foot-by-16-foot frame kitchen in a wooden lean-to. The middle room served as the bedroom in which all eleven of the Sugg children were born. As the family grew, Sugg added bedrooms on the first and second floors as well as a frame kitchen. In the 1880s he built a two-story gallery across the front.

When nearby hotels were full, hotel managers referred guests to the Sugg House, where a rule stipulated that no "lewd women" could stay there. The Sugg family took in visitors until 1921, when the city began to require hot and cold running water and inside bathrooms in facilities rented to the public. Because the cost of making these conversions was more than the family could afford, the Suggs had to stop taking in boarders. In fact, the house had no indoor toilet until the 1940s.

William Sugg returned to Merced in 1877, a year after the birth of their last child. Mary Sugg remained in Sonora. Although high school classes were not offered in Tuolumne County until the late 1890s, Mary Sugg worked hard to see that all eleven children received at least an elementary school education. She died in 1915, and her grandson, Vernon Sugg McDonald, died at the Sugg House in May 1982.

Sugg House was built by a manumitted slave and his wife during the gold rush years. The house also is unique in California's gold rush country and Tuolumne County as one of the few remaining adobe buildings in the region. As of 1994 it was in use by a video productions organization.

DATE BUILT: 1857
ADDRESS: 37 Theall Street, Sonora
VISITING HOURS: Private, visitors may walk or drive by
SOURCE: NRHPINF.

Stockton

Moses Rodgers House

Moses Rodgers was born a slave in Missouri. While still a young man he acquired skill as a mining engineer. When the gold rush swept California in 1849, he went west to participate and moved to Hornitos, where he established a reputation as a superior mining engineer. His opinion was valued so highly throughout the state that investors often consulted him before purchasing mining claims or stock.

Rodgers acquired a number of mines in the Mariposa district. He also became a mining superintendent for the Washington mine established in 1869. In some years more than half a million dollars in gold was taken from this mine.

Rodgers married Sahra Quivers in the 1860s. They had five daughters. As the girls grew up, the family moved to Stockton because of the superior school facilities in that town. Rodgers built a fine, two-story frame home for his family on one of the best residential streets in Stockton. He continued his mining interests, becoming the first person to drill successfully for natural gas in Stockton. He didn't gain financially from his discovery, however, because he was not able to persuade investors to back the operation.

Rodgers lived in his house on South Joaquin Street until his death after the turn of the century. The house remained in the same family until 1971.

DATE BUILT:	1898
ADDRESS:	921 S. San Joaquin Street, Stockton
VISITING HOURS:	Private, visitors may walk or drive by
FEES:	None
SOURCES:	NRHPINF. "A History of Black Americans in California," 65.

Whittier

Pio Pico State Historic Park*

Pio Pico, a man of mixed Black heritage, was the last Mexican governor of California. He served as governor in 1832 and again in 1845–1846 until his last term was cut short by the United States invasion. Governor Pico used his wealth and influence to support the development of education and banking and to develop town sites. He was an important figure in California's transition from Mexican to American rule and led in California's cultural and economic development.

After the United States acquired California, Pico spent time as a rancher, a Los Angeles city councilman, and a business-owner. He invested in the state's first oil venture and built the Pico House, a one and one-half–story adobe hotel in Los Angeles.

Pico's mansion in Whittier, an adobe structure with a veranda and a central courtyard, once was a center of social activity. Pico built the house near the San Gabriel River to ensure a ready supply of water; there was no well at the site until the 1870s. The river, however, proved troublesome—three floods in the 1880s damaged the house. The third and most severe flood inundated the mansion in 1883–1884, damaging it so seriously that the structure was rebuilt. The west wing, which had ten or twelve rooms, was not rebuilt because it led in the direction of the river. A kitchen wing was built in the opposite direction.

The state-owned mansion was restored in 1946 and opened to the public as a museum. But disaster struck again, first with the October 1987 Whittier Narrows earthquake and again in January 1994 with the Northridge earthquake. Workers removed furniture, put up a chain-link fence around Pico House, and began using an injection method to stabilize the cracked adobe walls. In inspecting the damage,

workers discovered that the house had not been completely rebuilt after the 1883–1884 flood as had been thought; on the contrary, five of the rooms were from the original 1852 mansion.

Pico House is worth seeing both for its architecture and for its place in Black history. Architecturally, the mansion is interesting because its construction reflects both Spanish and American influences. The first floor, of adobe construction, is Mexican-Spanish in style. The second story shows influences from the eastern United States—construction is of wood and there are dormer windows that are not typical in California construction. In the final restoration a section with two rooms on the first floor and two on the second will be rebuilt. An old photograph shows Pico sitting on the balcony of this section and shows an American-style Victorian railing on the balcony.

Governor Pico, who was born May 5, 1801, died September 11, 1894. Although forgotten by many Californians today, Pico should be remembered again as an accomplished business person and as the last Mexican governor of California. His ethnic heritage, which included Spanish, African, Indian, and Italian ancestors, reflects the ancestry of many of today's Californians. His Black heritage, which Pico acknowledged, was the heritage of many of California's early settlers; Pico House, therefore, is a part of California's Black history.

DATE BUILT:	1852; rebuilt 1884; restored 1946 and 1995
ADDRESS:	6003 Pioneer Boulevard at Whittier Boulevard, Whittier
TELEPHONE:	(562) 695-1217
VISITING HOURS:	Wed.–Sun. 10–4; closed New Year's Day, Thanksgiving, Christmas 👫
SOURCES:	Telephone conversation Apr. 22, 1995, Jeanne Ekstrom, state park interpreter, Pio Pico State Historic Park. Manuel Bergado, chief ranger, Historic Sites. State Park Units with Black Culture Influence. *National Register of Historic Places.*

Works Consulted

The African American Encyclopedia. Vols. 1, 4. Michael W. Williams, ed. New York: Marshall Cavendish, 1993.

Biddy Mason's Place: A Midwife's Homestead, The Power of Place. Dolores Hayden. Los Angeles: The Power of

Place, 1988. [poster]

*Black Angelenos: The Afro-American in Los Angeles,
1850–1950.* Los Angeles: California Afro-American
Museum, June 1988. [exhibit guide]

The Black West: A Documentary and Pictorial History. Rev.
ed. William Loren Katz. New York:
Anchor/Doubleday, 1973.

California Afro-American Museum. Los Angeles:
California Afro-American Museum. [brochure]

California Weekly Explorer. Irvine, Calif.: California
Weekly Explorer, 1980. [newspaper]

"Grandma Mason Remembered." Clipping files, vol.
13, no. 1, p. 4, history department, Los Angeles Public
Library. [newsletter]

"A Guide to Black History in Los Angeles." Emily
Gibson. *Los Angeles Herald Examiner,* Jan. 30, 1987.

"A History of Black Americans in California." Eleanor
M. Ramsey and Janice S. Lewis. In *Five Views: An Ethnic
Sites Survey for California.* Sacramento, Calif.: State of
California, Department of Parks and Recreation, 1988.

*International Library of Negro Life and History: Historical
Negro Biographies.* Wilhelmena S. Robinson. New York:
Publishers, 1970.

Los Angeles County Historical Directory. Janet I. Atkinson.
Jefferson, N.C.: McFarland, 1988.

Museums of Southern California. Sara LeBien. Salt Lake
City, Utah: Gibbs-Smith, Peregrine, 1988.

National Register of Historic Places. Washington, D.C.:
National Park Service, 1976.

"Return of the Dunbar." I. Posey and F. Finley
McRae. *Los Angeles Weekly,* 19–25 Feb. 1988.

A Salute to Black Pioneers. Richard L. Green, ed.
Chicago: Empak, 1986.

State Park Units with Black Culture Influence.
Sacramento, Calif.: California Department of Parks
and Recreation. [list]

The Story of the Negro Pioneer. Kate B. Carter. Salt Lake
City, Utah: Daughters of Utah Pioneers, 1965.

"Ten Benchmarks and Landmarks: Black History
on View in LA." Toni Tipton. *Los Angeles Times,*
Jan. 15, 1987.

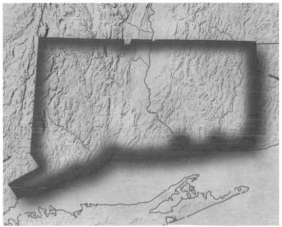

Canterbury

Prudence Crandall House

When Prudence Crandall admitted Sarah Harris, a
Black girl, to her school, the town of Canterbury
erupted into violence. Angry townspeople directed
their wrath at Crandall and at her girls school on
Canterbury Green. There is an interesting background to this incident.

Prudence Crandall was well known in Canterbury,
where she had lived from the time she was ten years
old. As a young woman, Crandall moved to nearby
Plainfield to teach at a girls school. Then, in 1831, a
group of Canterbury citizens asked her to return there
to establish a school. She agreed and opened the
school in January 1832 with strong citizen support.

A few months later, Crandall, a Quaker, received a request from Sarah Harris to enter the school. Following is how Crandall described Harris's first visit to the school:

> A colored girl of respectability—a professor of religion—and daughter of honorable parents called on me sometime during the month of September last and said in a very earnest manner "Miss Crandall, I want to get a little more learning. If possible, enough to teach colored children and if you will admit me to your school, I shall forever be under greatest obligation to you. If you think it will be the means of injuring you, I will not insist on the favor.[1]

There were immediate reactions to Sarah's admission. Some parents threatened to withdraw their daughters if the Black girl did not leave; others withdrew their financial support. Crandall sought the advice of well-known abolitionist William Lloyd Garrison of Boston. After carefully considering the alternatives, she made a decision that would prove even more controversial. Instead of dismissing Sarah, Crandall dismissed the remaining white students and reopened the institution as a school for young Black girls. Even young women from other towns were allowed to enroll.

Local outrage and violence exploded. White citizens gathered outside to taunt the students as they left the school. They called out names and hurled eggs, mud, and rocks at the building and the students. The church across from the school refused to allow the girls to worship there. A shopkeeper refused to sell them food and supplies, and local physicians refused to give them medical treatment. When someone tried to set a fire at the school, white citizens accused a Black supporter of the school, George Olney, of starting the fire. He was tried and later acquitted.

Canterburians then encouraged state lawmakers to pass a law designed to destroy the school. The 1833 legislation known as the *Black Law* made it illegal to operate a school that brought Black or brown students into Connecticut. Crandall was arrested for breaking this law, and later released. When she returned to the school, violence erupted again. A mob attacked the building at midnight on September 9, 1834, using clubs and iron bars to break more than ninety windowpanes.

Fearing that the girls were in great physical danger, Prudence Crandall and her husband finally decided to close the school. They fled from Connecticut. Prudence Crandall spent her later years in Kansas.

In 1886 the townspeople of Canterbury, recognizing the immense wrong the town had committed against Crandall and her students, granted an annuity of $400 per year to Crandall for the rest of her life. Sarah Harris later married and lived in Rhode Island. (See the listing for George and Sarah Fayerweather in Kingston, Rhode Island.)

The Prudence Crandall House opened as a state-operated museum in 1984. The sixteen-room, two and one-half–story house is a reminder of a period of segregation and racism in Connecticut. Today the museum has an exhibit that includes information about the Black experience in pre-Civil War Connecticut.

DATE ESTABLISHED:	c1805; school, 1833–1834; museum, 1984
ADDRESS:	Junction of CT 14 and CT 169, Canterbury
TELEPHONE:	(860) 546-9916
VISITING HOURS:	Jan. 15–Dec. 15, Wed.–Sun. 10–4:30; closed Mon., Tues., Thanksgiving ⛓
FEES:	Adults, $2; senior citizens and children, $1; school groups, free; adult and youth groups, special rates
SOURCES:	Ms. Kazimiera Kozlowski, museum curator I, Prudence Crandall Museum. *The Prudence Crandall House. National Register of Historic Places*, 102. *The Prudence Crandall Museum: A Teachers Resource Guide. The Underground Railroad in New England. The Underground Railroad in Connecticut. Classic Connecticut, Vacation Guide 1989–1990.* "Letter to the *Windham County Advertiser*."

Farmington

Samuel Deming House

Fugitive slaves entering Connecticut at Stamford, New Haven, or Old Lyme usually next found their way to Farmington, called the "Grand Central Station" of Connecticut. Leaving Farmington, they traveled north to Westfield or Springfield in Massachusetts.

In Farmington Samuel Deming's house was a stop on the underground railroad. It also was associated with the Africans from the schooner *Amistad* (see First Church of Christ, Congregational and Austin Williams House, following). The Deming House later became the home of the headmaster of Miss Porter's School.

ADDRESS: 66 Main Street, Farmington

TELEPHONE: Miss Porter's School, (860) 546-9916

VISITING HOURS: Private faculty residence; visitors can drive by

SOURCES: Telephone call Apr. 5, 1994, Miss Porter's School. *The Underground Railroad in New England. The Underground Railroad in Connecticut.*

First Church of Christ, Congregational

A group of Africans who had been kidnapped from the West Coast of Africa for sale into slavery worshiped at this church while awaiting their trial to determine whether they would be slaves or free. Their ordeal began in 1839 when they were taken from Africa to Cuba. There they were purchased by two Spanish (Cuban) slave traders, Señores Ruiz and Montez, and were taken aboard the schooner *Amistad* to be delivered to Puerto Principe, Cuba. One of the slaves, Joseph Cinque, the son of a Mendi chief, was a man of high intelligence and leadership ability.

The Africans, numbering about fifty, were kept chained by the neck below deck, subsisting only on some bread, one plantain, and one cup of water per day. They had been terrified when the ship's captain killed a man with his knife, then used the knife to slash others among the Mendi. Moreover, the cook had threatened them with cannibalism. As a storm began to rage and the crew struggled to keep the schooner afloat, Cinque and his companions plotted their escape. Within four days some of the Africans broke loose from the hold, seized and killed the ship's captain and cook, and gave orders to Ruiz and Montez to return the ship to Africa.

During the day, the two Spaniards seemed to comply with their directions, but at night they sailed in a different direction, hoping to reach safety in a southern slave state. They had been at sea for weeks when crewmen from a Navy brig, the *U.S.S. Washington*, spotted the *Amistad* off Montauk Point in Long Island Sound. Seizing the schooner, the Navy crew captured the Africans and jailed them in New Haven, Connecticut. Later the Africans were transferred to Hartford, Connecticut, where they were to stand trial for mutiny, piracy, and murder.

An African slave from Mendi, who was working on a ship docked in New York, was brought in as an interpreter. Through the interpreter the prisoners told that they were not slaves but were freeborn Africans who had been kidnapped and sold to the Spaniards. After the Africans told their story, abolitionist sentiment rose for emancipating the group. The opening trial was scheduled for September 1839 in the State House at 800 Main Street in Hartford. The trial resumed in 1840 in the District Court of New Haven. When the Spanish government, regarding the slaves as property, demanded their return to the Cubans, the *Amistad*

mutiny became an international affair. U.S. President Martin Van Buren sought to resolve the issue in favor of Spain, even offering to send a brig to take the Africans back to slavery in Cuba.

Meanwhile, the *Amistad* case was brought to the U.S. Supreme Court in 1841. While awaiting the decision, the Africans were taken to Farmington, where they became part of the community. They attended services at the First Church of Christ, Congregational during their nine months in Farmington. Former President John Quincy Adams served as counsel for the Africans before the Supreme Court. In March 1841 the Court declared the Africans to be free and upheld their right to return to their homeland. Sadly, on their return to Africa, they learned that members of their families had been sold into slavery.

DATE BUILT:	1771; *Amistad* Africans attended services, 1841
ADDRESS:	75 Main Street, Farmington
TELEPHONE:	(860) 677-2601
VISITING HOURS:	Mon.–Fri. 8–4; tours by request
SOURCES:	David O. White, director of education, Connecticut State Library. NRHPINF. *International Library of Negro Life and History*, 63–64. *The Underground Railroad in Connecticut. The Underground Railroad in New England.* "Farmington Was the Grand Central on the Route North." *Race Racism and American Law*, 29–31.

Austin F. Williams House

When the Africans from the schooner *Amistad* came to Farmington, they lived in the carriage house of the Austin Williams House. Runaway slaves also stayed in the cellar under the carriage house. Twentieth-century owners of the house found five layers of flooring over the trap door leading to the cellar. The layers of flooring would have deadened any sounds made by the people hidden below.

DATE OF SIGNIFICANCE:	1839
ADDRESS:	127 Main Street, Farmington
VISITING HOURS:	Private; visitors may walk or drive by
SOURCE:	*The Underground Railroad in New England.*

Groton Heights

Fort Griswold State Park

Fort Griswold State Park is across the Thames River from New London, Connecticut, in the town of Groton. In September 1781 British troops under the leadership of the treacherous Benedict Arnold sailed up the Thames River, intent on burning the towns of Groton and New London. They attacked the small earthwork garrison called Fort Griswold. The British believed the attack was justified because ships from Connecticut towns along Long Island Sound had raided British shipping vessels throughout the war.

As the British soldiers sailed toward the fort, they were observed by a white farmer named Latham and his slave, Lambert Latham, who were tending cattle in a field. They rushed to assist fort commander Lieutenant Colonel William Ledyard and the other Americans at the fort. Latham and his slave were among those who refused to surrender even though they were surrounded by the enemy. Although Lambert Latham had a bullet wound in his hand, he was able to reload and fire again and again. During the attack Jordan Freeman, a Black slave and orderly, killed a British officer.

Although the Americans fought valiantly, they were outnumbered, and Colonel Ledyard finally offered his sword in surrender. The British officer, angered at the death of his colleague, took the sword and suddenly ran it through Ledyard to the hilt. Lambert Latham then stabbed the British officer with his bayonet, thus drawing upon himself the fury of the British, who pierced him thirty-three times with their bayonets. The British slaughtered eighty-four Americans, even though most of them had already surrendered. Both of the African American soldiers, Freeman and Latham, died in the massacre.

The 135-foot-high Groton Monument near Fort Griswold lists the names of the massacre victims. The placement of names on the monument reflects racism. The names of the white men who died were placed at the top while Lambert Latham and Freeman were listed below under the heading "Colored Men" and Latham, who had the nickname "Lambo," was listed as "Sambo."

DATE OF SIGNIFICANCE:	1781		DATE BUILT:	1871
ADDRESS:	At the junction of Monument Street and Park Avenue, Groton Heights		ADDRESS:	Stowe House, 73 Forest Street; Carriage House, 71 Forest Street; Stowe Library in the Katherine Day House, 77 Forest Street; Twain Home, 351 Farmington Avenue, Hartford
VISITING HOURS:	Park, daily 8–sunset; museum and monument, Memorial Day–Labor Day, daily 9–5, Labor Day–Columbus Day, weekends 9–5		TELEPHONE:	(860) 525-9317; Twain Home, (860) 493-6411
FEES:	None		VISITING HOURS:	Stowe House, Tues.–Sat. 9:30–4, Sun. 12–4, June 1–Columbus Day and Dec., daily, last tour at 4, closed New Year's Day, Easter, Labor Day, Thanksgiving, Dec. 24–Christmas; Library, Mon.–Fri. 9–5, closed Sat.–Sun., holidays, Thanksgiving and the following Fri., Dec. 24–25 👫
SOURCES:	David O. White, director of education, Connecticut State Library. William E. Hare II, curator, The New London County Historical Society. Jonathan Lincoln, park manager, Fort Griswold State Park. *Black Heroes of the American Revolution.*		FEES:	Admission for both the Stowe House and the Day House, adults, $6.50; children 6–16, $2.75
			SOURCES:	Telephone conversation June 9, 1994, Althea Sorensen, senior guide. The Stowe-Day Foundation. *National Register of Historic Places*, 97.

Hartford

Harriet Beecher Stowe House and Library
Mark Twain Home

The residence at 73 Forest Street was home to Harriet Beecher Stowe (1811–1896), a white woman who influenced thousands through her stories about the horrors of slavery. After listening to African Americans describe their experiences, Stowe used some of the details they had supplied in her 1852 book, *Uncle Tom's Cabin*. Publishers translated the story into more than forty languages, and the narrative impelled many previously uncommitted readers to work actively against slavery.

Stowe lived in this home from 1878 until her death. Today the restored house is filled with original furnishings and family memorabilia, and visitors are offered guided tours. The Stowe-Day Library at 77 Forest Street, next to the Stowe House, is open to researchers studying the works of Harriet Beecher Stowe.

Visitors to the Stowe House have the opportunity to see the neighboring Mark Twain House where plans are proceeding to restore the third floor room of Black servant George Griffin. A former slave, Griffin came to the house in 1874 to wash windows and remained almost eighteen years as the household butler. A deacon in the Methodist Episcopal Church, he had a knack for making money and was remembered for lending funds to others in the African American community.

Wadsworth Atheneum

The Amistad Foundation of the Wadsworth Atheneum in 1987 acquired the Simpson Collection of African-American Art, a world-class record of the Black experience in America from the Middle Passage to the present. The Amistad Foundation Collection contains more than 6,000 paintings, sculptures, photographs, posters, books, historical documents, and artifacts. It began with Randolph Linsly Simpson who, as a boy, lived near the cemetery where Frederick Douglass was buried. Simpson's family had a strong antislavery tradition, and the boy became aware of the contributions of African Americans to American life. Deeply disturbed to realize that objects and pictures associated with Black history were rapidly disappearing, he became passionately dedicated to saving as much of this record as he could. The Simpson Collection found a permanent home in Connecticut's Wadsworth Atheneum.

The collection is extensive. More than 2,200 photographs, including some of Black abolitionists, show slave life in the early 1840s. The museum also includes slave narratives and objects made by slaves or used in the slave trade—from a pair of rare handmade chairs used in a slave cabin to shackles and chains. A bronze sculpture, *The Negro Looks Ahead, 1944,* was created by Richmond Barthe, who was born in Bay St. Louis, Mississippi, of African American, French, and American Indian parentage. Barthe was one of the first artists to use African motifs in his work.

The museum library includes historical documents such as letters, slave contracts, manuscripts, and more than 350 books.

DATE ACQUIRED:	1987
ADDRESS:	600 Main Street, Hartford
TELEPHONE:	(860) 278-2670; program/tour information, (203) 278-2670, ext. 3049
VISITING HOURS:	Tues.–Sun. 11–5; closed Mon., New Year's Day, July 4, Thanksgiving, Christmas
FEES:	Adults, $3; students and senior citizens, $1.50; members and children under 13, free; Thurs. 11–1, free; Sat., free; annual student pass available
SOURCES:	Barbara A. Hudson, African-American art curator, Amistad Foundation Collection. David O. White, director of education, Connecticut State Library. Telephone conversation Apr. 5, 1994, Eugene Gaddis and William G. Delana, archivist, Wadsworth Atheneum. *The Amistad Foundation.*

Milford

Black Soldiers from the Revolutionary War Marker

The town of Milford has erected a marker on the town green to honor three Black soldiers from the locality who fought in the American Revolution. During the Revolution African Americans made up about 3 percent of Connecticut's population and 2 percent of its armed forces. Some Black men were sent to serve in the army in the "master's" place, and of these, some were freed after completing their service in the army.

DATE OF SIGNIFICANCE:	Revolutionary War
ADDRESS:	Town Green, Milford
VISITING HOURS:	Daily, 24 hours
SOURCES:	David O. White, director of education, Connecticut State Library. "Town Records Tell Story of Black Residents."

New Haven

Connecticut Afro-American Historical Society

In 1971 a group of African American citizens formed the New Haven Afro-American Historical Society. Now called the Connecticut Afro-American Historical Society, the group operates a museum in a small turn-of-the-century house donated by a founding member. The original goal was to collect and preserve historical African American biographies, diaries, photographs, periodicals, and artifacts describing the early community of African Americans in New Haven, but the project expanded to include the state of Connecticut. The collections, displayed in five rooms on two levels of the house, include poster-sized photographs on the walls of each room, a Civil War rifle that belonged to an African American soldier from New Haven, uniforms from fraternal associations, and other items.

The historical association helped to plan the erection of a monument commemorating the *Amistad* incident (see the Farmington, Connecticut, listings for the Samuel Deming House; the First Church of Christ, Congregational; and the Austin F. Williams House). Dedicated in 1992 and rededicated in 1994, the triangular monument features three life-sized figures of Cinque, the leader of the African Mendi people who were kidnapped in Africa and who were later jailed in New Haven. Cinque is shown at three different points of his stay in America. Ed Hamilton, a nationally recognized African American artist and a resident of Louisville, Kentucky, won a national competition to create the sculpture. The *Amistad* monument is located in front of the New Haven City Hall on the New Haven Green, on the site where the jail once stood that housed the *Amistad* people.

As of January 1995 the Connecticut Afro-American Historical Society was seeking more space for its museum. Its most exciting project, however, is one recently initiated in conjunction with the Mystic Seaport Museum in Mystic, Connecticut, with $2.5 million in funding from the state of Connecticut. The museums plan to have built a full-sized replica of the schooner *Amistad* to serve as a floating museum. The home bases for the schooner, described as a Baltimore clipper, will be in New Haven and Mystic Seaport. If plans work out as desired, the ship will sail from port to port in Connecticut as well as throughout the United States, manned in part by inner-city youth trained to work on the schooner. The anticipated date of completion is summer 1998.

DATE ESTABLISHED:	1971
ADDRESS:	444 Orchard Street, New Haven
TELEPHONE:	(203) 432-4131
VISITING HOURS:	By appointment 👫
FEES:	Donations appreciated
SOURCES:	Telephone call Mar. 16, 1990, Russell Hamilton, Connecticut Afro-American Historical Society. David O. White, director of education, Connecticut State Library. Edna B. Carnegie, volunteer, Connecticut Afro-American Historical Society. Telephone conversation Apr. 12, 1994, Lucinda Hamilton, board member, Connecticut Afro-American Historical Society. Telephone conversation Jan. 15, 1995, Khalid Lum, president, Connecticut Afro-American Historical Society.

Goffe Street Special School for Colored Children *

Before 1869 Black children were barred from attending New Haven's public schools. Some African American children received instruction in private homes, but this arrangement was inadequate to meet the needs of the community. In 1864 a group of influential citizens met and resolved to establish a school for "the intellectual and moral well being of the colored people of the Town of New Haven and especially of their children."[2]

Henry Austin, one of Connecticut's most-influential architects of the mid-nineteenth century, designed the Goffe Street School, and starting in 1866, Black people used the facilities at night. By 1871 state and local leaders modified laws to permit the public education of Black children. Soon the African American community was using the building for sewing classes, a boys club, a masonry school, and an athletic club. The athletic club was chartered in 1895 as the Colored

Young Men's Christian Association. After World War I, St. Luke's Episcopal Church used the building as a parish house and Black community center.

When the Dixwell Community Center was constructed nearby in 1924, use of the Goffe Street School decreased. The Grand Lodge of Negro Masons purchased the building in 1929 with the intent of preserving it for New Haven's Black community.

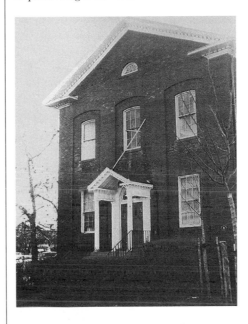

The Goffe Street School is a brick structure with two stories and attic. An interior staircase features heavy, turned balusters and an oak handrail. Although the exterior has been remodeled to serve as a parish house for St. Luke's Episcopal Church and later for use as a Masonic Lodge meeting hall, it still retains its basic original design.

Goffe Street School is significant in a state that has few remaining sites directly connected with Black history.

DATE BUILT:	1864
ADDRESS:	106 Goffe Street, New Haven
TELEPHONE:	Prince Hall Masonic Lodge, No listing
VISITING HOURS:	Call for information 👫
SOURCE:	NRHPINF.

Yale University

The Beinecke Library at Yale University houses the James Weldon Johnson Memorial Collection of Negro Arts and Letters, historic items from African American literature and culture. Named for prominent Black author, composer, and civil rights leader James Weldon Johnson, the collection is a large and scholarly set of manuscripts, musical scores, prints, recordings, photographic slides, and letters written by well-known authors. It is open to researchers rather than to the general public.

ADDRESS: Beinecke Library, Yale University, 121 Wall Street, New Haven

TELEPHONE: (203) 432-2962

VISITING HOURS: Mon.–Fri. 8:30–5

FEES: None

SOURCE: Telephone conversation June 10, 1994, Suzanne Eggleston, reference librarian, Sterling Memorial Library.

Stratford

Judson House and Museum

The cellar of the Judson House once served as slave quarters. Today, the restored and furnished colonial home has a collection of farm and craft tools that fill the former slave quarters. An adjacent museum, operated by the Stratford Historical Society, has some Black history items, including manuscripts and a list of eighteen local Black men who fought in the American Revolution. One was Robert Freeman, whose descendants still live in Stratford. The museum also has an account of Jack Arabas, a local Black man who had been promised his freedom for joining the army. When his master, Thomas Ivers, refused to grant his freedom, Jack Arabas took his master to court. He won both his case and his freedom.

The museum library has such materials as a copy of the autobiography of Aunt Hagar Merriman, a local African American woman born in the 1790s; the secretary's book of the local abolition society, dating from the 1850s; and a rare collage silhouette and bill of sale, both of a slave named Flora who died in 1815.

DATE BUILT: c1750

ADDRESS: 967 Academy Hill, Stratford

TELEPHONE: (203) 378-0630

VISITING HOURS: Apr. 15–Oct. 31, Wed., Sat., Sun. 11–4; closed July 4 👥

FEES: Adults, $2; children, $1; senior citizens, $1.50; $5 per family if more than $5 individually

SOURCES: Hiram Tindall, curator, Stratford Historical Society. *Classic Connecticut, Vacation Guide 1989–1990.*

Notes

1. Prudence Crandall, "Letter to the *Windham County Advertiser*," May 1833. In Randy Ross-Ganguly, *The Prudence Crandall Museum: A Teachers Resource Guide* (Hartford, Conn.: Connecticut Historical Commission, 1988), 66.
2. Leroy Fitch, "History of the Goffe Street Special School," quoted in NRHPINF for Goffe Street Special School for Colored Children, 2.

Works Consulted

The Amistad Foundation: The Simpson Collection at the Wadsworth Atheneum, Hartford, Connecticut. Hartford, Conn.: The Foundation. [brochure]

Black Heroes of the American Revolution. Burke Davis. New York: Odyssey/Harcourt Brace Jovanovich, 1976.

Classic Connecticut, Vacation Guide 1989–1990. Rocky Hill, Conn.: Department of Economic Development, 1989.

"Farmington Was the Grand Central on the Route North." Lin Noble. *(Farmington) Herald*, Mar. 1989. Newcomers Section.

International Library of Negro Life and History: Historical Negro Biographies. Wilhelmena S. Robinson. New York: Publishers, 1970.

"Letter to the *Windham County Advertiser*." May 1833. In *The Prudence Crandall Museum: A Teachers Resource Guide.* Randy Ross-Ganguly. Hartford, Conn.: Connecticut Historical Commission, 1988.

National Register of Historic Places. Washington, D.C.: National Park Service, 1976.

The Prudence Crandall House. Connecticut Historical Commission. Hartford, Conn.: The Commission, n.d.

The Prudence Crandall Museum: A Teachers Resource Guide. Randy Ross-Ganguly. Hartford, Conn.: Connecticut Historical Commission, 1988.

Race Racism and American Law. Derrick A. Bell Jr. Boston: Little, Brown, 1973.

"Town Records Tell Story of Black Residents." Mary L. Nason. *(Simsbury) News,* 19 Feb. 1987, 22.

The Underground Railroad in Connecticut. American Bicentennial Commission of Connecticut. Hartford, Conn.: Connecticut Historical Commission, 1976.

The Underground Railroad in New England. Richard R. Kuns and John Sabino, eds. Boston: American Bicentennial Administration, Region I, with Boston 200, the Bicentennial and Historical Commissions of the Six New England States, and the Underground Railroad Task Force, 1976.

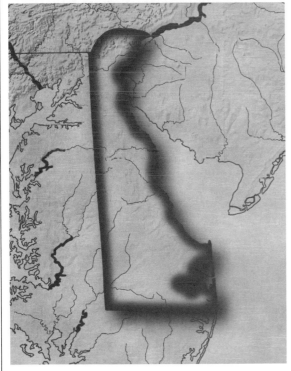

Dover

Delaware State College

The historically Black Delaware State College opened in 1891 as a land-grant college that grew out of the Second Morrill Act of 1890. An earlier land-grant act of 1862, known as the Morrill Act because it was introduced by Congressman (and later Senator) Justin S. Morrill, had offered federal land tracts as an incentive for establishing college programs in science, agriculture, industry, and the military. The 1890 Morrill Act specified that states practicing racial segregation had to establish Black colleges in order to receive land-grant act funds; Delaware State College was established as a result of that second act.

The first African American colleges, whether they were publicly or privately funded, enrolled Black students who were former slaves or who had been free Black Americans with very limited opportunities to attend school; their students often had to begin their studies at an elementary school level. For this reason it was not until 1898 that Delaware State produced its first graduates, a fine achievement considering the starting point of its students.

The current student body is made up of approximately 58 percent African American students who study on a 400-acre campus that has 24 buildings. Loockerman Hall, constructed between 1772 and 1790, is one of the historic buildings on the campus. Restored in the 1970s, it retains some of the original interior woodwork.

DATE ESTABLISHED:	College, 1891; Loockerman Hall, c1772–1790
ADDRESS:	US 13, Dover
TELEPHONE:	(302) 739-4924
VISITING HOURS:	By appointment with the Public Relations Office, Mon.–Fri. 8:30–4:30; closed weekends and holidays ♀♂
FEES:	None
SOURCES:	Drexel B. Ball, director, Office of Public Relations, Delaware State College. *National Register of Historic Places,* 109.

John Dickinson Plantation

Although the slave houses are no longer standing at the Dickinson Plantation, site interpreters give a comprehensive look at the lives of African Americans who lived here. The Delaware Bureau of Museums and Historic Sites has gleaned information from more than 400 documents pertaining to slavery and to John Dickinson's manumission practices. The researchers used tax-assessment records, orphans-court records, daybooks, account books, receipts, manumission records, probate inventories, period legislation, petitions, and newspapers to reconstruct the lifestyles of slaves and manumitted African Americans between 1750 and 1808.

The plantation belonged to John Dickinson (1732–1808), a lawyer of great wealth who was known as the "penman of the Revolution." He was a Delaware delegate to the United States Constitutional Convention. Although Dickinson wrote many essays on colonial rights and liberty, ironically slaves lived on his plantation.

DATE BUILT:	Mansion, 1740, rebuilt 1804; opened as a museum, 1956
ADDRESS:	8 miles south of Dover on Kitts Hummock Road just off US 113 and southeast of the Dover Air Force Base
TELEPHONE:	(302) 739-3277
VISITING HOURS:	Tues.–Sat. 10–3:30, Sun. 1:30–4:30; group tours by arrangement; closed Mon., holidays ♀♂
FEES:	None
SOURCES:	Letter Sept. 27, 1989, Madeline D. Thomas, curator of education, Bureau of Museums and Historic Sites. *The John Dickinson Plantation.*

Wilmington

Afro-American Historical Society of Delaware

The Afro-American Historical Society of Delaware has identified several sites in Wilmington associated with the Black history of the city. One of the historic sites is the Walnut Street Young Men's Christian Association. Referred to at one time as the "Colored Y," for years it was the only YMCA that allowed Black participation.

Today the YMCA of Delaware remains active, providing housing for young men in its rooms and sponsoring activities for young people including a daycare program, weightlifting, and swimming.

For more information about Delaware's Black historic sites, call the Afro-American Historical Society of Delaware.

DATE ESTABLISHED:	1939
ADDRESS:	Historical society administrative office, 512 E. 4th Street; "Y," 1000A Walnut Street, Wilmington
TELEPHONE:	Administrative office, Afro-American Historical Society of Delaware, (302) 571-9300; "Y," (302) 571-6935
VISITING HOURS:	Mon.–Fri. 1–5
FEES:	Contact the "Y" for information
SOURCES:	Harmon Carey, executive assistant for African-American Affairs, Delaware Division of Historical and Cultural Affairs. Telephone conversation June 11, 1994, Mrs. Ruth Peebles of the YMCA. *Potentially Significant Afro-American Historic Sites.*

Works Consulted

The John Dickinson Plantation. Dover, Del.: Department of State, Delaware Division of Historical and Cultural Affairs. [brochure]

National Register of Historic Places. Washington, D.C.: National Park Service, 1976.

Potentially Significant Afro-American Historic Sites. Patricia B. Koeker. Dover, Del.: State of Delaware, Division of Historical and Cultural Affairs, Oct. 1989. [list]

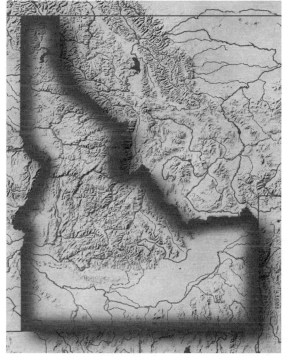

Boise

St. Paul Missionary Baptist Church

The Black population of Boise was small during the city's era of early growth, and African American worshipers attended church services with white congregations before St. Paul's congregation was organized. By 1909 African Americans had established their own separate church, meeting at first in a small building in Boise's commercial district. Within a year they received

a donation of land south of Warm Springs Avenue.

In 1921 the Reverend William Riley Hardy, first pastor of the church, and church members built the present structure themselves. The building they created is a frame, rectangular structure with arched stained-glass windows. The interior has a raised central pulpit and pews made of oak. The church built a parsonage in the 1950s—a structure that later housed an office for the local chapter of the National Association for the Advancement of Colored People.

St. Paul Missionary Baptist Church is one of two remaining predominantly Black churches in Idaho. The building is listed in the *National Register of Historic Places.*

DATE BUILT: 1921
ADDRESS: 124 Broadway Avenue, Boise
TELEPHONE: (208) 344-0674
VISITING HOURS: By appointment, Mon.–Fri.
SOURCES: NRHPINF. Telephone conversation June 21, 1994, Mrs. Evelena Lady Ashley, wife of Pastor Bobby C. Ashley.

Spalding

Nez Percé National Historical Park

The Black man, York, who traveled with the Lewis and Clark Expedition of 1803 to 1806, may have been one of the first African Americans to explore the territory now called Idaho. York, a slave, was a man of great size and strength, and he became a valued member of the expedition. He traveled with the explorers to the areas of Idaho now within the Nez Percé National Historical Park, the Lolo Trail, and Weippe Prairie. The Nez Percé National Historical Park extends from Wallowa Lake, Oregon, to Bear Paw Battlefield near Chinook, Montana (the site of the Nez Percé surrender). The park consists of thirty-eight sites, of which Lolo Trail and Weippe Prairie are in Idaho.

In 1805 the explorers traveled over the Lolo Trail, slowly and steadily moving in the direction of the Pacific Ocean. The expedition members became the first non–Native Americans to contact the Nez Percé Indians. The journey had been very difficult, and the group was half-starved after crossing the Bitterroot Range from Montana into the Idaho territory. There they decided to rest for twelve days. Although the Nez Percés graciously provided camas roots and dried fish, the travelers were not accustomed to this type of food, and they suffered from dysentery.

When members of the expedition were well enough to continue, they cut down some large trees at this site and burned out the trunks to construct five dugout canoes. In this way they were able to paddle down rivers and streams to the Pacific, their goal. This rugged and beautiful land in the Nez Percé park covers 12,000 square miles of northern Idaho. The Canoe Camp today has an exhibit of a modern dugout canoe and an interpretive marker. Although visitors are able to see the terrain through which members of the Lewis and Clark expedition traveled, the interpretive emphasis at the park is almost entirely on the Nez Percé. Visitors, however, can purchase three books at the site that describe the expedition, and a twenty-three-minute movie, *Nez Percé: Portrait of a People*, tells how the meeting with members of the Lewis and Clark expedition changed the lives of the Nez Percé.

DATE ESTABLISHED: The Lewis and Clark Expedition crossed this area, 1805; Natl. Historical Park, 1968

ADDRESS: P. O. Box 93, Spalding, ID 83551 (Nez Percé County); headquarters and Visitors Center, at the park unit in Spalding, ten miles east of Lewiston, Idaho

TELEPHONE: (208) 843-2262

VISITING HOURS: Memorial Day–Labor Day daily 8–7; rest of the year, 8–4:30; closed New Year's Day, Christmas

FEES: None

SOURCES: Telephone conversation June 21, 1994, Mary Lou Tiede, business manager, Northwest Interpretive Association of the Nez Percé Branch. Telephone conversation Apr. 1, 1995, Judy Wohlert, interpreter, National Park Service, Nez Percé National Historical Park.

Work Consulted

Idaho's Ethnic Heritage Historical Overviews. Laurie Mercier and Carole Simon-Smolinski, project codirectors and eds. Boise, Idaho: Idaho Ethnic Heritage Project; cosponsored by Idaho Centennial Commission; National Park Service, U.S. Department of the Interior; and Idaho Historical Society, Mar. 1990.

Illinois

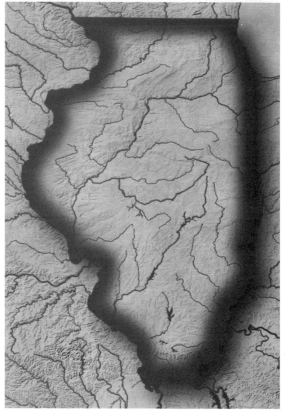

Alton

Alton Museum of History and Art

In 1987 the Alton Museum established the Committee on Black Pioneers, a group charged with documenting African American cultural activities in Alton from the 1830s to the present day. Each year the museum highlights a different theme from local Black history. One exhibit, for example, featured local Black pioneers who changed conditions for the better; it also displayed the work of African American artist Regina Shaw. A room in the Alton Museum of History and Art shows how a printing press was set up for martyred white abolitionist Elijah Lovejoy. The room contains a press similar to the Lovejoy press that an angry mob threw into the Mississippi River.

Elijah Lovejoy (1802–1837) was born in Albion, Maine, the son of Reverend Daniel Lovejoy and Elizabeth Pattee Lovejoy. He graduated from Waterville College in Maine (now Colby College). In 1836 he came to Alton, at that time the most prosperous city in Illinois. Previously he had edited *The Observer*, published at St. Louis, Missouri. Because Missouri was a slave state, Elijah and his views soon became highly unpopular. He decided, therefore, to move his activities to Alton, across the Mississippi River from St. Louis. Many Alton citizens originally were from New England and other eastern states, and they believed slavery was evil. When Lovejoy began anew to edit the *Alton Observer* and to express antislavery views in the paper, many townspeople supported him. In spite of their support, however, and despite the status of Illinois as a free state, Lovejoy and his paper became targets of violence. An incident occurred when a press arrived on a Sunday morning. Lovejoy's religious convictions prevented him from caring for the business of shipping the press on the sabbath, and he left it unguarded on the wharf. That Sunday night the press was dumped into the river. The citizens of Alton condemned the act and pledged money for a new press. Two other presses were destroyed by mobs, but the Ohio Antislavery Society, hearing of the outrageous vandalism, replaced them. The rage of proslavery forces escalated, however, after the founding of a state antislavery society at Alton; soon the proslavery mobs destroyed another press. Armed abolitionists then came from nearby towns to protect a new press that was on the way from Ohio. When the press arrived on November 7, 1837, armed guards stood watch over the warehouse where it was placed. The entire city of Alton was in a state of apprehension as night fell.

That night a mob came and tried to set the warehouse on fire. Lovejoy rushed out to try to stop them, and they shot and killed him, then dumped the press into the Mississippi River.

Elijah Lovejoy was buried in the Alton Cemetery, and a monument of the winged statue of Victory was erected to his memory. The statue symbolized triumph of the causes for which Lovejoy fought—freedom for Black people and freedom of the press.

Visitors should call the museum to check for current Black history themes. The African American cookbook is on sale for $8.50 at the museum and at the Alton Visitors Center, 200 Piasa Street.

DATE ESTABLISHED:	Museum, 1987; memorial monument, 1897
ADDRESS:	829 E. Fourth Street, Alton
TELEPHONE:	(618) 462-2763
VISITING HOURS:	Tues.–Wed., Thurs., Sun. 1–4; closed Mon., Fri., Sat., Christmas, Easter 👫
FEES:	None
SOURCES:	Letter from Lottie M. Pendergrass, Committee on Black Pioneers, Alton Museum of History and Art, Mar. 6, 1990. "Making History, Black History." *Dictionary of American Biography*, 434–5.

Chicago

Robert S. Abbott House

Robert Sengstacke Abbott was born in 1870 at St. Simon Island off the coast of Georgia. After attending the Beach Institute in Savannah (see the listing for Savannah, King-Tisdell Cottage), he studied at Claflin University in South Carolina and at Hampton Institute in Virginia. At Hampton, he learned the printer's trade, which proved useful in his future work. Although he had moved to Chicago to study at the Kent School of Law, Abbott was unable to earn a living as a lawyer, so he took a job working in a printing house.

Abbott wanted to print his own newspaper. He knew that the Black community had important concerns that needed to be widely shared, so he took his savings, borrowed money, and set up his first office in his landlady's dining room. In 1905 he began printing the *Chicago Daily Defender* in a small handbill size. He walked through the streets, delivering his precious first copies door to door to small Black-owned businesses. Within two decades the *Defender* was known in Black households across the country.

Abbott was brash and outspoken in his words and phrases. Where other Black newspaper writers of the day were careful not to offend white readers, the *Defender's* articles attacked racism and discrimination in searing terms. Abbott also used his newspaper for another purpose—to encourage African Americans to migrate north for better living conditions.

By 1929 Abbott was wealthy and able to publish his newspaper in a three-story building. The *Defender* became the senior partner of a chain of papers that included the *Michigan Chronicle, New Pittsburgh Courier, New National Courier,* and *Tri-State Defender.*

The most-successful Black publisher of his era, Abbott had nearly a half million dollars in cash. He purchased a fine home on South Park Way (now Martin Luther King Jr. Drive). This was in a Chicago South Side community known for the grand mansions and the opulent lifestyle of its African American residents. The Abbott house originally was built as a duplex with an elegant coach house in the rear. The interior featured carved-oak pilasters and exposed beams that framed the main rooms. Abbott lived in one section of the duplex between 1926 and 1940. When he died in 1940, Abbott's nephew, John H. Sengstacke, became the new head of the group of newspapers. The *Defender* continued to bring inspiration to thousands of Black people by offering the hope of relief from oppressive racism.

DATE OF SIGNIFICANCE: Abbott residence, 1926–1940

ADDRESS: Abbott House, 4742 Martin Luther King Jr. Drive; newspaper office, 2400 S. Michigan Avenue, Chicago

TELEPHONE: Newspaper, (312) 225-2400

VISITING HOURS: House, private, visitors may drive by; newspaper office, by appointment during business hours

FEES: None

SOURCES: Telephone call to the newspaper, June 24, 1994. NRHPINF. *International Library of Negro Life and History,* 153.

Black Metropolis

The historic area listed in the *National Register of Historic Places* under the theme of "Black Metropolis" consists of several commercial and civic buildings and a sculpture. Together they represent a once-thriving area of African American civic, commercial, and cultural activity. The structures are the Overton Hygienic Building, the Chicago Bee Building, Eighth Regiment Armory, Victory Sculpture, Unity Hall, and Wabash Avenue YMCA.

Development began in this area in the 1850s with the establishment of a grid of streets in an area three miles south of Chicago's central business district. A decade earlier African Americans had begun to leave oppressive conditions in the South. Many came to Chicago and settled throughout the city. Between 1900 and 1920 this geographic area changed from a white upper-middle class to a predominantly Black neighborhood, and several Black businesses prospered in the vicinity of State and Thirty-fifth Streets. Included in the district were the first Black-owned bank, restaurants, and theaters and nightclubs where patrons could listen to Louis Armstrong, Jelly Roll Morton, Florence Mills, and other popular entertainers.

After 1925 the Black Metropolis area began to decline. Fewer new arrivals meant a decline in the need for goods and services. White business owners began to realize the potential profits from providing services and goods to the Black population, and their businesses along Forty-seventh Street began to siphon off customers from Black enterprises. The greatest impact, however, came from financial hardships of the Great Depression years, which dealt a fatal blow to many Black businesses. Many buildings became vacant or fell into disrepair, and urban renewal projects of the 1950s and 1960s brought about the demolition of many houses and commercial buildings. By mid-year 1994 a strong resurgence of interest in rehabilitating some of the buildings in the Black Metropolis area was showing results, with projects in varying stages of progress.

The Chicago Bee Building, the Eighth Regiment Armory, the Overton Hygienic Building, Unity Hall, the Victory Sculpture, and the Wabash Avenue

YMCA all represent a once-thriving commercial and cultural area of the city. These structures are among the most significant Black historical landmarks in the United States and may once again be restored as places representing the pride of the community.

SOURCES: NRHPINF. Telephone conversation June 24, 1994, Alicia Mazur, preservation planner, City of Chicago, Department of Planning and Development. Telephone conversation June 24, 1994, Pat Dowell-Cerasoli, Mid-South Planning and Development Commission.

Chicago Bee Building

Anthony Overton built another landmark building in this community, the Chicago Bee Building at 3647–3655 South State Street. Overton had first published the *Chicago Bee* from his own building, the Overton Hygienic Building. Later he printed the newspaper from a storefront on State Street. Wanting to establish one location for the complete operation, he commissioned the Chicago Bee Building in 1929 as a combination newspaper office and apartment building. The three-story art deco structure had a facade ornamented with glazed terra cotta. It was ready for occupancy in 1931.

Unfortunately, with the onset of the Great Depression, Overton's bank and insurance company began to decline, and the bank failed. Overton gave up his Overton Hygienic Building and moved the cosmetics company into the Chicago Bee Building, where the two businesses shared quarters for many years. Although the newspaper ceased publication in the early 1940s, the cosmetics firm continued to operate from the Chicago Bee Building.

Today the Chicago Bee Building, which has had few alterations, remains as a landmark, the last major structure built in the Black Metropolis area. Plans are under way to renovate the Chicago Bee Building, which the City of Chicago has owned since 1987. Renovations were to begin in 1994 and to end in the fall of 1995. Plans call for restoring the original terra-cotta finish and first-floor storefronts.

DATE BUILT: 1929–1931
ADDRESS: 3647–3655 S. State Street, Chicago
VISITING HOURS: Visitors may drive by
SOURCE: NRHPINF.

The Eighth Regiment Armory

The Eighth Regiment Armory at 3533 South Giles Avenue is a third landmark in the Black Metropolis area. The Illinois National Guard built it as headquarters for the country's only regiment to be commanded entirely by Black men. Originally organized as a volunteer regiment drawn from the Black community in 1898 during the Spanish-American War, the regiment served as an infantry division of the Illinois National Guard. Although their first headquarters was in a former livery stable, the men distributed petitions as early as 1910 in which they asked for better facilities. Construction started in 1914, and the building was completed the following year.

The "Fighting Eighth" served during border conflicts with Mexico in 1916 and later fought on major battlefronts in France in World War I. It was recognized as the last regiment to drive the German forces from the Aisne-Marne region before the 1918 armistice. Almost every man in the regiment who returned had some kind of decoration for bravery in action. The name of the street on which the armory is located was changed to Giles Avenue to honor Lieutenant George Giles, the highest ranking officer killed in action. The Victory Sculpture on Thirty-fifth Street and Martin Luther King Jr. Drive, erected in 1927, also honors the bravery of this regiment.

The Eighth Regiment eventually became part of several specialized military divisions housed in a new armory on Cottage Grove Avenue. The historic Eighth Regiment Armory, a three-story building with limestone trim, was used for a time for community meetings and social functions, then it became vacant. The building still appears much as it was when designed, housing a drill hall, meeting rooms, dining facilities, and reception parlors. Discussions have begun on possible ways to renovate the building.

DATE BUILT:	1914–1915
ADDRESS:	3533 S. Giles Avenue, Chicago
VISITING HOURS:	Vacant, visitors may drive by
SOURCE:	NRHPINF.

Overton Hygienic Building

Between 1908 and 1931 the Black Metropolis area gained nationwide attention as a model of Black enterprise as capital raised by the African American community put up several new buildings. One of these landmarks was the Overton Hygienic Building, which was built in 1922–1923. Pioneer Anthony Overton constructed the building, which was considered a milestone in African American business achievement in Chicago. Its construction cost a quarter of a million dollars, and it was the first structure in the Black Metropolis to offer first-class rental offices.

Anthony Overton was a business genius who emphasized integrity in business relationships. He started with a small cosmetics firm, the Overton Hygienic Company, and developed other enterprises: the Victory Life Insurance Company, the *Chicago Bee* newspaper, the *Half Century Magazine,* and the Douglass National Bank—the first Black bank to receive a national charter.

Overton was born in slavery in Louisiana in March 1865. He studied at Washburn College in Topeka and earned a bachelor of law degree in 1888 at the University of Kansas. For a brief period Overton was proprietor of a general store in Oklahoma. He served as judge of the Municipal Court in Shawnee County, Kansas, and started the Overton Hygienic Company in Kansas City.

Needing larger facilities, Overton moved to Chicago. He established both his living quarters and his business in a former apartment building on South Wabash Avenue and began selling cosmetics, shoe polish, baking powder, and flavoring extracts to a wide market in the United States.

Overton broke into the publishing business in 1916 with the *Half Century Magazine* and the *Chicago Bee* newspaper. By 1922 his businesses were scattered in different buildings throughout the South Side. To consolidate them, he built the Overton Building. With more room for the different operations, Overton established an insurance company and, in 1922, the Douglass National Bank. The Black-owned bank solved many problems due to banking discrimination. A great many banks had taken funds from African American depositors but refused to employ them or give them loans.

In the Overton Building, quarters for the Douglass National Bank and Victory Life Insurance Company occupied most of the ground floor. The second floor housed quality rental offices for professionals. Overton used the third and fourth floors for his own businesses.

Overton's enterprises at first appeared to survive the Great Depression. Douglass National Bank was successful until financial panics and bank runs increased. The bank shut down in the early 1930s, and Overton's insurance company nearly became insolvent. Although the depletion of funds forced Overton to abandon the Overton Hygienic Building and to find smaller quarters in another building one block south, he retained control of the company until his death in 1946.

DATE BUILT:	1922–1923
ADDRESS:	3619–3627 S. State Street, Chicago
VISITING HOURS:	Private, visitors may drive by
SOURCE:	NRHPINF.

Unity Hall

Unity Hall was built in 1886 by a Jewish social organization, but became the headquarters of the People's Movement Club in 1917. This movement was started by Oscar Stanton DePriest, an African American who arrived in Chicago in 1889. DePriest became a city councilman and consistently sought jobs and better living conditions for his constituents. In 1917 DePriest, a Republican, created the People's Movement Club in order to establish a strong political base in the Black community. DePriest became the committeeman of the Third Ward in 1924. In 1928 he became the first Black person in the twentieth century and the first ever from the North elected to the U.S. House of Representatives. He served three consecutive terms before being defeated in 1934 by Arthur Mitchell, a Black Democrat.

The People's Movement Club used Unity Hall, a three-story building with red pressed-brick and terracotta ornamentation, as its headquarters. The interior had many small clubrooms and a large assembly hall in the rear. Later Unity Hall served for many years as headquarters for the Democratic politician William Dawson. The building later housed a church.

DATE BUILT: 1887; Unity Hall, 1917

ADDRESS: 3140 S. Indiana Avenue, Chicago

VISITING HOURS: Privately owned by a church

SOURCES: NRHPINF. *African Americans: Voices of Triumph*, vol. 2, *Leadership*, 212.

Victory Sculpture

The Victory Sculpture, located at the intersection of Thirty-fifth Street and Martin Luther King Jr. Drive, honors the courageous men of the Illinois Eighth Regiment, the first to be commanded entirely by Black men. The men served with distinction in France where they were incorporated into the 370th U.S. Infantry during World War I. By the end of World War I, General John J. Pershing had awarded the Distinguished Service Cross for extraordinary heroism to twelve members of the "Fighting Eighth." The French government awarded the *Croix de Guerre* to sixty-eight men from the unit.

At the close of World War I, Chicago's Black community requested a memorial to honor the achievements of the Eighth Regiment. In the mid-1920s they proposed that a monument be erected in the parkway of South Grand Boulevard (now Martin Luther King Jr. Drive). The South Park Commission, which controlled the boulevard system, firmly opposed the plan, maintaining that there was no space available for a monument.

Chicago's famed Black newspaper, the *Chicago Daily Defender*, began a campaign against the commission board. Editorials urged the Black community to vote against any South Park Commission projects until the city recognized its Black war heroes. The community maintained the pressure until the commission agreed to support the memorial. Eventually the commission and the state of Illinois jointly funded the project.

French-born sculptor Leonard Crunelle designed the Victory Sculpture, a circular, gray-granite shaft with three bronze panels finished with black patination. The memorial portrays a Black soldier, a Black woman symbolizing motherhood, and the figure of Columbia holding a tablet listing the locations of the regiment's main battles.

The sculpture, the second monument erected in the United States to honor Black war heroes, was dedicated in 1936 in a public ceremony. It has since become one of the best-known landmarks of Chicago's Black community.

The Victory Sculpture is part of a plan to improve the Martin Luther King Jr. Drive from

Thirty-fifth Street to the Stevenson overpass. Plans included planting trees along the way, refinishing the monument and providing special lighting for it, and raising the monument to a higher level. These changes are expected to make the underpass more visually inviting so that people would be encouraged to visit buildings in Black Metropolis.

DATE ESTABLISHED: 1936
ADDRESS: Thirty-fifth Street at Martin Luther King Jr. Drive
VISITING HOURS: Daily, 24 hours
SOURCE: NRHPINF.

Wabash Avenue Young Men's Christian Association

The Wabash Avenue YMCA opened its building to the public in 1913 after a successful three-year fund-raising drive. Julius Rosenwald, a white businessman, philanthropist, and chairman of Sears, Roebuck and Company, initiated the drive in 1911 by offering to advance $25,000 toward the erection of a YMCA building. Additional funds came from the Black community, which raised over $20,000, and from the contributions of business executives.

When the imposing five-story Wabash YMCA opened, it was one of the best-equipped of its type. Thousands of African American immigrants from the South were arriving in Chicago between 1910 and 1920, and, beginning in 1913, many were welcomed with housing and other services at the new "Y." The YMCA staff helped them find employment and pro-

vided job-training programs, including a popular auto repair class. Residents and newcomers enjoyed the assembly hall, gymnasium, and pool.

The YMCA served the community well for many years. However, by the late 1970s, the national YMCA office closed the Wabash Avenue "Y" and sold the building to a local church. The Wabash YMCA Building, which was used for a time by the church, was then purchased by a consortium of churches. With the help of a community association, the churches plan to develop the structure into a single-room occupancy building that would provide recreational and social support services, much as the old "Y" had done.

DATE BUILT: 1911–1913
ADDRESS: 3763 S. Wabash Avenue, Chicago
VISITING HOURS: Private, visitors may drive by
SOURCES: NRHPINF.

Chicago Historical Society Museum

In 1990 a major permanent exhibit opened at the Chicago Historical Museum: *A House Divided: America in the Age of Lincoln.* Museum displays focus on Black resistance to slavery, the role of Black soldiers, and the role of free Black people as abolitionists during the Civil War era.

The museum also has a small replica of Jean Baptiste Point du Sable's trading post. Du Sable, a man of mixed African ancestry, was Chicago's first non-Native American settler.

DATE ESTABLISHED: 1856
ADDRESS: 1601 N. Clark Street at North Avenue, Chicago
TELEPHONE: (312) 642-4600
VISITING HOURS: Mon.–Sat. 9–4:30, Sun. noon–5; closed Thanksgiving, Christmas, New Year's Day
FEES: Adults, $3; senior citizens and children 6–17, $1; Mon., free to all
SOURCES: Pat Manthei, public relations manager. Telephone call to site, June 25, 1994.

Du Sable Museum of African-American History *

The Du Sable Museum, one of America's oldest Black history museums, houses Chicago's most extensive collection of African American historical materials. The museum was named for Jean Baptiste Point du Sable, a Haitian pioneer of mixed African and European parentage; he was Chicago's first non-Native American settler.

The museum, which has an extensive permanent collection of African and African American art and artifacts, mounts more than six exhibitions each year. Its collection includes more than 800 artworks from the Works Progress Administration period of the Depression years and the 1960s Black arts movement. It features a monumental bas-relief carving by Robert Witt Ames that traces 400 years of African American history. The library also contains more than 10,000 volumes on African and African American life, history, and culture. Programs include tours for schools, lectures, and live performances of music and dance.

DATE ESTABLISHED:	1961
ADDRESS:	740 E. Fifty-sixth Place (Washington Park at Fifty-seventh Street and Cottage Grove Avenue), Chicago
TELEPHONE:	(312) 947-0600
VISITING HOURS:	Mon.–Sat. 10–5, Sun. noon–5; closed New Year's Day, Easter, Thanksgiving, Christmas ♀♂
FEES:	Adults, $2; senior citizens and students, $2; children under 6, free; Thurs., free to all
SOURCES:	Mildred B. Jourdain, Du Sable Museum. Brochure of the Du Sable Museum sent by the Chicago Tourism Council. Brochure on Chicago museums from the Illinois Department of Commerce and Community Affairs Office of Tourism. Telephone call to site, June 24, 1994.

Provident Hospital and Training School

Dr. Daniel Hale Williams, a pioneering African American physician, was born in Pennsylvania in 1858. He grew up in a home in which his parents worked for the abolitionist cause. His father died when he was eleven. As a young man, Williams moved about the country in search of jobs. After working as a waiter, a barber, and a musician, he was fortunate to find an employer in Wisconsin who encouraged him to complete high school. After graduation, a prominent local doctor, Henry Palmer, later sponsored Williams's admission to Chicago Medical College from which he graduated in 1883.

Williams became known as an outstanding physician in the Black community. Although he treated both Black and white patients, he was acutely aware of the discrimination that barred Black patients, nurses, and interns from white-owned hospitals and training programs. To remedy this situation, he founded Provident Hospital in 1891, which was the first training school for Black interns and nurses in the United States. It was also America's first hospital serving physicians and patients without regard to race.

Williams was a staff surgeon at Provident from 1891 to 1912, except for short periods spent at Freedmen's Hospital in Washington, D.C. In 1893 he made history when a young man was brought in unconscious and bleeding internally from a stab wound to the heart. Williams opened the chest and operated, becoming one of the first physicians to perform a successful surgical closure of a wound to the heart and pericardium.

The first two hospital buildings of Provident Hospital have been demolished, and the third building—the one that opened two years after Williams's death—also is in danger of being lost. Vacant, boarded up, surrounded by a high fence, and for sale in mid-1994, the historic building is accessible only for exterior viewing. Visitors should go by only if they can view the building as a once-fine, historic brownstone that still has possibilities for restoration.

DATE BUILT:	1891
ADDRESS:	500 E. Fifty-first Street and Vincennes Avenue, Chicago
TELEPHONE:	Newer Provident Hospital, (312) 572-2000 (not a historic structure)
VISITING HOURS:	Vacant, visitors may drive by
SOURCES:	Telephone conversation June 24, 1994, Carol Reliford, RN, Human Resource Department, Provident Hospital of Cook County. *Webster's New Biographical Dictionary*, 1061. *The African American Encyclopedia*, vol. 6, 1705–7. "The Provident Hospital Project," 457–75.

Quinn Chapel African Methodist Episcopal Church

Quinn Chapel houses Chicago's earliest Black congregation. The church was founded in 1844 when several Black Chicagoans organized a nonsectarian prayer group that met each week in the members' homes. In 1847 the group became known as part of the African Methodist Episcopal Congregation. Their church was named in honor of Bishop William P. Quinn.

More than fifty members of the congregation were ex-slaves. Some had purchased their freedom or had been manumitted, while others had escaped from bondage. Although technically free, they were bound together by a danger—even in Chicago. In 1793 the United States had passed a law, rooted in the fugitive slave clause of the Constitution, mandating that any person who was a slave in one state and escaped to another state should be apprehended and returned to his or her owner. Then in 1850 Congress passed a new and stronger Fugitive Slave Law—which placed every Black person in danger. With no more than a sworn affidavit, a white person could claim that an African American was an escaped slave and take him or her before a federal commissioner. Any citizen could be summoned to help in capturing the fugitive; anyone who interfered with such a capture could be fined a maximum of $1,000 and imprisoned up to six months.

African Americans had no right to a trial by jury or to testify in their own behalf. Thus, there was a strong incentive to send the person back into slavery because this would reward the commissioner (the official in charge of such cases) with a fee of $10. If the suspected escapee was released, the commissioner received only $5.

Reaction at Quinn Chapel to the new fugitive slave law was immediate. The church called a special meeting, which 300 people—more than half of Chicago's Black population—attended. The group passed a resolution declaring that its members would defend themselves at all costs, even at the risk of shedding human blood. In the words of the resolution, "We who have tasted of freedom are ready to exclaim, in the language of the brave Patrick Henry, `Give us liberty or give us death.'"[1] The group formed the Liberty Association and assigned teams of men to patrol the city and watch for possible slave hunters.

The Quinn Chapel congregation constructed their first church in 1853. True to their beliefs, they used the church as a station on the underground railroad. After the church was destroyed in the Chicago fire of 1871, church members met in several temporary locations until they could construct the present Quinn Chapel, a substantial brick and rusticated gray-stone structure, in 1892. The exterior of the church has remained virtually unchanged, and much of the interior is original. The second-floor chapel has the original wooden pews as well as the William H. Delle pipe organ purchased from the German pavilion at the 1893 Columbian Exposition. In 1940 church member Proctor Chisholm painted a mural in the sanctuary of Christ's resurrection.

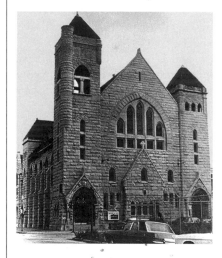

Members of Quinn Chapel have been active in community affairs. They assisted in founding the Bethel A.M.E. Church, Provident Hospital, and the Wabash Avenue YMCA. Some church members have served in both houses of the Illinois legislature. Quinn Chapel A.M.E. Church is listed in the *National Register of Historic Places.*

DATE ESTABLISHED:	Congregation, 1844; church, 1892
ADDRESS:	2401 S. Wabash Avenue, Chicago
VISITING HOURS:	By appointment, Mon.–Fri. 10–4
SOURCES:	NRHPINF. Telephone conversation June 24, 1994, Ms. Ruth Hawkins, receptionist, Quinn Chapel A.M.E. Church. *There Is a River,* 160–1.

Harold Washington Library Center

The Harold Washington Library Center, the main library of the Chicago Public Library, is the largest public library in the United States in volume. Appropriately, it is named for a man of high achievement, Harold Washington, the first African American mayor of Chicago.

Washington was born in Chicago in 1922. He graduated from Roosevelt University in 1949 and from Northwestern University Law School in 1952. Two years later he began his political career, serving as a Democratic Party precinct captain. Later he was elected to the Illinois House of Representatives and the Illinois Senate; from 1980 to 1983 he was a member of the U.S. House of Representatives.

In the February 1983 Democratic mayoral primary, Washington surprised many who had predicted that he would be defeated by incumbent mayor Jane Byrne or by Richard M. Daley, son of the late Mayor Richard J. Daley. After Washington's surprise victory in the primary election, he went on to win the mayor's seat in the April 1983 general election. Although his was a narrow victory, Washington had many loyal supporters and was reelected in 1987. The city was shocked and saddened when Washington died of a heart attack later that year.

Today the city honors its former mayor with a library that bears his name and carries an important collection of his papers. The ten-story building takes up a full city block and is designed in a classical tradition. Constructed of red granite, the library has a green roof with green metal owls perched in the corners, symbolic, perhaps, of the wisdom that resides inside. In addition to the Harold Washington Collection, the library contains a large collection of works on Black history and the Civil War.

DATE ESTABLISHED:	1991
ADDRESS:	400 S. State Street, Chicago
TELEPHONE:	(312) 747-4300
VISITING HOURS:	Mon. 9–7; Tues., Thurs. 11–7; Wed., Fri., Sat. 9–5; Sun. 1–5 ♟♟
SOURCES:	Telephone conversation June 25, 1994, Sue Puterko, librarian. Telephone call to site, Aug. 12, 1995. The Academic American Encyclopedia.

Ida B. Wells-Barnett House

Ida B. Wells Barnett, a nineteenth- and early twentieth-century journalist and crusader, fought racism throughout her adult life. Her pioneering research and publications decried the brutal lynchings that terrorized the Black community. They were a forerunner to the work of the National Association for the Advancement of Colored People in protesting violence and senseless killings.

Ida Wells was born in Holly Springs, Mississippi, in 1862. Her father was a skilled carpenter and a man of integrity. As Ida was attending Rust College, her education was suddenly interrupted when her parents died during the yellow fever epidemic of 1878. Although only sixteen at the time, she took over the responsibility for her younger brothers and sisters and earned some money by teaching school in a town near Holly Springs.

Later Wells moved to Memphis, where she taught school and continued her teacher training at LeMoyne Normal Institute and Fisk University. About that time Jim Crow laws were passed in Tennessee, and Wells rebelled against them one day by refusing to move from the first-class section into the smoking car, which had been set aside for African Americans. Upon her refusal to follow the conductor's order, she was dragged out of the car by three white men. She filed a lawsuit against the Chesapeake & Ohio Railroad as a result. At first she appeared to have won when a court awarded her $500 in damages. However, the state had no intention of setting a precedent in favor of equal rights; the Tennessee Supreme Court reversed the decision of the lower court.

Wells next became a journalist and purchased an interest in a small Memphis newspaper, *Free Speech and Headlight.* An article by her in the newspaper denouncing the inequities observed in the Memphis school district cost her her job as a teacher, but she persisted in her efforts to expose injustice. A tragedy in Memphis in 1892 was a crucial event in Wells's life. Three Black entrepreneurs had opened a grocery store in town. Its popularity grew, drawing customers away from a store run by a white man. Resentment grew in the white community against the Black businessmen. One day a group of white thugs began to harass the Black-run store, and a group of armed Black men repelled the invaders. Three of the white attackers were shot in the confusion. The white press soon printed inflammatory articles about the Black men, portraying them as brutes who had attacked innocent white citizens. Not long afterward, a mob invaded the jail where the Black entrepreneurs were being held, seized them, and lynched them. The store run by the three Black entrepreneurs was looted and then closed down. Wells had been a close friend of one of the Black grocery store owners and his wife. Shocked at the outrage, she wrote a series of scathing articles about the lynching in her newspaper, urging Black residents to leave Memphis since there was no justice for them there.

Wells pointed out that lynchings seemed to take place when Black people began to rise up and compete economically with white people. One of her articles analyzed 728 lynchings that had taken place over a decade. She pointed out that women and children as well as men were among the victims; she hinted that many lynchings may have occurred because of interracial relationships instigated by white women. Wells was out of town when this particular article appeared. It raised a fury, and a band of white citizens burned the newspaper office to the ground and ran Wells's coworkers out of town. Wells received a warning that

if she returned to Memphis, she would be hanged.

Wells stayed in the North for the next three years, lecturing in northeastern cities. She visited England for several months in 1893 and again for several months in 1894. In 1895 she ended the sojourn in the north, marrying Ferdinand Lee Barnett, a lawyer and founder of *The Conservator,* Chicago's first Black-owned newspaper. Settling in Chicago, Wells-Barnett raised a family and periodically wrote additional articles on the subject of lynching. She formed clubs for women, helped to organize the National Association for the Advancement of Colored People, went on speaking tours, and continued her outspoken attacks on lynchings and other forms of injustice. Some felt that she was too sharp in her criticism, but she never stopped crusading against lynching—the most savage act of racism.

Ida Wells-Barnett spent ten years with her husband and children at their home in Chicago on South Grand Boulevard, later called South Park Way, now renamed Dr. Martin Luther King Jr. Drive. The Barnett family moved to the three-story, fourteen-room house in 1919 where they lived until 1929. Ida Wells-Barnett died in 1931.

DATE BUILT:	c1890
ADDRESS:	3624 Martin Luther King Jr. Drive, Chicago
VISITING HOURS:	Private, visitors may drive by
SOURCES:	NRHPINF. *When and Where I Enter. National Register of Historic Places,* 206. *The African American Encyclopedia,* 1676–80.

Junction

Old Slave House

The Old Slave House in Gallatin County, Illinois, has chilling and tangible evidence to support statements that many kidnapped slaves were kept in bondage here. Although the house is in Illinois, a free state, it was just over the border from Kentucky, a slave state. According to legend, slaves were kept in this house to provide free labor for the Equality Salt Wells in Illinois. On the third floor one can see twenty-five cells where male slaves were kept as well as family rooms for the female slaves. Iron bars over the windows allowed a modicum of ventilation and prevented attempts at escape. Even though slavery was illegal in Illinois, the owner of the Old Slave House—a man named Crenshaw—kept up his nefarious work for years. Although Crenshaw stood trial for kidnapping slaves as they escaped across the river from Kentucky, he was always acquitted. The last male slave who at one time lived in this house is said to have died in 1949 at the age of 119 years.

The slave quarters, which are open to visitors, are approached through narrow doorways leading into the small rooms. This is an important and unique historic site for those who wish to see physical evidence of what slavery was like in one nonplantation setting. Unfortunately, plans have been made to close the museum in December 1997. In 1994 the local ferry closed for good; because the house is a long drive away from urban amenities, too few visitors came after the ferry's closing to justify keeping the museum open. Perhaps with the resurgence of interest in Black history, enough visitors will drive the distance to keep the Old Slave House open.

DATE BUILT:	1834
ADDRESS:	Junction vicinity, 9 miles west of Shawneetown, near intersection of IL 13 and IL 1
TELEPHONE:	(618) 276-4410
VISITING HOURS:	May–Oct., daily 9–5; closed winter 👫
FEES:	Adults, $4; children, $3
SOURCES:	Telephone conversation June 24, 1994, George M. Fisk, the Old Slave House. Janet Armstrong, secretary, White County Historical Society. *Hammond United States Atlas*, 222.

Princeton

Owen Lovejoy Homestead

Owen Lovejoy (1811–1864) was born in Albion, Maine. He studied at Bowdoin College in Maine but did not graduate. He studied law and taught school before moving in 1836 to Alton, Illinois, where he prepared for the ministry under the guidance of his older brother, Elijah. Owen soon joined in the antislavery campaigns championed by his brother. After Elijah was killed in 1837 by mobs that repeatedly had destroyed his printing press, Owen vowed never to forsake the antislavery cause. He became minister of the Congregational Church in Princeton, Illinois. During his seventeen years as minister at the church, he repeatedly testified against slavery in spite of frequently encountered violence. In January 1843 he married a widow, Eunice Dunham; they had seven children. The Lovejoys sheltered runaway slaves in this two-story, fifteen-room frame home, and Owen wrote a book about his brother, a volume that became important in the antislavery cause. The house owned by Owen and Eunice Lovejoy became the main underground railroad station in Princeton.

Owen Lovejoy served in the U.S. Congress from 1857 until his death in 1864. While in Congress, he continued to speak out against slavery. However, he did not join in when William Lloyd Garrison, another white abolitionist, made verbal attacks on President Lincoln. Lovejoy agreed with President Lincoln's reconstruction program, which some believed was too generous to the South, and he introduced a universal emancipation bill that, after many changes, became the heart of the Thirteenth Amendment. Unfortunately, he did not live to see the amendment adopted. He died in 1864 and was buried in the Oakland Cemetery in Princeton, Illinois. In 1972 the Lovejoy house was restored to its original state.

DATE BUILT:	1838; Lovejoy residence, 1843–1857
ADDRESS:	E. Peru Street (US 6), Princeton
TELEPHONE:	(815) 879-9151

VISITING HOURS:	May–Sept., Thurs. and Sun. 1–4; Oct., by appointment; closed Nov.–Apr. 👫
FEES:	Adults, $2; senior citizens, $1.50; students, $.50
SOURCES:	Telephone conversation June 24, 1994, Ezby Collins, member of Lovejoy House board of directors. NRHPINF. *National Register of Historic Places,* 203. State historical marker. *Dictionary of American Biography,* 435–6.

Springfield

Lincoln Home National Historic Site*

This frame, two-story house was home to Abraham Lincoln, his wife, and their three sons from 1844 until 1861. The home has been restored to look as it did at that time. During this period Lincoln worked as a lawyer, a state legislator, and a congressman. After winning the 1860 presidential election, Lincoln left Springfield and never returned.

Called the "Great Emancipator," Lincoln wavered over the question of slavery during his presidency. During the 1860 presidential campaign, the Republican Party to which he belonged opposed the extension of slavery into new territories but did not oppose existing slavery in the South. Although Lincoln may have had a deep personal dislike of the institution of slavery, he adhered to the policy of the party on this matter.

In 1860 H. Ford Douglass, a Black leader from Illinois, made a speech to an abolitionist audience at Framingham, Massachusetts. He expressed regret that Lincoln had not opposed the notorious Fugitive Slave Law that made it easier to capture escaped slaves. Douglass pointed out:

> In regard to the repeal of the Fugitive Slave Law, Abraham Lincoln occupies the same position that the old Whig party occupied in 1852....What did he say at Freeport? [Illinois, at the Lincoln–Douglas debates] Why, that the South was entitled to a Fugitive Slave Law; and although he thought the law could be modified a little, yet, he said, if he was in Congress, he would have it done in such a way as not to lessen its efficiency! Here, then, is Abraham Lincoln in favor of carrying out that infamous Fugitive Slave Law.[2]

Although Black abolitionist Frederick Douglass supported Lincoln's candidacy, Douglass became disillusioned as the campaign progressed. He was disturbed by Lincoln's reluctance to take a firm stand against slavery. Douglass and several other African Americans finally turned their support to the Radical Abolitionist Party, which stood firmly against slavery. Other Black community members, noting that Republicans had taken a partial stand against slavery, continued to support Lincoln and the Republican Party. Many of them rejoiced when he was elected President.

The Lincoln administration maintained that the purpose of the war was to restore the Union and had nothing to do with slavery. When General John Frémont issued a proclamation freeing slaves of all rebels in Missouri, President Lincoln worried that all Southerners might turn against the government. He softened Frémont's proclamation to the point of confiscating only slaves who had directly aided the Confederate military forces. Thousands of Missouri slaves thus lost an opportunity to be set free. These actions of the President greatly displeased the radical Republicans who wanted to put an end to slavery at any cost.

In March 1862 President Lincoln recommended to Congress that federal compensation be offered to any state adopting the gradual abolition of slavery. Although nothing came of this plan, Black people saw the policy as a positive shift and rejoiced. Their hopes were shattered again, however, on May 19 when Lincoln revoked General David Hunter's April 25 order proclaiming freedom for all slaves in South Carolina, Georgia, and Florida.

In July 1862, President Lincoln drafted an emancipation proclamation but withheld it from his cabinet until the Union Army won a great victory at Antietam on September 17 that year.

In August 1862 President Lincoln met with five Black men from the District of Columbia. Claiming that racial differences made it impossible for Black and white people to live together as equals, he advocated complete separation of the races. Black people could be colonized in Central America, he maintained, where they would work in coal mines under development there. Although Lincoln moved ahead with this plan, it never came to fruition. Later he arranged to send more than 400 African Americans from Washington, D.C., and Virginia to Haiti. Nearly 100 died from disease, starvation, or mutiny. This plan did not succeed, and it was necessary to send a ship to return the survivors to the United States.

At first, Black troops were not allowed officially to fight in the Union Army, although they could serve as laborers, carpenters, cooks, and nurses. Some African Americans built earthworks and bridges, unloaded cargoes, and served as spies and scouts. Black families had helped the Union cause by taking Union soldiers into their cabins, feeding them, and giving the weary soldiers a safe place to rest. In spite of their eagerness to serve, many white Northerners refused to fight beside Black soldiers, and many white people in the North and South believed Black soldiers would prove cowardly under battle conditions.

During the summer of 1862, as Union forces suffered a series of defeats, leaders at Washington began to realize that they needed Black participation to turn the tide. In July they agreed to enlist Black soldiers. From that point on nearly 10 percent of the Union Army was comprised of men in Black regiments.

Finally, Abraham Lincoln issued the Emancipation Proclamation on January 1, 1863. It stated that all slaves in the rebellious states would be free. Although the proclamation applied only to the Confederate states, all opposed to slavery rejoiced. In January 1865, when the war was nearly over, Congress adopted the Thirteenth Amendment abolishing slavery throughout the country.

Although President Lincoln had often compromised with the southern states on the issue of slavery, he eventually decided against it. Some Black Americans were critical because Lincoln had not done more to improve the lives of freed people, but many respected and revered him. Disbelief and grief were widespread when an assassin killed Lincoln on April 14, 1865. The *New Orleans Tribune,* an African American newspaper, expressed this grief.

> Brethren, we are mourning for a benefactor of our race. Sadness has taken hold of our hearts. No man can suppress his feeling at this hour of affliction. Lincoln and John Brown are two martyrs, whose memories will live united in our bosoms. Both have willingly jeopardized their lives for the sacred cause of freedom.[3]

DATE BUILT:	1839
ADDRESS:	Visitors Center, 426 S. Seventh Street; Lincoln Home, 413 S. Eighth Street (Eighth and Jackson Streets), Springfield
TELEPHONE:	(217) 492-4150
VISITING HOURS:	Daily; June 1–Aug. 15, 8–8; Aug. 16–Oct. 31, 8–6; Nov. 1–Mar. 31, 8–5; Apr. 1–May 31, 8–6; closed Thanksgiving, Christmas, New Year's Day ⛄
FEES:	None; visitors must obtain tickets at the Visitors Center on a first-come, first-served basis; tours last 15–20 minutes
SOURCES:	Telephone conversation June 24, 1994, Andre Jordan, park ranger. Telephone conversation Aug. 31, 1995, Joyce Mavis, secretary, Lincoln Home. Telephone conversation Sept. 3, 1995, Roy Tolbert, park ranger, Lincoln Home. *National Register of Historic Places,* 211. *The Negro's Civil War,* 5, 6, 20, 41, 43, 93, 94, 98, 99, 145, 241. *New Orleans Tribune.*

Lincoln's Tomb State Historic Site

A granite obelisk on a square base, a statue of Lincoln in front of the obelisk, a bust of Lincoln in front of the tomb—these are symbols at the final resting place of President Abraham Lincoln, his wife, and three of his four children.

When a funeral train brought Lincoln's body back to Springfield for burial, a regiment of Black troops with rifles reversed led the funeral procession to the state capitol. Almost all of Springfield's Black citizens joined in expressing respect for the assassinated leader. The tomb was dedicated in 1874. Lincoln's body, earlier laid to rest above ground in a marble sarcophagus, was placed beneath the burial chamber floor in 1901 after reconstruction of the tomb.

DATE ESTABLISHED:	1874
ADDRESS:	Oak Ridge Cemetery, 1441 Monument Avenue (Business Loop US 55, turn west on N. Grand Avenue to Monument Avenue, turn right, two blocks to the cemetery entrance), Springfield
TELEPHONE:	(217) 782-2717
VISITING HOURS:	Daily 9–5; closed New Year's Day, Veterans' Day, general election day, Thanksgiving, Christmas ⛄
FEES:	None

SOURCES: Telephone conversation June 24, 1994, Nan Wynn, site manager. Telephone conversation Aug. 12, 1995, Nancy Lugo, seasonal interpreter, Lincoln's Tomb. *National Register of Historic Places*, 211. *A Guide to Historic Illinois*, 24.

Notes

1. NRHPINF for site.
2. H. Ford Douglass lecture, annual Fourth of July abolitionists' picnic (Framingham, Mass.), originally printed in *Liberator* (13 July 1860), quoted in James M. McPherson, *The Negro's Civil War* (New York: Ballentine, 1991), 6.
3. *New Orleans Tribune* (20 Apr. 1865), quoted in James M. McPherson, *The Negro's Civil War* (New York: Ballentine, 1991), 312.

Works Consulted

The Academic American Encyclopedia. Danbury, Conn.: Grolier, 1993. [electronic version]

The African American Encyclopedia. Vol. 6. Michael W. Williams, ed. New York: Marshall Cavendish, 1993.

African Americans: Voices of Triumph. Vol. 2, *Leadership.* Alexandria, Va.: Time-Life, 1993.

Dictionary of American Biography. Vol. 6. Dumas Malone, ed. New York: Scribners, 1933, 1961.

A Guide to Historic Illinois. Illinois Historic Preservation Agency, Mar. 1988. [booklet]

Hammond United States Atlas. Maplewood, N.J.: Hammond, 1989.

International Library of Negro Life and History: Historical Negro Biographies. Wilhelmena S. Robinson. New York: Publishers, 1970.

"Making History, Black History Month: Exhibit Shows Contributions Black Residents Made to Area." Mary Ann Mazenko. *The (Alton) Telegraph*, 1 Feb. 1990.

National Register Information System. Washington, D.C.: National Park Service. [computer database]

National Register of Historic Places. Washington, D.C.: National Park Service, 1976.

The Negro's Civil War. James M. McPherson. New York: Ballentine, 1991.

New Orleans Tribune, 20 Apr. 1865. Quoted in *The Negro's Civil War*, James M. McPherson (New York: Ballentine, 1991), 312.

"The Provident Hospital Project: An Experiment in Race Relations and Medical Education." Vanessa Northington Gamble. *Bulletin of the History of Medicine* 65 (1991): 457–75.

There Is a River: The Black Struggle for Freedom in America. Vincent Harding. New York: Vintage Books, 1983.

Webster's New Biographical Dictionary. Springfield, Mass.: Merriam-Webster, 1988.

When and Where I Enter: The Impact of Black Women on Race and Sex in America. Paula Giddings. New York: William Morrow, 1984; New York: Bantam, 1988.

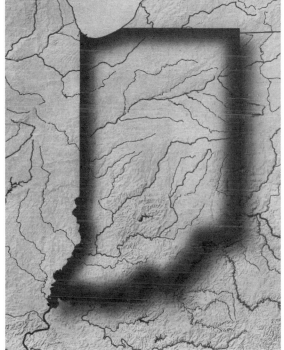

Evansville

Liberty Baptist Church

Liberty Baptist Church is the oldest African American congregation in Evansville. The church arose within a community living in a section of Evansville known as "Baptist Town." In 1860 there were only ninety-five African Americans in Evansville, but after the Civil War many former slaves crossed the Ohio River and settled

there, seeking to leave behind the harsh living conditions of the postwar South. As a result, the Black population of the city rose to almost two thousand by 1870.

The Liberty Baptist congregation formed around 1865. Its first minister was a white man named Colonel Woods. All the deacons and members of the congregation were Black. After worshiping in inadequate quarters for a number of years, the church members erected a brick church in 1880 at a cost of about $10,000. Church members were shocked when, six years later, a tornado completely destroyed it. Undaunted, the congregation immediately began to collect funds to rebuild. In December 1886—just six months later— Liberty Baptist members were able to worship again in their new church, a structure that stands today.

Through the years this church has provided a center for religious, cultural, and political affairs in the Black community. Church members have offered day-care services, recreational activities for young people, and housing assistance.

DATE BUILT:	1886
ADDRESS:	701 Oak Street (corner of Seventh Street), Evansville
TELEPHONE:	(812) 422-4628
VISITING HOURS:	By appointment, Mon.–Fri. 10–2
SOURCES:	NRHPINF. Telephone conversation June 17, 1994, Mr. David Fisher, custodian.

Fountain City

Levi Coffin House

Prior to the Civil War, slaves escaping from the South to freedom in Canada traveled along a great many routes. Many passing through the Midwest came through Fountain City, Indiana, which at that time was known as Newport. They received there a warm welcome and assistance from a white merchant named Levi Coffin. Originally from a Quaker community in the Carolinas, Coffin and his wife, Catherine, had come to this area in 1826 along with a group of Quakers vigorously opposed to slavery. Some years later—about 1839—the Coffins erected this house. Both Coffin and his wife joined with the free African

Americans of the community in an effort to defy the Fugitive Slave Law of 1850. Some thirty families cooperated in this effort.

Coffin's home, which was built right up to the sidewalk on the main street in town, became a major stop on the underground railroad in this area. Slaves were hidden in a secret area attached to a maid's room on the second floor. This room had a ceiling sharply sloping down to a four-foot-high south wall. A low bed hid a small panel door that led to a crawl space under the roof where fugitives could hide. Many runaways remained with the Coffins for days or weeks until they had regained enough strength to continue their journey.

The Coffins also were active in establishing two schools in Randolph County—the Cabin Creek School and the Union Literary Institute—that taught freed slaves and their children. In 1847 the Coffin family moved to Cincinnati, where they continued to help approximately 1,000 additional slaves find their way to freedom. After the Civil War, the Coffins continued to assist the freedmen.

Coffin House was one of the most important underground railroad sites in the country, providing refuge for more than 2,000 slaves before and during the Civil War. The house was altered in 1910 to serve as a rural hotel but later was restored to its original condition.

DATE BUILT: 1839

ADDRESS: 113 U.S. 27 North, Fountain City

TELEPHONE: (317) 847-2432

VISITING HOURS: June–Aug., Tues.–Sun. 1–4; Sept.–Oct., Sat.–Sun. 1–4; groups at other times by appointment; closed July 4, Labor Day, Nov.–May 👫

FEES: Adults, $1; students 6–18, $.50; children under 6, free

SOURCES: Personal visit to site, summer 1990. Telephone conversation June 17, 1994, and Aug. 27, 1995, Saundra Jackson, secretary, Levi Coffin House Association. Jeffrey Tenuth, registrar/historian, Indiana State Museum and Historic Sites, Aug. 25, 1989. Division of Historic Preservation and Archaeology. Survey and brochure from Saundra Jackson, secretary-treasurer of Levi Coffin House Association. *National Register of Historic Places*, 224.

Indianapolis

Crispus Attucks High School

During the nineteenth century, education in Indianapolis was segregated. Certain elementary schools were designated for "Coloreds only." Even though Black high schoolers were comparatively few in number, their presence was resented by the white community. In 1908 the superintendent of schools suggested that a separate high school be set up for African Americans. Nothing was done about this proposal until after World War I, when racial tensions increased and the Ku Klux Klan in Indiana grew rapidly. White citizens repeatedly petitioned for the removal of Black students from the public high schools.

In 1922 the Indianapolis school board began to make plans to build a separate Black high school despite strong opposition from the Black community. Among the groups protesting were the Black churches and the Better Indianapolis League, an African American civic organization; they forwarded protests to the school board, pointing out that separation would be divisive and unjust. Archie Greathouse, a leader of the Black community, was able to delay the school board's plans in a series of court battles. In the end, however, the courts upheld the right of the school authorities to establish a segregated school.

The school board then went ahead with construction plans and announced that some 800 Black pupils would attend what was to be known as the "Thomas Jefferson High School." The Black community was able to persuade the board to change the name to honor Crispus Attucks, a Black man who was one of the first persons to die in the Boston Massacre of 1780. (See the Boston, Massachusetts, section of this book for more information about Attucks.)

Crispus Attucks High School was completed in 1927. Until 1949 it was the only free public school for Black students in Indianapolis. Although Indiana outlawed school segregation in 1949, the school remained almost exclusively Black until the 1970s, when busing was initiated to achieve integration. Today the school is known as Attucks Middle School. Recent extensive renovations retained the original appearance of the exterior facade and the marble flooring and marble columns in the entryway. However, some interior floors were carpeted, and classrooms were enlarged to modern standards.

DATE BUILT:	1927; addition, 1938
ADDRESS:	1140 N. Martin Luther King Jr. Street, Indianapolis
TELEPHONE:	(317) 226-4007
VISITING HOURS:	By appointment, Mon.–Fri. 8–3
SOURCES:	NRHPRF. Personal visit, summer 1990. Telephone conversation Feb. 13, 1995, Kay Gootee, school secretary.

Indiana State Museum: Freetown Village

The story of Indiana's Black history is told at the Indiana State Museum through Freetown Village, a living-history exhibit within the museum. There a house facade is set up, and a woman sits on the front porch, telling her story to those who pass by. By re-creating such scenes, the Freetown Village actors and storytellers teach Indiana's African American history.

Their stories begin in the nineteenth century when many runaway slaves passed through this border state in their search for freedom. Some of the fugitives settled in Indiana, where they and other African Americans increased the state's Black population to approximately 3,000 in the 1870s.

Freetown Village actors and storytellers regularly present living history exhibits, plays, and workshops, portraying Indiana's African American community after the Civil War. Some of the actors tour midwestern states, teaching Black history by taking the roles of a barber named Isaiah Cuffee, a woman known as Mother Eudora, and other nineteenth-century villagers. Although Freetown Village actors perform regularly at the Indiana State Museum, it is a separate and independent organization.

DATE ESTABLISHED:	1982
ADDRESS:	Indiana State Museum, 202 N. Alabama Street; Freetown Village office, Walker Building, 617 Indiana Avenue, Room 900, Indianapolis
TELEPHONE:	Indiana State Museum, (317) 232-1641; Freetown Village, (317) 631-1870
VISITING HOURS:	Mon.–Sat. 9–4:45, Sun. 12–4:45; closed Christmas 🏃
FEES:	Museum, free; tours, fee
SOURCES:	Ophelia Umar Wellington. Letter, Aug. 25, 1989, Jeffrey Tenuth, registrar/historian, Indiana State Museum and Historic Sites. Telephone conversation June 17, 1994, Goldie Roberts, administrative assistant, Freetown Village. Telephone conversation Feb. 16, 1995, Patti Means, executive secretary, Indiana State Museum.

Indiana Avenue Historic District

Black settlers arrived in Indianapolis before emancipation and lived near the White River as early as the 1860s. This area was open to them, to other immigrants, and to white laborers because upper-income white families found the area undesirable. In 1921 malaria had caused the death of one eighth of the city's population, and some city dwellers believed the river attracted the malaria-infested mosquitoes that had caused the pestilence. Therefore, the early newcomers found an abundance of inexpensive, unsettled land near the river, and they moved into the racially mixed area.

By the 1920s much of the city had become segregated. The 500 block of Indiana Avenue became a thriving area for Black-owned businesses; there African Americans established a restaurant, a saloon, clubs, theaters, an undertaking establishment, and the office of the *Indianapolis Recorder,* the third-oldest Black-owned newspaper in the United States. Today, the 500 block of Indiana Avenue contains eleven buildings that are historically significant as the only remaining examples of business establishments from an early, predominantly Black district. The historic avenue is of interest, too, as one of four diagonal streets laid out in the city's original 1921 plan. Where the diagonal streets intersected the regular rectangular grid, triangular building lots resulted; there some flatiron buildings were constructed to conform to the triangular lots. Two good examples of such buildings are the structures at 502–504 and 547–551 Indiana Avenue.

DATE ESTABLISHED: 1869–1935

ADDRESS: 500 block of Indiana Avenue between West, North, and Michigan Streets and Central Canal, Indianapolis

VISITING HOURS: Public and private ownership; some restricted access; visitors may walk or drive by

FEES: Public area, free

SOURCE: NRHPINF.

Madame C. J. Walker Urban Life Center

The Madame Walker Urban Life Center in Indianapolis is a cultural center founded by Madame C. J. Walker, an entrepreneur and the nation's first Black female millionaire. The center served as headquarters of Madame Walker's cosmetics business, housing business offices, storefronts, and a theater.

In 1867 Walker was born as Sarah Breedlove on a cotton plantation in Delta, Louisiana. The first member of her family to be born free, she lived in extreme poverty in a one-room cabin with her sharecropper parents, Owen and Minerva Breedlove, and her brother and sister, Alex and Louvenia. After the parents died from yellow fever, Alex went to Vicksburg to look for work, and Sarah went to live with her sister, Louvenia, in Vicksburg, Mississippi. Louvenia later married, but Sarah was treated harshly by Louvenia's husband; to escape this environment Sarah married Moses McWilliams at the age of fourteen. At the age of seventeen she gave birth to a daughter, Lelia. Two years later, McWilliams was killed in an accident. Mother and daughter moved to St. Louis where Walker worked hard for eighteen years as a laundress. In spite of hardships, she was able to observe well-educated, elegantly dressed African American women, and she vowed to become like them. Saving what money she could, she managed to send Lelia to public schools in St. Louis and to Knoxville College in Tennessee.

In 1906 Sarah married Charles Walker. She previously had noted the trouble Black women had in caring for their hair and had developed highly successful formulas that were well accepted. She soon was manufacturing beauty products that were sold widely and established training programs and beauty shops throughout the country. Walker, now owner of the Madame C. J. Walker Manufacturing Company, had much-larger plans than her husband had, and they divorced in 1912.

Although Walker's business was first established in Denver, she decided to consolidate her operations in Indianapolis in 1910. At first, employees manufactured the products in a building behind Walker's home, but soon she drew up plans to construct a building that would provide adequate space. Although Walker initiated these plans, the building was not completed until after her death in 1919.

The four-story Madame Walker Urban Life Center was constructed on Indiana Avenue in a commercial area of Indianapolis just northwest of the area now called the Indiana Avenue Historic District. The building had a distinctive triangular design because it had to fit into one of the area's original diagonal streets. The first floor contained storefronts and the entrance to the Walker Theater. First-floor decorations included brightly colored African motifs such as terracotta masks adapted from Yoruba designs.

The Walker Theater, which occupies the most space in the center, once was an Indianapolis showcase of motion pictures and traveling shows. Doorways on both sides of the stage have Egyptian or Moorish designs. The ceiling has an intricate pattern of masks, animals, and other African symbols. The building also contains a ballroom and stage on the fourth floor. Among the many businesses here were the Walker Drug Store, the Coffee Pot Restaurant, and the Walker Beauty College, an institution that trained thousands of Walker agents.

In the early fifties the neighborhood deteriorated, and the theater closed. However, the Madame Walker Urban Life Center, Inc., purchased the building in 1979 and restored it for use as a community cultural center. The Walker Theater reopened in 1988.

Although Walker died more than seventy years ago, she left a legacy of her business acumen and her sense of dignity and worth as well as her generous philanthropy to Black charities. (For additional information on Madame Walker, see the entry for Irvington, New York.)

DATE BUILT:	1927
ADDRESS:	617 Indiana Avenue, Indianapolis
TELEPHONE:	(317) 236-2099
VISITING HOURS:	Mon.–Sat. 8:30–5; tours by appointment
FEES:	Tours, $2
SOURCES:	Letter, Aug. 25, 1989, Jeffrey Tenuth, registrar/historian Indiana State Museum and Historic Sites. Personal visit, summer 1990. NRHPINF. *The African American Encyclopedia,* 1642–4. *Madame C. J. Walker, Entrepreneur.*

Kendallville

Anderson Building

Alonzo (Lon) Anderson, a successful Black businessman, built the commercial building at 113 North Main. Anderson was born in 1845 in Terre Haute, Indiana. As a young man, he enlisted in 1864 in the Twenty-eighth U.S. Colored Regiment and marched with the regiment into Richmond, Virginia. He was mustered out of the army in 1868.

When the Civil War ended, Anderson and his brother, Jerry, took up the barbering trade in Kendallville. His brother's five children are thought to be the only Black children to have graduated from Kendallville High School until recent years.

Anderson moved his barbershop into this building in 1896. The Anderson building is in the Iddings/Gilbert/Leader/Anderson Block, a row of five connected buildings constructed in the late nineteenth century. These buildings are distinctive because of their decorative panels with raised scrollwork and rosettes.

The building at 113 North Main remained in the Anderson family until the year following Alonzo Anderson's death in 1899. It then changed hands many times, housing a buggy and implement business; a plumbing, heating, and roofing business; a store; a pool hall; and in 1983, the American State Bank and, later, the Society Bank. The bank did extensive remodeling to the Queen Anne-style building, giving the building a new brick facade.

There are no plaques to identify the Anderson Building. Be forewarned: in this Indiana town, while the author was photographing the Anderson building, a police officer drove up and took her license number.

When she asked why he was doing so, he said he was investigating because she was photographing a bank. She asked him if bank robbers usually operated with a tripod and a camera. Then thinking better of it, she explained the Black history of the building to him and left. The building remains an example of Black entrepreneurship in the late-nineteenth century.

DATE BUILT: 1894

ADDRESS: 113 N. Main Street, Kendallville

VISITING HOURS: Private, visitors may walk or drive by

SOURCES: NRHPINF. Personal visit, summer 1990.

Rushville

Booker T. Washington School

Because Indiana legislation of 1869 called for the state to provide education for African Americans, local officials began to build segregated facilities. About 1905 the state built the Booker T. Washington School in Rushville. Students attended grades one through six here, and a large room upstairs served as a community center for social and political meetings, plays, and dances. Beginning in 1910, the National Association for the Advancement of Colored People met in the upstairs room. Local chapters of the Odd Fellows and Masons also met on the second floor. Noted educator Mary McLeod Bethune visited the school about 1919. When the Booker T. Washington School was in operation, there was only one other school for Black students in Rush county.

Dwindling enrollment and a poor economy led to the closing of the Washington School in 1932. Seventy individuals signed a petition to keep the school open, but their efforts were in vain. Yet in 1990 community residents, who remembered the school with pride, spearheaded efforts to restore the building and to reopen it. The Black community, a local preservation group, and the city of Rushville were involved in the restoration. The restoration effort, spearheaded by the dreams of local resident Billy Rae Goins, gained a national award from the Historic Landmark Foundation in 1993.

The stately two-story brick building stands in an open area on a small rise. The recessed entrance is marked by paneled wooden double doors. The interior of the school has retained much of its historic appearance. In 1990, before restoration began, there were two large classrooms in the main section of the first floor. Just inside the front entrance, a wide central stairway led upstairs; on either side of the staircase was a very narrow hall of single-file width.

Today the historic schoolhouse is used by a variety of community agencies—Head Start, the Interlocal Community Action Program, Rush County Heritage, and Big Brothers-Big Sisters. The large hall upstairs is used for community meetings. Although the building has regained its luster and a new status, community residents have insisted on keeping certain reminders of its history—the old basketball goal and the segregated wading pool outside.

DATE BUILT: 1905

ADDRESS: 525 E. Seventh at 614 Fort Wayne Road, Rushville

TELEPHONE: (317) 932-2863

VISITING HOURS: Mon.–Fri. 8–5; call in advance to arrange to see the interior 👥

FEES: Donations welcome

SOURCES: NRHPRF. Personal visit, 1990. Conversation at Washington School July 5, 1990, Bill R. Goins, president, Booker T. Washington Community Center, Inc., and the late Reverend Peter Fletcher of Rushville, Indiana. Telephone conversation Sept. 3, 1995, Mr. Paul Davis of Rushville, who donated the schoolhouse to the community. Telephone conversation June 17, 1994, Eileen Briscoe, Community Action Representative.

Works Consulted

The African American Encyclopedia. Vol. 6. Michael W. Williams, ed. New York: Marshall Cavendish, 1993.

Madame C. J. Walker, Entrepreneur. A'Lelia Perry Bundles. Black Americans of Achievement Series. New York: Chelsea House, 1991.

National Register of Historic Places. Washington, D.C.: National Park Service, 1976.

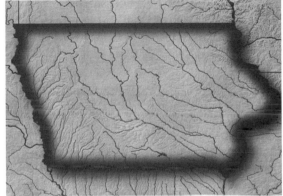

Cedar Rapids

Iowa Masonic Library

The Masonic Library has an extensive collection of literature and history relating to Prince Hall Masonry and Prince Hall Masonic Grand Lodges. Prince Hall, the founder of Black Masonry, was born in Bridgetown, Barbados, about 1735. His father was English and his mother was a free Black woman. Hall's training and trade primarily involved working with leather. He immigrated to Boston, Massachusetts, in 1765, where he became a minister and a leader in the African American community.

Prince Hall served in the militia during the Revolutionary War; in this same period, he organized the first Black Masonic Lodge in America. Having sought out a British regiment encamped near Boston, Hall successfully persuaded the British

lodge of Masons in that group to initiate him and fourteen others into the association in March 1775. The British withdrew from Boston the following year, and Hall then organized a Masonic lodge in that city, the first in the United States for African Americans. In 1787 (the Iowa Masonic Library gives the date as September 29, 1784), Hall obtained a charter from England for the African Lodge Number 459, and five years later served as Grand Master of a recently organized interstate Grand Lodge. What is not clear is why the British favored a patriot who had served in the American Army by inducting him and others into their association. After Hall's death in 1807 the lodge changed its name to Prince Hall Grand Lodge.

DATE OF SIGNIFICANCE:	The African Lodge, chartered 1784 or 1787; Iowa Masonic Library, established 1885, moved to the present building 1955
ADDRESS:	813 First Avenue 3E, Cedar Rapids
TELEPHONE:	(319) 365-1438
VISITING HOURS:	Mon.–Fri. 8–noon, 1–5; closed most holidays
FEES:	None
SOURCES:	Telephone conversation May 10, 1994, Paul H. Wieck, Grand Secretary and Grand Librarian, Iowa Masonic Library. Keith Arrington, librarian. Telephone conversation Aug. 31 and Sept. 5, 1995, Ken Hurmence, deputy secretary of the Iowa Masonic Grand Lodge, and Joe Nolte, library assistant, Iowa Masonic Library. *International Library of Negro Life and History*, 21. *Historical and Cultural Atlas of African Americans. The Shaping of Black America.*

Davenport

Bethel African Methodist Episcopal Church

The Bethel A.M.E. congregation was one of several established in many states by African Americans after the Civil War. It was founded in 1875 to provide a separate worship facility for Black Methodists in Iowa.

By 1909 the congregation had fifty members and had become an important central point in Davenport's Black community. As a result, the congregation was able to build the present church in 1909 on a corner lot in a turn-of-the-century Black neighborhood. The rectangular concrete building had high, round-arched, stained-glass windows and half timberwork with stucco. The pastor, William W. Williams, lived in the parsonage next door to the church. Bethel African Methodist Episcopal Church is listed in the *National Register of Historic Places.*

DATE ESTABLISHED:	Congregation, 1875; church, 1909
ADDRESS:	325 W. Eleventh Street, Davenport
TELEPHONE:	(319) 322-6622
VISITING HOURS:	By appointment
FEES:	None
SOURCES:	Davenport Community Development Department, Iowa Division of Historic Preservation. Telephone conversation May 29, 1994, Pastor Moody, Bethel A.M.E. Church.

Des Moines

Burns United Methodist Church

Burns United Methodist Church was organized in 1866 in a decade when there were only thirteen Black persons in Polk County. The first African American church of this denomination in Des Moines, it was named for Francis Burns (1809–1863), who was elected in 1852 by the Northern Methodist Episcopal Church as its first Black bishop. Elected as a missionary bishop to serve in Africa, he had no authority to supervise white churches.

This congregation has had six different places of worship. The first was a building that also housed the city's segregated school for Black children. The congregation built a small chapel in 1873 and then moved to a larger building between 1885 and 1887.

In each location the church offered a variety of religious and community activities. Members sponsored Sunday School programs, literary societies, musical programs, group dinners, and charitable activities. A quartet sang in different locations around the state to raise money to purchase the present church on Crocker Street and acquired sufficient funds to do so by 1930.

Members purchased a building constructed in 1912 on gently sloping land near downtown Des Moines. The one-story brick structure with stained-glass windows and Tudor arches was located in a neighborhood of small houses and apartment buildings.

DATE ESTABLISHED:	Congregation, 1866; present church, 1912; purchased by the Burns United Methodist congregation, 1930
ADDRESS:	811 Crocker Street, Des Moines
TELEPHONE:	(515) 244-5883
VISITING HOURS:	Office hours, Mon.–Fri. 10–4; Sun. school, 9:30; Sun. service, 11
SOURCES:	Telephone conversation May 29, 1994, Reverend Leon Herndon. NRHPINF. *The Black Church in the African American Experience,* 66.

Public Library of Des Moines National Bar Association Collection

The Public Library of Des Moines is the depository for the National Bar Association's historical papers. In 1991 the association unveiled a limestone sculpture at the library as a memorial to its founders.

The National Bar Association, formerly known as the Negro Bar Association, began in Des Moines in 1925. Founders Gertrude Rush, S. Joe Brown, James B. Morris, Charles P. Howard Sr., and George H. Woodson all were active in the early legal history of Des Moines. Rush lived in Des Moines for sixty years and was the first African American woman admitted to the Iowa Bar.

DATE ESTABLISHED:	National Bar Association, 1925
ADDRESS:	100 Locust Street, Des Moines
TELEPHONE:	(515) 283-4152
VISITING HOURS:	Mon.–Thurs. 9–9, Fri. 9–6, Sat. 9–5; closed Memorial Day–Labor Day Thurs. at 6; closed holidays
FEES:	None
SOURCES:	Library press release, July 5, 1991. Shirley Aluster, head of reference, Public Library of Des Moines. Telephone call to site, May 10, 1994.

Lewis

Hitchcock House

Hitchcock House, built in 1856, is one of Iowa's few remaining underground railroad stations. The two-story, sandstone house was located approximately two miles from the conjunction of the Oregon and Mormon trails. Its location is on a hill providing a 360-degree view, and its inhabitants could see anyone, whether runaway slave or slave catcher, twenty minutes before the person's arrival. The fugitives came primarily from Missouri into Nebraska City and moved from there into Tabor, Iowa, and then to Lewis, where they found safety in this house. They left by foot or by false-bottomed wagon for Anita, Iowa. The journey was risky because they had to cross a river between Des Moines and Council Bluffs; sometimes slave catchers waited at the river.

Abolitionist John Brown set up an underground railroad route through Iowa that included a stop here at the home of a sympathetic Congregational circuit-riding preacher, George B. Hitchcock. Hitchcock had moved here in 1851 and built a log cabin; then, in 1854–1856 he erected the present house with abolitionist activity in mind. Hitchcock, his wife, and their eight children provided a haven here.

Visitors can see a house with four bedrooms upstairs (there may earlier have been fewer) and a kitchen, pantry, dining area, and sickroom/birthing room downstairs. There are two basement rooms, one of which was secret. Because many buildings of that era did not have basements, visitors would have assumed that the one room, with its limestone hearth and fireplace, was all there was on that level. A large cabinet, however, covered an opening to the second half of the 60-foot-by-50-foot basement. The opening, 3.5 feet by 6 feet, concealed a hiding place that today has a few items that suggest what the furnishings might have been like at that time—wood pallets with straw tick coverings and a toilet container.

Hitchcock House was abandoned in the late 1950s or early 1960s. In 1978 a grant made possible the restoration of the house and furnishing it in the time period. Its authenticity as an underground railroad site is suggested by still-existing letters mentioning that John Brown stayed at the house or that he soon would be arriving there.

The house is operated by the Cass County Conservation Board. In addition to the house, visitors today see a barn that has displays of crafts and that shelters occasional picnics. A 1.75-mile nature trail features native plants and animals.

DATE BUILT:	1856
ADDRESS:	R.R. 1, Lewis vicinity (take I-80 to Atlantic, Iowa, exit 57; go south on US 6 about 8 miles to a sign for Lewis and Hitchcock House; go south to Lewis; turn right at first street in Lewis; go approximately 1 mile; follow the sign at the top of a hill and take the road south to Hitchcock House)
TELEPHONE:	(712) 769-2323
VISITING HOURS:	Apr. 15–Oct. 15, Fri.–Wed. 1–5; by appointment Oct. 16–Apr. 14 and on Thurs.; guided tours by appointment
FEES:	Donations appreciated
SOURCES:	Telephone conversation Apr. 30, 1994, Jeff Hauser, caretaker. Telephone conversation Feb. 14, 1995, Dessie Hansen, caretaker. Flier from Hitchcock House.

Muscatine

Alexander Clark House

Alexander Clark (1826–1891) became Iowa's most prominent African American in the years following the Civil War. In addition, he was in his time one of the most outstanding Black leaders in America. Clark pressed for civil rights gains in voting and education and led the fight to enact a statewide Black suffrage amendment. When the Muscatine school board refused to admit his ten-year-old daughter, Susan, to the local grammar school because of her race, Clark sued. The celebrated case involved appeals, after which the Iowa Supreme Court ruled that a pupil could not be excluded from the public schools because of race, nationality, or religion. Because of Clark's persistence, Iowa was one of the first states to ban school segregation. Clark gained a fine education for himself, too, becoming the second African American in Iowa to graduate from the University of Iowa Law School (his own son was the first African American to do so). Black law students at the university honor him today through the Alexander Clark Society established at the university's law school.

Clark was born free prior to the Civil War to a white father and a Black mother. He matured into a well-educated individual who was successful as a business and property owner in Muscatine. His sphere of influence widened during the Reconstruction Era when he was chosen as a delegate to the 1869 National Colored Convention in Washington, D.C. There he chaired a committee that presented to Congress claims of Black soldiers and seamen. Throughout the 1860s Clark was Grand Master in the Masonic Order, overseeing Missouri, Iowa, Colorado, and Minnesota. He also owned and edited a Chicago newspaper that strongly advocated the rights of Black citizens. In 1880 President Benjamin Harrison appointed Clark minister resident and consul general to Liberia. He served in Liberia until his death the following year.

Prior to 1879 the Clark family lived in a frame dwelling facing West Third Street. In 1878 the home burned in a fire suspected to have been caused by arsonists. By December of that year, Clark had spent $4,000 on construction of a new double, brick, two-story residence with arched windows and scroll brackets. It is believed that he lived in the number 207 side of the double house, which today is one of the few double brick houses remaining in Muscatine.

When construction plans were made to build a housing project on the site, Clark House, in danger of being demolished, was moved to a sloping land area one-half block from the original site, and plans were initiated to convert the structure into a museum. Although the museum was not developed, Clark House, now listed in the *National Register of Historic Places,* remains of interest to many who drive by to see this symbol of an outstanding Black American from Iowa.

DATE BUILT: 1878; moved, 1975
ADDRESS: 205–207 W. Third Street, Muscatine
VISITING HOURS: Private, visitors may walk or drive by 👫
SOURCES: NRHPINF. Telephone conversation May 15, 1994, D. Kent Sissel, area resident.

Salem

Henderson Lewelling Quaker House

In 1994 a fortunate and serendipitous discovery was made at this site. After a century and a half of concealment, workers remodeling floorboards in the Lewelling Quaker House found a second trap door—a secret place where fugitive slaves were concealed. The directors of the shrine could scarcely conceal their delight at the discovery. Henderson Lewelling, a Quaker who was determined to share in the abolitionists' battle, had built this house in 1840 to be a part of the underground railroad. He had built it so well that after more than a century even friends of the cause had not found out all of its secrets.

People knew, of course, about the tunnel, a dirt passageway discovered earlier when workers pulled up a floor for repair work. Today, visitors may look down into that tunnel, but the passageway leading from the kitchen to the basement is something that those who were hiding had to crawl through. Basements were unheard of in the 1840s when Lewelling built his stone house in the Quaker town of Salem as a safe place for hiding slaves. No one would have suspected the trapdoor and tunnel that led to safety in the basement. Lewelling House is interesting in its own light. When workers pulled down the plaster upstairs, they saw beams made of rough logs with the bark still on them.

There once were five other underground railroad houses in Salem, each one possibly as interesting as the Lewelling House, but they are no longer standing. The only remaining relic from one of the other houses is a large wheel once situated in an attic. A stout rope could drop from the wheel down inside the wall; a turning of the wheel could raise a portion of the first-story floor, opening up a trapdoor leading to a hiding area for fugitives.

Of the approximately one hundred underground railroad stations in Iowa, few are still standing. In addition to Lewelling House, they include the Reverend Todd House in Tabor, the Jordan House in West Des Moines, and the Hitchcock House in Lewis. These three sites are also open to the public.

DATE BUILT:	1840
ADDRESS:	From Mount Pleasant, 10 miles south on US 218, then 3 miles west on Salem Road
TELEPHONE:	Not available; to make an appointment to visit, write Lewelling Shrine, Box 28, Salem, IA 52649
VISITING HOURS:	May–Sept., Sun. 1–4; tours by appointment 🧒🧑
FEES:	Adults, $1; students and children, $.50
SOURCES:	Vicki Baker, president, West Des Moines Historical Society. Telephone conversation May 17, 1994, Fay Heartsill, president, Board of Directors, and Judy Feeham, member of the Board of Directors.

West Des Moines

Jordan House Museum

The Jordan House Museum, a national historic site, was once a station on the underground railroad. The Victorian mansion belonged to James Cunningham Jordan, the first white settler in West Des Moines. He constructed the house in 1850 when the area was a pioneer farming settlement.

Jordan is considered to have been the chief conductor of the underground railroad in Polk County, Iowa. He made decisions about where the fugitives would stay and determined when it was safe for them to move on along the route to freedom. Community legend, family stories, and older history books document the role of this house as a station on the underground railroad. Escaping slaves on their way to freedom in Canada stayed in the kitchen or hid in a sleeping room in the basement. On one occasion twenty-four fugitives were in the house at the same time.

The famous abolitionist John Brown also stayed here on December 17, 1858. A group of slaves had been traveling through Tabor, Iowa, with their masters, and Brown helped them to escape. Brown stayed at the Jordan house again in February 1859 while planning his raid on the arsenal at Harpers Ferry. He trained followers at the Maxham farm in Springdale, Iowa, and stored ammunition at Reverend Todd's home in Tabor, Iowa. Ten months later he was hanged for treason for leading the raid. (See the listings for sites related to John Brown in Chambersburg, Pennsylvania; Harpers Ferry, West Virginia; Akron, Ohio; Lake Placid, New York; and Kansas City and Osawatomie, Kansas.)

The Italian Gothic house originally had only six rooms during the underground railroad period; more rooms were added in the 1870s. The West Des Moines Historical Society purchased Jordan House in 1978 and transformed it into a museum. A display in the basement room where the fugitives stayed tells of its story in the underground railroad. Local schools have used the house as part of their fifth grade curriculum.

DATE BUILT:	1850; addition, 1870
ADDRESS:	2001 Fuller Road, West Des Moines
TELEPHONE:	(515) 225-1286
VISITING HOURS:	May–Oct., Wed., Sat. 1–4; Sun. 2–5; closed federal holidays 🧒🧑
FEES:	Adults, $2; school-aged children, $.50
SOURCES:	Telephone call to site, May 2, 1994. Vicki Baker, president, West Des Moines Historical Society. Flier from Jordan House Museum.

Works Consulted

The Black Church in the African American Experience. C. Eric Lincoln and Lawrence H. Mamiya. Durham, N.C.: Duke University Press, 1990.

Historical and Cultural Atlas of African Americans. Molefi K. Asante and Mark T. Mattson.

New York: Penguin, 1992.

International Library of Negro Life and History: Historical Negro Biography. Wilhelmena S. Robinson. New York: Publishers, 1970.

The Shaping of Black America. Lerone Bennett Jr. New York: Penguin, 1993.

Maine

Brunswick

Bowdoin College

Bowdoin College, located 25 miles northeast of Portland and a few miles away from Maine's rugged coastline, is the state's oldest institution of higher learning. Founded in 1794 as a college for men, the institu-

tion became coeducational in 1971. Among Bowdoin's illustrious nineteenth-century students were poet Henry Wadsworth Longfellow, novelist Nathaniel Hawthorne, and newspaper editor John Brown Russwurm, who in 1826 became Bowdoin's first Black graduate.

In 1827 Russwurm established *Freedom's Journal*, the nation's first newspaper edited by a Black person (see the entry on the Russwurm House in Portland, Maine). Today a center at Bowdoin is named in his honor.

The Little-Mitchell House, once a stop on the underground railroad, houses the offices of the Africana Studies Program and the John Brown Russwurm Afro-American Center. The center's library contains archival materials on the Black experience including 2,000 volumes on the subject of the Black diaspora.

The Hawthorne-Longfellow Library contains the original manuscript of a Phillis Wheatley poem, records of the Freedmen's Bureau, and papers of General Oliver O. Howard, founder of Howard University. This library and the Russwurm Center library are used by researchers from across the United States.

DATE ESTABLISHED:	1794
ADDRESS:	John Brown Russwurm Afro-American Center Library, 6–8 College Street; Hawthorne-Longfellow Library, Maine, Bath, and College Streets, Brunswick
TELEPHONE:	(207) 725-3000
VISITING HOURS:	Russwurm Center, summer Mon.–Fri. 8:30–5, winter Sun.–Fri. 7 A.M.–11 P.M.; library, Mon.–Sat. 8:30 A.M.–midnight, Sun. 10 A.M.–midnight, spring and summer breaks Mon.–Fri. 8:30–5
FEES:	None
SOURCES:	Telephone conversation Apr. 13, 1994, Harriet Richards, academic coordinator, Africana Studies Program, Bowdoin College. *Bowdoin, The Offer of the College. African-American Studies at Bowdoin.* The Academic American Encyclopedia.

Harriet Beecher Stowe House

Author Harriet Beecher Stowe awakened the conscience of thousands of Americans with her novel, *Uncle Tom's Cabin* (1852). During the eighteen years she lived in Cincinnati, Ohio, she met several fugitive slaves and listened to the stories of their lives. On a visit to Kentucky, she saw a slave auction site and learned more about the lives of slaves in the South.

In 1850 Stowe's husband became a professor at Bowdoin College, and the Stowes moved to the house at 63 Federal Street in Brunswick, Maine, where Stowe began writing her story using composite characters developed from true incidents that had been related to her. The resulting book, *Uncle Tom's Cabin,* was a moving story of slavery and flight from bondage. Sympathetic readers bought 10,000 copies in the first week, while slaveholders violently opposed the book, proclaiming that much of the content was false.

After two years in Brunswick, the Stowe family moved to Massachusetts. The house in Brunswick later was altered for use as a restaurant, motel, and gift shop. The first floor is used for the front desk and gift shop of the hotel, and private quarters are upstairs. The barn is used today as a restaurant. The exterior of Stowe house is largely unaltered, and much of the original woodwork remains inside.

DATE OF SIGNIFICANCE:	Stowe residence, 1850–1852
ADDRESS:	63 Federal Street, Brunswick
TELEPHONE:	(207) 725-5543
VISITING HOURS:	Private; call to see interior
SOURCES:	Telephone conversation Mar. 31, 1994, April Glass, front desk clerk, Stowe House Restaurant. NRHPINF. *National Register of Historic Places,* 289. *Uncle Tom's Cabin.*

Gardiner

Nathaniel Kimball House

Although Maine's sea captains were heavily involved in the slave trade, residents of some towns in Maine opposed the trade and gave assistance to fleeing slaves. Sometimes they used boats to transport individuals or families from one town to the next on the underground railroad.

The Lamb House, a large Colonial home, is located about 200 feet from the west bank of the Kennebec River. Captain Nathaniel Kimball, a sea captain, built the residence in 1846 as a wedding gift for his daughter. The house later became part of the underground railroad. After fugitives arrived by boat, the family hid them in a cellar archway or under the eaves in the large attic.

In 1912 Dr. Bert Lamb purchased the house. Since that time, the residence has been used as a convalescent home and an office building, and the cellar hiding place was converted to storage use. Today it houses the Gardiner Family Chiropractic.

DATE BUILT:	1846
ADDRESS:	220 Main Street, Gardiner
VISITING HOURS:	Private office; visitors may view the exterior from nearby parking lots by permission
SOURCES:	*The Underground Railroad in New England.* "An Architectural and Historical Survey of the Gardiner Area."

Portland

Green Memorial African Methodist Episcopal Zion Church

Green Memorial African Methodist Episcopal Zion Church is the oldest Black congregation in Maine. Its parent organization, the Abyssinian Society, was incorporated in 1828. When the church was organized, members first worshiped in a brick-and-stone meeting house on Newbury Street in Portland, a structure that no longer exists.

The present two and one-half–story structure was built in 1914, and when completed, it was considered one of the finest Black churches in New England. The church is constructed of rough-textured concrete block. Rectangular windows on the first floor admit daylight, while arched second floor windows create a diamond pattern in stained glass. A two-story, shingled rectory stands adjacent to the church.

The congregation named the church in 1943 for Moses Green, a man who was born a slave and who worked for fifty-two years at Portland's Union Station. Records indicate that Green Memorial A.M.E. Zion Church was the only all-Black congregation in Maine's history. This church and the John B. Russwurm House in Portland are the only sites where physical evidence remains of African American history in Maine.

By 1993 the congregation had dwindled to fifteen members, but there was a rewarding increase in membership and attendance starting in 1993 and 1994. Reverend Margaret R. E. Lawson, who became pastor in May 1993, noted that a recent video entitled *Anchor of the Soul* told of the struggle and survival of Black people in Maine. The videotape brought focus on Green Memorial Church, and some members of the Green family who were related to the original founders of the church were located. Many hundreds of viewers of the videotape have described it as a moving experience. Green Memorial Church is listed in the *National Register of Historic Places*.

DATE ESTABLISHED: Congregation, 1828; church, 1914

ADDRESS: 46 Sheridan Street, Portland

TELEPHONE: (207) 772-1409

VISITING HOURS: Sun. school, 9:45; Sun. service, 11; other hours by appointment

FEES: None

SOURCES: Telephone conversation Apr. 10, 1994, Reverend Margaret R. E. Lawson, Green Memorial African Methodist Episcopal Zion Church. NRHPINF. *National Register of Historic Places*, 291. *Anchor of the Soul*.

John B. Russwurm House

John Brown Russwurm (1799–1851) was one of the first African Americans to graduate from a college in the United States. He was founder and editor of *Freedom's Journal*, the nation's first Black-owned newspaper, and through his press he sharpened the debate about the future of free Black people in America.

Russwurm's father was a white planter in Virginia; his mother, a slave on his father's plantation in Virginia. Father and son relocated to Portland in 1812. The boy already had received some schooling in Canada; in the 1920s he began attending Maine's Hebron Academy. When his father died in 1815, John continued to live in the Portland house as a family member except during the school year.

After graduating from Hebron Academy preparatory school in Maine in the early 1820s, Russwurm studied medicine at Bowdoin College in Brunswick. Perhaps because of discrimination, although this is not certain, Russwurm was the only student in his class to live off campus. He boarded with a blacksmith outside Brunswick. Graduating in 1826, Russwurm then moved to New York City, where he began his newspaper career by founding *Freedom's Journal*. The journal's coeditor and cofounder was Samuel Cornish, a man who had been born free in Delaware in 1790 and had attended school in Philadelphia.

The growth of *Freedom's Journal* coincided with the growth in the United States of an organization called the American Colonization Society, founded in 1816 to encourage former slaves to emigrate to Africa. The society established the colony of Liberia in 1822; in 1824 the colony was named for U.S. President James Monroe. More than 2,600 Black Americans migrated to Liberia in the next decade, settling in Monrovia or establishing separate colonies. The colonies amalgamated in 1847, making Liberia the first independent republic in Black Africa.

In the United States Black people and white people were debating the idea of Black emigration to Africa. As coeditor of *Freedom's Journal*, Russwurm was silent about his emigrationist views; after becoming editor, however, he gradually began using the paper as a forum to promote the idea of emigration. He admired and praised Paul Cuffee, a Black man from Massachusetts who also promoted colonization (see the Cuffe listing for Westport, Massachusetts). Some African Americans, however, harshly criticized Russwurm—they believed slaveowners wanted to eliminate free Black people from their communities by sending them to Africa because the slaveowners feared the influence of free Black people on their slaves. Those African Americans who were opposed to emigration knew they had helped to build America and had shed their blood in America's wars; therefore, they claimed their future was in America.

On the other hand, African American emigrationists believed Black people could never control their destinies in America. On a daily basis they faced hostility and indifference in both the North and the South, and they strongly felt the grip of the tentacles of slavery. These people believed their lives would be better in Africa where they could practice self-determination and live unmolested by daily rebuffs of discrimination.

In 1829 Russwurm acted on his beliefs and moved to the new colony of Liberia. He later became governor of the neighboring colony of Las Palmas. During his seventeen years as governor, Russwurm introduced currency and established education programs. He eventually merged his colony with others to create the Republic of Liberia. He died in Las Palmas in 1851. Although he did not live to see the emancipation of America's slaves, he contributed to the struggle for freedom and raised questions about self-determination that African Americans continue to debate today.

Russwurm resided in Portland between 1812 and 1827. The house, one of two sites in Maine directly related to African American history, is listed in the *National Register of Historic Places.*

DATE OF SIGNIFICANCE: Russwurm residence, 1812–1827
ADDRESS: 238 Ocean Avenue, Portland
VISITING HOURS: Private residence; visitors may drive by
SOURCES: Telephone call June 10, 1994, Maine Office for Historic Preservation. NRHPINF. *International Library of Negro Life and History,* 68. The Academic American Encyclopedia.

Works Consulted

The Academic American Encyclopedia. New York: Grolier, 1993. [electronic version]

African-American Studies at Bowdoin. Brunswick, Maine: Bowdoin College, Nov. 1990. [brochure]

Anchor of the Soul. Shoshanna House and Karine Odlin, prods. Distr. by Northeast Historic Film. Buckport, Maine. 1994. [videotape]

An Architectural and Historical Survey of the Gardiner Area. Augusta, Maine: Maine Historic Preservation Commission, 1984. [booklet]

Bowdoin, The Offer of the College: The Bowdoin Viewbook 1993–1994. Brunswick, Maine: Office of Admissions and the Office of Communications, Bowdoin College, 1993. [booklet]

International Library of Negro Life and History: Historical Negro Biographies. Wilhelmena S. Robinson. New York: Publishers, 1970.

National Register of Historic Places. Washington, D.C.: National Park Service, 1976.

Uncle Tom's Cabin. Harriet Beecher Stowe. Bantam Books. 1981.

The Underground Railroad in New England. Richard R. Kuns and John Sabino, eds. Boston: American Revolution Bicentennial Administration, Region I, with Boston 200, the Bicentennial and Historical Commissions of the Six New England States and the Underground Railroad Task Force, 1976.

Amherst

W. E. B. Du Bois Library, Special Collections and Archives

The University of Massachusetts at Amherst houses an outstanding collection of papers by and about W. E. B. Du Bois, an African American who was a Harvard University graduate, scholar and author, and a leader in establishing the NAACP and its journal, *The Crisis*. In an era when many leaders advocated an industrial model of education for Black students, Du Bois insisted on a quality classical curriculum, especially for the talented tenth of Black students who would lead others of the race in the struggle for equality.

The Special Collections Archives is located in the University of Massachusetts, Amherst, main library, recently renamed the W. E. B. Du Bois Library. The collection spans the years from 1803 to 1979 (1877 through 1963 for Du Bois's own writings) and includes manuscripts and printed versions of his speeches,

newspaper columns and articles, pamphlets and leaflets, book reviews, petitions, essays, nonfiction books, and an eighty-nine-reel microfilm collection.

ADDRESS: University of Massachusetts, 154 Hicks Way, Amherst

TELEPHONE: (413) 545-2780, or (413) 545-0150

VISITING HOURS: Mon.–Fri. 10–3

SOURCES: Daniel Lombardo, curator of special collections, Jones Library, Inc. Telephone conversation June 11, 1994, Lori Mestere, education reference librarian, University of Massachusetts. Telephone conversation Jan. 20, 1995, Mike Milewski, archives assistant, Special Collections and Archives.

Ashley Falls

Colonel John Ashley House

The Ashley House, the oldest dwelling in Berkshire County, was home not only to a prominent white family, the Ashleys, but also to Elizabeth Freeman, a slave who changed the course of Black history in Massachusetts. Freeman was the first African American to win freedom under a court test of the Massachusetts Bill of Rights. The 1760s decision, known as *Brom & Bett* v. *Ashley*, was a landmark civil rights case.

The Ashley property, owned by John and Hannah Ashley in the eighteenth century, stood in an area of farmland, meadows, and the winding Housatonic River. John Ashley—a Yale graduate, attorney, surveyor, and justice of the peace—owned more than 3,000 acres of land. Although he had Black servants, John, Zack, and Harry, John Ashley appeared to have had some sentiment against the institution of slavery. He had been brought up in the tradition of the Congregational Church, which opposed slavery as an institution. His church urged slave owners to treat their slaves as indentured servants. John Ashley, in his will, referred to John, Zack, and Harry as servants rather than as slaves.

Mrs. Ashley, however, had a different, more harsh view of slavery. She had grown up with the beliefs of the Dutch Reformed Church, which taught that God approved the enslavement of Black people. Although Mr. and Mrs. Ashley had different beliefs, he may have accommodated himself somewhat to her beliefs, perhaps because of her strong personality. A neighbor, Catharine Sedgwick, once referred to Hannah Ashley as a "shrew untamable."[1] The harshness of Mrs. Ashley's character led to the conflict that caused Elizabeth to seek her freedom.

In September 1735 John Ashley married Hannah Hogeboom and purchased two children on the slave market, Elizabeth (later known as "Mum Bett") and her younger sister Lizzie, to serve as maids to his wife in her new home. The field and household servants lived in an east wing of the house, which had its own fireplaces for heat and cooking. Elizabeth became indispensable in the household and was respected as a nurse, midwife, friend, and counselor to the village children.

In the late 1760s, the Massachusetts Bay Colony was planning to adopt a new constitution. When Colonel Ashley and his friends discussed the details of the proposed constitution, Elizabeth served refreshments to visitors in the upstairs meeting room and listened. One day Mrs. Ashley became enraged at some transgression of Lizzie, Elizabeth's younger sister, and reached out with a red-hot kitchen implement to burn the girl. Elizabeth moved between the two and received the blow herself, suffering a severe burn on her arm. Although she had been a slave for thirty years, she left the house at once, walking three miles in freezing weather to the home of a neighboring family, the Sedgwicks.

Citing the provisions of the new Massachusetts Constitution of 1780 and its Declaration of Rights clause, Elizabeth asked Theodore Sedgwick to go to court on her behalf. She told him that she had overheard that the clause specified that all men were born free and equal. Sedgwick was surprised at Elizabeth's knowledge because he knew she was illiterate. When he asked how she knew about the provisions of the Constitution, she replied that she had learned by keeping still and minding things. Sedgwick took the case, even though he was John Ashley's friend. Ashley appeared to welcome the test case and did nothing about his wife's demand that Elizabeth should be brought back to their household. In fact, he resigned his lifetime appointment as a judge because he did not want a conflict of interest in a case in which he was part of the lawsuit.

Because women had no standing in court, a Black man called Brom was made codefendant with Bett. Sedgwick and another attorney, Reeve, argued that slavery had never received legal sanction in Massachusetts, and that regardless of the prior situation, slavery was now outlawed by the Declaration of Rights of the new Constitution. They won the case and won a later appeal, setting a precedent in the arena of human rights in Massachusetts. Brom and Bett were freed. Bett took the name Elizabeth Freeman at some point.

Theodore Sedgwick later became a judge, a member and speaker of the Continental Congress, a member of the United States House of Representatives, and a Justice of the Massachusetts Supreme Court. Even though Hannah Ashley never again allowed Sedgwick to enter her house, he and John Ashley remained friends.

The Ashleys pleaded with Elizabeth to return to their household, but she refused and went to work, instead, in the Sedgwick household. There she remained, a loved, respected, and valued member of the household, for twenty years. She later bought land in Stockbridge and raised a large family of children and grandchildren. Elizabeth Freeman died in 1792 at the age of eighty-five and was buried in the Sedgwick family plot in the old burying ground at Stockbridge next to Catherine Maria, the Sedgwick daughter.

The Ashley House is a museum today, open to visitors. The house, now the property of The Trustees of Reservations, has been moved one-quarter mile to its present location, and has been restored to its early character.

DATE BUILT:	1735
ADDRESS:	Cooper Hill Road, Ashley Falls
TELEPHONE:	(413) 229-8600
VISITING HOURS:	Memorial Day–last Tues. in June, Sat.–Sun. and holidays 1–5; last Wed. in June–Labor Day, Wed.–Sun., and Mon. that fall on holidays 1–5; day after Labor Day–Columbus Day, weekends and holidays 1–5; days subject to change 👫
FEES:	Adults, $5; children 6–12, $2.50; members and children under 6, free; groups, reduced fees

SOURCES: Lisa McFadden, assistant director for public information, The Trustees of Reservations. Telephone conversation May 21, 1994, and Aug. 9, 1995, Don Reid, western regional ecologist, The Trustees of Reservations. Telephone conversation Jan. 20, 1995, Mark Miller, editor, *The Berkshire Eagle. Webster's New Biographical Dictionary*, 900. *W. E. B. Du Bois: Biography of a Race. The Ashleys: A Pioneer Berkshire Family.* "Mum Bett's Heroism." "A Monument to History and High Purposes."

Boston

Black Heritage Trail™*

The Black Heritage Trail is a walking tour of fourteen Black history structures known formally as the Boston African American National Historic Site. The fourteen structures on the trail were constructed before the Civil War and represent the largest grouping of pre-Civil War Black historic sites in the United States.

Among the structures are the African Meeting House, the oldest standing Black church in the United States, the Abiel Smith School, and the Phillips School, which was integrated in 1855.

Boston's first African Americans arrived as slaves in 1638, eight years after the city was founded. However, by the end of the Revolutionary War, more free Black individuals than slaves lived in Boston. By the nineteenth century, most of the city's African Americans had their homes in the West End between Pinckney and Cambridge Streets and between Joy and Charles Streets in an area known today as Beacon Hill's north slope. Many of their leaders lived in this community, including Prince Hall, founder of the African American Lodge of Masons.

Slavery was outlawed in Massachusetts by the end of the 1700s. By 1790 the federal census recorded no slaves in Massachusetts, the only state in the Union at that time to have no slaves recorded. Thus, African Americans belonged to a free Black community. They were concerned with improving their social and educational status and abolishing slavery in the rest of the country.

The sequence for visiting the sites as recommended in the *Black Heritage Trail* brochure is the African Meeting House, Smith Court Residences (and the house on Holmes Alley), Abiel Smith School, Middleton House, Robert Gould Shaw and Fifty-fourth Regiment Memorial, Phillips School, Smith House, Charles Street Meeting House, Lewis and Harriet Hayden House, Charles Street A.M.E. Church, and Coburn's Gaming House. Visitors also may take a guided tour led by rangers from the National Park Service. Of the fourteen sites in the historic area, five are listed in alphabetical order and described in greater detail. Four are associated with nineteenth-century African American leaders, and one is associated with soldiers who served in the Civil War. The following sites that have a briefer overview are listed in sequence by proximity. They are included for their historical value and for their architecture that shows how African Americans lived in this nineteenth-century Boston community. Of sites on the Black Heritage Trail, only the African Meeting House and the monument to Robert Gould Shaw and the Fifty-fourth Massachusetts Colored Infantry Regiment are public; the rest are private and may be viewed from the street.

In the nineteenth century there were alleys where back yards stand today; the alleys in the middle of the blocks contained houses. NUMBER 7A IN HOLMES ALLEY is to the rear of Number 7 on Smith Court and is similar to several other houses that once stood in Holmes Alley. A mariner and a hairdresser once lived in 7A.

The GEORGE WASHINGTON HOUSE at 5 Smith Court was built between 1815 and 1828. Washington, a laborer and a deacon in the African Meeting House, purchased the house in 1849. The Washington family, which included nine children, lived in the upper part and rented out the first floor.

The JOSEPH SCARLETT HOUSE at Number 10 Smith Court was originally owned by Black chimneysweep and entrepreneur Joseph Scarlett. Built in 1853, this house is next to the African Meeting House. Scarlett owned fifteen real estate parcels at the time of his death and left bequests to the African Methodist Episcopal Zion Church and to the Home for Aged Colored Women.

The GEORGE MIDDLETON HOUSE at 5–7 Pinckney Street was built in 1797. Two Black men, George Middleton and Lewis Glapion, were the original owners. This is the oldest existing home on Beacon Hill built by an African American. Middleton was a veteran of the American Revolution and led an all-Black company from Boston, the Bucks of America, one of two all-Black units in the Continental Army.

The PHILLIPS SCHOOL at Anderson and Pinckney Streets was built in 1824. Until 1855 the school was open only to white children. When the state legislature abolished separate schools in 1855, this became one of Boston's first integrated schools.

The JOHN J. SMITH HOUSE at 86 Pinckney Street belonged to a man who was born free in Virginia in 1820 and moved to Boston at the age of twenty-eight. Smith's barber shop, at the corner of Howard and Bulfinch Streets, became a center for Black abolitionists and fugitive slaves. Smith worked in Washington, D.C., as recruiting officer for the all-Black Fifth Cavalry during the Civil War. He was elected between 1868 and 1872 to the Massachusetts House of Representatives and later was appointed to the Boston Common Council. Smith, who died in 1906, lived at this address from 1878 to 1893.

CHARLES STREET MEETING HOUSE, at the corner of Mt. Vernon and Charles Streets, was built in 1807 for the white Third Baptist Church of Boston (later known as the Charles Street Baptist Church). In the mid-1830s an abolitionist member, Timothy Gilbert, challenged the segregated seating patterns in the church by bringing some Black friends into his pew. Expelled from the church, he with other white abolitionists founded Tremont Temple, one of America's first integrated churches.

The CHARLES STREET AFRICAN METHODIST EPISCOPAL CHURCH used the old meeting house on Charles Street until 1939. The last African American institution to leave Beacon Hill, it moved in 1939 to Dorchester, a district of Boston, where it is located today.

John Coburn was born in Massachusetts in 1811 and worked as a clothing dealer. He hired Boston architect Asher Benjamin to design COBURN's GAMING HOUSE at Phillips and Irving Streets, which was built in 1843–1844, as a home for himself, his wife Emmeline, and his adopted son Wendell. He also established there a private gaming house. Emmeline Coburn died in 1872. When John Coburn died the following year, he left substantial holdings of real estate and cash, a testament to his financial acumen.

DATE BUILT:	19th century
ADDRESS:	Sponsored by the Museum of Afro-American History located in Abiel Smith School, 46 Joy Street, Boston
TELEPHONE:	(617) 742-1854
VISITING HOURS:	Visitors can see the exteriors from street; rangers from the National Park Service lead guided tours Memorial Day–Labor Day at 10, noon, and 2 starting at the Robert Gould Shaw and Fifty-fourth Massachusetts Colored Infantry Regiment Monument at Beacon and Park Streets 🏃🏃
FEES:	None; donations are appreciated
SOURCES:	Telephone conversation June 11, 1994, Kevin Wall, park ranger. The Black Heritage Trail concept was devised by Sue Bailey Thurman and refined by J. Marcus and Gaunzetta L. Mitchell. Marilyn Richardson, curator, Museum of Afro-American History. Maurice Nobles Jr., site manager, African Meeting House. Representative Byron Rushing, Commonwealth of Massachusetts, House of Representatives. NRHPINF. *Black Heritage Trail. A Documentary History of the Negro People in the United States*, 221, 244, 320–1, 336–41, 357–9, 376–7, 406, 481. *Before the Mayflower*, 171. *African Americans: Voices of Triumph*, Vol. 1, *Perseverance*, 65. *The Underground Railroad in New England*.

African Meeting House

The Museum of Afro-American History is the owner of the African Meeting House, the oldest extant Black church structure in the United States. Built in 1806 to accommodate the First African Baptist Church, it was the center of Boston's Black community for more than ninety years.

In the early nineteenth century members of the Black community needed a church of their own—in white churches they were required to sit in a segregated gallery and were denied voting privileges. Then Reverend Thomas Paul, a Black preacher from New Hampshire, began leading worship meetings for African Americans in Boston's Faneuil Hall. In 1805 Reverend Paul and the twenty members of his congregation purchased land in the West End; a year later they completed the African Meeting House, making it the first Black church in the United States. The three-story brick building was designed by Asher Benjamin, an architectural designer of Federal-style buildings throughout Boston's Beacon Hill area. Located on Beacon Hill, which at one time was the heart of Boston's Black community, the church was constructed almost entirely by Black labor. Its two-story interior contained meeting space with a gallery on three sides. Ironically, when the congregation dedicated the new building in December 1806, Black members chose to sit in the gallery and reserved the seats below for white worshipers who had been friends to the Black community.

Beginning in 1808 the basement of the African Meeting House served as a school for Black chil-dren. It was the site of so many historic meetings that dur-ing the abolitionist era the building was called the Abolition Church and the Black Faneuil Hall. Here, in 1832, white abolitionist William Lloyd Garrison and his followers founded the New England Anti-Slavery Society, New England's first abolitionist orga-nization. Frederick Douglass; U.S. Senator Charles Sumner, a white man who was a passionately outspo-ken member of the antislavery movement; and women's rights advocate Maria Stewart, an African American teacher and speaker who opposed slavery, racism, and sexism, were some of the noted Americans who spoke from the African Meeting

House platform. When Black Americans finally received authorization to serve in the Civil War, members of the Massachusetts Fifty-fourth Regiment enlisted here. This regiment was portrayed in *Glory,* a much-acclaimed book and motion picture.

The congregation remodeled the Meeting House in the 1850s. By the end of the nineteenth century, the Black community had begun to migrate to the South End and Roxbury. They sold the building to a Jewish congregation, which used it as a synagogue until it was purchased by the Museum of Afro-American History.

This national historic site has been restored to its appearance in the mid-1850s and is open to the pub-lic. The red-brick, Federal-style structure, symbol of the early search for independence, now is called the Museum of Afro-American History. Although there are changing art exhibits inside, the primary emphasis is the historic structure itself.

DATE ESTABLISHED: Congregation, 1805; Meeting House, 1806
ADDRESS: 8 Smith Court, Boston
TELEPHONE: (617) 742-1854
VISITING HOURS: Mon.–Fri. 10–4; closed New Year's Day, July 4 Thanksgiving, Christmas 👥
FEES: None; donations are appreciated

Lewis and Harriet Hayden House

This four-story building was home to Lewis and Harriet Hayden, outstanding Boston citizens of the nineteenth century. Lewis was born a slave in Kentucky in 1816 but escaped on the underground railroad. He and his wife, Harriet, lived in Detroit before moving to Boston. This home was built in 1833, and the Haydens moved into the dwelling about 1849.

Lewis Hayden became a leader in Boston's abolitionist movement. The Hayden home became a haven for fugitive slaves, even though passage of the 1850 Fugitive Slave Law imposed severe penalties for providing such assistance. Hayden operated underground railroad activities from his home and from his store on Cambridge Street. When William and Ellen Craft escaped from slavery by posing as master and slave, they lived for a period in the Hayden house. Craft and his wife first met as slaves in Macon, Georgia. Both had been separated from their families in childhood, and both yearned to live in a place where they would be able to raise and protect their own children. Ellen's skin was nearly white, and they based their escape on a plan in which Ellen would disguise herself as a white gentleman while William would pose as her slave. The dangerous plan worked, and they lived in Philadelphia and, for a period, in Boston. Other fugitive slaves as well were sheltered here. In one of the boldest actions in defiance of the Fugitive Slave Law, in 1851 Hayden and other Black men forcibly rescued a slave named Shadrach from United States custody.

When Harriet Beecher Stowe came to Boston to seek material for her *Key to Uncle Tom's Cabin*, she visited the Hayden home, and thirteen fugitive slaves were brought into a room for her to see.

Lewis Hayden was a leader in the Black community's efforts to become politically active and to gain equality of rights. When Boston's Jim Crow school, the Abiel Smith School, was closed in 1855, Hayden was one of those who sponsored a dinner honoring William Nell, who had led the struggle to close the school.

Hayden served as a recruiting agent for the Fifty-fourth Regiment during the Civil War. His only son died serving in the Union Navy. Hayden, who was one of two Black men elected to the state legislature in 1873, died in 1889. Harriet Hayden, who survived her husband, provided in her will a scholarship for African American students at Harvard Medical School.

DATE BUILT: 1833; Hayden residence, from c1849
ADDRESS: 66 Phillips Street, Boston
VISITING HOURS: Private; visitors may walk or drive by

William Nell House

White bricklayers built this residence in 1799. Around 1825 or 1830 Black families rented the double house with its common entryway. William Nell, a prominent community activist and possibly the first published Black historian in America, boarded here from 1851 to 1856. Nell served on many committees that sought to gain equality for Black people, including one that sought rights for Black Americans in seafaring occupations. Beginning in 1822, after a slave rebellion led by Denmark Vesey, several states passed laws forbidding free Black seamen to leave their ships when at port. In 1842 Nell, with other African Americans in Boston, protested the laws and petitioned the Massachusetts legislature and the U.S. Congress to pronounce such laws unconstitutional.

Nell, who once had studied law, was one of the primary leaders in the pre-Civil War struggle to integrate Boston's public schools. For years Boston's Black community had petitioned the school committee to allow their children to attend school in the community where they resided, but the committee voted to continue separate schools. The African American parents held a series of mass meetings in 1844 and adopted a resolution recommending withdrawal of their children from Abiel Smith School, the only school Black students were allowed to attend. By 1849 Boston's abolitionists, led by William Nell, had collected funds to hire Charles Sumner as attorney to plead their case. Unfortunately the Boston court ignored Sumner's plea and delivered a "separate but equal" decision. Nell continued to lead the group in sit-ins and stand-ins until the state legislature finally passed a law banning segregation in schools.

Nell joined Boston citizens in protesting slavery and in protesting the ban on allowing Black Americans to serve in the U.S. Army. In 1865 an African American clothing dealer, James Scott, purchased the house.

DATE BUILT: 1799; Nell residence, 1851–1856

ADDRESS: William Nell House, 3 Smith Court, Boston

VISITING HOURS: Private; visitors may walk or drive by

Robert Gould Shaw Memorial Fifty-fourth Massachusetts Colored Infantry Regiment Monument

In 1863 President Lincoln's administration first allowed Black soldiers to officially join the Union forces in the Civil War. The North's first Black regiment was recruited in Massachusetts and was commanded by Robert Gould Shaw, a young white officer. Black men were eager to serve as soldiers. They understood that freedom for African Americans could depend on the outcome of the battle. Distinguished African Americans were involved in the recruiting, including the great Black abolitionist Frederick Douglass, who wrote a lengthy editorial in his newspaper on March 2, 1863. The editorial, entitled "Men of Color, to Arms!" said in part:

> There is no time to delay. The tide is at its flood that leads on to fortune. From East to West, from North to South, the sky is written all over, "Now or Never," "Liberty won by white men would lose half its luster." "Who would be free themselves must strike the blow." "Better even die free, than to live slaves." This is the sentiment of every brave colored man amongst us....
>
> The day dawns; the morning star is bright upon the horizon! The iron gate of our prison stands half open,…while four millions of our brothers and sisters shall march out into liberty. The chance is now given you to end in a day the bondage of centuries, and to rise in one bound from social degradation to the plane of common equality with all other varieties of men.[2]

In July 1863 the all-Black regiment led an attack on Fort Wagner in South Carolina. The new troops were tired from marching and had received little food for two days. Nevertheless, they showed magnificent bravery in battle. Under the leadership of Colonel Shaw and under crossfire from Confederate guns, ninety men with Shaw made their way to the parapet of the fort. Shaw was killed and half of the 600 men in his regiment were killed, wounded, or taken prisoner.

Although the regiment was not successful in taking the fort, it had distinguished itself at Fort Wagner. Sergeant William Carney earned the Congressional Medal of Honor because he had saved the American flag from the Confederates by wrapping it around his body. He was one of nine Black men to be awarded the Congressional Medal of Honor during the Civil War. (See the listing for Carney House in New Bedford, Massachusetts.) That flag is now on display in the State House Hall of Flags in Boston.

Joshua B. Smith initiated the collecting of funds to build the memorial to the regiment. Smith, a fugitive from North Carolina, had worked in the Shaw household. He became a state representative in 1873–1874. Sergeant Carney, veterans of the Fifty-fourth and Fifty-fifth Regiments and the Fifth Cavalry, and speakers including Booker T. Washington were present for dedication ceremonies in 1897.

DATE OF SIGNIFICANCE: July 1863; monument dedicated 1897

ADDRESS: Memorial: entrance to the Boston Common, Beacon and Park Streets; State House Hall of Flags, Beacon Street across from the Memorial, Boston

VISITING HOURS: Memorial always accessible; Memorial Day–Labor Day, starting point for tour of Black Heritage Trail sites at 10, noon, 2; Hall of Flags, Mon.–Fri. 9–5

Abiel Smith School

Prince Hall, an African American leader in Boston, petitioned the Massachusetts legislature for access to the public school system for Black children. After this petition and others presented by Black parents were denied, the parents organized a grammar school. The school first met in a Beacon Hill home but moved in 1808 to the basement of the African Meeting House.

In the 1820s, the city of Boston established two primary schools for Black children. White business-man Abiel Smith left a bequest to the city for the education of Black children, and in 1834 the Abiel Smith School was constructed. The Smith School replaced the Meeting House School and served Black children from all over the city of Boston.

In 1848 Benjamin Roberts sued for the right of his daughter Sarah to attend any of the five white schools that stood between his home and the Smith School. Roberts sued on the basis of an 1845 statute that provided recovery of damages for any child unlawfully denied public school instruction. William C. Nell, a Black leader in the struggle to integrate the schools, sought the aid of abolitionists in obtaining funds to have the well-known abolitionist Charles Sumner represent Sarah Roberts. The case was a lengthy one, and Sumner and the Black community lost. Nell and his association then initiated a boycott, asking all of the Black parents to remove their chil-dren from the segregated schools. Within six months the state legislature passed a bill ending segregation in public schools in Massachusetts. In appreciation a din-ner was given in honor of William C. Nell for his long efforts in leading the struggle to abolish segregated schools in Boston.

Black children were permitted to attend the school closest to their homes, and in 1855 the Smith School closed. For many years the building was used to store school furniture. In 1887 Black Civil War vet-erans began to use the building as their headquarters. Abiel Smith School currently is used for offices of the Afro-American History Museum and the National Park Service. Museum leaders hope to restore the interior and open the school to the public.

DATE BUILT:	1834
ADDRESS:	46 Joy Street, corner of Smith Court, Boston
TELEPHONE:	(617) 742-5415
VISITING HOURS:	Tours of interior not currently available; National Park Services offices on upstairs level, daily, 9–5 Memorial Day–Labor Day and Mon.–Fri. Labor Day–Memorial Day; closed Christmas, Thanksgiving, other hol-idays; closings vary, so check ahead
FEES:	None; donations are appreciated

Bunker Hill Monument

During the American Revolution Black soldiers were among those who fought in an important battle that took place in Boston's Charlestown district. The site was actually Breed's Hill, but the battle is mistakenly known today as the Battle of Bunker Hill, after the name of a neighboring hill.

Among the Black soldiers who fought in this bat-tle were Salem Poor, Peter Salem, Pomp Fisk, and George Middleton. Peter Salem's owner—a man who owned property at Framingham, Massachusetts—granted Peter his freedom so that he could fight in the Continental Army of the American colonists. By some accounts Peter Salem fired the shot that killed the British commander, Major Pitcairn.

Both Peter Salem and Salem Poor were cited as outstanding soldiers in this action. Fourteen officers later commended Poor for his bravery, commenting that he behaved like an experienced officer. His offi-cers presented a petition to the General Court of Massachusetts in 1775, saying, "We would only beg leave to say, in the person of this said negro, centers a brave and gallant soldier."[3] Poor later served in the battles at Valley Forge and White Plains.

Each year thousands of visitors come to see the Bunker Hill Monument, which is located in the Charlestown neighborhood of Boston. A lodge con-tains a diorama and other displays depicting the battle that took place on Breed's Hill. There are booklets, a free brochure, and an interpretive talk by a ranger. From the lodge visitors proceed to the monument itself, a 221-foot- high obelisk with 294 steps to the top. Those who are hardy enough to reach the top are rewarded with a view of the land on which the battle was fought. Although there is little to see and hear about Black history at this site, visitors have informa-tion from this entry about the role of some of the African Americans in the battle.

DATES OF SIGNIFICANCE:	Battle, June 17, 1775; monument built 1827–1842, dedicated 1843
ADDRESS:	Breed's Hill (from downtown Boston fol-low the Freedom Trail Line, painted on the street pavement, across bridge, past Charlestown Naval Yard), Monument Square, Charlestown District, Boston

TELEPHONE:	(617) 242-5641
VISITING HOURS:	Daily including holidays 9–5 👫
FEES:	None
SOURCES:	Telephone conversation May 26, 1994, Joe Damico, park ranger. Telephone conversation June 11, 1994, Emily Prigot, interpretive ranger. *Before the Mayflower*, 62, 64. *International Library of Negro Life and History*, 28, 30.

Bunker Hill Pavilion

After seeing the Bunker Hill Monument and the land where the battle actually took place, visitors may wish to see a multimedia show that portrays some of the sights and sounds of the battle. The show, called *Whites of Their Eyes*, contains 1,000 slides, 14 screens, and 7 channels of sound.

DATE OF SIGNIFICANCE:	1775
ADDRESS:	55 Constitution Road, Charlestown (from Boston, follow the red line in the pavement, the Freedom Trail line, from the Boston Common to nearby Bunker Hill Monument)
TELEPHONE:	(617) 241-7575
VISITING HOURS:	Daily 9:30–4; shows every half hour starting at 9:30 👫
FEES:	Adults, $3; senior citizens, $2; children, $1.50; special school and group rates
SOURCE:	Mary J. Morrissey, supervisor.

Charles Street African Methodist Episcopal Church

Charles Street African Methodist Episcopal Church is one of the historic Black churches in Boston. It is located in the Roxbury section of Boston in a residential neighborhood of Queen Anne and Victorian houses. A white congregation, Mount Pleasant Congregational Church (All Souls Church), erected the building in 1888–1889. In 1939 the Charles Street A.M.E. Church bought the building.

The African American congregation originated before Civil War days, meeting on Anderson Street in Boston. They held many antislavery meetings at the earlier site that included such outstanding speakers as Frederick Douglass, William Lloyd Garrison, and Wendell Phillips. The congregation owned the Charles Street Meeting House on Beacon Hill from 1876 through 1939. As population patterns changed and African Americans began to move from Beacon Hill to Roxbury, the Charles Street Church was the last Black congregation to leave Beacon Hill.

Architect J. Williams Beal designed the Roxbury church that the Black congregation purchased. He used a combination of Gothic-revival and Tudor-revival elements. The exterior features local materials such as Roxbury puddingstone and Quincy granite trim. The interior is finished in cypress. Although some of the stained-glass windows were removed when the church was sold in 1939, some remain, including windows by John LaFarge, an outstanding nineteenth-century stained-glass designer. The sanctuary, a broad, low space, has varnished wainscoting and roof timbers. The ceiling is supported by a complicated system of rafters and beams.

DATE BUILT:	1888–1889; purchased by African American congregation, 1939
ADDRESS:	551 Warren Street at Elm Hill Avenue, Boston
TELEPHONE:	(617) 427-1298
VISITING HOURS:	Office, Mon.–Fri. 10–4; Sun. services, 8, 11 👫
FEES:	None
SOURCES:	Candace Jenkins, preservation planning director. Telephone conversation May 26, 1994, Lisa Radcliffe, secretary. NRHPINF.

Faneuil Hall *

Faneuil Hall originally was built as a market and meeting hall. It was given to the city by a merchant named Peter Faneuil in 1740. Destroyed by fire in 1761, it was rebuilt two years later and then enlarged and restored during the nineteenth century. The building was a focal point for Boston citizens protesting against English rule. Among the five men killed by British soldiers in Boston on March 5, 1770, the first to die was a Black man, Crispus Attucks. (See the listing for Old Granary Burying Ground in Boston.) Three days after the massacre a public funeral was held with a large procession starting from Faneuil Hall where the five men had lain in state.

Faneuil Hall became an important focal point for religious meetings of the African American community and for meetings of nineteenth-century abolitionists. Thomas Paul, a Black preacher from New Hampshire, led worship meetings here for the Black community. In 1805 his twenty-member group formed the First African Baptist Church. In that same year they purchased land and began building the African Meeting House (which still stands in Boston). Black abolitionist Frederick Douglass was a speaker at Faneuil Hall. Black Bostonians met here in 1850 and formed the Black Vigilance Committee to provide assistance to fugitive slaves. In August 1907 W. E. B. Du Bois addressed an audience of about 800 at Faneuil Hall at the third annual meeting of the Niagara Movement.

Faneuil Hall is a brick, three-story building with an octagonal cupola. It has a great hall on the second floor. This historic building currently is used as both a marketplace and a museum.

DATE BUILT:	1740–1742
ADDRESS:	Faneuil Hall Square, Merchants Row, Boston
TELEPHONE:	(617) 635-3105, or (617) 242-5675
VISITING HOURS:	Mon.–Fri. 10–5 👫
FEES:	None
SOURCES:	*National Register of Historic Places*, 345. *W. E. B. Du Bois: Biography of a Race*, 339. *The Negro in the Making of America*, 52.

Farwell Mansion/League of Women for Community Service

This fine old brownstone mansion twice has played a role in Black history—once as a site on the underground railroad and again, for the past seventy-five years, as the home of the League of Women for Community Service.

William Rice Carnes built the mansion about 1858. He had built another home nearby, but that one did not meet his high standards; he believed this represented his better effort. The mansion had gold and brass chandeliers and hand-carved furnishings.

The house is of interest in Black history because abolitionists hid fugitive slaves at this site. If they anticipated a dangerous situation, they would send the fugitives to the original Carnes mansion, which was kept in total darkness to make it appear uninhabited. The fugitives would be returned to this site at 558 Massachusetts Avenue when the danger was over.

Boston was a center of abolitionist activity, and the Farwell House, as it was known for the family that purchased it from the Carnes estate, was only one of many places in which slaves were hidden. Many Black abolitionists lived on Beacon Hill (then called West End) in the nineteenth century, and the African Meeting House was the center of many abolitionist meetings. White abolitionist William Lloyd Garrison lived in Roxbury.

The Farwell house was empty for about ten to fifteen years before it was purchased by an African American organization, the League of Women for Community Service, a benevolent society that used the house for many years as a temporary residence for young women.

DATE BUILT:	c1858
ADDRESS:	558 Massachusetts Avenue, Boston
TELEPHONE:	Answering service, (617) 536-3747
VISITING HOURS:	By appointment; closed June and July 👫
SOURCES:	Telephone conversation May 22, 1994, Muriel Turk, League of Women for Community Service. Telephone conversation May 25, 1994, Jacqueline Arrington, League of Women for Community Service. *The Underground Railroad in New England*.

Museum of the National Center of Afro-American Artists

The Museum of the National Center of Afro-American Artists highlights contemporary and historical Afro-American art in displays that include thousands of items of African, African American, and Caribbean art. The structure housing the museum is worth seeing, too. Resembling an old stone castle, it was originally the Oak Bend mansion that was built in the early 1870s by Aaron Davis Williams. The 20,000-square-foot mansion is constructed of Roxbury puddingstone and Nova Scotia sandstone and is one of the best examples of neo-Gothic architecture in Boston. At a cost of more than $365,000, it was the most expensive house in Boston at the time of construction. The old "castle" served as a residence until the mid-1920s when it became a school for boys with discipline problems. Later it became an annex to the David Ellis School. The building closed and fell into ruin until the museum acquired it in the mid-1970s and began the still-ongoing process of restoration; the museum occupies half of the mansion. Visitors can also enjoy the surroundings that include a large lawn shaded by oak trees and surrounded by a low stone wall.

DATE ESTABLISHED: 1969
ADDRESS: 300 Walnut Avenue, Boston
TELEPHONE: (617) 442-8014
VISITING HOURS: Tues.–Sun. 1–5; closed New Year's Day, Thanksgiving, July 4, Christmas 🕇🕇
FEES: Adults, $1.25; students and senior citizens, $.50; members, free
SOURCES: Edmund Barry Gaither, curator/director. Telephone conversation May 26, 1994, Mr. Gaither.

Old Granary Burying Ground

The Old Granary Burying Ground has a place in Black history because among the victims of the Boston Massacre buried here is Crispus Attucks, the first person to die in the struggle against Britain that led to the War of Independence.

In 1770 the antagonism between British troops and Black and white patriots reached a peak in Boston. The city was tense as a result of numerous fights and skirmishes. On March 5, as some soldiers emerged from their barracks near the center of town, a crowd gathered, trading insults with the soldiers and taunting them with snowballs and stones. Among the crowd was a Black man, Crispus Attucks (c1723–1770), who had escaped from slavery and had worked for twenty years as a merchant seaman.

According to one report, when the crowd began to draw back, Attucks rallied them to continue and a fight broke out. Soon the fire bell rang at the Old Brick Meeting House, and more frightened and angry citizens joined the crowd. The British troops panicked and opened fire. Attucks was the first to fall in the conflict that later became known as the Boston

Massacre. A plaque in the middle of State Street commemorates the massacre.

The Old Granary Burying Ground, which contains the remains of Paul Revere and John Hancock, also contains the bodies of the five victims of the massacre. Crispus Attucks is further honored by the Crispus Attucks Monument, which citizens of Boston erected in 1888 on the Tremont Street side of the Boston Common.

DATE OF SIGNIFICANCE: Mar. 5, 1770
ADDRESS: Park Street District, Tremont, Park, and Beacon Streets, Boston
VISITING HOURS: Daily, dawn–dusk 🕇🕇
SOURCES: *Before the Mayflower*, 61. *National Register of Historic Places*, 346. *International Library of Negro Life and History*, 8.

Dorchester

William Monroe Trotter Home

William Monroe Trotter was born in 1872 to a life of privilege in a Black family of Boston. He excelled in his studies and was elected president of his senior class at Hyde Park High School. After spending a year as a shipping clerk, Trotter attended Harvard College, graduating *magna cum laude* in 1895. He was the first African American elected to the Phi Beta Kappa chapter at Harvard.

The 1890s were a period of racial tensions and hatreds. Intimidation and a tangled web of restrictive laws were used to bar African Americans from voting. The 1896 U.S. Supreme Court decision in the *Plessy v. Ferguson* case established the infamous "separate but equal doctrine." Under it, Louisiana was entitled to segregate Black travelers in railroad cars. This decision led to a court-approved system of segregation for the next sixty years.

During the 1890s white Americans were raising Booker T. Washington to national prominence. They approved of his statements that the races could remain separate and that Black people should not concern themselves with political power, and they supported Washington's emphasis on industrial training in schools for Black students.

Trotter, however, vigorously opposed such ideas. He spoke out for political involvement against segregation, becoming more militant as he saw racist views spreading from the South into the North. In 1901 Trotter helped organize the Boston Literary and Historical Association, which served as a forum for expressing militant political opinion.

That same year Trotter and his friend George Forbes founded *The Guardian,* a weekly newspaper that opposed compromises on civil rights. Trotter spoke out against Booker T. Washington's ideas, which he believed relegated African Americans to a lower place in society, and he insisted on the right to vote as essential for achieving power.

On July 30, 1903, Booker T. Washington was the featured speaker at the Columbus Avenue African Zion Church in Boston. As Washington started to speak, Trotter stood on a chair and attempted to read nine questions he had prepared concerning Washington's program. Trotter and his sister were arrested, leaving Washington free to deliver his speech. The press, giving widespread coverage to the incident, called it the "Boston riot."

Trotter's sentence of thirty days in jail drew national attention to his views and encouraged another leader, W. E. B. Du Bois, to join forces with him. Trotter continued to work for justice, forming another group, the Boston Suffrage League, and assisting in founding the Niagara Movement in 1905.

(See the listing for Harpers Ferry, West Virginia.) However, he would not join the 1909 initial meeting of the NAACP because he believed the association was dominated by white people.

Since Trotter devoted so much time to civil rights causes, he had less time for his business. As a result, he eventually lost the property inherited from his father and the house on Sawyer Avenue where he had lived from 1899 to 1909. He slipped into poverty, and many of his old friends abandoned him.

Although he lived in poverty, Trotter continued to fight energetically for better conditions for African Americans in *The Guardian.* Twenty thousand people from thirty-six states signed a petition on civil rights that he drafted and presented to President Woodrow Wilson. Although Trotter met twice with the President, Wilson made no commitment for a change.

When the Paris Peace Conference convened in 1919, Trotter was denied a passport that would have allowed him to attend and to place the plight of Black people before the world's leaders. Despite this setback, he found a job as a cook on a transatlantic steamer in order to reach France. There he attended the conference as a delegate of the National Equal Rights League and presented the cause of African Americans. Neither President Wilson nor the newly created League of Nations gave any response to Trotter's plea to end racial discrimination. In America conditions continued to deteriorate as white groups in 1919 took up arms against Black people in cities throughout America. Trotter continued his work, speaking out for racial justice before a Senate committee and supporting an antilynching bill.

Trotter's later years were overshadowed by financial problems and other disappointments, yet he never flinched from speaking out and never drew back from working for justice for African Americans. William Monroe Trotter died in April 1934. His home is listed as a national historic site.

DATE OF SIGNIFICANCE: Trotter residence, 1899–1909

ADDRESS: 97 Sawyer Avenue, Dorchester

VISITING HOURS: Private, visitors may drive by

SOURCES: NRHPINF. *Before the Mayflower,* 329–30, 333. *International Library of Negro Life and History, Historical Negro Biographies,* 154, 254–5.

Framingham

Old Burial Ground

Framingham was home to two Black men who gained fame in the Revolutionary War period. One was Crispus Attucks; he was born a slave but escaped from his owner in 1750. Attucks was the first person killed in the Boston Massacre, one of a series of events that led to the Revolutionary War. (See the entry on the Old Granary Burying Ground in Boston.)

The other Black man from Framingham was Peter Salem, whose master freed him so that Peter could serve in the Continental Army. Peter took part in the first conflicts of the Revolutionary War at Lexington and Concord in 1775. Later that same year Peter Salem and another Black man, Salem Poor, showed outstanding courage at Breed's Hill, in the conflict known today as the Battle of Bunker Hill. Peter is credited with shooting the British commander, Major Pitcairn, at Breed's Hill.

Peter Salem died in Framingham and was buried in that city.

DATE ESTABLISHED:	Prior to 1698
ADDRESS:	Main Street, Framingham
TELEPHONE:	Framingham Historical Association, (508) 872-3780; Framingham Public Library, (508) 879-3570
VISITING HOURS:	Daily dawn–dusk 👫
FEES:	None
SOURCE:	Bonita M. Bryant, corresponding secretary pro tem, Framingham Historical & Natural History Society.

Great Barrington

W. E. B. Du Bois Boyhood Home

William Edward Burghardt Du Bois, one of the most brilliant scholars of his time, was born on Church Street in New Barrington on February 23, 1868, the son of Alfred Duboise and Mary (according to his birth certificate). Although there may have been fewer than thirty Black families in the village, Du Bois had a strong attachment to the region; he claimed that Burghardts had lived there for more than 200 years.

Du Bois spent the first seventeen years of his life in Great Barrington. Before he was two years old, however, his parents' marriage failed and his father left; his mother then had to leave the child with his grandparents on South Egremont Road. When Willie (as he was called then) was five years old, his grandfather died and his grandmother, Sarah, had to sell the family property to pay debts. She moved in with Willie's mother and his half-brother Adelbert above some stables on an estate south of Main Street. The family moved again, to a run-down house near the tracks on Railroad Street that they shared with a poor white family. By the time Du Bois was in high school, some townspeople who were interested in his family's welfare helped them to find a small house to rent on Church Street; it was located behind the property of a white family, the Casses.

Du Bois's mother encouraged him to do well in school. No one in his family had attended school beyond the elementary level, but he showed promise. The only Black student in his high school, he was recognized as the outstanding scholar in his graduating class. He attended Fisk University on a scholarship, graduating in 1888, then continued his studies at Harvard University, where he received his bachelor's degree with honors in philosophy in 1890.

Du Bois began studying for a doctorate degree at Harvard University. Before completing his dissertation at Harvard, he studied at the University of Berlin for two years. In 1895 he became the first African

American to receive a Ph.D. degree from Harvard University. Harvard published his Ph.D. dissertation.

Du Bois began writing and publishing at an early age. He also taught at Wilberforce University in Ohio, the University of Pennsylvania, and Atlanta University. While teaching in Atlanta, he began to challenge the views of Booker T. Washington, who had recommended industrial training rather than a classical education. Du Bois believed that Washington's curriculum prepared for manual-labor careers rather than for leadership positions that would challenge the status quo. Moreover, Du Bois believed that Washington was too accommodating of racial segregation. In contrast, Du Bois sought to educate the "talented tenth" of Black people through a rigorous classical education. His ideas were widely influential at many Black colleges and universities.

In 1905 Du Bois called for a national meeting of leaders to initiate the Niagara Movement, which was superseded in 1909–1910 by the NAACP. In 1910 he became founder and editor of the NAACP magazine, *The Crisis*. Because of his independent stance, Du Bois at times came into conflict with NAACP fellow directors. In 1934 he resigned from the NAACP and returned to Atlanta University for a decade.

For most of his career Du Bois was interested in Africa. He gathered and shared valuable information about the European colonies in Black Africa and served as a consultant on matters about Africa.

In 1958 Du Bois made his fifteenth trip abroad, visiting the Soviet Union and the People's Republic of China. In 1961 he applied for membership in the American Communist Party and accepted an invitation from President Kwame Nkrumah of Ghana to reside in Ghana. He became a citizen of Ghana in 1963 and died there the same year. He was given a state funeral and buried in Accra.

The outspoken scholar, Du Bois, was the great-grandson by marriage of another intelligent, respected, and outspoken African American, Elizabeth Freeman. (See the listing for the Colonel John Ashley House in Ashley Falls, Massachusetts.)

Du Bois owned the Burghardt house from 1928 to 1954. He never acquired great wealth, and his friends, recognizing his love for the place in Great Barrington, purchased his boyhood home for him. The two-story clapboard house where he once lived is no longer standing. The property is a park today, five acres of land in an open field, clustered with pine, maple, and elm trees.

DATE OF SIGNIFICANCE: 1868–c1885

ADDRESS: North side of MA 23, between Great Barrington and South Egremont Streets, Great Barrington

VISITING HOURS: Privately owned, but accessible to the public as a park during daylight hours

FEES: None

SOURCES: Mr. Walter Wilson, W. E. B. Du Bois Memorial Foundation. NRHPINF. *W. E. B. Du Bois.*

Lynn

Jan Ernst Matzeliger Monument

A monument in Lynn honors the Black man who invented the mechanical shoe-lasting machine. As a young man, Jan Matzeliger worked for several years to perfect a machine that made possible the routine mass production of shoes. He worked on his model in between his regular working hours in a shoe factory. The device Matzeliger created was credited with improving wages and working conditions for thousands of people. While the manual method of shoe-making produced only fifty pairs of shoes a day, Matzeliger's method could turn out 150 to 600 pairs.

Matzeliger was born in 1852, the son of a Dutch colonial engineer father and a Black Guianese mother in Dutch Guiana (now Suriname). At the age of ten, he began an apprenticeship in his father's machine shop. At age nineteen, he left home to become a sailor and earned his passage to the United States. He worked in Philadelphia for five years, and then came to Lynn. He attended evening school and went to work in Lynn's major industry, the shoe industry. Matzeliger had worked in a shoe factory in Philadelphia, but in Lynn he began the painstaking process of creating a machine that could automatically fit leather over the sole of a shoe. Before his invention, this task had to be completed by hand.

Although he worked fourteen years to perfect the process, Matzeliger never gained the major financial benefit from his invention. He had to sell the majority ownership in the device to finance its production. The U.S. Shoe Company was the beneficiary and became the industry leader. Matzeliger died in 1889 of tuberculosis at the age of thirty-six.

ADDRESS: Pine Grove Cemetery, Boston Street, Lynn

TELEPHONE: (781) 477-7049

SOURCES: *I Have a Dream*, 25. *Webster's New Biographical Dictionary*, 666. *Hippocrene U.S.A. Guide to Black America*, 167. *International Library of Negro Life and History*, 99.

Nantucket

African Baptist Society Church

The historic African Baptist Church in Nantucket, built in 1830, may be the second-oldest surviving Black church in the United States. The church is a rectangular building with a double-door entrance. Its origins are associated with people from the west coast of Africa. In 1826 trustees of the African Baptist Society bought land at Pleasant and York Streets, and sea captain Absalom Boston and four of his crew built the church. Boston, who also put up a home for himself on Nantucket Island, had an all-Black crew on his ship, *Harmony*. The crew were representative of the many African Americans who worked aboard whaling vessels in the nineteenth century.

The African Baptist Church became important to runaway slaves who had escaped by becoming stowaways on vessels sailing north from Maryland and Virginia. Upon reaching Nantucket the runaway people became free. Many of them settled in a small area west of Orange Street and south of Silver Street known as New Guinea. There they developed their own community with shops, stores, and the African Baptist Church. The church provided a place of worship, a school, and a meeting center. From 1847 to 1888, the years when the church was active, Reverend James Crawford, also a barber, served as its minister.

The whaling industry prospered until 1850 or 1860 when the sailing ships became obsolete as steamships replaced them. Now unemployed, some of Nantucket's African Americans left for New Bedford or other ports. This may explain why the church ceased to operate by 1888.

In 1911 C. Chase bought the church for $250. He installed large garage-type doors, strengthened the floors, extended the building so that trucks could be parked inside, and transformed the house of worship into a warehouse and garage.

In 1933 Florence Higginbotham bought the church for $3,000 from the estate of Henry Chase. The building could have been torn down, but Mrs. Higginbotham's son, who was attending a Black preparatory school in North Carolina at the time, learned the history of the building in a Black history course. Years later he donated the building to Boston's Museum of African-American History. Although the church is not yet open to visitors, the Boston museum intends to restore it and to research the history of the Africans who established it.

DATE ESTABLISHED: c1827

ADDRESS: North side of York Street at corner of Pleasant Street, Nantucket

TELEPHONE: Boston Afro-American Museum, (617) 742-1854

VISITING HOURS: Interior not open to public, but visitors can walk or drive by; contact the museum to find out when the restoration will be complete

SOURCES: Nantucket Historical Association. Historic American Buildings Survey HABS No. MASS-909, 1967 Historic American Buildings Survey summer project on Nantucket, Massachusetts. "Hub Museum to Restore Black Church."

Nantucket Historical Association

The collection of the Nantucket Historical Association includes portraits of sea captain Absalom Boston and Arthur Cooper, two of Nantucket's most prominent Black citizens. The library and research center has detailed information on Nantucket's Black history, including diaries, letters, and newspaper clippings.

Nantucket was the birthplace of Lucretia Coffin Mott, a white advocate of Black rights and women's rights. Mott lived in Nantucket throughout her childhood years and often returned to the island. (For additional information about Mott, see the La Mott, Pennsylvania, listing.)

ADDRESS:	Peter Folge Museum Building, Broad Street, Nantucket
TELEPHONE:	(508) 325-4015
VISITING HOURS:	Portraits and facilities by appointment Mon.–Fri. 10–3; closed holidays
FEES:	$5 per day research fee
SOURCES:	Elizabeth A. Codding, assistant curator, Nantucket Historical Association. Telephone conversation May 12, 1994, Peter MacGlashan, audiovisual librarian.

New Bedford

New Bedford Heritage Trail

Five sites in New Bedford show the history of the city's Black and Cape Verdean citizens. Many runaway slaves found the city of New Bedford hospitable and decided to live here instead of continuing to Canada. A second and distinct Black population originated with the Cape Verdeans who also arrived in New Bedford in the nineteenth century. They came from the dry and infertile Cape Verde Islands off the most western point of Africa; the islands were Portuguese territory until independence in 1975. They had functioned for centuries as a way station and slave depot on slave routes to the New World and had served as an administrative center for the Portuguese colony of Guinea. Ethnically the Cape Verdeans were Black Africans or Black/Portuguese who spoke Portuguese or a Creole form of Portuguese called "crioulo."

Many Cape Verdeans came to New Bedford on whaling ships in the late eighteenth and early nineteenth centuries, and some chose to settle in that important whaling port. There they sometimes disagreed over their identity. Catholic in religion and with a language based on Portuguese, many considered themselves Portuguese; the white population, on the other hand, often saw the Cape Verdeans as Black. During the 1970s, an era of emphasis on racial pride, some Cape Verdeans formed alliances with

Black Americans. They shared a common heritage related to working in seafaring occupations.

A group of New Bedford's Black historical sites follow in alphabetical order. Tina Furtado, archivist at the New Bedford Free Public Library, notes that all of the sites can be viewed in a pleasant two-hour walk.

ADDRESS:	Visitors Center, 42 S. Second Street, New Bedford
TELEPHONE:	(508) 991-6200
SOURCES:	Tina Furtado, archivist, New Bedford Free Public Library. *We The People*. The Academic American Encyclopedia.

Sergeant William H. Carney House

Sergeant Carney of the Fifty-fourth Massachusetts Volunteers was the first African American to win the Congressional Medal of Honor. In the Union assault on Fort Wagner, South Carolina, in 1863, Carney rescued the colors from the mortally wounded standard bearer. Even though severely wounded twice, Carney held the colors as he led a charge to the parapet.

The Carney house was built in 1850 and until 1939 was occupied by members of the Carney family. Today the small frame, story-and-a-half home is owned by the Martha Briggs Educational Club, a Black women's organization founded in 1920 to provide scholarships to young people. Although the house generally is not open to the public, it is open once a year for a week when the local historical association gives tours of New Bedford's historic sites.

DATE BUILT:	1850
ADDRESS:	128 Mill Street, New Bedford
TELEPHONE:	New Bedford Preservation Society, (508) 997-6425; New Bedford Chamber of Commerce, (508) 999-5231; New Bedford Free Public Library, (508) 991-6278; New Bedford Library, (508) 991-6275
VISITING HOURS:	Not open to public except once yearly during tour of historic homes
SOURCES:	Telephone conversation June 12, 1994, Annette Morton, president, Martha Briggs Educational Club. *Historical and Cultural Atlas of African Americans*, 88. *Before the Mayflower*, 94.

Nathan Johnson Home

When New Bedford was a refuge for slaves who ran away via a sea route, this house was a safe haven and a stop on the underground railroad. One of the most famous fugitives to stay at this house was Frederick Augustus Washington Bailey who, at the age of twenty-one, escaped from slavery and arrived in Newport by sea with his wife. They were transported to New Bedford where they were sheltered by Nathan and Mary Johnson. Nathan Johnson was an officer in the Antislavery Society of New Bedford and his wife, Mary, ran a successful confectionary and catering business from the home.

Nathan Johnson was reading Sir Walter Scott's *Lady of the Lake* at the time of their visitors' stay, and Frederick Bailey, taking his new name from one of the characters of that book, became known from then on as Frederick Douglass.

DATE BUILT:	Early 1800s
ADDRESS:	21 Seventh Street, New Bedford
VISITING HOURS:	Private, visitors may drive or walk by
SOURCES:	Telephone conversation May 21, 1994, Paul Cyr, curator, New Bedford Free Public Library. *The Underground Railroad in New England.*

Liberty Bell

Only a small piece of the old New Bedford liberty bell remains because most of it burned up in a fire. After the United States passed the 1850 Fugitive Slave Law that made it easier to capture slaves, New Bedford used this bell to warn escaped slaves of imminent danger. People would ring the liberty bell to warn the runaways when a schooner was on its way to capture fugitives.

DATE OF SIGNIFICANCE:	1850–Civil War
ADDRESS:	Corner of William Street and Purchase Street, New Bedford
VISITING HOURS:	Always accessible

New Bedford Whaling Museum

The New Bedford Whaling Museum has in its collection an example of a toggle harpoon invented by the Black metalsmith Lewis Temple. The contributions of other African Americans who participated in seafaring industries are also described in museum exhibits that include models of the vessels of shipbuilder John Mashow and the papers of wealthy sea captain Paul Cuffe. Mashow, who was born in South Carolina in 1805, was the son of an African American mother and a white father. His father sent him to New Bedford to learn the trade of ship building. Mashow became New Bedford's second-largest builder of whaling ships. Although he was talented enough to establish his own shipyard at the age of twenty-seven, his business was destroyed nearly thirty years later by an oversupply of whale oil on the market. The man and his accomplishments were nearly forgotten when he died in 1893.

ADDRESS:	18 Johnny Cake Hill, New Bedford
TELEPHONE:	(508) 997-0046
VISITING HOURS:	Mon.–Sat. 9–5, Sun. 1–5 🏃🏻
FEES:	Adults, $4.50; senior citizens, $3.50; children 6–14, $3; children under 6, free
SOURCES:	Telephone call to site May 21, 1994. *African Americans,* 92.

Lewis Temple Statue

Lewis Temple, a Black metalsmith who operated a whalecraft shop in New Bedford, invented the toggle harpoon in 1848. Unlike older harpoons that often slipped out allowing the whale to escape, Temple's toggle device snapped shut and anchored firmly at a right angle. Although the harpoon greatly increased the whalers' profits, Temple did not patent his invention, and like Jan Matzeliger of Lynn, he did not benefit from his work. As a result, Temple died in poverty. Today he is honored with a statue crafted by Black sculptor James Toatley. The statue is located in front of the New Bedford Free Public Library. As one faces the library, Temple's statue is on the left; on the right is a statue of a whaleman holding the toggle harpoon invented by Temple.

ADDRESS:	613 Pleasant Street, New Bedford
TELEPHONE:	(508) 991-6275
VISITING HOURS:	Statue always visible
SOURCES:	Telephone conversation May 21, 1994, Ernestine Furtado, archivist, and Paul Cyr, curator, New Bedford Free Public Library. *African Americans,* 92.

Newton

Jackson House

Many sites of the underground railroad have been identified by oral tradition but lack specific written documentation. In contrast, the Jackson House has been identified and described as such a site by an account written in 1874 by Ellen D. Jackson. Jackson told how the women of Newton used to hold sewing circles at the house to prepare clothing for fugitive slaves. Because slave owners often searched Boston for their slaves, the fugitives were often sent west of Boston to make the connection to Canada. Notice of their arrival was signaled by pebbles tossed against the window. The family rushed the visitors inside. If there was danger nearby, they hid the fugitives between two chimney supports and covered the area with boards and sacks of vegetables.

Today the house serves as the Newton City Museum, where interpreters describe the Jackson family role in the abolitionist movement. To school groups, interpreters tell about specific families who made their way to Massachusetts or Canada, and they describe the Jackson family's role on the local Vigilance Committee.

ADDRESS: 527 Washington Street, Newton

TELEPHONE: (617) 552-7238

VISITING HOURS: Mon.–Thurs. 1–5

FEES: Adults, $2; children, $1

SOURCES: Telephone conversation May 21 and May 24, 1994, Susan Abele, director. *The Underground Railroad in New England.*

Roxbury

Dillaway–Thomas House

According to oral tradition passed on by older members of the Roxbury Historical Society, the Dillaway–Thomas House, built as a parsonage by Reverend Oliver Peabody between 1750 and 1754, served as a station on Boston's underground railroad. A hidden trapdoor in the kitchen and other evidence of the underground railroad have been destroyed by a major fire in the house. The house still stands, however, and is now a part of the Roxbury Heritage Park. Located on the north side of John Eliot Square, the dwelling at one time was called Dillaway House because it was occupied by a Roxbury teacher named Charles K. Dillaway.

Before the fire occurred, the author, having heard that the Dillaway House—then boarded up and empty—was a part of the underground railroad, made a request to the Roxbury Historical Society to open the house for her inspection. Although the interior was interesting with its wide floorboards and large kitchen fireplace, the most meaningful area was the hidden trapdoor. It totally resembled the other floorboards in the kitchen, but once grasped in a certain way, it lifted to reveal in the darkness below a small rectangular area where fugitive slaves were hidden. To see such a place was an extremely moving experience. Unfortunately, knowledge of the hiding place seems to have been forgotten.

The site is operated today by the state of Massachusetts as part of the Roxbury Heritage State Park. Community groups use the house for community activities and exhibits and the garden area for concerts. The gambrel-roofed structure has retained its exterior appearance. The interior has been extensively remodeled, but sections of the original have been retained to show how it once looked. It is located in the Roxbury town square, also called John Eliot Square, an area of nineteen buildings from the eighteenth and nineteenth centuries. The John Eliot Square District is listed in the *National Register of Historic Places.*

DATE BUILT: 1750

ADDRESS: John Eliot Square, 183 Roxbury Street, Roxbury

TELEPHONE: (617) 445-3399

VISITING HOURS: Wed.–Fri. 10–4, Sat.–Sun. 12–5, or by appointment

SOURCES: Personal visit to site c1965. Telephone conversation May 28, 1994, Walter Vaughn of the Dillaway–Thomas House. *National Register of Historic Places,* 348.

William Lloyd Garrison House

William Lloyd Garrison (1805–1879), who was born in Newburyport, Massachusetts, was a well-known white abolitionist. He was born in poverty, and once was an indentured servant.

Although Garrison began his work as an abolitionist by advocating the gradual emancipation of the slaves, he became more radical in his views over time. Influenced by Black people, he founded *The Liberator,* an antislavery journal published between 1831 and 1865. The well-known journal was influential in making the antislavery cause known. Individuals in Black communities were among the newspaper's strongest supporters. In the first years of publication, almost 90 percent of its subscribers were African Americans.

Considered a radical abolitionist, Garrison founded the American Anti-Slavery Society in 1833 and was the society's president between 1843 and 1865. The first board of managers of this society included five Black abolitionists.

Garrison was well known to Black abolitionists of the day. They communicated with each other on a regular basis, discussing how best to end the institution of slavery. When the American Colonization Society proposed relocating numbers of Black Americans to Africa, Black abolitionists helped turn Garrison and other white abolitionists against that idea.

Garrison lived in this house, a two and one-half–story frame structure with clapboarding, from 1864 to 1879.

DATE BUILT:	19th century
ADDRESS:	125 Highland Street, Roxbury
VISITING HOURS:	Private, visitors may walk or drive by
SOURCES:	*Webster's New Biographical Dictionary,* 388. *National Register of Historic Places,* 348. *Before the Mayflower,* 144, 152, 153.

Salem

Peabody Museum of Salem

The Peabody Museum, founded in 1799 by Salem sea captains, contains in its collections some artifacts from African culture that the captains had brought back to their home port. One exhibit, *Tribal Style,* is a selection of artifacts from the museum's subSaharan art collection. The exhibit includes sculpture, masks, utensils, musical instruments, and weapons— priceless documents of a vanished way of life.

DATE ESTABLISHED:	1799
ADDRESS:	East India Square, Salem
TELEPHONE:	(508) 745-1876
VISITING HOURS:	Mon.–Sat. 10–5, Thurs. 10–9, Sun. 12–5; closed Thanksgiving, Christmas, New Year's Day
FEES:	Adults, $4; children 6–16, $1.50; senior citizens and students, $3
SOURCE:	Ellen Soares, Peabody Museum of Salem.

Westport

Paul Cuffe Monument

Paul Cuffe was born in 1759 near New Bedford, Massachusetts, to a former slave father and an Indian mother. The family lived on a marginal farm as he grew up and had few material resources. As a young man Paul went to sea. Earning money from whaling, ship building, transporting whale oil and whalebone to Europe, and retail storekeeping, he became one of the wealthiest Black men of his day.

At the age of forty-nine, Cuffe became a member of the Society of Friends. Attending services at the Friends' Meeting House in Westport, he soon established personal and business ties with his Quaker associates. According to his own account, in 1813 he advanced over $500 in materials toward the total cost of $1,198.08 needed to build the present meeting house in Westport.

Cuffe gained an international reputation for his efforts to advance the cause of Black settlement in Sierra Leone and trade with that African nation. His work in furthering trade with Africa brought him to the attention of President James Madison. Cuffe's petition for special trading privileges to Africa received a favorable vote in the U.S. Senate.

Cuffe also sought gains in minority rights in Massachusetts. With other African Americans he submitted petitions to local and state governments seeking tax relief. The petitioners reasoned that African Americans and Indians should not have to pay taxes if they were not allowed to vote. Although the petitions were rejected, a court decision in 1783 eventually granted African Americans the right to vote.

The Friends' Meeting House in Westport, built in part through Cuffe's generosity, is open to visitors today. Cuffe, who died in 1817, was buried in the adjacent cemetery. The Society of Friends dedicated the monument at his grave, and a plaque in the town hall honors his memory.

DATE BUILT:	c1813
ADDRESS:	938 Main Street, Westport
TELEPHONE:	(508) 636-4963
VISITING HOURS:	Call to arrange to see interior
SOURCES:	Telephone conversation May 21, 1994, Jean Kennisor, member of the Westport Monthly Meeting of Friends NRHPINF. *National Register of Historic Places*, 332–3.

Notes

1. Arthur M. Chase, *The Ashleys: A Pioneer Berkshire Family* (Ashley Falls, Mass.: The Trustees of Reservations, 1978), 20.
2. Frederick Douglass, "Men of Color, to Arms!" *Frederick Douglass's Paper* (Mar. 2, 1863), quoted in Herbert Aptheker, ed., *A Documentary History of the Negro People in the United States*, vol. 1 (New York: Citadel, 1990), 478–9.
3. Wilhelmena S. Robinson, *International Library of Negro Life and History: Historical Negro Biographies* (New York: Publishers, 1970), 28.

Works Consulted

The Academic American Encyclopedia. New York: Grolier, 1993. [electronic version]

African Americans: Voices of Triumph. Vol. 1, *Perseverance*. Alexandria, Va.: Time-Life, 1993.

African Americans: Voices of Triumph. Vol. 2, *Leadership*. Alexandria, Va.: Time-Life, 1993.

The Ashleys: A Pioneer Berkshire Family. Arthur C. Chase. Ashley Falls, Mass.: The Trustees of Reservations, 1978.

Before the Mayflower: A History of Black America. 5th ed. Lerone Bennett Jr. New York: Penguin, 1988.

Black Heritage Trail. Byron Rushing and Staff of the Museum of Afro-American History. Boston: Boston National Historical Park, National Park Service.

A Documentary History of the Negro People in the United States. Vol. 1. Herbert A. Aptheker, ed. New York: Citadel, 1990.

Hippocrene U.S.A. Guide to Black America: A Directory of Historic and Cultural Sites Relating to Black America. Marcella Thum. New York: Hippocrene, 1992.

Historical and Cultural Atlas of African Americans. Molefi K. Asante and Mark T. Mattson. New York: Macmillan, 1991.

"Hub Museum to Restore Black Church." Diana Lewis. *Boston Globe* (6 Feb. 1989).

I Have a Dream: A Collection of Black Americans on U.S. Postage Stamps. Washington, D.C.: U.S. Postal Service, 1991.

International Library of Negro Life and History: Historical Negro Biographies. Wilhelmena S. Robinson. New York: Publishers, 1970.

"A Monument to History and High Purposes." Hal Borland. *The Berkshire Evening Eagle*, 3 Sept. 1958.

"Mum Bett's Heroism." Gerard Chapman. *The Berkshire Eagle*, 24 Feb. 1987.

National Register of Historic Places. Washington, D.C.: National Park Service, 1976.

The Negro in the Making of America. Benjamin Quarles. New York: Collier, 1987.

The Underground Railroad in New England. Richard R. Kuns and John Sabino, eds. Boston: American Revolution Bicentennial Administration, Region I, with Boston 200, the Bicentennial and Historical Commissions of the Six New England States and the Underground Railroad Task Force, 1976.

We the People: An Atlas of America's Ethnic Diversity. James Paul Allen and Eugene James Turner. New York: Macmillan, 1988.

W. E. B. Du Bois: Biography of a Race. David Levering Lewis. New York: Henry Holt, 1993.

Webster's New Biographical Dictionary. Springfield, Mass.: Merriam-Webster, 1988.

Adrian

Second Baptist Church

Second Baptist Church was organized in 1866, shortly after the end of the Civil War. This was Adrian's second African American church, and many of the founding members were former slaves. Prior to the war, the church had been a stop on the underground railroad; its members provided shelter for slaves fleeing to the North.

The congregation constructed the present clapboard structure in 1900. The one-story church with a basement is located in a residential neighborhood. Minor alterations in 1985 included the installation of pews to replace the wooden folding chairs.

DATE ESTABLISHED:	Congregation, 1866; present building, 1900
ADDRESS:	607 N. Broad Street, Adrian
TELEPHONE:	(517) 263-2486 or (517) 263-1020
VISITING HOURS:	Some Fri. and Sun. mornings; call for appointment 👥
SOURCES:	Telephone conversation Dec. 29, 1991, Reverend Russell Henagan, associate pastor Second Baptist Church. Lawrence Richardson Jr., Second Baptist Church. Personal visit, summer 1990. *Pathways to Michigan's Black Heritage.*

Dearborn

Henry Ford Museum, Greenfield Village

This open-air and indoor museum complex, the nation's largest, has displays showing the interaction of agriculture and industry in American life. Industrialist Henry Ford had historic homes and shops moved from many sites in the United States to Greenfield Village, where they were reassembled on streets and in green areas.

Several of the historic structures relate to African American history because Black families once lived in some of them. These include an 1860 Tidewater, Maryland, plantation building; two brick slave quarters from a Georgia rice/industrial plantation; an early-twentieth-century Black landowner's house that was brought to this site from near Saranson, Georgia; and a replica of the three-room cabin in which Dr. George Washington Carver was born.

The Henry Ford Museum contains inventions of Black scientist Elijah McCoy, including his hydrostatic lubricator.

DATE ESTABLISHED:	Museum, 1929; buildings, 17th–19th centuries
ADDRESS:	20900 Oakwood Boulevard (bounded by Michigan Avenue, Village Road, Southfield Expressway, and Oakland Boulevard), Dearborn
TELEPHONE:	(313) 271-1620
VISITING HOURS:	Daily 10–5; closed Thanksgiving, Christmas, Jan. 1–mid-March 👥
FEES:	For either museum or village, persons 13 and older, $12.50; children 5–12, $6.25; senior citizens 62 and older, $11.50; for

both museum and village, persons 13 and older, $22; children 5–12, $11; combination ticket is good 2 consecutive days; parking, free

SOURCES: Ed Merrell, manager of interpretation, Greenfield Village. Personal visit, summer 1990. Telephone calls to site Jan. 18, 1992, Apr. 24, 1994, Aug. 13, 1995. *National Register of Historic Places,* 367.

Detroit

Alpha Phi Alpha Fraternity House

Detroit's Gamma Lambda chapter is the third graduate chapter of Alpha Phi Alpha fraternity. The fraternity, America's oldest Greek fraternal organization for Black students, was founded in 1906 at Cornell University in New York. The Gamma Lambda chapter in Detroit was installed in 1919. Members purchased the house at 239 Eliot Street in 1939.

The fraternity's motto is "Manly deeds, scholarship, and love for all mankind." Members have carried out the ideals expressed in the motto through voter registration programs, educational programs for high school and college students, and participation in the 1950s and 1960s Civil Rights Movement.

When the Alpha Phi Alpha fraternity purchased this site in 1939, most public entertainment and dining facilities were segregated. Fraternities and sororities provided opportunities by sponsoring cultural, educational, and entertainment programs for Detroit's African American community. Currently fraternity members participate in a tutoring program in the Spain Middle School and participate in a joint project with other fraternities and the Masons to develop and revitalize the Brush Park area.

Prominent former members of the fraternity are the following: Dr. Martin Luther King Jr., Dr. W. E. B. Du Bois, and Paul Robeson. John Dancy, the former director of Detroit's Urban League, and Dr. Haley Bell, founder of radio station WCHB, are also members who were well known in the community.

The three-story Alpha Phi Alpha Fraternity House is open to the public by appointment. The site has a Michigan historical marker and is listed in the *State Register of Historic Sites.*

DATE ESTABLISHED: House, 1939
ADDRESS: 293 Eliot Street, Detroit
TELEPHONE: (313) 831-5485
VISITING HOURS: By appointment
FEES: None
SOURCES: Personal visit, summer 1990. Telephone call Dec. 1991, Mr. Kenneth Jordan, Alpha Phi Alpha House. *Pathways to Michigan's Black Heritage. Black Historic Sites in Detroit.*

Ambassador Bridge
Detroit–Windsor Tunnel

Cornelius Langston Henderson Sr. was the second African American to graduate from the University of Michigan in the field of engineering. Henderson was born in 1887 or 1888 in Detroit. His father was president of Atlanta's Morris Brown College, and Cornelius received his early education in the South. He excelled in mathematics, studying at Morris Brown College, Wayne State University, and the University of Michigan, where he received his degree in civil engineering.

Henderson designed portions of the Detroit–Windsor Tunnel as well as the Canadian approaches to the Ambassador Bridge that connects Detroit and Windsor, Canada. He also designed the Detroit Memorial Park and Toronto's General Electric Building. Henderson died in 1976.

ADDRESS: Detroit River; tunnel approached via Randolph Street, Detroit
VISITING HOURS: Always open
SOURCES: *Pathways to Michigan's Black Heritage. International Library of Negro Life and History,* 202.

Detroit Urban League

The Urban League was organized in New York City in 1910 to help meet the needs of migrants from the South. Branches later opened in other major cities in the North. In the first decades of the twentieth century, a major migration of Black people from the rural South came north seeking jobs. The Detroit Urban League office began its work in 1916 under the leadership of Forrester Washington and Henry G. Stevens.

The first wave of Black migrants faced tremendous problems—housing shortages, unemployment, and a death rate twice that of their white contemporaries. The Urban League was the major organization concerned with the problems of the migrants.

The first community center under the Urban League's direction opened in 1919. It was located at 553 East Columbia near St. Antoine. The Detroit Urban League in 1919 hosted the first National Urban League meeting outside New York City.

John C. Dancy served as executive director from 1918 to 1960, a period when more and more African Americans were attracted to the city to work in the automobile factories. Although there was not a Black "ghetto" in Detroit, and although those with money could live wherever they chose (within limits), newcomers were crowded into congested tenement districts. Both races lived in the tenements, but white families had more opportunity to move to better quarters. Under John Dancy's direction, the Urban League grew to prominence as an institution that could help Black people obtain employment, housing, recreation, and other social services.

This Urban League headquarters has a Michigan historical marker and is listed in the *State Register of Historic Sites.*

DATE ESTABLISHED:	1916
ADDRESS:	208 Mack Avenue, Detroit
TELEPHONE:	(313) 832-4600
VISITING HOURS:	By appointment
FEES:	None
SOURCES:	Telephone call to site, Jan. 2, 1992, and Feb. 24, 1995. Personal visit, summer 1988. *Pathways to Michigan's Black Heritage. Black Historic Sites in Detroit.*

East Ferry Historic District

The East Ferry Historic District includes approximately twenty-four buildings, constructed around 1900. The neighborhood at one time was predominantly white, but in the 1940s it began to house many African American businesses.

Toward the end of World War I, wealthy families were beginning to move out to Detroit's suburbs. War industries were attracting thousands of African Americans to the city. By 1917, 30,000 had moved into Detroit, and some had begun to move into this fashionable neighborhood.

Landmarks still remaining include Dunbar Hospital at 580 Frederick Avenue, the former site of the Lewis Business School, Slade Gragg Academy, Fritz Funeral Home, the Omega Psi Phi fraternity house, and the Detroit Association of Women's Clubs.

The East Ferry Historic District, with its turn-of-the-century buildings that house Black businesses, is listed in the *National Register of Historic Places.*

DATE ESTABLISHED:	c1900
ADDRESS:	E. Ferry Avenue between Woodward Avenue and Brush Street
TELEPHONE:	See individual site information
VISITING HOURS:	See individual site information

Detroit Association of Women's Clubs
Detroit Association of Colored Women's Clubs

The Michigan State Association of Colored Women was founded in 1898; its mission was to promote education and philanthropy. The association adopted its current name in 1920. In 1941 Ms. Rosa Gragg mortgaged her home, furnishings, car, and her husband's business to secure the $2,000 down payment for the elegant house on Brush Street and East Ferry Avenue.

The Detroit Association of Colored Women's Clubs consisted of eight clubs in the early years, and by 1945 it reached a peak of seventy-five clubs with a membership of 3,000 Black women. The association has had a tradition of community service, providing financial support for needy school children and senior citizens, assisting youth clubs, and awarding scholarship programs. Its motto is "Lifting as We Climb."

Gragg, whose strong commitment to the association led her to purchase this house, was inducted in 1987 into the Michigan Women's Hall of Fame. The state historic marker at the headquarters was dedicated in 1986. The headquarters building is listed in the *State Register of Historical Sites.*

DATE ESTABLISHED:	Association, 1895; house purchased, 1941
ADDRESS:	5461 Brush Street (at E. Ferry Ave.), Detroit
TELEPHONE:	(313) 873-1727
VISITING HOURS:	By appointment
SOURCES:	Personal visit, summer 1990. Telephone conversation May 26, 1994, Ms. Senora Smith, historian and active member since 1945 in the Detroit Association of Colored Women's Clubs. *Pathways to Michigan's Black Heritage. Black Historic Sites in Detroit.*

Dunbar Hospital

Dunbar Hospital, a landmark of the East Ferry Historic District, was Detroit's first nonprofit hospital for the Black community. The building later served as home to two of Michigan's first Black men elected to state and national political offices. The townhouse-style building originally was built in 1892 as a residence for a prosperous jeweler and real estate developer.

In an era of racial segregation, the Black community did not have adequate access to Detroit's hospitals. Black physicians who attended sick people in their homes eventually became overburdened by the need for health care. To address this crisis, Black physicians formed the Allied Medical Society (forerunner of the Detroit Medical Society) and raised money to establish a hospital. By 1918 the society acquired the house on Frederick Avenue and a year later opened Dunbar Hospital.

Dunbar Hospital moved to Brush and Illinois Streets in 1928 and was renamed Parkside Hospital, which operated until 1960 when the building was razed as part of an urban renewal project. While it was in existence, Parkside housed Detroit's first Black nursing school and provided advanced training for Black doctors and interns.

Charles C. Diggs Sr. and his family acquired the original buildings of Dunbar Hospital in 1928. They lived in number 580 and operated an undertaking business in 584. In 1937 he was elected as Michigan's first Black Democratic state senator. His son, Charles Jr., who lived in this house from the age of six years, succeeded his father in the Michigan Senate from 1951 to 1954. He served as Michigan's first Black member of the U.S. House of Representatives from 1954 to 1980. The Diggs family later moved from these properties. The house at 584 Frederick Avenue no longer stands.

The Dunbar Memorial Hospital Building is a red-brick townhouse-style structure on a narrow lot. The interior features an open staircase and originally had spacious bedrooms on the second and third floors. When other neighborhood buildings were cleared for urban renewal, the Dunbar Hospital Building was spared. The Detroit Medical Society purchased the site in 1978 to house its activities and to establish a museum featuring the history of medicine in Detroit's Black community. Dunbar Memorial Hospital Historical Museum exhibits include old medical equipment, photographs, and historical papers.

DATE ESTABLISHED:	1918
ADDRESS:	580 Frederick Avenue, Detroit
TELEPHONE:	Detroit Medical Society/Dunbar Memorial Hospital Historical Museum, (313) 832-7800
VISITING HOURS:	Mon.–Fri. 10–5; closed most holidays 👫
FEES:	None
SOURCES:	Personal visit, summer 1990. Telephone conversation Dec. 26, 1991, Ms. Dorothy Aldridge of the Dunbar Hospital Building. NRHPINF. *Pathways to Michigan's Black Heritage. Black Historic Sites in Detroit.*

Fritz Funeral Home

The Fritz Funeral Home, another landmark of the East Ferry Historic District, is one of the oldest Black-owned firms of this type in Detroit. M. Kelly Fritz came to Detroit in 1919 from Toledo, Ohio. His first business site was on Livingston and St. Antoine Streets, the central part of the Black community. The firm moved to Garfield Avenue and Brush Street, where it became the first Black firm in that area (the building was demolished in 1991).

The Fritz Funeral home moved to 246 East Ferry Avenue in 1946. The area was practically all white, and the house that Fritz chose had been built in 1914 for a prominent Jewish family. This family sold the house to a Jewish wholesale meat dealer. The next owner was Prophet Jones, a well-known religious leader in Detroit. Prophet Jones operated 246 East Ferry Avenue as a rooming house for twelve couples.

Fritz Funeral Home is a large, elegant structure, consisting of three floors and a basement. The third floor, once a dance hall and entertainment room, has a high ceiling and a hardwood floor. The original designs painted on the walls are still there, even though the third floor is now used for storage. The second floor had bedrooms for the family as well as quarters for the maid. The first floor had a large living room, a dining room, and a sun room.

In 1991 Fritz, eighty-seven years of age, personally remembered many years of Detroit history. He had seen the changes that took place when Detroit was desegregated. His son attended Northwestern High School but was not allowed to use the YMCA facilities across the street from the school because it was for white men only.

Fritz vividly remembered the trial of Dr. Ossian Sweet. When Sweet defended his home against a white mob, three white men were killed in the melée. During the trial Fritz worked as headwaiter in Detroit's Wolverine Hotel. One day Dr. Sweet, Mrs. Sweet, and famed attorney Clarence Darrow entered the Wolverine and sat down at a table for lunch. Fritz was amazed to see African Americans seated at a table in the hotel. Until then they had been allowed to stay in the hotel but were not allowed to eat in the dining room; they had to take their meals in their rooms. On that day Fritz saw the dining room integrated for the first time.

Fritz also remembered the numerous Black businesses that thrived in Detroit in the 1930s, including a wholesale coffee business, an automobile dealership, barber shops, drugstores, hotels and cabarets, dry-cleaning shops, and grocery stores. An omen of the decline of these businesses occurred about 1940 at a meeting of the local Black Business League. Detroit's mayor (possibly Mayor Frank Cousins) asked to speak to the group. In his speech the mayor stated that segregation in Detroit would soon end. A prominent Black business owner of a chain of drugstores responded by saying that integration would be a one-way street in which Black people would patronize white businesses without receiving reverse business from the white community.

According to Fritz, this prediction was correct. African American businesses began to dwindle or even disappear until there were few to patronize. Where two Black-owned barbershops once had ten chairs each, now the average barber-shop for Black people had only one chair.

Fritz Funeral Home is located a block and a half east of Woodward Avenue in an area designated as the East Ferry Historic District, which is called "Preservation Wayne" because of the restoration being done in some of the buildings by Wayne State University. The home at East Ferry Avenue is significant in Black history for its association with M. Kelly Fritz, a prominent Black businessowner for more than four decades.

DATE ESTABLISHED: 1914; purchased by Fritz family, 1946
ADDRESS: 246 E. Ferry Avenue, Detroit
TELEPHONE: (313) 871-6090
VISITING HOURS: By appointment
FEES: None
SOURCE: Telephone conversation Nov. 1991, Mr. M. Kelly Fritz.

Lewis Business School Building

The former Lewis Business School Building is another landmark of the East Ferry Historic District. This structure on John R. Street near East Ferry Avenue is the second of three sites for this Detroit business. Dr.

Violet T. Lewis came to Detroit from Indianapolis in 1939 in response to an invitation from the Detroit Chamber of Commerce. She soon had organized the Lewis Business College.

The college outgrew an earlier site at the corner of McGraw and Warren Avenue, and moved to 5040 John R. It adapted two old mansions for classroom and office use and used a third house as a student dormitory. Lewis and her family lived on the second floor of one of the mansions.

In the 1970s the Lewis College of Business expanded and began to offer associate degrees rather than certificates. The college moved in 1970 to 17370 Meyers in northwest Detroit.

ADDRESS:	Historic site, 5040 John R. Street; college, 17370 Meyers, Detroit
TELEPHONE:	(313) 862-6300
VISITING HOURS:	Visitors may walk or drive by
SOURCES:	Personal visit, summer 1990. *Black Historic Sites in Detroit.*

Omega Psi Phi Fraternity House

The Omega Psi Phi fraternity house, also in the East Ferry Historic District, was founded in 1911 at Howard University, the first national Greek-letter fraternity established at a Black university. In 1923 three men—Dr. DeWitt T. Burton, Francis Dent, and O. T. Davis—founded Detroit's Nu Omega graduate chapter. Nu Sigma, the undergraduate chapter, was established at Wayne State University in 1938. The Nu Omega Detroit chapter purchased this spacious house on East Ferry Avenue in 1942. The large structure served as a home for Nu Omega.

The rooms in this Victorian house were given new functions for fraternity use. The first floor has a foyer with a piano for entertainment as well as an office, a living room, and a dining room converted to a meeting room. On the second floor, two front rooms have showcases that house archives for the local chapter and the Tenth District. The second floor has a game room. Two back rooms once were used for a caretaker's quarters. The third floor has recreation rooms, including a large room with stage that is rented for parties and weddings. A basement lounge runs the full length of the house.

The Omega House is open on a regular basis on Friday afternoons and on special occasions. Fraternity members, who meet on the second and fourth Saturdays of the month, sponsor projects that match their motto: "Manhood, scholarship, perseverance and uplift." These projects include tutoring students and giving college scholarships to achieving students.

This Omega Psi Phi fraternity house has a Michigan historical marker, and is listed in the *State Register of Historic Sites* and the *National Register of Historic Places.*

DATE ESTABLISHED:	1942
ADDRESS:	235 E. Ferry Avenue, Detroit
TELEPHONE:	(313) 872-1646
VISITING HOURS:	Lounge, Fri. 6 P.M.–10 P.M.; closed Sun.–Thurs., holidays
FEES:	None
SOURCES:	Personal visit, summer 1990. Telephone conversation Nov. 29, 1991, Mr. James Wood, Omega Psi Phi Fraternity. *Pathways to Michigan's Black Heritage. Black Historic Sites in Detroit.*

Orsel McGhee House

The home of Orsel McGhee was the site of a conflict over the rights of African Americans to live where they chose. The conflict led to a United States Supreme Court decision over the issue of restrictive covenants.

In 1944 Orsel and Minnie McGhee and their two children moved into this house on Seebaldt Avenue. Their next door neighbors, Benjamin and Anna Sipes, protested, filing a legal suit against the McGhees. They claimed that a restrictive covenant prohibited Black occupancy of the house next to theirs. The McGhees received court orders to leave their home but refused to do so. Aided by the National Association for the Advancement of Colored People, with Thurgood Marshall as attorney, the McGhees appealed the case to the United States Supreme Court. The case was argued as a class action suit. In 1948 the United States Supreme Court ruled in *Sipes* v. *McGhee* that restrictive covenants could not be enforced because such covenants violated protections ensured by the Fourteenth Amendment to the Constitution. The McGhees and the NAACP triumphed, and the family remained in the home on Seebaldt Avenue. Thurgood Marshall later was named a United States Supreme Court Justice.

The Orsel McGhee House has a Michigan historical marker and is listed in the *State Register of Historic Sites.*

DATE ESTABLISHED:	African American family residence, 1944
ADDRESS:	4626 Seebaldt Avenue, Detroit
VISITING HOURS:	Private; visitors may drive by
SOURCES:	Personal visit, summer 1990. *Pathways to Michigan's Black Heritage. Black Historic Sites in Detroit.*

Motown Museum

The famed Motown sound began in 1957 when songwriter Berry Gordy Jr. quit his job at the Ford Motor Company to devote his time to music. He borrowed $800 from his family's savings club and turned the loan into the thriving business that produced the 1960s Motown sound.

In 1969 Gordy purchased the house at 2648 West Grand Boulevard for $10,500 and established offices and recording studios there. Well-known stars and future stars—the Supremes, Michael Jackson, the Four Tops, Smokey Robinson and the Miracles, the Temptations, Lionel Richie, the Commodores, Stevie Wonder, the Spinners, and Gladys Knight and the Pips—recorded at Detroit's Motown Studio

between 1959 and 1972. Their talent and Gordy's business acumen propelled Motown into a multimillion-dollar enterprise.

Although the studio moved to Hollywood, California, in 1972, visitors kept asking to see the original Motown recording studio and control room; as a result, the Motown Museum, Hitsville USA, was incorporated in 1985. Since the museum opened, thousands of tourists from all over the world have come to see studio A and its equipment used to record famous hits, the wall of photographs, and the Michael Jackson room.

The complex has four houses, two for the museum, one for offices, and one for conference rooms. Berry Gordy moved into the first house (now called Hitsville) in 1959. He lived upstairs and located the original recording studio downstairs. With the recording studio left open twenty-four hours a day, musicians came in freely to record at any hour when they felt most creative. As the business grew, Motown bought the house next door.

Today, a souvenir shop is located upstairs in the original house where Gordy and his family lived. Motown/Hitsville USA has a Michigan historical marker in the yard and is listed in the *State Register of Historic Sites.*

DATE ESTABLISHED:	1985
ADDRESS:	2648 W. Grand Boulevard (Lodge Freeway to W. Grand Boulevard exit), Detroit
TELEPHONE:	(313) 875-2264 or (313) 875-2266
VISITING HOURS:	Mon. noon–5, Tues.–Sat. 10–5, Sun. 2–5
FEES:	Adults, $3; children 12 and under, $2
SOURCES:	Personal visit, summer 1990. Telephone call Dec. 1, 1991, Ms. Barbara Leftwich Reed, Hitsville USA. Telephone call to site, Apr. 24, 1994. *Black Historic Sites in Detroit. Pathways to Michigan's Black Heritage.*

Museum of African American History

The Museum of African American History was founded in 1965 by obstetrician Dr. Charles Wright and thirty-three residents of the Detroit area. The museum originally was housed in three row houses on West Grand Boulevard close to a public library and the

Carter Metropolitan Christian Methodist Episcopal Church. More space was needed, and recognizing the museum's value, the city of Detroit provided $3.5 million for construction of a new building, which was dedicated in 1987. This section of the street in the new location was renamed Frederick Douglass Street.

The museum's contemporary, trapezoidal-shaped building has red conical shapes near the entrance that symbolize African culture. The two-story, 28,000-square-foot museum includes exhibit space, a library, a laboratory, and administrative space.

In 1983 the museum initiated the African World Festival, one of Detroit's largest summer festivals, which features speakers, musicians, and special exhibits. It offers outstanding changing exhibitions such as the featured exhibit *I Dream a World*, portraits of Black women who have changed America.

DATE ESTABLISHED: 1965; new site, 1987

ADDRESS: 301 Frederick Douglass Avenue (northbound I-75 to Warren exit), Detroit

TELEPHONE: (313) 494-5800

VISITING HOURS: Wed.–Sat. 9–5, Sun. 1–5; closed Mon., Tues., and federal holidays with the exception of Dr. Martin Luther King Jr. Day 🏛🏛

FEES: Donations welcome

SOURCES: Lenda Jackson, Museum of African American History. Personal visit, Aug. 9, 1990. Telephone call to site, Apr. 24, 1994, and Feb. 23, 1995. *Black Historic Sites in Detroit. Pathways to Michigan's Black Heritage.*

Paradise Valley/Black Bottom

Three buildings remain today from a once-thriving Detroit community known as Paradise Valley/Black Bottom. With the exception of St. Matthew's Episcopal Church (the historic building), the Lucy Thurman Young Women's Christian Association Building, and the 606 Horseshoe Lounge at Gratiot Avenue and St. Antoine Street, nothing remains but memories of a community demolished for highway construction and urban renewal.

Before the Civil War, Italian, Greek, Jewish, and Polish Detroiters began to move out of a community located between Brush and Elmwood Streets and extending from Gratiot Avenue south to Larned Street, and African Americans gradually moved in. The newcomers formed a tightly knit community that became known informally as Black Bottom. In the first three decades of the twentieth century, African Americans began leaving oppressive conditions in the South; attracted by the five-dollar-a-day wage that Henry Ford was paying to automotive workers, they migrated in waves to Detroit. By the 1930s and 1940s, local residents were referring to the commercial center of Detroit's Black community as Paradise Valley. African Americans had become the predominant ethnic group, and the streets were alive with families patronizing Black businesses, churches, and social organizations. They enjoyed restaurants, hotels, bowling alleys, grocery stores, music shops, and clubs that provided music and entertainment by nationally known artists.

ST. MATTHEWS EPISCOPAL CHURCH, a religious landmark in the community, was founded in 1846; it became one of Detroit's most-prominent Black churches. Although the congregation grew in the decade and a half that preceded the Civil War, church members became tense about the prospect of being captured under the 1850 Fugitive Slave Law, and many fled to Canada. They knew the federal law made it easier for slave owners to recapture their former slaves who had fled North, and they foundered in their belief that Detroit was a safe haven. So many left that remaining members could not pay their debt on the new church that they had erected on Congress and St. Antoine Streets, and the structure was never consecrated.

The church reorganized in 1881 and began to worship on the southwest corner of East Elizabeth and St. Antoine Streets. The historic brick, one-story church and parish house still stand in that location. In 1972, however, the congregation merged with St. Joseph's and began to worship at 8850 Woodward Avenue. Visitors can still drive by to view the exterior of the old church at East Elizabeth and St. Antoine Streets.

The 606 HORSESHOE LOUNGE, established in 1936, is the last survivor in an area that once included seventeen nightclubs. It was owned for many years by the Michael Pye family and was moved to this site from a nearby location.

As segregation decreased in Detroit, many African Americans moved to other sections of the city. The Chrysler Freeway devoured land in this community, and commercial development led to demolition of most of the old buildings.

The LUCY THURMAN YOUNG WOMEN3S CHRISTIAN ASSOCIATION BUILDING stands as a landmark of a bygone era. The Detroit Urban League helped to establish the branch in 1918 in an old building on St. Aubin and Maple Streets. The branch was named for Lucy Thurman, a nationally prominent temperance lecturer from Jackson, Michigan. In 1932 a new structure was erected on East Elizabeth and St. Antoine Streets. The thriving Lucy Thurman branch sponsored many programs but closed in 1963 after "Y" programs were integrated. The building now houses a social services agency. The Lucy Thurman YWCA received a state historical designation in 1993 as part of the Centennial Program of the Metropolitan YWCA.

DATEs ESTABLISHED: St. Matthews congregation, 1846; church, c1881; YWCA branch, 1918, structure, 1932; 606 Horseshoe Lounge, 1936

ADDRESS: Church historic structure, E. Elizabeth and St. Antoine Streets; Thurman YWCA, 569 E. Elizabeth Street; 606 Horseshoe Lounge, 1907 St. Antoine Street, Detroit

TELEPHONE: St. Matthew–St. Joseph Episcopal Church, (313) 871-4750; Horseshoe Lounge, (313) 962-4124

VISITING HOURS: 606 Horseshoe Lounge, Mon.–Fri. 10 A.M.–2 A.M., Sat. noon–2 A.M.; Lounge closed Sun., most holidays

FEES: Church, none; lounge, none

SOURCES: Telephone conversation Feb. 24, 1995, Mr. Selby Jones, kitchen manager, St. Matthews–St. Joseph Episcopal Church. Telephone conversation Dec. 27, 1991, Miss Stella Jackson, St. Matthews Church. Telephone conversation Dec. 23, 1991, Ms. Ellen Bostic, Detroit YMCA. Telephone conversation Dec. 23, 1991, Mr. John W. Copeland, former executive director, St. Antoine Branch YMCA. Telephone conversation Jan. 2, 1992, Ms. Jacqueline Steingold, YWCA. Personal visit to Horseshoe Lounge, summer 1990. Telephone conversation Nov. 29, 1991, Mr. Ralph Madison, Horseshoe Lounge manager. *Black Historic Sites in Detroit. Pathways to Michigan's Black Heritage.*

Sacred Heart Roman Catholic Church, Convent, and Rectory

The Sacred Heart Roman Catholic Church complex has the only remaining buildings in an area cleared for urban renewal. It represents an important part of Detroit's African American history as the mother church of Black Catholic churches in the city and as the former site of Detroit's only Roman Catholic school for Black students. The church is significant architecturally as the sole Italianate-style church in Detroit.

Sacred Heart was established when the corner of Eliot and Rivard Streets was a rural area on the outskirts of Detroit. A German community developed in this area, and a mission school was established for them in 1874. This grew into the Sacred Heart parish; a church, convent, and school were established within a few years. By 1920 the residents of German origin began to disperse to newer residential areas in the city.

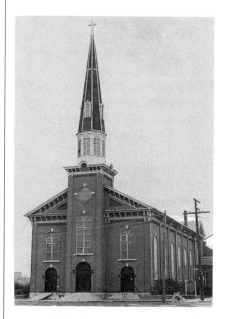

In 1911 Father Joseph Wuest had established a Black mission at St. Mary's School in an area now known as Greektown. The parish took the name of Peter Claver (1581–1654), a Spanish priest who ministered to African slaves in the Caribbean area. The new mission, which worshiped in a converted classroom for three years, moved in 1914 to a vacant church building on Eliot and Beaubien Streets. Black people were migrating to this area, and church membership among them increased. The parish dedicated a new kindergarten and primary school in 1936.

St. Peter Claver was just a block south of Sacred Heart Church. As St. Peter Claver's congregation diminished, the congregations merged. The church building at Eliot and Beaubien Streets became a community center, and in 1938 the St. Peter Claver congregation took possession of the new church.

Sacred Heart began to grow again after the merger and had at one time as many as 1,500 parishioners. The parish also maintained a grade school and Detroit's only Black Roman Catholic high school. Urban renewal eventually destroyed much of the neighborhood, and church members began to move to new areas throughout the city. They established new parishes that originated from Sacred Heart.

The Sacred Heart complex stands today in a cleared area next to the Chrysler Freeway. The church, built in 1875, is a two-story red-brick building with a wooden belfry and an eight-sided slate spire. The rectory is a red-brick building located behind the church on Eliot Street. There is a garden now where a school once stood between the rectory and the church. The school, built in 1889, was demolished in 1973. The convent, located at Eliot Street and Chrysler Service Drive, is a two-story wooden house built in the late 1870s.

Sacred Heart Church, which has stood more than 100 years in this area, is listed in the *National Register of Historic Places.*

DATE BUILT:	Church, 1875; convent, late 1870s; rectory, 1884
ADDRESS:	1000 Eliot Street, Detroit
TELEPHONE:	(313) 831-1356
VISITING HOURS:	Church, Sun. 7–3; Sun. services, 8:30 and 10:30; Sat. evening; call for appointment
FEES:	None
SOURCES:	Personal visit, summer 1990. Telephone conversation, Reverend Norman Thomas, Sacred Heart Church. NRHPINF. *Pathways to Michigan's Black Heritage.*

St. James Colored Methodist Episcopal Church

St. James Colored Methodist Episcopal Church (now the New Mount Gilead Missionary Baptist Church) is housed in one of the few examples of the small frame churches of Detroit. Most of these churches were destroyed early in the twentieth century because the congregations had purchased more elaborate structures. This church is located at the corner of Vinewood and East Kirby Streets in a quiet residential neighborhood. The simple, one-room, white, frame building sheathed in clapboard has stairs leading up to the front entrance. It was constructed by members of the St. James Colored Methodist Episcopal Church, a congregation that originated in 1924 with only eight members. They met for a number of years in modest quarters.

In 1929, when the congregation had increased to forty-eight members, larger facilities were clearly needed. Reverend Alexander Turner, the newly appointed pastor, encouraged several men in the congregation to build a church. They agreed to donate their labor one day per week and soon were able to complete the present church.

In the early years a pot-bellied stove in the middle of the room heated the interior. Children sat in different areas of the room for Sunday School lessons, with the youngest placed close to the stove to ensure that they would be warm. People seated farther away were not as fortunate and often felt the cold. The church is heated now by a gas furnace in one corner of the room.

The one-room church had no basement and no facilities for social events. Therefore, when members had a tea or small dinner, they had to bring small card tables to the church and decorate them. Since there were no facilities for cooking or for refrigerating food, members brought food from home or from the parsonage next door. When the church hosted summer conferences, soft drinks were kept cold on the lawn in tin tubs that held blocks of ice.

As the Great Depression ended and the economy improved, members were able to contribute fifty cents per week rather than twenty-five cents; the minister was paid approximately $75 per month.

By 1945 the congregation needed a larger church because their small church seated only 125 persons. The white congregation of a Congregational church four blocks away from St. James planned to move away because the neighborhood was undergoing racial change. Their substantial brick church was offered for $100,000 in cash. This offer was accepted, and St. James's congregation members walked in a joyful procession to their new church, which was renamed the Carter Metropolitan Christian Methodist Episcopal Church.

The historic building on Vinewood Street was taken over by different congregations. Since the 1960s it has housed the New Mount Gilead Missionary Baptist Church.

DATE ESTABLISHED: Congregation, 1924; church, 1929

ADDRESS: Church, 5330 Vinewood Street; parish house, 3875 W. Kirby Street, Detroit

TELEPHONE: (313) 898-2802 or (313) 898-2808

VISITING HOURS: Sun. service, 11; call for appointment 👫

SOURCES: Author's childhood church. Personal visit, summer 1990. Telephone conversation Dec. 27, 1991, Reverend Singleton, pastor, New Mount Gilead Church. Telephone conversation Dec. 27, 1991, Reverend Clyde Walker, New Mount Gilead Church. *Milestones of Carter.*

Second Baptist Church of Detroit

Second Baptist Church is the oldest Black congregation in Michigan and perhaps the second oldest in the Midwest. It was established in 1836 when thirteen former slaves withdrew from the First Baptist Church of Detroit because of discriminatory practices encountered there. Their meetings took place in a hall until they were able to purchase the First German Reformed Zion Church, which was located on the site of the present church.

Even before that date, Second Baptist was active as a station on the underground railroad. It formed antislavery societies and its members helped form the Amherstburg Baptist Association that helped escaping slaves reach Canada. Second Baptist also helped establish the Canadian Anti-Slavery Baptist Association. Second Baptist's first minister, William C. Monroe, led the congregation during its work for the underground railroad. He also established Detroit's first school for Black children, which operated in the church basement from 1839 to 1842. In 1843 and 1846 church members sponsored state conventions that petitioned for the right of Blacks to vote. The congregation was associated with a number of Americans involved in the struggle for equality. Frederick Douglass addressed Detroit's Black populace at the church in March 1859. During the Civil War Black volunteers met at Second Baptist in 1863 to form the First Michigan Colored Infantry Regiment. Fannie Richards, Detroit's first Black schoolteacher, was a church member. Much later, Dr. Ralph Bunche, winner of the Nobel Peace Prize and Undersecretary General of the United Nations, was baptized at Second Baptist in 1927. Here was held the first celebration in Detroit of the Emancipation Proclamation. A plaque in the church reads as follows:

President Abraham Lincoln finally issued the Emancipation Proclamation on January 1, 1863. The first celebration in honor of that event in Detroit was held in the Second Baptist Church on January 6, 1863.

Second Baptist Church has occupied its present site since 1857. The original one-story church was converted to two stories in 1880, and an auditorium was added. After fire almost destroyed the church in 1914, remodeling created a new structure around the original one. The congregation constructed an activities building west of the church in 1926 and an office and educational building to the east in 1968.

Second Baptist Church has a Michigan State historical marker and is listed in the *State Register of Historic Sites* and the *National Register of Historic Places*. A tour of the church includes the underground area where slaves slept before they continued on their way on the underground railroad.

DATE ESTABLISHED:	1836
ADDRESS:	441 Monroe, corner of Beaubien, Detroit
TELEPHONE:	(313) 961-0920
VISITING HOURS:	Mon. Fri. 10 4:30; Sun. services; tours by appointment 👫
FEES:	None
SOURCES:	Personal visit, summer 1990. Telephone call to church Dec. 1, 1991. *Doorway to Freedom: Detroit and the Underground Railroad. Pathways to Michigan's Black Heritage. Black Historic Sites in Detroit.*

Shiloh Baptist Church

Shiloh Baptist Church, the second-oldest Baptist congregation in Detroit, was organized in 1881, growing out of the Second Baptist Church. Detroit's Black community was increasing at that period. As families moved north of Gratiot Avenue, some found it difficult to travel the distance to Second Baptist Church. Twenty-five members of Second Baptist left in 1881 to form Shiloh Baptist.

Shiloh Baptist Church held some services in homes during the early years, and early services also were held in a small hall on Gratiot Avenue, a building that no longer is standing.

Reverend Moses Hill became pastor in 1911. Under his leadership, the congregation purchased two houses on the site of the present church. They joined the houses together to accommodate the congregation and built a basement under the houses. Church member Ms. Daveen McKinney remembers hearing, as a little girl, stories about the early building. On rainy Sundays, rain came into the structure, and members had to use umbrellas inside the building.

Although there were many churches in the neighborhood, Shiloh Baptist was the first Black church to build its own edifice from the ground up, using Black contractors. Other churches had purchased existing buildings and moved into them. Shiloh Baptist broke ground for the church in 1920 and had its cornerstone observance that same year. Because of funding problems, the church was not completed until 1926.

The 1930s were the years of the Great Depression when Black people in Detroit were making pleas for decent housing. Historic Brewster/Douglas Housing Project, a federal housing project, developed around the church, which was slated for demolition when the projects were completed. However, the Reverend Solomon David Ross, pastor of Shiloh Baptist, led efforts to save the church. An independent thinker, he did not go along with the tradition in which a white minister's group served as a go-between with banks when Black churches needed loans. Reverend Ross realized that Shiloh was not being offered a fair price for the church and realized that Black churches were paying exorbitant interest rates on loans. As a graduate of Morehouse College, he was determined that Black churches should deal directly with banks rather than with white go-betweens. Under his leadership Shiloh remained in the area and was not demolished. Of approximately forty churches in the area, Shiloh was the only one to stand.

Church historian Daveen McKinney notes that in 1949 famed concert artist Paul Robeson (see listing for New York City) gave a concert at Shiloh Baptist. Robeson had been blackballed because he was outspoken against racism and because he refused to cooperate when the House Un-American Activities Committee called on him to testify. When officials would not permit him to perform in Detroit,

Reverend Hill of Hartford Baptist, Reverend Ross of Shiloh Baptist, Coleman Young (later mayor of Detroit), David Moore, and others looked for a place where Robeson could perform. Ms. McKinney remembers that Robeson came to her home for a planning session for the concert, and she remembers that an overflow crowd came to hear the concert at Shiloh Baptist Church.

In 1977, under the leadership of the Reverend Dr. William Crews, the church was renovated at a cost of nearly $300,000. In the late 1980s, the Brewster projects became vacant. Shiloh Baptist still stood, an oasis in a nearly deserted community. In 1992 new housing was planned for the site where the historic Brewster projects recently had been demolished. Shiloh Baptist Church remains an important part of the history of this community. The Bentley Library at the University of Michigan in Ann Arbor has a complete copy of the church historical records and pictures. The church also has its own museum of mementos, photographs, church programs, and such memorabilia as the birth certificate of the first pastor, a document that described his color as "yellow."

DATE ESTABLISHED:	Congregation, 1881; present church, 1926
ADDRESS:	557 Benton Avenue, Detroit
TELEPHONE:	(313) 831-6466
VISITING HOURS:	Mon., Wed.–Fri. 11–3 by appointment 👫
SOURCES:	Telephone conversation Dec. 1991, Ms. Daveen Ross McKinney, church historian, Shiloh Baptist Church. Patricia Coleman-Burns, Burns Funeral Home. Telephone conversation Dec. 1991, Mr. John Burns II. Personal visit, summer 1990. *Pathways to Michigan's Black Heritage.*

Ossian Sweet Home

The Dr. Ossian Sweet House symbolizes the determination of a Black family to live in the house of their choice. Their move first provoked violence but later served as a step in breaking down barriers of residential segregation in Detroit. The Sweets selected a one and one-half–story house in a residential district on Detroit's east side. Dr. Ossian Sweet (1895–1960) purchased the house on the corner of Garland Avenue

and Charlevoix Avenue for $18,500 and moved into the house in the summer of 1925.

Sweet, a physician and gynecologist, was educated at Wilberforce University and Howard Medical School. In spite of his profession, he was not welcome in this all-white neighborhood. On hearing that their new neighbors would be Black, white residents held a mass meeting at the nearby Howe School on July 14, 1925. Intent on keeping the neighborhood white, they formed the Waterworks Park Improvement Association. Their methods were violent—the organization threatened to blow up the house on Garland Avenue if the Sweets moved in.

Sweet and his wife, Gladys—with the help of nine associates—moved into the house on September 8, 1925. They were armed and under police escort because of the threats. The next evening a crowd gathered, throwing rocks and bottles at the house, breaking windows, and finally rushing toward the house. As the crowd moved forward, gunfire came from an upstairs window. It killed a man sitting on his porch across the street and seriously injured a bystander. The next evening police arrested Dr. Sweet and ten of his companions, booking them all for first-degree murder. Eventually, only Sweet and his brother, Henry, were tried.

The National Association for the Advancement of Colored People hired famed attorney Clarence Darrow to represent Sweet. Judge Frank Murphy (later the mayor of Detroit, governor of Michigan, and member of the U.S. Supreme Court) presided over the three-week trial, which resulted in a hung jury. A second trial involving Sweet's younger brother, Henry, ended with acquittal after less than four hours of deliberation. The decision was based on the right of the Sweet family to defend their home against an attack. Sweet and his brother were released; there were no further efforts to prosecute others who were in the house at the time of the violence.

Sweet returned to his home on Garland Avenue in 1928 and lived there without further incident until 1944. He was politically active for a period but became reclusive in later life. In 1960, alone, despondent, and suffering from painful arthritis, he committed suicide.

The Ossian Sweet House is significant in the history of race relations in Detroit. His trial affirmed that citizens had a right to defend life and property and affirmed that these rights extended to African Americans. The milestone case did not usher in a period of harmony and integration in housing but moved a step in that direction because of Sweet's courageous stand.

The Dr. Ossian Sweet House is listed in the *National Register of Historic Places.*

DATE BUILT: House, 1919; Sweet residence, 1925–1944
ADDRESS: 2905 Garland Avenue, Detroit
VISITING HOURS: Private, visitors may drive or walk by 👫
SOURCES: Personal visit, summer 1990. *Pathways to Michigan's Black Heritage. Black Historic Sites in Detroit.*

Grosse Ile

St. James Episcopal Church

Elizabeth Denison Forth represents the African Americans who not only sought their own freedom but who were generous in giving something of lasting benefit to the community. A former slave, she bequeathed her life savings for building the original chapel at this site. The funds were supplemented by the family she had worked for, and the chapel was erected.

Elizabeth (Lisette) Denison was born about 1787 in the post of Detroit, an area then part of upper Canada. The Denisons were slaves owned by William and Catherine Tucker. After William Tucker died, Elizabeth's parents were freed, but the children

remained slaves. A lawsuit later filed against Mrs. Tucker requested the freedom of the Denison children. Judge Woodward ruled that the youngest child was to be free, but the older children were to remain slaves. Then Lisette and her brother heard about another ruling that stated that slaves who went to Canada for their freedom and later returned were to be considered free. Lisette and her brother went to Canada, and when they returned to Michigan, they returned free. The year was about 1815.

In 1827 Lisette married Scipio Forth, a man who operated a freight business. Their marriage was recorded in September 1827 in records of St. Paul's Church in Detroit.

Lisette showed business ability. She purchased land in Detroit and Pontiac, and with advice from some white Detroit businessmen, purchased stock in the steamboat *Michigan.* In 1831 Forth joined the Biddle household, where she worked as a servant for thirty years. She and Mrs. Eliza Falconer Biddle became good friends, and the two eventually made a vow jointly to build a chapel.

When Lisette Forth died August 1866, she had kept the vow, leaving a portion of her estate to her family and a portion to be used to build a church. This money, along with money from the Biddle family, provided funding for building St. James Episcopal Church on Grosse Ile. The frame, one-story church was built in Gothic-revival style with board-and-batten siding; corner and side buttresses; pointed, arched stained-glass windows; and a large Tiffany-glass tracery window. The original structure serves today as a chapel for a larger church built in 1958. The chapel doors are dedicated to Elizabeth Denison Forth. The congregation members revere the original chapel.

DATE BUILT: 1867
ADDRESS: 25150 E. River Road, Grosse Ile
TELEPHONE: (313) 676-1727
VISITING HOURS: Sun. services, 8, 10; by appointment 👫
FEES: None
SOURCES: Telephone conversation Dec. 29, 1991, Reverend Scott Krejci, St. James Episcopal Church. *National Register of Historic Places,* 369. *The Ark of God. Pathways to Michigan's Black Heritage.*

Idlewild

Idlewild Historic District

The Idlewild Historic District consists of more than 1,000 acres of rolling hills, woods, and lakes. It is a resort community consisting of some 500 structures, cottages, and commercial buildings. Idlewild, which developed in Lake County, Michigan, as a self-contained community, became one of America's most popular resorts for African Americans. Middle-class professionals and business leaders came to enjoy Idlewild's attractive recreational setting away from the noise and confusion of the city.

The resort began in 1915 when two white entrepreneurs organized the Idlewild Resort Company and began marketing lots. The company erected a large clubhouse on an island in Idlewild Lake and made plans to develop a golf course and ball park. Eventually Black owners and entrepreneurs took over the business, and Black real estate agents began to sponsor tours for prospective buyers from different cities. Owners who put up small summer cottages took care to preserve the natural landscape with its many trees and shrubs.

Many influential members of the Black community built cottages at Idlewild, including Dr. Daniel Hale Williams, a well-known surgeon from Chicago and a pioneer in cardiac surgery, as well as noted scholar and historian W. E. B. Du Bois. By the 1920s Idlewild was well known to middle-class Black people in many states. As the resort continued to grow, Black businessman Herman Wilson developed Paradise Garden, a subdivision near the original settlement. One of its features was the Paradise Club, a center where Black artists could perform. The club is no longer standing.

After World War II an entrepreneur purchased Williams Island and developed it into a night entertainment place. Such well-known entertainers as Sarah Vaughn, Sammy Davis Jr., and Aretha Franklin performed here.

The boom years for the resort extended from 1920 through 1960. Affluent Black people from throughout North America came to buy land or vacation at the resort. After the 1950s, however, integration opened up other vacation and recreation areas, and a slow decline began. Some residents were disturbed by trends in commercial development in a resort that originally had a rural, recreational character. By 1970 Idlewild was nearing extinction as a community. The clubhouse was gone, and many of the cottages stood vacant.

Idlewild residents have organized recently to revitalize the community. The district still contains many of its original buildings as well as the original street plan and setting. Those who drive through may see such attractions as the Solomon House dating from 1920, the Dr. Daniel Hale Williams House (1921), and the central business district, which contains a concrete-block grocery store (around 1935) and its bar-restaurant (around 1928). Idlewild is listed in the *National Register of Historic Places*.

DATE ESTABLISHED: 1915

ADDRESS: South of US 10 (east of Baldwin, Michigan, at the junction of MI 37 and US 10); Township office, in the fire station on Lake Drive, Idlewild

TELEPHONE: Township office, (616) 745-3940

VISITING HOURS: Private; the best days of the week to visit are Mon. and Fri.; call the Township Office for directions and an appointment

SOURCES: NRHPINF. Telephone conversation Feb. 27, 1995, Mrs. Janet Gordon, deputy treasurer, Yates Township. *Pathways to Michigan's Black Heritage*.

Marshall

Crosswhite Marker

A marker at this site commemorates an incident in which neighbors helped Adam Crosswhite and his family escape to Canada. Crosswhite, who had escaped from slavery in Kentucky in 1844, brought his family to Marshall, Michigan, where they lived in relative safety. They knew, however, that there was always danger that slave catchers might try to pick them up and return them to their former owners. Therefore, they made arrangements to signal neighbors if they might need help. In 1847, three years after the Crosswhites arrived in Marshall, a group of slave catchers found them and attempted to return them to the South. When the Crosswhites gave their danger signal, their neighbors helped the family escape to safety in Canada. The slave owner then sought restitution and took to court the neighbors, who had to pay a fine of $1,925 (a very substantial amount in that era). A historical marker consisting of a boulder with a plaque marks the site where citizens defended the Crosswhite family.

DATE OF SIGNIFICANCE: 1847

ADDRESS: Near Triangle Park, Michigan Avenue and Madison Street, Marshall

VISITING HOURS: Daily, 24 hours

SOURCE: *Pathways to Michigan's Black Heritage.*

Muskegon

Jonathan Walker Memorial

The Jonathan Walker memorial, a huge obelisk with text, honors a white man who was branded on his right hand with the letters SS for "slave stealer." In 1844 Captain Jonathan Walker was captured with seven fugitive slaves off the coast of Pensacola, Florida. A federal court ordered him branded and sentenced him to one year in prison. He was the only man ever ordered branded by a federal court. John Greenleaf Whittier, the Quaker abolitionist poet from Massachusetts, commemorated this incident in his poem, "The Man with the Branded Hand."

After his release from prison, Walker moved to Muskegon, Michigan, where he died in 1862. Since 1955 the Greater Urban League in Muskegon, Michigan, has given the Jonathan Walker Award to any citizen who has worked to improve race relations.

DATE OF SIGNIFICANCE: Prior to the Civil War

ADDRESS: 391 Irwin Avenue, Muskegon

TELEPHONE: Muskegon Cemetery and Forestry Department, (616) 724-6783

VISITING HOURS: Daily, dawn–dusk

SOURCES: Telephone conversation Feb. 27, 1995, Gloria Coburn, department secretary, Muskegon Cemetery and Forestry Department. *Pathways to Michigan's Black Heritage. Webster's New Biographical Dictionary,* 1055.

Niles

Ferry Street School

Ferry Street School is a restored nineteenth-century schoolhouse for Black students. The one-room, brick building opened in 1868 as a school for "colored" children; forty-nine students enrolled. The original building opened at a cost of $2,726.28. There were only two grades, which met in the single classroom.

When the city schools were integrated in 1870, the Ferry Street School was closed. A nearby church used the building while church facilities were remodeled. As other city schools became overcrowded, the schoolhouse was reopened in 1875. A west wing was added in 1903. Niles schools became overcrowded again, and the city began renting rooms in houses and stores, converting them to classrooms. By 1951 the city had built several new elementary schools, and the old Ferry Street School no longer was needed. The building was used for storage and briefly as a center for exceptional children. In 1975 the building was abandoned.

Concerned citizens, treasuring the historic building, began restoring the one-room section of the school to its presumed 1868 appearance. The citizens held rummage sales and raffles and sought donations for the project. The city council provided some funds for removing exterior paint. With the project completed, the building was turned over to the Niles Community School District. The Michiana Literacy Council, Rescue Read, uses half of the schoolhouse today, while the restored schoolroom is seen in the side entered through the double doors. The Ferry Street School is significant as a restored schoolhouse that originated as a one-room school for Black children.

DATE BUILT: 1868

ADDRESS: 620 Ferry Street, Niles

TELEPHONE: (616) 683-3313

VISITING HOURS: Mon.–Thurs. 10–4; closed Martin Luther King Jr. Day, Memorial Day, July 4, Labor Day, Thanksgiving, Christmas 👫

SOURCES: Personal visit, summer 1990. Telephone conversation May 4, 1994, Phyllis Lutin, executive director, Michiana Literacy Council. *Ferry Street School.*

Remus

Wheatland Church of Christ

When Wheatland Church of Christ was organized in 1876, it was the first Black church in Mecosta County. Originally it was known as the Cross Church in honor of the Reverend Thomas Cross, who built it in 1883 and served as its pastor until his death in 1897. Although the structure has been somewhat altered, it is virtually the same church that Cross built in the nineteenth century—a simple one-story frame structure with white clapboard siding and double-entry doors. The interior has seen little alteration with the exception of carpeting and more efficient windows. The original pews are there, and two of four lights in the sanctuary that hang from long chains have the original globes.

Wheatland Church of Christ is listed in the *Michigan State Register of Historic Sites.*

DATE ESTABLISHED:	Congregation, 1876; church, 1883
ADDRESS:	3025 Eleven Mile Road, Remus
TELEPHONE:	(517) 967-8861
VISITING HOURS:	By appointment
SOURCES:	Telephone conversation Apr. 24, 1994, Rev. Randy Piatt, pastor, Wheatland Church of Christ. *Pathways to Michigan's Black Heritage.*

Works Consulted

The Ark of God. Isabella E. Swan. Grosse Ile, Mich.: St. James Church of Grosse Ile, 1968.

Black Historic Sites in Detroit. Detroit: Black Historic Site Committee, Detroit Historical Department, 1989.

Doorway to Freedom: Detroit and the Underground Railroad. Detroit, Mich.: Detroit Historical Department, n.d.

Ferry Street School. Niles, Mich. [flier]

International Library of Negro Life and History: Historical Negro Biographies. Wilhelmena S. Robinson. New York: Publishers, 1970.

Milestones of Carter. Detroit: Carter Metropolitan Church, 1970. [booklet]

National Register of Historic Places. Washington, D.C.: National Park Service, 1976.

Pathways to Michigan's Black Heritage. Bertha H. Miller, ed. Lansing: Bureau of History, Mich. Dept. of State, 1987.

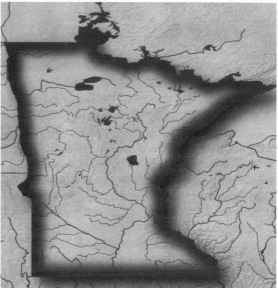

Rochester

Avalon Hotel

The Avalon Hotel, built in 1919, stands at the edge of downtown Rochester on North Broadway Avenue. The three-story, red-brick building, which is located next to one of the city's railroad depots, provided rental rooms in an era when African Americans faced the color barrier in accommodations.

In the early twentieth century, Rochester's Mayo Clinic grew in fame as an international medical center. Out-of-town patients coming for medical services needed short-term accommodations while they received medical treatments. White patients were housed in a variety of guest houses and hotels, but the Avalon Hotel was the only place in Rochester that accommodated Black visitors.

While some visitors came seeking medical help, others came to see the many outstanding entertainers who performed at the Avalon—well- known personalities such as Duke Ellington and his band, the Ink Spots, and boxer Henry Armstrong. Purchased in 1988 and restored, the site is now the Hamilton Music Building.

DATE BUILT: 1919
ADDRESS: 301 N. Broadway, Rochester
TELEPHONE: (507) 288-6311
VISITING HOURS: By appointment
SOURCES: NRHPINF. Telephone conversation June 20, 1994, Myrna Kay Hamilton, owner.

St. Paul Vicinity

Fort Snelling State Historical Park *

The Louisiana Purchase gave the United States jurisdiction over land extending from the Mississippi River to the Rocky Mountains. But this vast territory lay beyond American settlement and was inhabited only by fur traders and Native Americans who were still loyal to the British. After the War of 1812, the U.S. government began to establish its presence there by erecting a chain of forts from Lake Michigan to the Missouri River.

Fort Snelling was established in 1820 near the confluence of the Minnesota and Mississippi Rivers.

The outpost was used for transportation, exploration, commerce, and the protection of U.S. citizens for approximately forty years. Traders stopped at the fort while their goods were inspected; missionaries called on the fort for help as they worked with Native Americans; and government officials visited the fort for lodging and supplies.

Free Black people and slaves arrived with the U.S. Army in the early years of Fort Snelling. Some of them participated in the local fur trade. Other Black Americans, however, arrived as slaves of the military staff. Of the slaves, the one who was to become the best known in history was Dred Scott, who was born about 1795 in Southampton County, Virginia; he arrived at Fort Snelling from St. Louis in 1836 with his owner, Dr. John Emerson, the fort's new army surgeon. Earlier, Emerson had taken Scott to Illinois, a state where slavery was prohibited by the Northwest Ordinance of 1787. When Emerson took Scott to Fort Snelling, he was taking him into Louisiana Territory where slavery was forbidden by the Missouri Compromise. Emerson had ignored the ban against slavery both in Illinois and in the Louisiana Territory where he continued to treat Scott as his slave.

In 1837 Dred Scott married Harriet Robinson, another slave at Fort Snelling, who was sold by Major Lawrence Taliaferro, a federal Indian agent, to Dr. Emerson. The Scotts had a child, Eliza, during this period; Eliza was born north of the Missouri Compromise line and, therefore, was not legally a slave. However, she was treated as a slave by Emerson.

Later, when Emerson brought Scott and his family back to Missouri and sold them to a man named Sanford, Scott sued for freedom for himself, his wife, and his two daughters, one of whom was born after the family returned to Missouri. Scott claimed the right to freedom as a result of having lived in Illinois and in Minnesota Territory, regions where slavery was prohibited. Having lived in free territory, he should be considered free.

Similar claims—that a slave who had lived in a free state should be considered free even if returned by the owner to a slaveholding state—had been brought before courts in several states with varying results. A slave girl named Rachel, who at one time had lived at Fort Snelling, successfully sued for her freedom on a similar basis in a St. Louis court. Stockton, an army officer, had bought Rachel as a slave in Missouri and later took her with him to Fort Snelling, where they lived for a year. He then took her to Prairie du Chien (then in Michigan/Wisconsin Territory, where slavery was forbidden) for four years before taking her back to Missouri and selling her as a slave. Rachel was successful in gaining her freedom on the basis of having been taken to live in free territory.

Dred Scott won his case at a lower court level, but the Supreme Court of Missouri ruled that he remained a slave. The case was taken to the U.S. Supreme Court, where the court ruled against Scott. In the infamous decision Justice Roger Taney wrote the opinion of the court. He maintained that slaves were property and that any act of Congress prohibiting ownership of slaves (property) in a specific territory was not warranted by the Constitution and was, therefore, void. He also made the chilling statement that Black people did not have the rights of citizens, that for more than a century before the Constitution of the United States was adopted, they were regarded as so inferior that they had no rights that white people were bound to respect.

The 1857 U.S. Supreme Court decision was an outrage to abolitionists and increased the bitterness between the North and the South that a few years later led to the Civil War. Soon after the decision Dred Scott was emancipated, and he began working as a hotel porter in St. Louis. He died a year after gaining his freedom.

After the Civil War Fort Snelling served as a center for administering Indian affairs. During the Indian wars, the all-Black Twenty-fifth U.S. Infantry was stationed at Fort Snelling from 1882 to 1888. The fort served as a recruitment center in the twentieth century, until it was closed after World War II.

In 1963 the process of restoring buildings at Fort Snelling began. Today historic Fort Snelling consists of a large fort complex, eighteen fully furnished stone-and-wood buildings within a stone wall, erected over a 150-year period.

The History Center includes a film every thirty minutes, an exhibit area, and a museum. Although elements of Black history are covered through exhibits and through the costumed living-history program, the amount of information included about Black history may vary according to the interpreter. Restoration includes a uniformed mannequin representing a soldier from the Twenty-fifth Infantry Regiment, panels representing the service of Black soldiers, and the servant/slave quarters. Plans are made for an outdoor sculpture commemorating the role of Black people in the early years of Fort Snelling. Although Black history is a minor part of the interpretation at the fort, visitors to the site will be able to see where and how Black soldiers lived at this frontier site and will see the environment that was a part of the famed Dred Scott case. (For more information on Dred Scott, see the listing for St. Louis, Missouri.)

DATE ESTABLISHED: 1820–1824

ADDRESS: Fort Snelling exits on MN 5 and MN 55 near the Minneapolis-St. Paul International Airport

TELEPHONE: (612) 726-1171

VISITING HOURS: Fort, daily May 1–Oct. 1, Mon.–Sat. 9:30–5 and Sun. 11:30–5, closed Nov. 1–Apr. 30 but gift shop open weekends 9–4:30 (call ahead) 👫; History Center, Mon.–Sat. 9:30–5 and Sun. 11:30–5; closed weekends and holidays in winter 👫

FEES: Adults 16 and up, $4; children 6–15, $2; children 5 and under, free

SOURCES: Stephen E. Osman, site manager, Historic Fort Snelling. Telephone conversation June 19, 1994, Florence Olson, museum shop. Telephone call to site, Sept. 4, 1995. George Ryan, Minnesota Historical Society. *Webster's New Biographical Dictionary*, 897. *National Register of Historic Places*, 377. *Historic Fort Snelling. Dred Scott v. Sandford.*

Highland Park Tower

Clarence W. Wigington, one of St. Paul's few African American architects, designed the Highland Park water tower and belatedly was honored for his accomplishment. For many years the design was attributed to a white man, Wigington's supervisor. The tower, built in 1928, is significant both as a vital part of the city's water system and for its architectural distinction.

Clarence Wigington, who was born in Lawrence, Kansas, in 1883, attended high school in Omaha and an architectural school for a year before beginning to work for Thomas Kimball, who was at the time president of the American Institute of Architects. While employed by Kimball, Wigington studied for six years at Professor Wallace's Western School of Art. When Wigington took the city architectural examination, he received the highest grade anyone had ever scored on the test. As a young architect Wigington designed a church and two apartment buildings in Omaha as well as the administration building for North Carolina State University at Durham.

After moving to St. Paul in 1915, Wigington received commissions to design creameries at Elk River and Northfield. He also drew up the plans for the St. James African Methodist Episcopal Church at Central Avenue and Dale Street in St. Paul; the church has since been remodeled. Wigington worked on other buildings in St. Paul, including the Keller Golf Course clubhouse, the Municipal Auditorium, ice palaces, several park structures including the Harriet Island Pavilion, and schools including the Monroe School. Wigington was active in community organizations. He was a member of the Urban League, the Elks Lodge, and the Episcopal Church. He and his wife lived at 679 St. Anthony Avenue during most of their years in St. Paul.

The Highland Park Water Tower is an octagonal, brick-and-cut-stone structure consisting of a base, a shaft, and a lookout area. It has a 200,000-gallon steel tank with a circular staircase around it. One hundred fifty-one steps lead to an observation platform topped by a tile roof and small cupola. The lookout provides a panoramic view of the Twin Cities. Water is pumped from a reservoir into the tower, then flows by gravity to approximately 9,000 homes in the area.

Wigington designed the water tower in 1928, but his accomplishments were not recognized until 1976 (he died in 1967). Ironically, his supervisor's name had appeared in numerous sources as the architect of the building and still appeared on a plaque on the building. In a public ceremony in 1976 the community finally honored Wigington for his "excellence in design of the Highland Park Tower."

The tower is open to the public on special occasions. This significant landmark, designed by an African American registered architect, is listed in the *National Register of Historic Places.*

DATE BUILT: 1928
ADDRESS: 1570 Highland Parkway, St. Paul
VISITING HOURS: Daily, 24 hours
SOURCE: NRHPINF.

Holman Field Administration Building

The Holman Field Administration Building is a large rectangular structure located within the St. Paul Downtown Airport. Black architect Clarence Wesley Wigington's limestone building with its four-story octagonal control tower is considered the finest of his works. One of his Works Progress Administration projects, it was completed in cooperation with the city of St. Paul as a program during the Great Depression.

While Wigington designed many buildings for St. Paul between 1915 and 1949 (see also the entry for Highland Park Tower), all designs from his city office were stamped with the name of the city architect. Only recently were many of the structures realized to be Wigington's designs.

Of his surviving buildings, the Holman Field Administration Building is one of the best preserved. It was completed as part of a project to improve St. Paul's municipal airport, which is separate from the main St. Paul airport. The building is noted for its execution of the moderne architectural style, the fine use of salvaged Kasota stone, and the high standard of craftsmanship.

DATE BUILT:	1939
ADDRESS:	644 Bayfield Street, St. Paul
VISITING HOURS:	Daily, 9–dusk
SOURCES:	NRHPRF. Telephone call June 19, 1994, Capitol Air, Holman Field Administration Building.

Pilgrim Baptist Church

In 1863 a group of former slaves came to St. Paul from Missouri with their leader, Robert Hickman. That same year they founded Pilgrim Baptist Church, the second-oldest Black congregation in Minnesota and the oldest in St. Paul.

In the early years St. Paul's African American residents lived in different areas of the city. By the 1920s and 1930s, however, they began to cluster increasingly in the area that is now Concordia Avenue.

Members of Pilgrim Baptist Church worked actively to help newcomers to the area to adjust. They assisted in finding jobs, worked for better educational and recreation facilities in the community, and sought protection in the realm of civil liberties. The church history was closely related to the establishment in St. Paul of local chapters of the National Association for the Advancement of Colored People (1913), the Urban League (1923), and the Hallie Q. Brown Community Center (1929).

The first two church buildings of Pilgrim Baptist Church no longer exist. When the present church was constructed in 1928, the location matched the movement of the Black population from the old city uphill to the Rondo neighborhood. This neighborhood began to attract larger numbers of Africans in the 1920s and 1930s; it became predominantly Black in the 1950s and 1960s.

Pilgrim Baptist Church is a large structure constructed of brick with concrete trim. A series of stained-glass windows in the clerestory portray Dr. Martin Luther King Jr. and past ministers of the church.

DATE BUILT:	1928
ADDRESS:	732 W. Central Avenue, St. Paul
TELEPHONE:	(612) 227-3220
VISITING HOURS:	Private, visitors may drive or walk by
SOURCE:	NRHPRF.

Works Consulted

Dred Scott v. *Sandford.* 60 U.S. (19 How.), 393–633.

Historic Fort Snelling. St. Paul, Minn.: Minnesota Historical Society, 1989. [brochure]

National Register of Historic Places. Washington, D.C.: National Park Service, 1976.

Webster's New Biographical Dictionary. Springfield, Mass.: Merriam-Webster, 1988.

Montana

Havre

Fort Assiniboine

When Fort Assiniboine was built in 1879, it was a Montana-Territory frontier post thirty miles south of the Canadian border. General John J. Pershing (1860–1948), an Army lieutenant at the time, led a troop of black soldiers of the Tenth Cavalry from South Carolina to Fort Assiniboine, where he directed them in raids against Native Americans. They also led raids against outlaws.

Pershing earned the nickname "Black Jack" because he was a leader of African American men. Assignments leading Black troops were not sought after at the time, and some officers refused to accept them.

Pershing, however, had been raised among Black people. Some of his childhood playmates in Laclede, Missouri, were African Americans. Because of his positive stance, Pershing related to the soldiers well. He required excellence of the men in his regiment and treated them with respect and consideration.

Although the Black soldiers at Fort Assiniboine were regarded as tough and capable, there was some racism in the surrounding areas, and relationships between the soldiers and the community were strained at first. Apparently the soldiers were fully willing to protect themselves, and this resulted in a few physical conflicts.

In spite of the racism that they met at times, men of the Tenth formed a courageous, disciplined unit that became a legend in the West. Years later, in 1921, General John J. Pershing wrote these words about the Tenth Cavalry:

> It has been an honor which I am proud to claim to have been at one time a member of that intrepid organization of the Army which has always added glory to the military history of America— the 10th Cavalry.[1]

Most of Fort Assiniboine's 104 buildings were torn down in the late 1920s, leaving only fourteen standing structures. Today the buildings at old Fort Assiniboine are used for agricultural research offices, laboratories, and shops. The Fort Assiniboine Preservation Association sponsors summer tours that take approximately two hours and include all the buildings of the fort. Travel is by vehicle. Gary Wilson of the Preservation Association says that winter tours are not generally offered because Montana's usually frigid winter temperatures seem a little too cool for most visitors.

DATE ESTABLISHED:	1879
ADDRESS:	Star Rt. 36, Havre
TELEPHONE:	Mr. Gary Wilson, tour guide, Fort Assiniboine, (406) 265-8336; Montana Agricultural Experimental Station, (406) 265-6115; Clark Museum, (406) 265-4000
VISITING HOURS:	Summertime tours Sat., Sun. at 5; winter tours by appointment 👫
FEES:	Adults, $2; students, $1; children under 6, free

SOURCES: Telephone conversation June 22, 1994, Gary Wilson, Fort Assiniboine Preservation Association. Don Anderson, superintendent, Fort Assiniboine–Northern Agricultural Research Center. "John J. Pershing at Fort Assiniboine," 19. *The Black West,* 210–12.

Helena

Montana Historical Society

Although Black culture is not a primary emphasis in the Montana Historical Society's collection, the society does have several artifacts relating to Montana's African American history, including a painting of York, the Black man who was on the Lewis and Clark Expedition. The artifacts are displayed when they fit into other temporary exhibits. Visitors may call to request information on Montana's African American history.

ADDRESS: 225 N. Roberts Street, Helena

TELEPHONE: (406) 444-2694

VISITING HOURS: Mon.–Fri. 8–6, Sat.–Sun. 9–5; closed holidays

FEES: None

SOURCE: Kirby Lambert, curator of collections, Montana Historical Society.

Missoula

The Historical Museum at Fort Missoula

Fort Missoula was established in 1877 when local settlers asked for protection in the event of conflicts with nearby Native Americans. This was the period of the Nez Percé uprising, and the fort was to be a major outpost for the entire region.

The Twenty-fifth Infantry Regiment, a unit of Black soldiers led by white officers, arrived at Fort Missoula in 1888. The men became part of an Army experiment to test the use of bicycles by the military when, in 1896, Lieutenant James Moss organized the Twenty-fifth Infantry Bicycle Corps. The plan was to find out if bicycles could successfully replace the mounted patrol-duty horses. Men from the Twenty-fifth Infantry traveled by bicycle from Fort Missoula

up the Bitterroot Valley to Yellowstone Park. In another experiment, in 1897, the bicycle corps traveled 1,900 miles from Missoula to St. Louis. This trip marked the end of these experiments; the Twenty-fifth Infantry returned by train to Missoula. The Army had decided that the bicycle had only a limited potential and would not be used to replace horses.

The Twenty-fifth Infantry was one of the first Army units called to fight in the Spanish-American War of 1898. When the unit was suddenly summoned to duty, the entire population of Missoula postponed their Easter church services to turn out and bid the soldiers farewell. After serving in the Philippines, men from the Twenty-fifth were assigned to other posts.

Fort Missoula, a complex of concrete buildings with red-tile roofs, was remodeled between 1908 and 1914. During the Depression years the fort served as a regional headquarters for the Civilian Conservation Corps. After Pearl Harbor 650 Japanese Americans were interned here. The post was decommissioned in 1947, and many of the buildings were sold or dismantled.

The fort does not appear as it did when the Black soldiers were stationed here, but it remains important in Black history as a place where Black men served in the late nineteenth century. Although African American history is not a primary focus of the museum's interpretation, a portion of the permanent exhibit on the fort's history—half of a wall—tells about the Twenty-fifth U.S. Infantry and the bicycle corps. The museum staff hopes to re-create the bicycle "dash" to St. Louis in 1997, the one hundredth anniversary of Fort Missoula, and to present an exhibit about the Buffalo Soldiers.

DATE ESTABLISHED: Fort Missoula, 1877; historical museum, 1975

ADDRESS: Building 322, Fort Missoula, Missoula

TELEPHONE: (406) 728-3476

VISITING HOURS: Memorial Day–Labor Day, Mon.–Sat. 10–5; rest of year, Tues.–Sun. 12–5; closed New Year's Day, Thanksgiving, Christmas

FEES: Donations accepted

SOURCES: Telephone conversation June 22, 1994, and Mar. 29, 1995, Dr. Robert M. Brown, director, The Historical Museum at Fort Missoula. *Historical Museum at Fort Missoula. The Black West,* 219.

Note

1. William Loren Katz, *The Black West* (Seattle, Wash.: Open Hand Publishing, 1987), 212.

Works Consulted

The Black West: A Documentary and Pictorial History. 3d ed. rev. William Loren Katz. Seattle, Wash.: Open Hand, 1987.

Historical Museum at Fort Missoula. Missoula: the Museum. [brochure]

"John J. Pershing at Fort Assiniboine." Donald Smythe, S.J. *Montana Magazine of Western History* 18, no. 1 (winter 1968), 19.

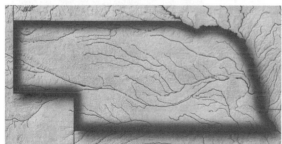

Aurora

Plainsman Museum

Although the Plainsman Museum is not a Black historical site, it has a showcase that depicts the Black history of Nebraska's Hamilton County, including that of the David Patrick family. The museum has murals, mosaics, and exhibits that trace the region's history from prehistoric times to the present, including a sod house, a schoolhouse, a log cabin, an agricultural museum, and the showcase on Black pioneers. Children especially enjoy the doll case with its collection of 800 dolls, the juke box, and the working player pianos.

Black homesteaders were among the pioneers in Hamilton County. In 1873, for example, David Patrick began to farm 120 acres of land northeast of Aurora. Another African American, Frank Harris, established a large orchard in the area in 1880. He managed this fruit farm throughout his lifetime, employing as many as thirty workers at "picking time."

Aurora also was home to General Delevan Bates, a white commander who in 1864 was appointed Colonel of the Thirtieth Infantry Regiment, United States Colored Troops. After the siege at Petersburg, Virginia (1864–1865), Bates's brigade was sent to North Carolina, where it joined General William T. Sherman's Army. A description of the service of Black regiments at Petersburg is included in the listing for Petersburg, Virginia.

DATE ESTABLISHED:	1976
ADDRESS:	210 Sixteenth Street (3 miles north of the I-80 Interchange on NE 14), Aurora
TELEPHONE:	(402) 694-6531
VISITING HOURS:	Apr. 1–Oct. 31, Mon.–Sat. 9–5, Sun. 1–5, Nov. 1–Mar. 31, daily 1–5; closed Thanksgiving, Christmas, New Year's Day, Easter 👫
FEES:	Adults, $4; senior citizens ages 62 and up, $3; children 5–16, $1; children under 5, free; AAA discount
SOURCES:	Telephone conversation Aug. 12, 1995, Mrs. Gwen Allen, director, Plainsman Museum. Telephone conversation June 18, 1994, John H. Green, assistant director.

Bayard

Chimney Rock National Historic Site

Extensive exploration of the area that is now Nebraska began in 1804 when President Thomas Jefferson sent Meriwether Lewis and William Clark to the Missouri River to explore the Louisiana Territory for the United States. A Black servant named York was an important part of this expedition and was with the group when its members explored many sites in Nebraska, including the Chimney Rock National Historic Site. (For more information about York, see the listings for St. Charles, Missouri; Washburn, North Dakota; Spalding, Idaho; Astoria, Oregon; and Ilwaco, Washington.)

The Nebraska State Historical Society operates the Chimney Rock Visitors Center as a branch museum. The new building at the site opened in July 1994 with exhibits associated with the site. Visitors are able to see the landmark geological formation called Chimney Rock, but due to deterioration of the formation, they are not able to get close to it. Children will enjoy seeing the rugged prairie terrain that still has many dirt roads and will enjoy thinking about the wagon trains that passed through this main crossing.

ADDRESS:	South of Bayard on US 26 and NE 92
TELEPHONE:	(308) 586-2581, Fax (308) 586-2589
VISITING HOURS:	Memorial Day–Labor Day, 9–6
FEES:	None
SOURCES:	Telephone conversation June 18, 1994, Linda Wagaman, reference assistant, Nebraska State Historical Society. *Nebraska Guide to Museums and Historic Sites.*

Crawford

Fort Robinson Museum

Fort Robinson, now Fort Robinson State Park, is a former frontier Army post whose history spans seven decades (1874–1948). It contains sixty buildings associated with the period of its active use. Black history is associated with the post because it was the regimental headquarters for the Ninth Cavalry between 1887 and 1898. Between 1902 and 1907 it served as regimental headquarters for the Tenth Cavalry. For seventeen years the post was garrisoned by Black cavalry.

Fort Robinson was established in 1874 in Nebraska's Pine Ridge country near the Red Cloud Agency. It took part in the last days of the wars between the United States and the Plains Indians. Here the Oglala warrior, Crazy Horse, met his death in 1877. Thirteen years later, Black soldiers, called

the Buffalo Soldiers, patrolled the Pine Ridge Reservation in the difficult days after the Battle of Wounded Knee in 1890.

Charles Young, the third Black man to graduate from West Point in 1889, was assigned to the Ninth Cavalry that same year. He spent part of his military career at Fort Robinson. Young later became the first Black colonel in the United States Army. (See the listing under Wilberforce, Ohio.)

The Ninth Cavalry Regiment left Fort Robinson in 1898 to fight in Cuba during the Spanish-American War. The Tenth Cavalry then served at the fort until it was assigned to duties along the Mexican border in 1910.

Original and reconstructed buildings tell the story of the fort's past. Interpretive exhibits in the 1905 Post Headquarters show items from the fort's seventy-year history, including several exhibits on the Ninth and Tenth Cavalry Regiments.

DATE ESTABLISHED:	1874
ADDRESS:	Fort Robinson State Park, US 20, 3 miles west of Crawford
TELEPHONE:	Disconnected
VISITING HOURS:	Apr. 1–Nov. 1, Mon.–Sat. 8–5, Sun. 9–5; Nov. 1–Apr. 1, hours vary, phone ahead 👫
FEES:	Museum: adults, $1; children with adults, free; State Historical Society members and immediate families, free; group rates available
SOURCES:	Thomas R. Buecker, curator, Fort Robinson Museum. Information page from Fort Robinson Museum.

Dorchester

Saline County Museum

Among the structures exhibited at the Saline County Museum is the Burden House, home of the only Black pioneer family in Saline County. The museum and the Burden House contain family pictures and interesting articles used by the Burden family. One picture from 1893 shows the entire family outside the home. Documents include their homestead certificate and discharge papers.

Henry Burden was born about 1844 in Petersburg, West Virginia, of slave parentage. He escaped from the Confederate Army and enlisted as a private in Company B, Seventeenth U.S. Infantry. After being honorably discharged from the Union Army on February 17, 1866, he moved to Nebraska. There he filed a homestead claim on Saline County land two and one half miles south of Pleasant Hill. Mr. and Mrs. Henry Burden and their sons, Henry and George, are buried in the Pleasant Hill Cemetery.

DATE ESTABLISHED:	1964
ADDRESS:	NE 33, south of Main Street, Dorchester
TELEPHONE:	Contact Ms. Norma Knoche, (402) 947-2911, or Ms. Bertha Zak, (402) 946-7441
VISITING HOURS:	Sun. 2–5; or by appointment; closed Easter, Thanksgiving, Christmas 🕴🏽
FEES:	Donations accepted
SOURCE:	Norma E. Renner, board member, Saline County Museum. Telephone conversation Aug. 10, 1995, Norma Knoche, president, Saline County Museum.

Fort Calhoun

Fort Atkinson State Historical Park

York, a Black slave, traveled with the Lewis and Clark expedition when its members explored vast new territories in the western United States. The explorations may have originated with an idea that fascinated President Thomas Jefferson from his childhood. Long before the Louisiana purchase of 1803, Jefferson thought that a water route might connect the Mississippi River with the Pacific Ocean. After the land purchase, Congress appropriated funds for the discovery of this water route (that later was found not to exist). Two former army officers, also close friends, Meriwether Lewis and William Clark, were selected to lead the expedition. With them was York, a Black man who was a servant to Clark but who also was a strong contributor to the success of the expedition. York may have been the first Black American to traverse this rugged, treacherous, and marvelous terrain.

Fort Atkinson State Historic Park marks the site of Lewis and Clark's Council on the Bluff, at which they met with local Indians in 1804. From 1819 to 1827 Fort

Atkinson was a United States Army Post. Today the post is partially restored and has a Visitors Center. There people can see a film about the Lewis and Clark expedition and another film depicting the process of restoring the fort. The center exhibits various artifacts and processes common to an earlier period; for example, staff members bake bread in a recently built mud oven. Walking trails lead to a blacksmith's shop, a settlers' store, the council house, and the fort itself.

ADDRESS:	US 73 to Fort Calhoun, east on Madison Street, Fort Calhoun
TELEPHONE:	(402) 468-5611
VISITING HOURS:	Visitors Center, Memorial Day–Labor Day, daily 9–5; grounds, Memorial Day–Labor Day, daily 9–7 🕴🏽
FEES:	$2.50 per vehicle per day or $14 annually
SOURCES:	Telephone conversation June 18, 1994, Delores Holder, tour guide. "The Lewis and Clark Expedition."

Lincoln

Museum of Nebraska History
Nebraska State Historical Society

The Museum of Nebraska History has a modest amount of information about African Americans on the frontier. The museum's exhibit on the topic consists of one showcase on the second floor that features one or two pictures of the sod houses in which some Black families lived and a picture of a former slave and sharpshooter named Nate Love. Black pioneers came to the region in search of opportunity and freedom, and they settled on the Nebraska frontier as early as 1867. Staff members can talk with visitors about the settlers' experiences—the all-Black homesteading towns as well as the Ninth and Tenth Cavalry stationed at Fort Robinson.

The museum contains three floors of exhibits, including a first-floor museum store, a World War II exhibit, a third-floor general store, an exhibit about Native Americans, and a toy exhibit. The Nebraska State Historical Society's research department, which is appropriate for adults, has the largest collection of newspapers in the state as well as photographs, history books, and census data.

DATE ESTABLISHED:	1957
ADDRESS:	Museum of Nebraska History, 131 Centennial Mall North, Fifteenth and P Streets; Nebraska State Historical Society, 1500 R Street, Lincoln
TELEPHONE:	Museum, (402) 471-4754; Historical Society, (402) 471-4751
VISITING HOURS:	Museum, Mon.–Sat. 9–5, Sun. 1:30–5 ♟; Historical Society Library, Mon.–Fri. 10–5, Sat. 8–5, Sun. 1:30–5; closed Veterans Day, Thanksgiving, Christmas, New Year's Day
FEES:	None
SOURCES:	Lynne Ireland, coordinator of museum programs, Nebraska State Historical Society. Telephone conversation June 18, 1994, Domingo Colón, chief of security. *Nebraska Guide to Museums and Historic Sites.*

Nebraska City Vicinity

John Brown's Cave and Museum

The frontier town of Nebraska City once served as part of the underground railroad. Residents friendly to the abolitionist cause used to provide assistance to slaves who had escaped from the Missouri and Kansas Territories. After sheltering and feeding the fugitives, the abolitionists guided them on to Iowa, a free state. From there many of the slaves were helped to reach Canada.

This site shows how one underground railroad site operated. Located in the vicinity of Nebraska City, it was named for abolitionist John Brown, who may have assisted here. The John Kagi Cabin nearby had an underground passage that led to caves along the river, providing a safe way to move on in times of danger. John Henry Kagi served as John Brown's secretary of war during the period of the raid on Harpers Ferry. He lived in this Mayhew cabin, which was built in 1851 and which is the oldest extant building in Nebraska. The Mayhews lived in the cabin with their six sons and with Kagi, Mrs. Mayhew's brother. Captain Kagi was assigned by John Brown to the command of the rifle factory in the raid on Harpers Ferry, where he supervised the five Black men who were part of the original group that took part in the raid—Shields Green, Dangerfield Newby, Sherrard Lewis Leary, John A. Copeland, and Osborne P. Anderson. Kagi and the men whom he led were overwhelmed at the rifle factory by as many as five hundred Virginians. Only Anderson escaped. John Copeland surrendered after the others (except Anderson) were killed, but later Copeland was executed. (See the listing for Harpers Ferry, Virginia).

The cave is still there for visitors to inspect. Entered in an earlier period through a trap door in the cabin, the cave is explored now by walking down steps. Once inside, to add to the realism, there are two manikins who represent slaves; one is lying down on a bed, the other is standing up and seems to be waiting for an opportunity to leave. Visitors go through the cave and emerge at the other end to explore the rest of the site. There they will find a little village consisting of a school, a depot, a washhouse inside a barn, and an African Methodist church that was originally in Nebraska City. The museum's interior has wooden-front stores including a candy shop, a barber shop, a dentist's office, a harness shop, a shoe shop, and tool and music shops on an old-fashioned street. Visitors can explore all of this on their own.

ADDRESS:	2000 Fourth Coorso (3 miles west of Nebraska City on NE 2), Nebraska City
TELEPHONE:	(402) 873-3115
VISITING HOURS:	Apr. 1–Nov. 30, Mon.–Sat. 10–5, Sun. 12–5
FEES:	Adults, $5; children, $2; seniors, $3; group rates available
SOURCE:	Telephone conversation June 18, 1994, Marge Johnson, receptionist.

Omaha

Black Americana Museum

The Black Americana Museum is a house of African American treasures that will delight children and history fans of all ages. The museum was founded by Oran Belgrave, a cosmetologist/hairdresser who traveled from city to city teaching the art of hairstyling while keeping an eye open wherever he went for gems of Black history. Noting his interest, others have added to his collection. Here the visitor sees life-sized figures of Black heroes, each in individually appropriate settings, including leader-to-freedom Harriet Tubman; inventor Granville T. Woods; Malcolm X, orating from a podium; George Washington Carver, pouring a substance from a laboratory beaker; Louis Armstrong, making his trumpet wail in a New Orleans setting; and Muhammed Ali, preparing to float like a butterfly and sting like a bee. Also present is a figure of Matthew Henson, warmly dressed for his run to the North Pole.

For sports fans the museum contains large, life-sized cardboard sports figures and memorabilia collected from members of a Black baseball league. There are assorted hair products and implements as well as authentic "white only" and "colored only" signs collected from around the country. The doll collection here is one described by volunteer Linda Batch as "the biggest Black doll collection I've ever seen." It includes hundreds of dolls, some from England and dating from the 1800s on up to all kinds of Barbie\T dolls. Included are ceramic dolls, composition dolls, and rag dolls, but a favorite of visitors is the Topsy-Turvy Doll, which has two faces. Turn the dress up one way and the face of the doll is Black; turn the dress up the other way and the face of the doll is white.

The Black Rainbow Gallery next to the museum features the work of local multicultural artists. Complete with a reception area, the gallery provides an opportunity to show local talent.

Although the museum has an admissions charge, those who cannot pay may leave a donation of any amount they choose.

DATE ESTABLISHED: 1991

ADDRESS: 1238–40 S. Thirteenth Street, Omaha

TELEPHONE: (402) 341-6908

VISITING HOURS: Daily 11–4 including holidays 👫

FEES: Adults, $3; children, $1.50; children under 5, free; donations accepted in lieu of standard admissions

SOURCE: Telephone conversation June 18, 1994, Linda Batch, volunteer.

Great Plains Black Museum

When the Civil War ended, a large number of Black families found their way to Nebraska. Most of these African American newcomers chose to live in Omaha. For two or three decades, they were free to live wherever they chose in the city. By the turn of the century, however, this freedom of choice diminished, and Black families increasingly were guided to the Near North Side, an area centered on Twenty-fourth and Lake Streets, or to another area in South Omaha near the stockyards. Many new African Americans arrived between 1910 and 1920 seeking industrial jobs. The growing presence of the Black immigrants was met with increasing hostility until an angry white mob lynched a Black man in a riot in 1919.

The Black history of Omaha and the surrounding region today is told in the Great Plains Black Museum, housed in the former Webster Telephone Exchange Building, a thirty-seven-room brick structure located in the heart of the Black community.

The structure is closely associated with Omaha's Black history from 1933 when American Bell donated the Webster Exchange Building to the Urban League. After a previously existing Black community center was consolidated with the Urban League, the building was remodeled for use as the Mid-City Community Center. In the 1950s, Whitney Young, later the director of the National Urban League, had his offices in this building. The Mid-City Community Center has provided a variety of services for African Americans including employment assistance, a library, a nursery, a medical and dental clinic, adult education classes, and youth groups.

The community center operated until about 1950 when the building was sold. The Exchange Building was first an apartment house, and then it became the headquarters of the Greater Omaha Community Action. Since 1975 the Great Plains Black Museum has used the historic structure.

The Great Plains Black Museum is the only museum in this area dedicated to preserving the history of the African Americans in the Midwest after the Civil War. The museum interprets life of Black people in the Great Plains from the pre–Civil

War–underground railroad years to the present. Displays include information on and artifacts of Black homesteaders, including Black women of the Great Plains. Museum activities include guided tours, temporary exhibits, and films. Facilities are available for community meetings and programs, achievement projects, and arts/crafts exhibitions.

The site is listed in the *National Register of Historic Places.*

DATE ESTABLISHED:	Building, 1906; museum, 1976
ADDRESS:	2213 Lake Street, Omaha
TELEPHONE:	(402) 345-2212
VISITING HOURS:	By appointment, Mon.–Fri. 8–4, Sat.–Sun.; open for Kwanzaa celebration Dec. 29–Jan. 6; closed Sat., Sun., Christmas Eve, Christmas Day, New Year's Eve, New Year's Day, July 4, Labor Day 👫
FEES:	$2
SOURCES:	NRHPINF. R. D. Waller, assistant director, Great Plains Black Museum. *Nebraska Guide to Museums and Historic Sites.*

Jewell Building
The Dreamland Ballroom

James C. Jewell and his son lived in one of the apartments of the Jewell Building while they operated the barbershop, billiard parlor, and Dreamland Ballroom. The Jewells built the building in 1923, an era when Black people were moving into the Near North Side neighborhood surrounding Twenty-fourth and Lake Streets. During World War I expanding wartime industries had attracted Black workers to Omaha, and the Black business district, previously at Fourteenth and Dodge Streets, shifted to this location.

From the 1920s through the 1950s, Dreamland Ballroom gained national prominence as a center for some of America's greatest jazz entertainers. Duke Ellington, Nat "King" Cole, Count Basie, Lionel Hampton, Dizzy Gillespie, Ray Charles, Dinah Washington, Sarah Vaughn, Louis Armstrong, and many others provided entertainment there.

In spite of potential loss of revenues, James Jewell refused to obtain a liquor license, thus allowing young people to attend the performances. After Jewell Sr. died in 1930, his son continued to operate the business.

During World War II the U.S. government took the Dreamland Ballroom away from the Jewell family and turned it into a U.S.O. Center for Black soldiers. A year later, when the government returned the building, Jewell sued for damages. The court awarded him $3,000 in a landmark case. The Dreamland Ballroom continued to operate until 1965, and the first-floor barbershop and pool hall were open through the mid 1970s.

In 1983 the building was sold to the community-based Omaha Economic Development Corporation. Having been vacant for years, the building was, as corporation president Alvin Goodwin said, "in disrepair and ready for the wrecking ball." Instead, the development corporation decided to rehabilitate it. The old, two-story floor plan had two storefronts on the first floor with two apartments at the rear and a dance hall with stage and a pressed-metal ceiling on the second floor. Today the two apartments have been renovated and leased. The rest of the building has been converted to office space and now houses offices of the Omaha Economic Development Corporation, the NAACP, the archdiocese, and a U.S. Post Office substation. The Jewell Building, one of Omaha's first important Black commercial buildings, a site associated with an influential Black business family, and a center of community entertainment for many years, is again an attractive and viable community structure. Designated a landmark by the City of Omaha Landmarks Heritage Preservation Commission, it is listed in the *National Register of Historic Places.*

DATE BUILT:	1923
ADDRESS:	2221–2225 N. Twenty-fourth Street, Omaha
TELEPHONE:	Omaha Economic Development Corporation, (402) 346-2300
VISITING HOURS:	Call for appointment
SOURCES:	NRHPINF. Telephone conversation June 20, 1994, Alvin Goodwin, president, Omaha Economic Development Corporation.

Works Consulted

"The Lewis and Clark Expedition." The Academic American Encyclopedia. Danbury, Conn.: Grolier, 1993. [electronic version]

Nebraska Guide to Museums and Historic Sites. Nebraska Department of Economic Development, Division of Travel and Tourism and Nebraska Museums Roundtable. Lincoln, Nebr.: The Division, n.d.

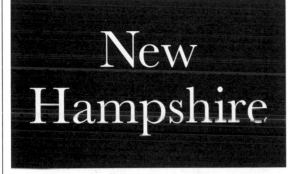

Jaffrey

Amos Fortune Homestead and Burial Site

Amos Fortune (1710–1801) was an African-born slave who was brought to Massachusetts as a youth. Sold at auction at the age of sixteen, he lived as a slave until he was able to purchase his freedom at the age of sixty. Having acquired expert skills in tanning hides, Fortune moved to Jaffrey, New Hampshire, where he established his own tannery. There he lived frugally, saving his money and using it to purchase freedom for other Black slaves. One of these slaves was a woman named Violate, whom he later married. He died a man well-respected in Jaffrey for his fine work and his achievements in life. In his will he left funds to the church and school in the town.

Today, many schoolchildren learn about Fortune by reading the book *Amos Fortune, Free Man.* Although the account is interesting and often moving, some statements may lead children to develop negative stereotypes. Black children could be devastated by reading the description of all African tribes as pagan (p. 5) or by reading that after two months at sea the Africans were forgetting their language and could make only meaningless sounds (p. 26–27). Caleb Copeland, the Quaker who bought Amos, described him as part-animal, one who would run wild without the white people's influence. Caleb's wife described Amos as a poor, black lamb, a description that could be excruciatingly humiliating to a Black child. These types of statements would lead to outrage in some Black communities that are trying to instill pride of heritage in their children; the statements detract from

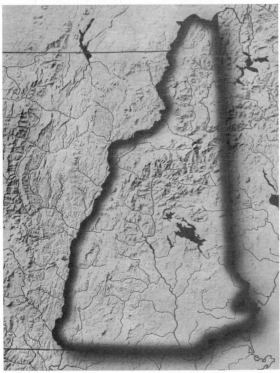

positive aspects of the story. Sensitive and aware teachers and parents who use the book may want to explain, when reaching these statements, that the author, writing in another era, inserted some bigoted ideas that were once widely held about African Americans.

Today's visitors can see the Amos Fortune Homestead on a road named in 1995 for Fortune. Fortune purchased the land in 1789 and probably erected the house and barn soon after. Today the small, white Cape Cod cottage and the barn are private, but visitors can drive by. Tyler Brook, a waterway used by Fortune for tanning purposes, still serves as the boundary line for Fortune's homestead. With advance notice, the Jaffrey Public Library will display for visitors some original documents relating to Fortune, a compass that he owned, and the book *Amos Fortune, Free Man*.

The gravestones of Amos Fortune and his wife are in the Meeting House Cemetery at Jaffrey. His inscription reads,

> *Sacred to the memory of Amos Fortune,*
> *who was born free in Africa a slave*
> *in America he purchased liberty,*
> *professed Christianity,*
> *lived reputably*
> *and died hopefully,*
> *Nov. 17, 1801, Aet. 91.*

The stone for Fortune's wife reads,

> *Sacred to the memory of Violate*
> *by sale the slave of Amos Fortune*
> *by marriage his wife*
> *by her fidelity his friend and solace*
> *she died his widow.*
> *Sept. 13, 1802, Aet. 73.*

DATE BUILT:	House, c1789
ADDRESS:	Amos Fortune Homestead, 19 Amos Fortune Road (from town center take NH 137 to Amos Fortune Road, turn right); Meeting House Cemetery (Old Burial Ground), follow NH 124 west to Jaffrey Center, turn right at flashing light (behind the meeting house is a stable, and the cemetery is behind the stable); Jaffrey Public Library, 38 Main Street, Jaffrey
TELEPHONE:	Jaffrey Public Library, (603) 532-7301
VISITING HOURS:	House private, visitors may walk or drive by; cemetery, always open; library Mon., Wed., Fri., 11–5:30; Tues. 1–8, Sat. 9–1

FEES:	None
SOURCES:	Alan F. Rumrill, Historical Society of Cheshire County. Telephone call to Jaffrey City Clerk's Office Aug. 22, 1995. Telephone conversation Aug. 26, 1995, Marilyn Simons, assistant librarian, Jaffrey Public Library. Telephone call Aug. 26, 1995, Tieger Realty Company, Jaffrey. *History of Jaffrey*, 752. *Amos Fortune, Free Man*.

Littleton

Carleton House

Edmund Carleton was a white attorney who served as a stationmaster on New Hampshire's underground railroad. Although Carleton was educated as a lawyer, he left the legal profession to begin operating a lumber business. Carleton was acquainted with the Boston abolitionist leader William Lloyd Garrison and kept one of the best collections of Garrison's antislavery newspaper, *The Liberator*.

Edmund and Mary Carleton were largely responsible for founding the Littleton Anti-Slavery Society in 1837. Carleton also defended two men, Nat Allen and Erastus Brown, who were arrested for interfering with church services by making abolitionist statements. The men rejected a choice of paying fines and were sent to the county jail.

ADDRESS:	32 Carleton Street, Littleton
VISITING HOURS:	Not accessible to public; visitors can walk or drive by
SOURCE:	*The Underground Railroad in New England*.

Works Consulted

Amos Fortune, Free Man. Elizabeth Yates. New York: Aladdin Books, 1951.

History of Jaffrey (Middle Monadnock). Albert Annell and Alice Lehtinen. Jaffrey, N.H.: Town of Jaffrey, 1937.

The Underground Railroad in New England. Richard R. Kuns and John Sabino, eds. Boston: American Revolution Bicentennial Administration, Region I, with Boston 200, The Bicentennial Commissions of the Six New England States and the Underground Railroad Task Force, 1976.

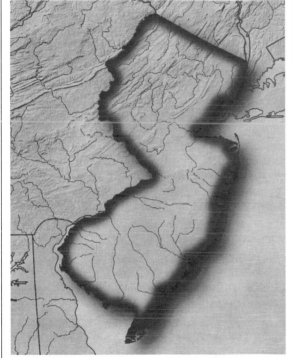

Burlington City

William R. Allen School

When the Civil War ended, New Jersey was divided on the issue of school segregation. A larger number of segregated schools were built in the state's southern counties than elsewhere in the state. The William R. Allen School is an example of one of New Jersey's segregated schools.

From the earliest time of their settlement in Burlington City, African Americans wanted schools for their children. As early as 1812 an African American teacher held classes in her home. By 1844 the state had begun to share public school funds with the Black community.

In 1866 Burlington City had built a frame school for Black children. The school was so small, however—approximately 20 feet square with a ceiling about 7 1/2 feet high—that only forty of the city's 110 to 120 Black children were able to squeeze inside. Seeing that the school clearly was inadequate, two businessmen donated land in 1868 and the city constructed the Federal Street School. From 1870 to 1900 the new schoolhouse served as the city's only school for African American students. Although a few Black students were admitted to white schools, most attended the Federal Street School. High school was not a possibility for Black students—they were refused admission.

In 1900 the city built the William R. Allen school at the Federal Street site. The new brick school, with its three rooms, was larger than the old school, and between 1914 and 1924—a period when Black families migrated to Burlington City from the South—the school was enlarged. In spite of a 1940s state constitution that explicitly forbade school segregation, Allen's student body remained almost entirely African American until the school closed in the 1960s.

After closure, the William R. Allen School reopened to house special education classes from the 1970s until the early 1980s; then the building became vacant. Today community members are discussing ways to have the schoolhouse restored so that it may be open to the public in the future. Although the interior is not accessible, it is worth driving by to see the historic 1900 schoolhouse.

DATE BUILT:	1900
ADDRESS:	Mitchell Avenue, Burlington City
VISITING HOURS:	Private, visitors can drive by
SOURCES:	NRHPINF. Conversation Mar. 24, 1994, Mark Henderson Jr., founder of MARABASH Museum. Conversation Mar. 26, 1994, Martha Henderson, president and founder, MARABASH Museum.

Fair Haven

African Methodist Episcopal Bethel Church

Free Black residents in Fair Haven organized two separate African Methodist Episcopal congregations before the Civil War. The St. James A.M.E. Zion congregation was formed in 1833, and its members built a church on the Port Washington Road that was destroyed by fire in 1873. The second church, Bethel A.M.E. Church, was organized in 1858.

When the Civil War ended, a group of African Americans came north and joined the Black population already established in this area. In 1882 General Clinton B. Fisk, the benefactor of Fisk University in Nashville, Tennessee, donated $3,000 for the erection of a chapel. He knew some members of the Black community at Fair Haven who worked on his estate in Rumson. Others were servants or farmhands in the community. Congregation members also donated money as well as their labor for the chapel, which was dedicated in 1882 and named in honor of General Fisk. A school for African American children was soon opened nearby. The school and its successor served Black children in Fair Haven for more than sixty years.

Fisk Chapel is the oldest religious building in the Rumson-Fair Haven area. The community not only used the building for religious services but also for meetings, concerts, and social activities.

The chapel is a 1,500-square-foot, white clapboard structure. It has Gothic windows, an exposed beam at each gable, and rose windows at each end of the building. The interior has four-foot-high mahogany-finished wainscoting and a tin ceiling painted white.

In the 1970s there were plans to demolish the chapel, but people mindful of its role in the past of the area saved it. It was moved to a residentially zoned site and dedicated in 1976 as a community center. The Fisk Chapel is listed in the *National Register of Historic Places.*

DATE BUILT:	1882
ADDRESS:	Lot No. 11, Cedar Avenue, Fair Haven
TELEPHONE:	Fair Haven city clerk, (908) 747-0241
VISITING HOURS:	Privately owned by Bethel A.M.E. Church, restricted access; call the city clerk for information
SOURCES:	NRHPINF. Telephone call to site, June 13, 1994.

Gloucester Township

Solomon Wesley United Methodist Church

Members of Solomon Wesley United Methodist Church still worship in the historic church constructed in 1850, and members of the founding Davis family still attend the church. One of two Black churches in Gloucester Township, Solomon Wesley is the only one remaining from the mid- nineteenth century. The church and its cemetery remain as symbols of African Americans who were given their freedom and who established the village of Davistown.

In his 1790 will, Daniel Bates left a mile-long parcel of land, $200, and freedom to Lindley Davis, a Black woman, and her family. The stretch of land grew into a Black village known as Davistown in which most residents were Davis family members who worked on nearby farms and marl pits.

In 1850 Zachariah and Catherine Davis deeded land to Solomon and Noble Davis and three other Black men for erecting a church and establishing burial grounds. Soon after, the leaders established Solomon Wesley Church as an African Wesleyan Methodist Episcopal Church.

Construction of the one-story church with clapboard siding encouraged the development of other facilities nearby. These included the camp meeting grounds and the Davistown Colored School, built beside the church in the 1870s. The school, which no longer stands, was the only one ever for Black children in Gloucester township.

Davistown had a population of between 100 and 200 residents at its height. However, the number of people in the village and in the congregation gradually decreased, and in the 1920s many of the founding families left Davistown. Modern homes replaced the early residences, leaving the one-story frame church and the cemetery to the rear of the church as symbols of the community's history. Members of the original Davis family, as well as veterans from the Civil War, Spanish War, and World Wars I and II are buried in the Solomon Wesley Cemetery. Solomon Wesley United Methodist Church is listed in the *National Register of Historic Places*.

DATE BUILT: 1850

ADDRESS: 292-B Davistown Road (Asyla Road), Blackwood, Gloucester Township

TELEPHONE: (609) 232-9067

VISITING HOURS: By appointment

SOURCES: NRHPINF. Telephone conversation Mar. 27, 1994, Reverend Johann Arnold, pastor, Solomon Wesley United Methodist Church.

Jersey City

Afro-American Historical and Cultural Society of Jersey City

The African American Historical Society Museum has exhibits from Black culture and history with emphasis on the New Jersey region. Visitors will enjoy seeing a kitchen of the 1930s, Black dolls dating back to the early 1900s, and a cluster of musical instruments including steel pan, banjo, and assorted drums. A section of statuettes is called "Black Giants in History." Panel boards illustrate the history of slavery in New Jersey, Black women's history, and the story of African American fraternal associations. A section on Africa includes dolls and other artifacts. The collection also includes African and African American art, photographs of outstanding New Jersey citizens, and posters from the 1960s Civil Rights Movement. The museum, which sponsors films, guided tours, and lectures, is housed in the former home of a sea captain who made his fortune transporting slaves from Africa.

DATE ESTABLISHED: 1977

ADDRESS: 1841 Kennedy Boulevard, Jersey City

TELEPHONE: (201) 547-5262

VISITING HOURS: Tues.–Sat. 10–5; closed national holidays ♟♟

FEES: None; donations encouraged

SOURCE: Telephone conversation Mar. 26, 1994, Theodore Brunson, director.

Manalapan

Monmouth Battlefield State Park

More than 800 African Americans were among the 13,000 Americans who fought at Monmouth during the Revolutionary War. One of the Black soldiers was Oliver Cromwell from Burlington, New Jersey, who fought throughout the war and who, at the age of one hundred, still remembered the battle at Monmouth. In 1783 his discharge signed by George Washington showed that he had received the Badge of Merit for long and faithful service.

Cromwell first volunteered to fight in the American Army as a twenty-year-old farm boy enlisting as a private in the Second New Jersey Regiment. He participated when General George Washington crossed the Delaware River on Christmas night 1776, and Cromwell fought in the January 3, 1777, battle in which Americans defeated the British in Trenton, New Jersey. On June 28, 1778, when Washington attacked the British near Monmouth Courthouse, New Jersey, the battle's outcome was not decisive.

Major Charles Lee, under orders from General George Washington to attack the British rear defenses, failed to carry out orders as directed, thus giving the British the chance to withdraw and complete their march to the sea.

Today, the Visitors Center at Monmouth Battlefield State Park gives information about the battle. Although there are no guided tours or markers and the land is relatively undeveloped, visitors can see the rolling terrain much as it originally appeared. The Visitors Center gift shop, a focal point of the site, includes a panel that tells about the men of color who fought at Monmouth.

DATE OF SIGNIFICANCE: June 28, 1778

ADDRESS:	347 Freehold Road (NJ Turnpike exit 8A, then right on NJ 33 East to the park), Manalapan
TELEPHONE:	(908) 462-9616
VISITING HOURS:	Park, daily, winter 9–4:30, spring 8–6, summer 8–8; Visitors Center, daily 9–4 ♦♦
FEES:	None
SOURCES:	Telephone conversation Mar. 26, 1994, Richard Walling, president, Friends of Monmouth Battlefield. *Black Heroes of the American Revolution*, 3–5. The Academic American Encyclopedia. *Men of Color at the Battle of Monmouth*.

Mount Laurel

Jacob's Chapel African Methodist Episcopal Church

Built in 1859, the original Jacob's Chapel is one of New Jersey's early Black churches. Although a newer structure stands close by, the congregation has lovingly preserved the historic building and uses it today for Sunday School and for special social occasions. They have even preserved, for history's sake, one of the two original outhouses (the other one was purchased). Although siding was added to the exterior, the original church has retained its basic appearance. The small, one-story building has three windows in front, an old-fashioned double door, and three windows on each side. The interior has wood paneling up to the

windows. Some of the original pews remain, but they have a new placement to make room for tables in the main area. Dr. James Still, in the 1840s one of the first Black doctors in the state, is buried in the churchyard.

DATE ESTABLISHED:	Congregation, 1813; church, 1859
ADDRESS:	Elbo Lane, Mount Laurel
TELEPHONE:	(609) 234-1728
VISITING HOURS:	Sun. service, 10–1
SOURCE:	Telephone conversation Mar. 27, 1994, Edith Cobb, stewardess and missionary.

Newark

State Street Public School

The State Street School, constructed in 1845 and one of the oldest school buildings in Newark, housed the Colored School of Newark between 1869 and 1873. James Miller Baxter Jr., the first Black principal in Newark's school system, was administrator of the State Street School at this site between 1869 and 1873. The school was later moved to three other locations as facilities grew inadequate at each site. However, the State Street structure is the only home of the school still standing. Having graduated with high honors from a Quaker-operated school, the Philadelphia Institute for Colored Youth, Baxter was offered a position in Newark at the age of nineteen. Two months later, he was appointed principal of the Colored School, a position he filled with distinction. Baxter improved the quality of the curriculum, established an evening school, and improved school facilities. He also was a community leader, a founder and Past Master in the Masons, a Congressional Convention delegate, and a member of the New Jersey Central Committee. The James M. Baxter Terrace, one of the city's first housing projects, was named in his honor.

Prior to 1872 Newark's public schools were segregated, and African American children were not permitted to enroll in secondary schools. Baxter and other Black community members successfully fought for the right of Irene Pataquam Mulford to become the first Black student to enroll in the Newark High School. Although Newark passed an ordinance in 1872 allowing Black children to enroll in schools throughout the city, the Colored School continued to operate until Baxter retired in 1909. The school's closing marked an end to segregated schools in Newark.

This two-story brick building is the oldest public school building still in use in Newark. State Street School contains eight classrooms, four on each floor. A newer 1882 addition has two classrooms on each floor, bathrooms, and a small kitchen. The school, with its wooden floors, transoms, and traditional school light fixtures, retains the atmosphere of a nineteenth-century schoolhouse. Today, the historic schoolhouse is home to the school district's art department.

DATE BUILT: 1845; addition, 1882
ADDRESS: 15 State Street, Newark
TELEPHONE: Art department, (978) 268-5188;
                 Main, (978) 733-7333
VISITING HOURS: Call or write for appointment
SOURCES: NRHPINF. Telephone call to Newark
                 School District Mar. 28, 1994.

Princeton

Witherspoon Presbyterian Church

William Drew Robeson, the father of Paul Robeson (see Paul Robeson site in New York City), was pastor of the Witherspoon Presbyterian Church between 1879 and 1899. His son, Paul, was born in Princeton, New Jersey, in 1898. Paul rose to prominence as an American actor, singer, and spokesperson for equality and justice. Although many white Americans rejected Paul Robeson because of the strong stand he took for dignity and justice, he continued to speak out for his beliefs.

The historic Witherspoon Congregational Church was founded in 1840; its members worship today in this white clapboard, one-story structure with a balcony. The site is significant as the church of an early Black congregation and as a church associated with the family of a gifted Black American, Paul Robeson.

DATE ESTABLISHED: 1840
ADDRESS: 124 Witherspoon Street, Princeton
TELEPHONE: (609) 924-1666
VISITING HOURS: Sun. service, 11; call to arrange to see the
                   interior
FEES: None
SOURCES: The Historical Society of Princeton,
                   New Jersey. Telephone conversation
                   Mar. 27, 1994, Reverend John E. White,
                   pastor, Witherspoon Presbyterian Church.

Red Bank

T. Thomas Fortune House

Thomas Fortune, Black leader, journalist, and outspoken advocate of the rights of African American people, owned and edited three newspapers: *New York Globe, New York Freeman,* and *New York Age.* Born in slavery in 1856 in Marianna, Florida, Fortune personally experienced discrimination and unjust treatment during slavery, Reconstruction, and the early part of the twentieth century. His strong reaction against bigotry led many to criticize his uncompromising and outspoken stance.

Fortune's father, Emanuel Fortune, had learned the basics of reading and writing as well as the trades of shoemaking and tanning, and he passed some of these skills on to his son. Emanuel also was politically active—so much so that his involvement in Reconstruction politics drew the wrath of local white citizens, including having the Ku Klux Klan place the family on a list of "troublemakers" and threaten their lives. The Fortunes gave up their profitable farm and escaped to Jacksonville, Florida, where they started anew. Thomas Fortune's mother died soon after this period.

Thomas attended Freedmen's Bureau Schools where he learned the printer's trade. At the age of thirteen he became a page in the State Senate; there he became aware of the political process that exploited Black people. He entered Howard University at the age of nineteen intending to study law. He married Carrie Smiley, and they lived for a period in Washington, D.C., but lack of funds forced him to withdraw from school and foreshadowed the financial difficulties that he would face throughout his adult years. Fortune began working for the *People's Advocate*. Then, in 1881, he started his own newspaper, the *New York Globe*. Soon his acrid criticism of Republicans for abandoning African Americans led many Black members of the Republican Party to withdraw their support for his newspaper; it failed within three years.

Undaunted, Fortune began publishing *Black and White* in 1884. He criticized both the white press for its distorted images of the Black community and the Supreme Court for declaring invalid the Civil Rights Act of 1875. Then financial difficulties caused him to shut down one newspaper after another, from the *New York Globe* to the *New York Freeman*, but he then went on to edit the *New York Age*. Still politically active, in 1887 he helped to establish the National Afro-American League, one of the forerunners of the National Association for the Advancement of Colored People. He also supported Black women in their crusade for better conditions in a period when poverty, lack of respect, and racial discrimination were widespread. When white townspeople destroyed the Memphis, Tennessee, newspaper office of Ida B. Wells, a Black antilynching crusader, Fortune offered her the use of the *New York Age* facilities so that she could continue her work.

Fortune's life of onerous financial burdens contrasted with that of the well-financed, nationally known educator Booker T. Washington. Washington believed as much as Fortune did in the need to uplift the Black race, but he was far more soft-spoken and accommodating in his words to the public. The two men worked together on some projects. Washington even contributed financially to Fortune's efforts and used Fortune's services at times as a ghostwriter, but their differences in approach led to an inevitable parting of ways. Perturbed at Fortune's seemingly radical comments, Washington warned him against making politically damaging statements, but Fortune continued to speak out. He lambasted racism in the Philippines and then turned to publicly criticizing President Theodore Roosevelt for his indictment of Black soldiers after a Brownsville, Texas, race riot. Finally, Washington withdrew financial support for the *New York Age* and severed his relationship with the journalist.

Fortune, now beset with difficulties, became depressed. He suffered an emotional breakdown and withdrew from public life, staying in his home on West Bergen Place. Then in 1915 he lost his home. He later worked for several newspapers, but he never regained his former stature.

Although Fortune was depressed at his apparent failures, he actually lived a worthy life. He shared vivid and prophetic insights. In his indictment of white newspapers he spoke words that are echoed in Black communities even today. He said such newspapers "are all on the side of the oppressor, or by silence preserve a dignified but ignominious neutrality. Day after day they weave a false picture of facts—facts which must measurably influence the future historian of the times in the composition of impartial history."[1] Timothy Thomas Fortune died in 1928, but many of his insights proved accurate, and questions and issues he raised are still being debated today.

The Thomas Fortune House, where the journalist resided from 1901 to 1915, was constructed between 1860 and 1885. Originally it was a two-story L-shaped building with living room, dining room, kitchen, and rear storage room on the first floor, three bedrooms on the second floor, and an unfinished attic. The structure was enlarged in 1917 and is listed in the *National Register of Historic Places*.

DATE BUILT:	1860–1885; purchased by Fortune, 1901
ADDRESS:	94 W. Bergen Place, Red Bank
VISITING HOURS:	Private, visitors may walk or drive by
SOURCES:	NRHPINF. *The Black 100*.

Somerville

Wallace House Historic Site

John Wallace was a wealthy merchant in Philadelphia who retired to this New Jersey location just as the Revolutionary War was beginning. He was sixty years old when he built and moved into Hope Farm. Few houses were built anywhere in the colonies during the war, and this two and one-half–story Georgian residence, white with green shutters, center hall, and elegant interior woodwork, was considered a fine residence in its day.

Some of the Wallace slaves—those who tended the house —lived in three small rooms above the kitchen. The rooms were approximately 8 feet wide by 8, 10, or 12 feet long. In his will John Wallace referred to two of the slaves as "my stock of negroes." Records indicate that one slave, Phyllis, was with the family for three generations; she was highly prized by the Wallace family for her skill in cooking and completing housework duties. Little is known about the slave named Greg other than that he was advertised for sale in 1788 along with a riding chair (an open, two-wheeled riding vehicle). For unknown reasons, Greg was not sold until 1791.

The slaves first were the property of John Wallace's mother-in-law; then they became Wallace's property. After the death of John's wife, Mary, in 1784 Greg and Phyllis passed into the hands of John's son, William Wallace. William died in 1796 and there are no records left to tell what happened to Phyllis after that date. There are no records either to describe the thoughts of the "highly prized" Phyllis—to tell what she thought of the family that valued her so highly through the generations for her usefulness as a servant. We do not know how often or how deeply she yearned for freedom.

The slave quarters are open on a limited basis. Because the staircase is fairly steep and winding, visitors are allowed only to look up the stairwell. However, there is a video tour of the second floor.

DATE BUILT: 1777
ADDRESS: 38 Washington Place, Somerville
TELEPHONE: (908) 725-1015

VISITING HOURS: Wed.–Sat. 10–noon, Sun. 1–4; closed holidays, Mon., Tues. 🧒
FEES: None; donation appreciated
SOURCE: Telephone conversation May 15, 1994, James Kurzenberger, historic preservation specialist.

Tenafly

African Art Museum of the S.M.A. Fathers

The African Art Museum of the S.M.A. Fathers (The Fathers of the Society of African Missions) contains one of the finest collections of African art in New Jersey. The large exhibition area houses more than 200 objects from sub-Saharan Africa including masks, statues, textiles, beadwork, and musical instruments.

The Society of African Missions was founded at Lyons, France, in 1856. Unlike some Christian missionaries who regarded African culture as inferior, members of the Society of African Missions sought to collect and preserve artifacts from West Africa. The collection includes works in wood, brass, bronze, and ivory. The objects show the African reverence for life in their symbols of spiritual forces and fertility. For example, young girls in Ghana tucked wooden dolls in their clothing to ensure their own fertility and their children's health and beauty.

In addition, the museum has carvings of antelope horns that were worn as a headdress in dances and pageants by the Bamana people of Mali. The collection includes Ashanti gold weights made by the "lost wax" method of casting.

Children will enjoy this site; approximately 2,000 schoolchildren visit the museum every year. There is a self-tour for children. By calling in advance, a group can schedule a ninety-minute presentation in which objects are shown close up. This is followed by a tour of the museum.

DATE ESTABLISHED: 1978
ADDRESS: 23 Bliss Avenue (County Road 501—Grand Avenue or Engle Street—to Bliss Avenue), Tenafly
TELEPHONE: (201) 567-0450
VISITING HOURS: Daily 9–5 🧒

FEES:	None; donations accepted
SOURCES:	Charles Bordogna, curator. Telephone conversation Mar. 25, 1994, Dr. Richard A. Barrows.

Trenton

Washington Crossing State Park

In October 1775 the Continental Congress approved a resolution that barred Black men from serving in the newly formed American Army. One month later, however, Lord Dunmore, the royal governor of Virginia, promised freedom to all male slaves who would join the British troops fighting against the colonists. As a result of Dunmore's proclamation, General George Washington reversed the resolution of the Congress and instructed his recruiting officers to enlist Black men as soldiers. In January 1776 Congress approved this decision.

Two Black men, Prince Whipple and Oliver Cromwell, accompanied Washington during the crossing of the Delaware River in 1776. Whipple had been born in Africa and was sold into slavery at the age of ten in Baltimore. He was bought as a servant by a white man named William Whipple, who lived in Portsmouth, New Hampshire. William Whipple became a general and one of George Washington's aides in the American Revolution, and Prince Whipple served during the war as a trusted bodyguard to his owner. Cromwell, another African American, was a farmer who volunteered for the colonial army when he was twenty-one years old.

Whipple and Cromwell were among the men who marched over icy roads in freezing rain in this region. In one of the important victories of the war, Washington's small army defeated the British in a surprise attack at Trenton, suffering only five casualties among the American troops. Cromwell survived the war. When he died in January 1853, one of his most-treasured possessions was his discharge paper signed by Washington in 1783 at the end of the war. Prince Whipple was given his freedom after the war, but only after he and twenty other men protested to the New Hampshire legislature that they had been born free in Africa and that under provisions of the Declaration of Independence, they should be free. His wife and several children also gained their freedom as a result of the petition. Prince, however, died in New Hampshire soon after the war ended. An engraving at the Visitors Center shows Prince Whipple in General Washington's boat.

DATE OF SIGNIFICANCE:	1776
ADDRESS:	8 miles northwest of Trenton on NJ 29, then northeast on County Road 546 to the park
TELEPHONE:	(609) 737-0623
VISITING HOURS:	Park, Memorial Day–Labor Day daily 8–8, rest of the year daily 8–4; Visitors Center, Memorial Day–Labor Day daily 9–5, rest of the year Wed.–Sun. 9–4:30 🕴🕴
FEES:	$2 parking fee Memorial Day weekend–Labor Day; free after Labor Day
SOURCES:	*Before the Mayflower*, 446. *International Library of Negro Life and History*, 37. *Black Heroes of the American Revolution*, 16–17.

Note

1. Columbus Salley, *The Black 100: A Ranking of the Most Influential African-Americans Past and Present* (New York: Citadel, 1993), 217.

Works Consulted

The Academic American Encyclopedia. New York: Grolier, 1993. [electronic version]

Before the Mayflower: A History of Black America. 5th ed. Lerone Bennett Jr. New York: Penguin, 1988.

Black Heroes of the American Revolution. Burke Davis. New York: Odyssey Book, Harcourt Brace Jovanovich, 1976.

The Black 100: A Ranking of the Most Influential African-Americans Past and Present. Columbus Salley. New York: Citadel, 1993.

International Library of Negro Life and History. Wilhelmena S. Robinson. New York: Publishers, 1970.

Men of Color at the Battle of Monmouth June 28, 1778: The Role of African Americans and Native Americans at Monmouth. Richard S. Walling. Hightstown, N.J.: Longstreet House, 1994.

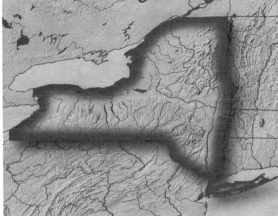

Auburn

William Seward House

Senator William Seward (1801–1872) and his Quaker wife, Frances Miller Seward, lived in the house at 33 South Street, a place where fugitive slaves found shelter. Seward was governor of New York and a leader of the Whig Party's antislavery wing. Later, as a U.S. Senator, he made a speech in Rochester, New York, in which he described the antagonism between freedom and slavery as a conflict between enduring forces.

Although Seward was known for negotiating the purchase of Alaska from Russia in 1867, equally as important were his outspoken views opposing slavery. His speeches on the topic were said to have made an impression on then Congressman Abraham Lincoln.

Seward was Lincoln's Secretary of State during the Civil War and was one of the intended victims of the plot to kill Lincoln in 1865. After Lincoln was assassinated, John Wilkes Booth's accomplice, a man named Paine, entered Seward's house and tried to kill Seward, too. Although he was severely wounded, Seward survived.

William Seward opposed slavery from his early childhood. In Florida when he was about five years old, he became friends with Zeno, a Black slave child who lived next door. One day Zeno was punished in the woodshed for some infraction and ran away from home. Seward tried unsuccessfully all of his life to find Zeno again. The incident probably influenced Seward to engage later in abolitionist activities.

As an adult, Seward provided financial support to Frederick Douglass and to underground railroad heroine Harriet Tubman. Knowing that Tubman was living in St. Catherines, Ontario, Canada, Seward wrote her. Describing her in his letter as an American hero, he urged her to live in her own country. In fact, Tubman did return to America. She came to Auburn to live and with Seward's assistance obtained a farm and a small pension from the government.

Frances Seward, who was brought up as a Quaker, gave refuge in the back of this house to fugitive slaves when her husband was a U.S. Senator. Slaves were hidden in a space above the woodshed, which they reached by stairway. While the actual room in which they hid is not open to visitors, it is still there. Visitors to the site can see the original house containing Seward's personal articles, a collection of articles that belonged to President Lincoln, and a fireplace carved by Brigham Young.

ADDRESS:	33 South Street, Auburn
TELEPHONE:	(315) 252-1283
VISITING HOURS:	Tues.–Sat. 1–4; closed Jan.–Mar. and federal holidays except Dr. Martin Luther King Jr. Day and Veterans' Day 👥
FEES:	Adults, $3; senior citizens, $2.50; AAA cardholders, $2.50; children under 6, free
SOURCES:	Telephone conversation Apr. 30, 1994, Paul McDonald, assistant curator. Betty Mae Lewis, the historic Seward House. *The African American Presence in New York State History*, 146. *Webster's New Biographical Dictionary*, 906.

Harriet Tubman Museum*

Harriet Tubman (c1820–1913) was one of the best-known and most courageous of abolitionists. Born in slavery in Maryland, she made a remarkable escape from bondage in 1849. Having gained her own freedom, she did not rest but returned directly into the heart of danger to rescue many others. Even though Tubman was targeted for capture by slavecatchers and by the law, she made the trip back nineteen times and was credited with leading at least 300 Black men and women to freedom. Tubman never lost a person along the way. Although rewards of up to $40,000 were offered for her capture, she was never taken. She helped her own aged parents to escape to Canada.

Tubman traveled through central New York many times as she conducted people along the underground railroad. She received support from many abolitionists who lived in this area. In 1857 Tubman moved to Auburn and in the following year she brought her parents back to Auburn. With the assistance of Senator William Seward, the former governor of New York, Tubman acquired a house and land on the outskirts of Auburn. She always was willing to share with others, and her home became known as a haven for poor and elderly Black people.

Harriet Tubman continued to help others throughout her life. She aided the Union side in the Civil War and later worked to improve women's rights and African American education.

In 1896 Tubman was successful in bidding for some acres of land adjoining her home. In 1903 she deeded her entire property to the African Methodist Episcopal Zion Church to be operated as a communi-

ty farm cooperative. Tubman died in 1913 in a home for the aged that she had founded. Tributes to her memory arrived from across America, and the city of Auburn erected a monument in her honor.

The Harriet Tubman House and Museum, designated as a state historic site and a national historic landmark, are located on her land. The restored house has a lean-to roof and a covered porch that extends along two sides of the house. The two-story frame structure contains Tubman's Bible and other items associated with her life. The museum, still owned by the African Methodist Episcopal Zion Church, is listed in the *National Register of Historic Places.*

Thompson Memorial A.M.E. Zion Church, which Harriet Tubman attended, and her burial site also are located in Auburn. The Harriet Tubman gravesite in Fort Hill Cemetery is marked with a small tombstone located under a large cedar tree. Thompson Memorial Church is located three blocks from Fort Hill Cemetery.

A bronze tablet at the Auburn Courthouse honors Harriet Tubman with these words:

> In memory of Harriet Tubman
> Born a Slave in Maryland About 1821
> Died in Auburn, NY, March 10, 1913
> Called the Moses of her People.
> During the Civil War, with Rare
> Courage She Led Over Three Hundred
> Negroes Up From Slavery to Freedom
> And Rendered Invaluable Service
> As a Nurse and Spy.
> With Implicit Trust in God
> She Braved Every Danger and
> Overcame Every Obstacle, Withal
> She Possessed Extraordinary
> Foresight and Judgement So That
> She Truthfully Said
> "On My Underground Railroad
> I NEBBER Run my Train off de Track
> An' I Nebber Los' A PASSENGER."

DATE BUILT:	c1908
ADDRESS:	180–182 South Street, Auburn
TELEPHONE:	(315) 252-2081
VISITING HOURS:	By appointment 👫

FEES: Donation

SOURCES: Jessie Thorpe, Afro-American Heritage Association, Rome, New York. NRHPINF. *National Register of Historic Places*, 496. *The African American Presence in New York State History*, 59–61, 151. *And Why Not Every Man?*, 136.

Brooklyn

Houses in the Hunterfly Road District *

Six houses on Hunterfly Road are the remaining houses from an early Black settlement called "Weeksville." This was the first major settlement of free Black people in the Bedford-Stuyvesant area.

Slavery was abolished in New York in 1827. Around that time Black people were coming to the Hunterfly Road area. They named their community for James Weeks, an African American landowner, stevedore, and community leader who chaired a committee that sought voting rights for Black citizens.

Weeksville became a refuge for Black families in July 1863 when the New York draft riots of the Civil War took place. Anger had been building among white townspeople who believed free Black workers were taking jobs away from them or driving down wages. At the same time, some poor white citizens believed they might be drafted for Civil War service while wealthier white citizens were exempted from the draft.

Civil unrest began, and white groups hurled insults and vicious comments at Black people as they walked through Brooklyn's streets. A mob of Irish workers forced their way into Lorillard and Watson, a tobacco company employing twenty-five African Americans, and tried to burn down the building with the workers, primarily women and children, inside. Although police arrived and saved the workers, tensions and fear ran high.

Eleven months later, four days of mob violence erupted in New York. The riots later were called the "draft riots," because the mobs, infuriated by seeing Black regiments pass through New York City on their way to the South, directed their greatest anger at the draft enrollment office. Roving gangs burned the Colored Orphan Asylum to the ground and lynched

African Americans in the streets and in their homes. Marching through all parts of the city, gangs of men, women, and children searched houses, raided businesses employing African Americans, and lynched the Black workers. Some were drowned in the river and others were hanged from the limbs of trees. Although hundreds of African Americans fled the city, those in Weeksville and Flatbush stood their ground, arming themselves and guarding their neighborhoods and families day and night. The people of Weeksville sheltered many African Americans from other parts of the city. Many in the city were ashamed of what had happened. Later, in 1864, the people of Weeksville must have felt immense pride when the Twentieth U.S. Colored Infantry marched down Broadway behind a military band while a crowd of thousands cheered.

The houses in Weeksville were forgotten until 1968 when college students under the direction of historian Jim Hurley began a research project on Brooklyn neighborhoods. Joseph Haynes, a Black engineer and pilot, discovered the historic houses on Hunterfly Road while exploring the area from the air. The clue was a lane that ran in a different direction from the other streets and the few wood-frame farmhouses on the lane. The houses were set in a different direction because they followed the old Hunterfly Road that no longer existed.

Archaeologists, students, and volunteers dug for artifacts and found several objects, including a tintype of a woman, an old coin, and a copy of the constitution of the Abyssinian Benevolent Daughters of Esther Association of the City of New York, a Black women's group formed in 1839. The pamphlet was printed in 1853 by a firm owned by a leading Black abolitionist.

The six houses in the historical district probably were erected around 1830. The wooden-frame structures vary from one and one-half to two and one-half stories. They are unique in this area as the only surviving houses built parallel to a colonial road and as the oldest known remnants of the nineteenth-century, free-Black community of Weeksville. Three of the former dwellings have been restored by master craftsmen and trainees from the local community and now house an educational facility and African American history museum. One house was in the process of being furnished in mid-1994. A costumed guide who is a graduate of the Banks Street College of Education shows the houses to visitors. The guide has noted that visitors have commented that the old houses with their greenery convey a calm, country atmosphere, often reminding them of a grandmother's place. Visitors see some old artifacts—a stove, an old iron, a washboard, a sewing machine, a butter churn—and learn about the process of restoration. The houses on Hunterfly Road project are a New York City landmark and are listed in the *National Register of Historic Places.* In 1992 Joan B. Maynard, executive director of the Weeksville Society, received the highest award from the National Trust for Historic Preservation for this restoration.

DATE BUILT:	1838–1865
ADDRESS:	1698, 1700, 1702–04, 1706–08 Bergen Street, Brooklyn
TELEPHONE:	(718) 756-5250
VISITING HOURS:	Office hours, Mon.–Fri. 10–4; tours by 3-week prearrangement Tues.–Thurs. and some holidays; closed Sat.–Sun., holidays 👥
FEES:	Adults, $3; children under 18, $1; senior citizens and students, $1.50
SOURCES:	Joan Maynard, executive director, Society for the Preservation of Weeksville & Bedford-Stuyvesant History. Patricia C. Gloster, The Center for African Art. Telephone conversation May 4, 1994, Anna French, administrator, Houses in the Hunterfly District. NRHPINF. *The Negro's Civil War,* 71–7, 212–13. *Weeksville Then & Now.*

Buffalo

Kush Museum of African and African-American Art and Antiquities

The Kush Museum, housed in the Langston Hughes Cultural Arts Center in Buffalo, exhibits a collection of African artifacts and several works of art by contemporary African and African American artists. The African collection concentrates on the Akan-speaking region and the Sudan region of Africa. Established in 1990, Kush Museum has programs for children of all ages. Associate Director Deborah Weeks is working with a group that plans to set up tours of under-

ground railroad sites in the Niagara area. The Langston Hughes Institute at this site also sponsors programs for children, including summer art activities.

DATE ESTABLISHED:	1990
ADDRESS:	Langston Hughes Institute, 25 High Street, Buffalo
TELEPHONE:	(716) 881-3266
VISITING HOURS:	Mon., Wed., Fri. 10–6 👥
FEES:	None
SOURCE:	Telephone conversation June 13, 1994, Deborah Weeks, associate director, Kush Museum.

Michigan Street Baptist Church

To many fugitive slaves, Michigan Street Baptist Church was the final stop on the underground railroad for those fleeing to Canada. The church played a major role in Buffalo's Black community from its establishment during the abolitionist movement. When the church was constructed in 1845, most of Buffalo's 350 African American residents lived in the Michigan–William Street area near the downtown district. Social life for this relatively small, cohesive group centered around church activities. Reverend Dr. Edward Nash, the pastor for 61 years starting in the 1890s, was a leader in the Buffalo Urban League and the local branch of the National Association for the Advancement of Colored People.

Today the El-Bethel congregation occupies the historic building. The church has the same basic appearance that it had when constructed except for such minor modifications as the addition of an outside stairway. In the lower level visitors can look down into the underground railroad room that has a tunnel leading out to the street, mute evidence of the importance of this church as the last stop before the slaves crossed into Canada.

DATE BUILT:	1845
ADDRESS:	511 Michigan Avenue, Buffalo
TELEPHONE:	(716) 854-7976
VISITING HOURS:	Sun. school, 10–11:30; Sun. service, 11:30–2; Sun. evening service, 6:30–9; Wed. evening Bible study, 6:30; Thurs. children's study group, 7–9 P.M.; Sat. 10–noon

SOURCES: Telephone conversation May 14, 1994, Mr. Larry Washington, pastor's assistant. NRHPINF.

Corona

Louis Armstrong House and Archives

Corona was the home of Louis "Satchmo" Armstrong, the grandson of former slaves and a man who became a major force in bringing recognition to jazz as an art form. Armstrong was born in 1900 in New Orleans and raised by his grandmother. He loved music and sang in his church choir. As he grew up, he often visited a section of New Orleans called Brick Row, where he would listen to musicians who played in the different buildings. "King" Joe Oliver, a cornetist in one of these New Orleans groups, had a great impact on Armstrong's career.

When Armstrong was twelve years old, he committed the illegal act of firing a gun filled with blanks. He was sent to the Colored Waifs Home for Boys. Armstrong had difficulty adjusting to life in the boys home, but Peter Davis, a music teacher and janitor at the home, recognized young Armstrong's musical talent and encouraged him. Armstrong became the band leader at the home and traveled with the band whenever the group played in city parades.

Armstrong was released from the home after a year and a half. His father, who had remarried, was given custody. However, his father lacked the means to care for the boy and sent him to live with the boy's mother. By the age of sixteen, he was working at odd jobs ranging from shoveling coal in a coalyard to playing his cornet. Gradually, Armstrong began playing full-time at clubs. He learned to read music and took the opportunity to play on steamers with Fate Marable's band, visiting different cities on a six-month tour.

In 1922 Armstrong left New Orleans for Chicago, where he joined the band of his idol "King" Joe Oliver. In 1942 he married Lillian Hardin, the pianist for the band. As Armstrong became well known, he played with different bands in the United States and Europe and began to make recordings.

By 1936 Armstrong's band was earning $8,000 per week. He and his wife, Lillian, purchased the home on 107th Street in Corona, where they lived for thirty-five years. Between 1961 and 1967 the U.S. State Department sponsored Armstrong in goodwill and concert tours for America, resulting in sell-out concerts in many countries. Thousands attended an open-air concert in Africa, and President Kwame Nkrumah of Ghana gave a reception at his guest house. Armstrong experienced severe illness in 1969 and again in 1971. He died in 1971 in New York.

The Armstrong House is a two and one-half-story, red-brick, detached rowhouse. The eleven-room house was renovated during the years when the Armstrongs lived there, and much of the interior remains as it was at that time. The house contains many of Armstrong's furnishings and his musical instruments. His recordings, manuscripts, and memoirs written in longhand have been moved to an archive at Queens College, City University of New York (CUNY), where they can be reviewed and enjoyed by researchers and jazz aficionados.

DATE ESTABLISHED:	Armstrong residence, 1940–1971; archives, May 24, 1994
ADDRESS:	Residence, 3456 107th Street, Corona, Long Island; archives, Rosenthal Library, Queens College/CUNY, 65–30 Kissena Boulevard, Flushing
TELEPHONE:	Residence, (718) 478-8274; archives, (718) 997-3670
VISITING HOURS:	House, small groups by appointment, Mon.–Fri. 9–5; archives by appointment, Mon.–Fri. 9–5
SOURCES:	NRHPINF. Telephone conversation May 3, 1994, Aishah Pacheco, assistant to the director.

Elmira

Woodlawn National Cemetery

Woodlawn National Cemetery is associated with John W. Jones, a stationmaster on Elmira's underground railroad. Jones was a runaway slave who had escaped from his master in Leesburg, Virginia. He settled in Elmira, situated in the Finger Lakes region of south central New York; there he became a leader of the underground railroad, personally helping hundreds of fleeing slaves.

The Woodlawn Cemetery, a Civil War prison camp, was at the rear of Jones's farm, and he was placed in charge of burying nearly 3,000 Confederate prisoners who had died during imprisonment at Camp Elmira in 1864. Jones, who once fled racism in the South, saw that the men were reverently buried. He erected wooden markers over their graves and kept a record of the name and location of each grave. As he tended the graves, he placed the name and other information about each soldier in a sealed bottle in the coffin. The information that he carefully recorded proved of value when Woodlawn became a national cemetery in 1877.

DATE OF SIGNIFICANCE:	1864
ADDRESS:	1825 Davis Street, Elmira
TELEPHONE:	(607) 732-5411
VISITING HOURS:	Always open; office, Mon.–Fri. 8:30–4:30, closed national holidays except Memorial Day
SOURCES:	Telephone conversation Jan. 25, 1995, Brian McCade, caretaker, Woodlawn National Cemetery. *And Why Not Every Man?*, 141–2. *The African American Presence in New York State History*, 58.

Flushing

Bowne House

Oral tradition maintains that the Bowne House in a large Quaker community once was a station on the underground railroad. The town of Flushing was founded in 1645 and the dwelling, built in 1661, was home to white abolitionist John Bowne, a founder of the Manumission Society in New York. After Bowne died in 1694, antislavery sentiment was passed on through the generations in this prominent family. Mary Bowne Parsons, John Bowne's great-great granddaughter, was a Quaker abolitionist.

Today the twenty-one–room Bowne House is a national shrine to religious freedom. With its labyrinth of nooks and passages it is a favorite place for children, who can learn about colonial history and New York's antislavery movement as they walk through it. Bowne House is a city and state landmark and is listed in the *National Register of Historic Places*.

DATE BUILT:	1661
ADDRESS:	37-01 Bowne Street, Flushing
TELEPHONE:	(718) 359-0528
VISITING HOURS:	Mon.–Fri. 9:30–4; Sat.–Sun. 2:30–4:30; closed mid-Dec.–mid-Jan., Easter 👫
FEES:	Adults, $2; children, $1
SOURCES:	Audrey Braver, director. Telephone conversation May 5, 1994, Donna Russo, executive director.

Fort Edward

Solomon Northup House

Northup House, originally built in the 1700s as Fort Edward, was built to guard the upper Hudson Valley but was abandoned after the French and Indian War. In 1777, General Burgoyne used the house as his headquarters during his march toward Saratoga. He was arrested and later joined other Loyalists in Canada.

This Fort Edward house once was the residence of Solomon Northup, a Black man who published the story of his life in a book called *Twelve Years a Slave*. In 1821, by Fort Edward board action, Solomon's father, Mintus Northup, was accepted as a free man. On Christmas Day 1829, Solomon Northup married Anne Hampton, and they began housekeeping in the Old Fort House. Northup worked with other men in repairing the Champlain Canal; he saved enough money to buy a horse and other items needed for canal-boat towing and then sought contracts for transporting rafts loaded with timber. With the earnings from this work, Solomon and Anne purchased a farm in Kingsbury in 1832.

Ten years later, however, Solomon was kidnapped and was sold into slavery in Louisiana, where he remained in bondage until he was rescued in 1853. He later told his story in a book that rivaled the popularity of Harriet Beecher Stowe's *Uncle Tom's Cabin* and that remains gripping in its descriptions of slave life.

Today the Old Fort House, the oldest frame building standing in Washington County, is a museum complex consisting of seven buildings, three of which are open for tours. Northup House was being restored at the time of this book's publication; visitors should call to find out if it is open. (For additional information on another house associated with Northup, read the listing for Bunkie, Louisiana.)

DATE BUILT:	1773; Northup residence, beginning Dec. 1829
ADDRESS:	29 Lower Broadway, Fort Edward
TELEPHONE:	(518) 747-0600
VISITING HOURS:	Mid-June–mid-Sept., daily 1–5; Dec., daily 1–4; closed all holidays and Nov., Jan.–Mar.; all groups by appointment 👥
FEES:	Individuals, free; bus tours, $1.50 per person
SOURCES:	Telephone call to site, May 9, 1994. R. Paul McCarty, director, and Pat Turner, tour director, Old Fort House. *Old House Museum.*

Hempstead

African American Museum of Nassau County

Established in 1970, the African-American Museum is the only one of its kind on Long Island. It highlights the history and contributions of local African Americans, many of whom made significant contributions to the nation. Special exhibits include art, books, and documents. Temporary exhibits provide a continuous public showcase for artists, and traveling exhibits from other institutions place the experience of Long Island within a broader world context. One exhibit presented *The World of Our Grandparents, African Americans on Long Island from 1880 to 1926.*

The museum is a facility of the division of Museum Services of the Nassau County Department of Recreation and Parks. Housed in a structure of approximately 11,000 square feet, it includes two galleries, an educational room, a music room, and a gift shop. The south wing is being expanded to include a theater with collapsible walls for concerts and conferences, a photography lab, and a reference room.

DATE ESTABLISHED:	1970
ADDRESS:	110 N. Franklin Street, Hempstead, Long Island (Southern State Parkway to exit 21, Nassau Road; northbound to Jackson Street)
TELEPHONE:	(516) 572-0730
VISITING HOURS:	Thurs.–Sun. 10–4:45; closed Mon.–Tues., holidays except Dr. Martin Luther King Jr. Day 👥
FEES:	None; charge for custom programs for groups with advance reservations
SOURCE:	Mildred Clayton, museum coordinator, March 1994.

Huntington

Bethel African Methodist Episcopal Church

Bethel African Methodist Episcopal Church is the oldest surviving African American church in Huntington. When Huntington was settled in the eighteenth century, most African Americans lived in the town as slaves on large properties. By the nineteenth century Huntington also had a free Black population. The Bethel A.M.E. congregation was incorporated in 1843. Most of the African American residents worked in agriculture, domestic service, or Huntington's brick-yards. The present church was designed and built in 1924 by church pastor George A. Lonzo. Prominently located on a busy village street in the city's historic district, Bethel Church, listed in the *National Register of Historic Places,* has played a central role in the spiritual life of the Black community.

DATE ESTABLISHED: 1843; African American congregation, 1860; present church, 1924

ADDRESS: 291 Park Avenue, Huntington

TELEPHONE: (516) 549-5014

VISITING HOURS: Sun. service, July–Aug. 10, rest of the year 11; Sun. school, July–Aug. 9, rest of the year 9:45

SOURCES: Telephone conversation May 1, 1994, Mrs. Jeanette Johns, wife of the pastor of Bethel A.M.E. Church. *The African American Presence in New York State History,* 118. Building Structure Inventory Form, Division for Historic Preservation New York State Parks and Recreation. *International Library of Negro Life and History,* 21. *The History of Bethel A.M.E. Church.*

Hurley

Historic Hurley

Hurley, New York, a village noted for its 250-year-old stone houses, once was the childhood home of outspoken Black activist Sojourner Truth. Although the Hardenberg house where she grew up is not open to the public, the town where slavery once existed still shows much about her early physical environment.

Before changing her name to Sojourner Truth as an adult, she was known as Isabella Baumfree. Although some believed that she was born a slave in New York's Ulster County around 1797, Sojourner claimed that she was born in Africa. She was brought to the Hardenberg house at an early age and spent the first eleven years of her life there. In the mid-1800s she spent years crusading for African American rights and women's rights, leaving a lasting impression on those who heard her speak.

Today Sojourner Truth's name is honored at several sites. In 1976 a plaque dedicated to Sojourner Truth was placed in front of the old courthouse on Wall Street in Kingston, New York. The library at State University of New York, New Paltz, is named for Sojourner Truth, and in 1986 a commemorative stamp was issued at the university in her honor.

Several houses in Hurley have links to Black history. The parsonage of the Reformed Church (1790), also called Crispell House, has a slave children's nook, an area where babies slept while their mothers did housework. A narrow stairway off the kitchen leads to the former slave quarters. Visitors may not enter the room because of the sloping stairs and the low ceiling, but they are able to look up the stairway.

The Dr. Richard Ten Eyck house (1780) allegedly was a stop on the underground railroad.

Two other houses, one on Old Route 109 and one on a side road in Hurley, are reputed to have been stations on the underground railroad. In 1790 a slave who lived at the Wyncoop house killed his master, Colonel Cornelius D. Wyncoop. Slave quarters can still be seen there.

Slave quarters for each stone house usually were located in the damp, dark basements; they consisted of cellars with several rooms. Men, women, and children slept in one room on straw or hay-covered boards placed on the cellar floor. Another room had a fireplace where cooking was done, including the food to be served to the household upstairs.

Each house usually had its own slave cemetery. Slave cemeteries were associated with the Cornelius Cool house, the William P. Cole house, the Mattys Ten Eyck house, and the Newkirk house. A cemetery on Eagles Nest, located on the top of the mountain off the Hurley Mountain Road, originated as a cemetery for white, Black, and Indian people.

In Hurley today twenty-five of its original houses from the 1700s are standing. The village has America's oldest concentration of stone houses, many with great hewn beams, floor and ceiling boards eighteen inches wide, sturdy oak doors, and thick stone walls in the basement.

A tour is sponsored by Hurley Reformed Church on Stone House Day, when about a dozen homes filled with antiques are open to the public. The tour includes the Ten Eyck house, which was part of the underground railway. A Revolutionary War encampment is set up in the streets, and there is a country fair in the church with crafts from the Revolutionary War era. Visitors may pick up a brochure giving directions for walking or driving around. They may see the village and the old Burial Ground on any day of the year.

DATE ESTABLISHED:	1700s; Hardenberg House, 1750; Hurley Reformed Church, 1850
ADDRESS:	Main Street, Hurley (exit 19 [Kingston] from New York State Thruway, take US 209 S toward Ellenville; Hurley is the first exit [right] on US 209 S, about 4 minutes from the Thruway; the Hurley Reformed Church is on the right)
TELEPHONE:	Hurley Reformed Church, (914) 331-4121
VISITING HOURS:	Interiors open only on Stone House Day (second Sat. in July) 10–4; walking tours all year 👬
FEES:	Tour of open houses: adults $10; children 12 and under, $1; senior citizens and students, $5; parking free; bus service to outlying houses, free
SOURCES:	Telephone conversation May 6, 1994, Reverend Stickley, Hurley Reformed Church. Olive M. Clearwater, co-historian for the town of Hurley. *Hurley in the Days of Slavery. Historic Hurley in the Mid-Hudson Valley. Walk, Drive Around Historic Hurley.* "Rocks 'n' Rolling, Hurley's Stones Also Its Homes."

Irvington

Madame Walker's Home

Villa Lewaro was built for Madame C. J. Walker, a nationally known cosmetics entrepreneur and possibly America's first Black, female self-made millionaire. In the early decades of the twentieth century, Madame Walker was attracted to New York City by its growing Black population and a myriad of commercial opportunities. She engaged Vertner Woodson Tandy, the first Black architect in New York State, to build an elegant three-story, red-brick townhouse at 108–110 West Thirty-sixth Street. The upper two stories served as her residence, while the lower floor housed her beauty shop and school. (The Countee Cullen Public Library later was built on this site.)

Later Madame Walker asked Tandy to build Villa Lewaro, the mansion that would become her new home. Born in Lexington, Kentucky, in the nineteenth century, he was the son of Henry A. Tandy, a prominent Lexington contractor who had erected some of that city's finest homes. The younger Tandy attended the Chandler Normal School in Lexington (see that listing in Lexington), studied architecture at Tuskegee Institute in Alabama, and continued his studies at Cornell University, where he completed the four-year program in three years. Tandy had his architectural office in New York City. Villa Lewaro is located on a beautiful five-acre site overlooking the Hudson River at Irvington-on-the-Hudson. Tandy designed the three-story residence as an Italian Renaissance palace with thirty-four luxurious rooms. The living room walls and ceiling gleamed with gold leaf, and gold-trimmed draperies hung at the windows. A marble stairway led to the second floor bedrooms and sleeping porches. The servants' quarters were on the third floor.

After Villa Lewaro was completed in 1918, Madame Walker began entertaining some of the most influential people of the day in her splendid mansion. Unfortunately, she died just eight months afterward. Her daughter, Lelia Walker Robinson, inherited the estate, which she later willed to the National Association for the Advancement of Colored People. Upkeep for the house was prohibitive, however, and in 1930 and 1931 the NAACP sold the house and auctioned off its contents. Villa Lewaro, originally valued at $400,000, sold for only $47,000 to a private nursing home. It is one of four African American sites designated as a Westchester County Tricentennial Historical Site.

DATE BUILT:	1918
ADDRESS:	N. Broadway, Greenburgh, Village of Irvington
VISITING HOURS:	Private, visitors may drive by
SOURCES:	NRHPINF. Telephone call June 13, 1994, Irvington Library. Westchester Historical Society. *"The Hills" in the Mid-Nineteenth Century.*

Ithaca

Alpha Phi Alpha Fraternity Founding Home

The house at 421 North Albany is associated with the founding of Alpha Phi Alpha Fraternity, a national Black fraternal organization. The fraternity had its first informal meeting at this house in 1905. The first African Americans who lived in the house were a group of seven students from Cornell University who used the house as a dormitory. Today Cornell students who are members of the fraternity still come by to see and photograph their founding house.

DATE ESTABLISHED: 1905

ADDRESS: 421 N. Albany, Ithaca

VISITING HOURS: Private, visitors may drive by

SOURCES: Telephone conversation May 22, 1994, Steven A. Centeno, community resident. Margaret Hobbie, director, DeWitt Historical Society. *Ithaca's Neighborhoods.*

Alex Haley Birthplace

The late Alex Haley (1921–1992), author of *Roots,* was born in the Cascadilla Street house and spent the first few weeks of his life here. The family included young Alex; his father, Simon, who was a graduate student; and his mother, Bertha.

Six weeks after Alex's birth, Alex and his mother went to stay with his grandparents in Henning, Tennessee, while Simon Haley stayed behind to complete his graduate studies. Simon Haley later came to Tennessee where he operated the Palmer family business. (See the Alex Haley Museum listing in Henning, Tennessee.)

DATE OF SIGNIFICANCE: 1921

ADDRESS: 212 Cascadilla Street (between Albany and Geneva Streets), Ithaca

VISITING HOURS: Private, visitors may drive by

SOURCES: Margaret Hobbie, director, DeWitt Historical Society. Telephone conversation May 22, 1994, Steven A. Centeno, community resident. *Ithaca's Neighborhoods.*

St. James African Methodist Episcopal Zion Church

St. James A.M.E. Zion Church was established by African Americans who at one time attended segregated services in a Methodist Episcopal church, that designated them as the "colored class" of the church. Upset by this discrimination, the Black members withdrew to found a church of their own. Ithaca was accessible to free Black people from different counties of New York State.

Between 1823 and 1825 the congregation had to meet in a private home but was able to build its own church on this site in the next decade. Peter Webb, the only slave in Ithaca ever allowed to purchase his freedom, bought the land for the church after he became a free person. From its earliest years, St. James Church was a station on the underground railroad. Church members along with white residents of Ithaca helped some fleeing slaves move to safety in Canada; they also provided assistance for those who chose to stay in Ithaca. One of the distinguished pastors was Jermaine Wesley Loguen, a man who had escaped from slavery in Tennessee. In the 1840s Loguen was active in the underground railroad in Syracuse, where he was a friend of Frederick Douglass. Douglass visited St.

James on one occasion. Another famous guest was Harriet Tubman, who attended St. James many times.

St. James continued its history of community involvement. In 1913 several Cornell students, unhappy at the discrimination they encountered in campus fraternities, founded the Alpha Phi Alpha Fraternity in the basement of St. James Church. More recently, church members have been involved in neighborhood preservation programs.

The 1830s construction date makes this the oldest church building in Ithaca, the oldest African American church in Tompkins County, and possibly one of the oldest churches built in the United States by an A.M.E. Zion congregation. The church started out as a modest wood structure on a high stone foundation. A second story—a wood frame structure—was added in 1861, and a belfry added about 1904. Steam heat and electricity were introduced in 1913, and a large rose window was installed in 1945. Although the church has expanded many times, the original stones are still visible in its foundation. Four streets near the church still have nineteenth-century homes of African Americans. The city of Ithaca plans to designate the church and community as a historic preservation site.

DATE BUILT:	1833
ADDRESS:	116–118 Cleveland Avenue, Ithaca
TELEPHONE:	(607) 272-4053
VISITING HOURS:	Sun. service, 11; by appointment Mon.–Fri.
SOURCES:	Margaret Hobbie, director, DeWitt Historical Society. Telephone conversation Jan 24, 1995, Linda Thornhill, wife of pastor, St. James Church. NRHPINF. *Ithaca's Neighborhoods,* 88–90.

Lake Placid

John Brown Farm State Historic Site *

The John Brown Farm state historic site, high in the Adirondack Mountains of New York, is the home and gravesite of the white abolitionist firebrand John Brown (1800–1859). He was born in Connecticut, grew up in Ohio, and later lived in Pennsylvania.

As a youth, Brown had seen a Black boy who was his friend beaten cruelly, an event that led him to believe that slavery was a sin against God. In 1855 Brown and five of his sons moved to Kansas, where Brown established a colony along the Osawatomie River. "Bleeding Kansas" had become a battleground for rival forces in favor of or against the institution of slavery. Brown was shaken by the raid a group of proslavery fanatics staged in 1856 on the capital of Kansas, Lawrence, which was noted for its abolitionist sympathies. In reprisal, Brown and some of his followers murdered five proslavery men on the banks of the Pottawatamie River a few days later. In 1859 Brown led the famous raid on Harpers Ferry, Virginia (now West Virginia). He was accompanied by twenty-two men, including five free Black men; his aim was to start an uprising that would lead to the overthrow of slavery in the South. Brown thought of himself as an Old Testament prophet and God's chosen instrument to eradicate the sin of slaveholding. Although the raid captured the town and its federal arsenal, most of the Black people in the area refused to join Brown's forces, believing that Brown's efforts would prove unsuccessful. In the end Brown and his men were besieged by a force of U.S. Marines led by Robert E. Lee. Many of Brown's party were killed in the fighting. Afterward, Brown was hanged for his rebellion against the state of Virginia. His death led to a wave of fear among white Southerners against the abolitionists, but in the North Brown often was regarded as a martyr. The raid on Harpers Ferry fueled the passions that led to the Civil War.

Although Brown's name will be forever connected with Harpers Ferry, he regarded North Elba (now Lake Placid) as his home. A well-known abolitionist named Gerrit Smith offered parcels of his vast land holdings in this area during the 1840s to free Black men and women. This land, it was thought, would give the free people an opportunity to develop farms. In 1849 John Brown and his family moved to North Elba to help the Black settlers. Brown surveyed the land and helped the settlers build homes and plant crops. Unfortunately, the climate was harsh and there were too few markets for the settlement's products. As a result, the settlement did not survive.

The site contains John Brown's cabin, which was his last home. It also encompasses Brown's grave, the graves of two of his sons killed at Harpers Ferry, and the graves of several of his followers in the ill-fated raid.

DATE ESTABLISHED: 1850, 1895

ADDRESS: John Brown Road (3/4 mile off NY 73, about 2 miles south of Lake Placid), Lake Placid

TELEPHONE: (518) 523-3900

VISITING HOURS: May 12–Oct. 31, Wed.–Sat. 10–5, Sun. 1–5; closed Mon.–Tues. ♟♟

FEES: None

SOURCES: Telephone conversation April 30, 1994, Mrs. Alice Cotter, wife of superintendent, John Brown Farm. Ben Kroup, New York State Office of Parks, Recreation and Historic Preservation, Bureau of Historic Sites-Peebles Island, Waterford, New York. *John Brown Farm. National Register of Historic Places*, 502.

New York

Abyssinian Baptist Church

Adam Clayton Powell Sr. was born in 1865 in a one-room log cabin. Robert E. Lee surrendered at Appomattox, in Virginia, just twenty-five days later. One of sixteen children, he was the son of a former slave. The family was poor and could not afford regular schooling, but young Powell was eager to learn when he could attend school. The family moved to West Virginia when Powell was about ten years old; after attending a revival meeting there, he decided to become a Baptist minister. He graduated from Virginia Union University (then Wayland Academy) and entered Yale Divinity School. In 1908 he was selected as pastor of the Abyssinian Baptist Church in New York City.

Abyssinian Church was established in 1808 when a group of African Americans refused to continue to sit in the racially segregated First Baptist Church. They withdrew their membership and organized their own church, meeting at various locations in the early 1900s. Although the church was small and deeply in debt, within a few years the Reverend Dr. Adam Clayton Powell Sr. had built it into one of the world's largest Protestant congregations. By 1920 the congregation had purchased lots on 138th Street; three years later it dedicated a new church and community house built at a cost of more than $330,000. Powell, who adopted many of the ideas of the influential Black leader Marcus Garvey, continued to lead the congregation until his retirement in 1937. He died in 1953.

Adam Clayton Powell Jr. was born in 1908 in New Haven, Connecticut. The only son of Mattie Fletcher Powell and Adam Powell Sr., he was noted for his intelligence, his confidence, and his oratorical skill. The young Powell attended Colgate University, graduating in 1930 and starting his career as assistant minister during the Great Depression. He led the free-meal program at Abyssinian Baptist, coordinated relief efforts throughout Harlem, and successfully garnered jobs for African Americans. The junior Powell continued to study and earned his master's degree in religious education from Columbia University in 1931.

Adam Clayton Powell Jr. succeeded his father as pastor of Abyssinian Baptist Church and served as its pastor from 1939 until 1971. Well known as a minister, Powell also was a fighter for civil rights. He organized boycotts to influence white merchants in Harlem to hire Black employees. As New York City's first Black city council member he initiated legislation to improve social and economic conditions for Black citizens. First elected to Congress in 1944, he wrote more than fifty pieces of social legislation during his time in office. Powell's flamboyant style and fearlessly outspoken speech earned him the enmity of many people, even of some Black leaders who felt that his forthright style was hurting their cause. After being stripped of his congressional seniority for defecting from the Democratic Party and for his abrasive behavior (and while he was being investigated by the U.S. Department of Justice for alleged misuse of federal funds), Powell steadfastly maintained that he was targeted because of racism and because of his power as a Black man. In 1967 the full House voted to exclude him from his congressional seat. Although the Supreme Court ruled in 1969 that the exclusion was unconstitutional, Powell did not return to serve in Washington. In 1970 he lost the primary election to another Black man, Charles Rangel. In 1971 Adam

Clayton Powell Jr. retired from the Abyssinian Baptist Church. He died in 1972 at the age of sixty-three. In recognition of his many positive contributions, the stretch of Seventh Avenue that goes through Harlem was renamed Adam Clayton Powell Jr. Boulevard.

DATE ESTABLISHED: Congregation, 1808; present building, 1923

ADDRESS: 132 W. 138th Street (between Lenox Avenue and Adam Clayton Powell Boulevard), New York

TELEPHONE: (212) 862-7474

VISITING HOURS: Mon.–Fri. 9–5, call in advance to arrange a visit

SOURCES: Telephone call to this site May 1, 1994. *The African American Encyclopedia*, vol. 1, 9–10. *The African American Presence in New York State History. Webster's New Biographical Dictionary*, 814. "Adam Clayton Powell Jr.," 1273–6.

Apollo Theater

For more than four decades, the Apollo Theater, one of America's leading entertainment centers, provided a premier performance hall for Black performers and served as a center of Black cultural awareness. At one time 125th Street was famed as the "Main Street" of Black Harlem.

The Apollo originally was built as a burlesque theater catering to a primarily white clientele. In 1934 two white businessmen purchased the building, renamed it the Apollo Theater, and began presenting a variety show featuring leading Black entertainers. Louis Armstrong, Duke Ellington, Count Basie, and Ella Fitzgerald were among those who performed at the Apollo. The Apollo's shows, which included drama, dance, comedy, gospel, blues, jazz, and rhythm and blues, led to Harlem's becoming known as the premier Black cultural and intellectual center in America.

The changing economy eventually led to the closing of the theater, but there was a later rebirth. After a multimillion-dollar renovation in 1989, the Apollo reopened, once again featuring the giants of entertainment and show business.

DATE BUILT: 1914

ADDRESS: 253 W. 125th Street, at Adam Clayton Powell Jr. Boulevard, New York

TELEPHONE: (212) 749-5838

VISITING HOURS: Contact theater for schedule of performances; New Amateur Night, Wed. 7:30

SOURCES: *The African American Presence in New York State History. Four Regional History Surveys*, 114.

Ralph Bunche House

Dr. Ralph Bunche, a man born in poverty in 1904 in Detroit, Michigan, became known worldwide as a scholar, the highest ranking African American in the United Nations Secretariat, and the first Black recipient of the Nobel Peace Prize.

Bunche's father was a barber, and his mother an amateur musician. The family moved to Toledo, Ohio, then to Albuquerque, New Mexico. However, both parents had poor health, and they died when Ralph was around twelve years old. Then Ralph, his sister, his grandmother, and his aunts moved to Los Angeles, California. (See the listing for the Ralph Bunche House in Los Angeles.) An outstanding student, Bunche won medals for debate, civics, English composition, and athletics. He won an athletic scholarship to the University of California, where he was elected to Phi Beta Kappa and graduated *summa cum laude*.

Bunche then studied at Harvard University, where he earned a master's degree in 1928 and a Ph.D. in 1934. Between his master's and doctoral studies, Bunche taught at Howard University, where he organized the political science department. He later returned to Howard as a full professor and assistant to the president. He received grants to study at the London School of Economics and the Capetown University of the Union of South Africa. Bunche's work took him on a world tour from which he gained expert knowledge about different cultures.

Bunche's life was marked by many achievements. He assisted Gunnar Myrdal in research for a comprehensive study of African American life in the United States. He was the first African American to hold a desk in the State Department. He also helped to draw up the United Nations charter.

In 1948 Bunche became secretary of the Palestine Commission. One of his greatest achievements came in 1949 when his negotiations brought an end to the Arab-Israeli War. When news of the armistice agreement reached the United States, Bunche began to receive honors from all over the world, including more than thirty honorary degrees and awards. During this period, in 1950 he was awarded the Nobel Peace Prize. Continuing to act as a catalyst for peace, Bunche was appointed undersecretary general of the United Nations. He died in 1971.

The Bunche residence is a two and one-half–story home in the Kew Gardens section of Queens, New York. The English Tudor Renaissance country house has a steep gable and a main roof with slate shingles and dormers. Wood, brick, and textured stucco were used in the construction. Many interior rooms remain furnished as they were when Bunche lived in the house.

DATE OF SIGNIFICANCE:	1952–1971
ADDRESS:	115–125 Grosvenor Road, Kew Gardens, vicinity of Queens, New York
VISITING HOURS:	Private, visitors may drive or walk by
SOURCES:	NRHPINF. *The African American Encyclopedia*, vol. 1, 241–3. Academic American Encyclopedia.

Center for African Art

The Center for African Art's mission is to create an understanding and appreciation of African art based on a cultural, cross-cultural, and historical perspective. The museum consists of two adjoining turn-of-the-century townhouses with exhibition space in small galleries on three levels. Hallways connecting the galleries afford additional viewing space.

The museum has a variety of exhibits. The exhibit entitled *Yoruba: Nine Centuries of African Art and Thought* displays art from the Yoruba people of West Africa, including ninth- and tenth-century objects excavated from archaeological sites in Nigeria. Among the works are naturalistic terra-cotta and bronze heads, some thought to portray African kings, called *onis*.

DATE ESTABLISHED:	1983
ADDRESS:	54 E. Sixty-eighth Street, New York
TELEPHONE:	(212) 966-1313
VISITING HOURS:	Tues.–Fri. 10–5, Sat. 11–5, Sun. noon–5; closed Mon. 👥
FEES:	Adults, $2.50; senior citizens, students, and children, $1.50
SOURCES:	Johanna Cooper for Carol Thompson, The Center for African Art. *Black Arts New York.*

Will Marion Cook House

The Will Cook residence is located in a neighborhood of Victorian townhouses built in 1891. So many outstanding, fashionable, and achieving Black African Americans lived in the community that it became known locally as "Strivers Row." Composer Will Marion Cook lived in Strivers Row in a three-story, buff-brick townhouse on West 138th Street. Cook was born in Washington, D.C., in 1869 to educated and talented parents. At the age of thirteen he began studying violin at the Oberlin Conservatory of Music. Three years later, he received funds to study violin in Germany, where he remained for nine years.

Although skilled in classical music, Cook developed interests in musical comedy and ragtime. He reached his peak as a musical composer between 1900 and 1910. Cook developed a Black jazz band and helped to organize the Clef Club's Syncopated Orchestra, comprising 125 Black musicians. When he died in 1944, he left an outstanding legacy of his compositions, innovative musical performances, and assistance for other creative artists.

Cook's residence on Strivers Row has Palladian windows on the second floor and wrought-iron balconies extending from the bottom of the first-floor windows as well as wrought-iron handrails on the steps. A cement post on one gate still bears the stern warning "Walk Your Horses," a relic from the days when exuberant ones were tempted to enter the gate at high speed. All four floors have been used since 1976 for a medical practice. The neighborhood, designated a historic district by the New York Landmarks Commission, is listed in the *National Register of Historic Places.*

DATE OF SIGNIFICANCE: Cook residence, 1918–1944

ADDRESS: 221 W. 138th Street, New York

VISITING HOURS: Private, visitors may walk or drive by

SOURCES: Telephone conversation May 14, 1994, Dr. Calvin Innis, community resident. NRHPINF.

Matthew Henson Residence
Dunbar Apartments

The Dunbar Apartments—a six-building, garden-apartment complex named for the poet Paul Lawrence Dunbar—was the first large cooperative in New York built for Black residents. The six structures contain some 511 apartments and occupy an entire block in Harlem. The Dunbar Apartments are significant architecturally and for their association with the following African American achievers who at one time lived here: Countee Cullen, poet; W. E. B. Du Bois, Fisk and Harvard University graduate, scholar, and writer; A. Philip Randolph, leader of the Brotherhood of Sleeping Car Porters and civil rights activist; actor Paul Robeson; and dancer Bill (Bojangles) Robinson. Famed explorer Matthew Henson, who is believed to be the first man to reach the North Pole, was another distinguished resident.

Matthew Henson was born in 1866 on a Maryland farm. As a young man he worked as a cabin attendant on a merchant ship. He received his first formal education from his ship's captain. When Henson was eighteen, he met U.S. Navy Lt. Robert Edwin Peary (1856–1920) and began working for him. Henson, who was highly skilled as a seaman, became one of the most highly valued members of Peary's team. Henson was able to communicate well with the Inuit people and saved Peary's life on several occasions.

In 1909 Henson was selected by Peary over five white men to accompany him on the famous expedition to the North Pole, a journey of 450 miles over ice and snow. Henson served as the trailblazer of the team that also included four Inuit explorers. Henson's task was to move ahead of the others, mark the path, build igloos at resting places, and prepare the way for the others. As a result, he was the first man to reach the North Pole. Henson recognized that when his compass no longer registered north, he had arrived at the goal, and he had the honor of placing the American flag at the Pole.

Even though Peary received many honors for this accomplishment, Henson's work was ignored for years. To support himself, Henson had to take jobs parking cars, and he worked as a messenger for the U.S. Customs Bureau in New York City, earning $900 a year at age forty-seven. Some honors and belated recognition finally came when President Truman honored Henson in 1953. President Eisenhower also cited Henson's accomplishments in 1955.

Matthew Henson lived at the Dunbar from 1925 until his death in 1955. In 1961 the state of Maryland, Henson's birthplace, placed a plaque in the State House to honor Henson as codiscoverer of the North Pole. Dunbar Apartments, the Matthew Henson residence, honored the explorer with a tablet at its Seventh Avenue entrance. The site is listed in the *National Register of Historic Places.*

DATE OF SIGNIFICANCE: Henson residence, 1925–1955

ADDRESS: 246 W. 150th Street, Apt. 3F, New York

VISITING HOURS: Private, visitors may walk or drive by

SOURCES: NRHPINF. City of New York Landmarks Preservation Commission. *The African American Encyclopedia*, vol. 3, 752–3.

Langston Hughes House

James Langston Hughes (1902–1967) was born in Joplin, Missouri. His parents separated when he was young, and he went to live with his grandmother, who told him stories about her husband, one of the Black men killed in John Brown's raid at Harpers Ferry.

Hughes worked in a variety of jobs during his lifetime—as a seaman, laundry sorter, waiter, bus-boy, and gardener. He lived for a while in Mexico and France, and studied at Lincoln University in Missouri. In 1926 his first book of poetry, *The Weary Blues,* called attention to his great literary ability. He gained special recognition for his poem "The Negro Speaks of Rivers." Hughes produced many other works, including the lyrics for the 1947 opera *Street Scene,* composed by Kurt Weill.

In the 1920s and 1930s a literary movement called the Harlem Renaissance highlighted the creative work of Black authors and artists. This flowering of literature and art focused on the question of Black identity, and Hughes was one of the movement's foremost figures.

The house on East 127th Street is typical of Harlem row houses built after the Civil War. Langston Hughes lived there during the last twenty years of his life. It is the best symbol of his association with Harlem and the Harlem Renaissance group.

DATE OF SIGNIFICANCE: Hughes residence, 1947–1967

ADDRESS: 20 E. 127th Street, New York

VISITING HOURS: Private, visitors may drive or walk by

SOURCES: *The African American Presence in New York State History,* 130. *Webster's New Biographical Dictionary,* 496.

James Weldon Johnson House

Civil rights leader and writer James Weldon Johnson (he changed his middle name from William to Weldon in 1913) was born in 1871 in Jacksonville, Florida. He grew up in a middle-class home. His father was a minister and a headwaiter, and his mother was a musician and music teacher. Although the Johnson boys attended the segregated Stanton School in Jacksonville, their parents taught James and their other son, John Rosamond, about literature, music, and racial pride. James never forgot the lessons about his heritage, and he set high goals for himself. Jacksonville offered no secondary education for Black students, so James attended a secondary school operated by Atlanta University and then earned his college degree in 1894 at Atlanta University.

Johnson was appointed principal of Stanton Grade School in Jacksonville and served in that capacity for four years. With a few friends he founded the *Daily American,* the first African American paper in Jacksonville. He also studied law and in 1899 was the first Black person admitted to the Florida bar. During a trip to New York in the summer of 1899 and meeting many artists in the theatrical world, he began to develop his talent for music. After returning to Jacksonville, Johnson wrote the lyrics to "Lift Every Voice and Sing," which later became known as the Negro national anthem.

Johnson and his brother returned to New York in 1900 and began a highly successful seven-year stint as the composers of more than 200 songs. The process of collaborating with others to write a campaign song for Theodore Roosevelt spurred an interest in political activity. In 1907 President Roosevelt appointed Johnson U.S. consul in Venezuela. In the next years he completed a novel, *The Autobiography of an Ex-Colored Man,* and became contributing editor of the *New York Age,* the city's oldest Black-owned newspaper.

Johnson joined the National Association for the Advancement of Colored People in 1916. He soon advanced, promoted first to field secretary, then to executive secretary, a position he held through 1930. In this capacity he increased NAACP membership dramatically by organizing branches in large cities in the South, a solid achievement considering the threats of reprisals that faced Southern African Americans for joining chapters. Johnson crusaded to halt segregation and lynchings, lobbying in support of the Dyer Anti-Lynching Bill. Even though the bill did not pass, he continued to confront Americans with the brutality of the lynchings that were taking place, and he vigorously promoted integration and political and cultural equality for African Americans. Throughout his career he stressed the view that Black Americans were active, creative, and important forces in American life.

While working with the NAACP, Johnson continued writing, publishing his own poems as well as an anthology, the *Book of American Negro Poetry.* He and his brother published two anthologies of African American spirituals. His musical work *The Creation* was produced at Town Hall, accompanied by members of the Boston Symphony Orchestra.

Johnson House is used today for a medical practice. James Weldon Johnson—author, musician, and activist—resided in this brick, five-story apartment building for more than thirteen years between 1925 and 1938, during his service as national executive secretary of the NAACP. After Johnson died in an automobile accident in 1938, he was widely mourned.

DATE OF SIGNIFICANCE: Johnson residence, 1925–1938
ADDRESS: 187 W. 135th Street, New York
VISITING HOURS: Private, visitors may walk or drive by
SOURCES: NRHPINF. Telephone conversation May 14, 1994, Dr. Fred Carter, community resident. *The Black 100*, 103–7. *The African American Encyclopedia*, vol. 3, 866–9.

Claude McKay Residence

The poet Claude McKay resided during the 1940s in the Young Men's Christian Association building. Born in Jamaica in 1890, he had moved as a young man to the United States. McKay worked at many odd jobs until he finally realized that his calling was to be a writer.

After World War I he noted with sorrow that Black soldiers who had served honorably in the U.S. armed forces returned home to face racial attacks and lynchings. Moved by this injustice, he wrote a stirring poem, "If We Must Die," later read by Winston Churchill in the British House of Commons. McKay's rousing poem was a catalyst that inspired many artists and writers of the Harlem Renaissance. Black writers finally were recognized for their creativity and ability to describe in their own words the African American experience in America.

The Great Depression was a time of financial difficulty for McKay, who also suffered emotionally. In 1937 when he published his autobiography, *A Long Way from Home*, his personal fortunes were very low. By 1942 he lacked money, he was in poor health, and he was unable to find work. He suffered a stroke, and although his last years were spent in poverty, he continued to write until his death in 1948 at the age of fifty-eight.

Claude McKay's home from 1941 to 1946 was in the Young Men's Christian Association building on 135th Street, which had residential space on its upper levels. A small plaque by the elevator confirms that

McKay lived here. Many well-known African Americans also lived in the hotel at the time. The fourteen-story red brick building contains a chapel, branch offices, conference rooms, and a basement kitchen. The site is listed in the *National Register of Historic Places*.

DATE OF SIGNIFICANCE: McKay residence, 1941–1946
ADDRESS: 180 W. 135th Street, New York
TELEPHONE: Harlem Branch of the YMCA, (212) 281-4100
VISITING HOURS: Private, visitors may walk or drive by
SOURCES: NRHPINF. Telephone call May 9, 1994, to site. "If We Must Die."

Florence Mills House

Florence Mills (1895–1927) was an internationally known entertainer in the early twentieth century. Although she had appeared regularly at the Keith and Orpheum Theaters before 1901, she gained wide recognition that year as a result of her performance in the musical *Shuffle Along*, that opened at the Sixty-third Street Theater in New York. The role of Ruth Little was to have been played by Gertrude Saunders, but Saunders became ill and Mills was chosen to replace her. The show made entertainment history as a musical composed, directed, and performed by African Americans, and Mills gained fame throughout the entertainment world for her stellar performance.

ADDRESS: 220 W. 135th Street, New York
VISITING HOURS: Private, visitors may walk or drive by
SOURCE: NRHPINF.

New York Amsterdam News Building

The *New York Amsterdam News* was located at one time in the center structure of a group of four-story row houses. The narrow structure—approximately fifteen feet wide at the street side—was the newspaper's second home. James H. Anderson founded the periodical in his home in 1909 using a few sheets of paper, a pencil, and a four-by-five-foot table. The newspaper met a need in the Black community. The National Association for the Advancement of Colored People was organized during this period, and the African American community was shifting away from the accommodationist philosophy of Booker T. Washington to the social action views advocated by W. E. B. Du Bois and William Monroe Trotter.

Impelled by racially motivated lynchings that were common occurrences at the time, the *New York Amsterdam News* condemned public officials for their failure to end these atrocities. When the Dyer Anti-Lynching Bill was defeated, the newspaper spoke out, maintaining that the bill still lived on in many hearts and minds.

By 1916 the journal needed more space and moved to Seventh Avenue (now Adam Clayton Powell Jr. Boulevard). There it expanded from a local paper in Harlem to one with nationwide appeal. Editors continued to condemn the discrimination and injustice faced by African Americans and provided a pow-

erful voice for African Americans in Harlem and throughout the United States.

In 1938 growth in circulation caused the newspaper to move again, this time to its present location on Eighth Avenue, where it has continued to be an effective voice for more than fifty-five years. The building on Adam Clayton Powell Jr. Boulevard, home of a distinguished Black newspaper for more than twenty-two years, is listed in the *National Register of Historic Places.*

DATE OF SIGNIFICANCE:	1916–1938
ADDRESS:	2293 Adam Clayton Powell Jr. Boulevard, New York
TELEPHONE:	Newspaper, (212) 932-7400
VISITING HOURS:	Private, visitors may drive by; newspaper operation at its current address, 2340 Frederick Douglass Boulevard, Thurs.–Fri. 11:30–12:30 or by appointment
SOURCES:	NRHPINF. Telephone conversation May 12, 1994, Selvin Michael, vice president and comptroller.

New York Historical Society

The New York Historical Society contains materials associated with African American history among its collections. The extensive pamphlet collection in the society's library, which dates from the colonial and Revolutionary War periods through the Civil War, is one of the largest ever assembled on American slavery and the abolitionist movement.

DATE ESTABLISHED:	1804
ADDRESS:	170 Central Park West, New York
TELEPHONE:	(212) 873-3400
VISITING HOURS:	Tues.–Sat. and some holidays 10–5
FEES:	Nonmembers, $1
SOURCE:	Brochure forwarded by Mary Carey, reference librarian, New York Historical Society.

Paul Robeson Residence

Paul Robeson (1898–1976) was an outstanding American scholar, actor, concert artist, and humanitarian. Because he took an uncompromising stand for justice, he was widely ostracized and shunned in his own country. In spite of the hostility he endured and the damage done to his reputation, Robeson ended his career as one of the most-respected men of the century.

Paul Robeson's father, William Drew Robeson, was a runaway slave who had demonstrated his own brand of courage by fleeing to freedom. He later earned a college degree, became a Methodist minister, and married Maria Louisa Bustill, a schoolteacher. Paul was born in Princeton, New Jersey, the youngest of eight children. Because his mother died when Paul was six years old, his father raised the family by himself, requiring excellence from each of the children.

Robeson entered Rutgers University in 1915, one of the first African Americans to study at that school. In spite of racism he encountered at Rutgers, he excelled in many fields. With twelve letters in sports, he was named all-American end in football and elected to the Phi Beta Kappa society. Robeson then entered Columbia University Law School, obtaining his law degree in 1923. About that time he married a chemist, Eslanda Cardozo Goode (1896–1965). Eslanda was brilliant in her own right. She was the granddaughter of Francis Lewis Cardozo, a graduate of Glasgow University, founder of the Avery Normal Institute (see the listing in Charleston, South Carolina), and state treasurer in South Carolina during Reconstruction years. Graduating at the age of sixteen from a high school in Chicago, Eslanda placed third in statewide examinations and received a full-tuition scholarship to the University of Illinois. There she majored in chemistry. After her junior year she transferred to Columbia University with plans to enter the field of medicine. She was the first Black staff member (in histological chemistry) at the Presbyterian Hospital of Columbia University. She met Paul Robeson while working at the hospital.

Despite his brilliance, Robeson had difficulties in the practice of law mainly because of racial prejudice against Black attorneys. Recognizing her husband's artistic talents, Eslanda urged him to become an actor and singer. Robeson joined the Provincetown Players and achieved a resounding success in New York and London in the title role of Eugene O'Neill's play, *The Emperor Jones*. He also played this same role in a film. Robeson's magnificent bass voice was noted by Larry Brown, an arranger of Black spirituals; this encounter was the impetus that made Robeson a star on the concert stage. He presented Black spirituals in Greenwich Village and on other stages around the country. He was acclaimed for his rendition of "Ol' Man River" in *Show Boat*. His performance in *Othello* on Broadway in 1943 was a memorable event.

Robeson, who was proud of his African American heritage, denounced Hollywood for the way in which films portrayed Black people, and he refused demeaning roles. Due to his demonstrations against segregation and his participation in pacifist and Communist-sponsored peace meetings, a shadow fell upon Robeson's career. When a Senate Judiciary Committee called upon him to testify in 1948, he refused on the basis of violation of his privacy. As a result, concert halls around the country were closed to him and the U.S. State Department refused to renew his passport. He accepted the Stalin Peace Prize in 1952 and settled in England with his family in 1958, the same year that a Supreme Court ruling restored his passport.

Later, in 1963, Robeson returned to the United States. Despite poor health, he was honored on his seventy-fifth birthday by a near-capacity crowd at Carnegie Hall in a three-hour celebration. He died in January 1976 at the age of seventy-seven.

DATE OF SIGNIFICANCE: Robeson residence, 1939 to 1941
ADDRESS: 555 Edgecombe Avenue, New York
VISITING HOURS: Private, visitors may walk or drive by
SOURCES: NRHPINF. *The African American Encyclopedia*, vol. 5, 1376–80.

Schomburg Center for Research in Black Culture *

The Schomburg Center for Research in Black Culture is the world's most complete collection of books, photographs, rare manuscripts, films, art, and other artifacts relating to African American culture. Individuals and institutions from the United States and abroad use the collection's more than 5 million items.

The three-story stone building in the middle of Harlem originally was the 135th Street branch of the New York Public Library. When the library opened in 1905, the neighborhood was a fashionable, predominantly Jewish community. African Americans were beginning to move into the area; within fifteen years this was one of the most important Black communities in the United States. Many Black residents came to New York to fill the labor shortage created by World War I. They settled in Harlem, and many of them patronized this library, which had begun to focus on the Black experience in America.

Ernestine Rose became the branch librarian in 1920. Five years later when the Harlem Renaissance was in full flower, the Department of Negro Literature and History was established here. In 1926 its collection won national acclaim with the addition of the personal library of the distinguished Black scholar Arthur A. Schomburg.

Schomburg, who was born in Puerto Rico in 1874, came to New York City in 1901. Carnegie funds were used to acquire his collection of materials on African American culture. Included were more than 5,000 volumes, 3,000 manuscripts, and 2,000 etchings and paintings. Schomburg served as curator of the department from 1932 until his death in 1938; the collection was renamed in his honor in 1940.

The Schomburg Center is engaged today in a massive expansion project. The landmark building housing the original collections will have study and storage space for special collections, an exhibition hall, the restored American Negro Theatre, and a new auditorium. The Schomburg Center is listed in the *National Register of Historic Places.*

DATE ESTABLISHED:	1905; as center, 1926
ADDRESS:	135th Street at Malcolm X Boulevard, New York
TELEPHONE:	(212) 491-2200
VISITING HOURS:	Mon.–Wed. noon–8, Thurs.–Sat. 10–6, Sun. (exhibits only) 1–5
FEES:	None
SOURCES:	Brochure from the Schomburg Center. NRHPINF. Telephone call to site, April 30, 1994. *The African American Presence in New York State History,* 12.

Studio Museum of Harlem

The Studio Museum of Harlem is an outstanding museum devoted to the art and artifacts of Black America and the African Diaspora. Incorporated in 1967 as a working space for artists, the museum quickly became the place to view the work of emerging and prominent Black and Hispanic artists.

In 1979 the museum received the gift of a half-empty, 60,000-square-foot office building, which was converted into the acclaimed Studio Museum. Serving the Harlem community, New York, the United States, and a growing international community as well, the Studio Museum has evolved into an internationally renowned cultural institution. Museum programs include temporary exhibitions; a permanent collection; and a schedule of interpretive, educational, and developmental programs.

DATE ESTABLISHED:	1967
ADDRESS:	144 W. 125th Street, New York
TELEPHONE:	(212) 864-4500
VISITING HOURS:	Wed.–Fri. 10–5, Sat.–Sun. 1–6; tours by appointment; closed Mon.–Tues. 👫
FEES:	Adults, $5; students and senior citizens, $3; children under 13, $1; members, free
SOURCE:	George Calderaro, public relations coordinator, Studio Museum in Harlem. Telephone call to site, Aug. 8, 1995.

The 369th Historical Society

The 369th Historical Society is named in honor of the 369th Regiment, an all-Black military unit that served with great distinction in France in World War I. The 369th Veterans Association housed at this site on Fifth Avenue preserves the achievements of Black Americans who served in the United States military and houses the largest collection of this type on the East Coast.

The 369th Regiment, originally called the Fifteenth Infantry Regiment, New York National Guard, was the first U.S. regiment to serve as an integral part of a foreign army. In 1918 the unit was designated the 369th Infantry and was sent to France. The U.S. government did not want to recognize a fully Black fighting unit; therefore, the 369th became the only unit in the United States to fight in World War I under a state flag—the men carried the state flag of New York throughout the war. The first Allied regiment to reach the Rhine River, the 369th fought continuously for 191 days on the front line and never had a man captured, never lost a trench, and never lost a foot of territory. The French government awarded the entire unit the Croix de Guerre for heroism and awarded the Croix de Guerre and the

Legion of Honor to 171 individual men for exceptional gallantry under fire. The 369th was the first combat regiment to arrive home in America and the first to march up Fifth Avenue under the Victory Arch.

The 369th Veterans Association is located on the first floor in this building and the museum is on the second level. During Black history month many school groups come to the museum to hear talks about African American veterans and to see the displays of old equipment and the photographs of African American officers from World War I through the 1990–1991 Desert Storm campaign.

ADDRESS:	2366 Fifth Avenue (142nd Street), New York
TELEPHONE:	(212) 281-3308
SOURCES:	Telephone conversation Jan. 27, 1995, Gladstone A. Dell, national vice president, 369th Veterans Association. *The Historical and Cultural Atlas of African Americans*, 116–17. *The African American Presence in New York State History.*

Port Chester

Bush-Lyon Homestead

The Bush-Lyon Homestead, one of the few residences in Port Chester constructed in pre-Revolutionary War days, contains a rare example in a northern state of slave quarters, which were part of a group of outbuildings to the northeast of the main house. Although the frame, two-story slave house is not open to the public, plans are under way to make the interior accessible. Other outbuildings at the site, which is operated by the Port Chester Historical Society, include a carriage house and a corn crib.

DATE BUILT:	1750
ADDRESS:	479 King Street (Lyon Park), Port Chester
TELEPHONE:	(914) 939-8918
VISITING HOURS:	Thurs. 1:30–4; closed holidays 👫
FEES:	Donations accepted
SOURCES:	Goldie Solomon, president, Port Chester Historical Society. Susan A. Morison, director, The Rye Historical Society. Telephone conversation May 11, 1994, James Charles, caretaker.

Rochester

Susan B. Anthony House
National Historic Landmark

Born in Adams, Massachusetts, the daughter of a Quaker abolitionist, Susan B. Anthony (1820–1906) was a prominent white abolitionist, temperance worker, and leader of the movement for women's rights. The Anthony family arrived in Rochester, New York, in the 1840s. Anthony was a teacher and an agitator for women's suffrage and equal pay for women. In 1848 she met Frederick Douglass, a well-known Black antislavery speaker. Members of the Douglass and Anthony families became friends and often met to discuss political issues, including the need to put an end to slavery in the United States.

Anthony's brother, Merritt Anthony, settled near Osawatomie, Kansas, where he became a supporter of John Brown, the white abolitionist leader. In August 1856 Merritt Anthony was wounded when he joined Brown and his followers in a battle against proslavery forces. This incident caused Susan Anthony to increase her antislavery campaign. On December 2, 1859, the night of Brown's execution, she rented Corinthian Hall in Rochester and urged the people of the city to mourn his death. Some 300 citizens attended the rally, even though many prominent Rochester residents refused to honor the memory of the controversial man.

In 1861 Anthony rented the hall again and staged a three-day antislavery convention. There was great tension in Rochester because at that very moment some of the southern states were seceding from the Union. On the first night of the convention a yelling, stamping mob broke into the hall and stopped the meeting. To avoid another violent confrontation, Anthony moved the convention on the next two nights to the Zion African Methodist Church.

During the Civil War Anthony strongly supported President Abraham Lincoln's emancipation policy. The petitions she gathered helped persuade Congress to pass the Thirteenth Amendment that abolished slavery in 1865.

After the war Anthony and her close associate Elizabeth Cady Stanton organized the National Women's Suffrage Association in 1869. Anthony agitated for extension of the right to vote to women. Even though she also favored giving the vote to freedmen, she was determined that the enfranchisement of Black men would not be emphasized over the drive for women's suffrage. Some had sought the vote for Black men before seeking it for women.

Despite the friendship between Douglass and Anthony, Douglass considered Anthony's position that "no Negro shall be enfranchised while woman is not" to be less than fair. He pointed out, "Now considering that while men have been enfranchised always, and colored men have not, the conduct of these white women [Anthony and Elizabeth Cady Stanton], whose husbands, fathers, and brothers are voters, does not seem generous."[1]

Still, more things brought Anthony and Douglass together than divided them. She was one of the eulogists at his funeral in Washington. A few days later Susan's sister, Mary Anthony, spoke at a memorial service for Douglass at a church in Rochester, recalling the ties of friendship between the two families over many years.

This two and one-half–story brick house was the home of Susan Anthony, a leader in the abolitionist crusade.

DATE BUILT:	c1860; Anthony residence, 1866–1906
ADDRESS:	17 Madison Street, Rochester
TELEPHONE:	(716) 235-6124
VISITING HOURS:	Thurs.–Sat. 1–4; closed Sun.–Wed. and holidays except by appointment 👥
FEES:	Adults, $5; senior citizens 62 and over and students, $3; children under 12, $1
SOURCES:	Telephone conversation May 5, 1994, and Aug. 10, 1995, Lorie Barnum, executive director, Susan B. Anthony House. "Griffing Papers," 469–70. *National Register of Historic Places*, 506. "Anti-Slavery Days in Rochester," 113–55. *Frederick Douglass*, 269.

Frederick Douglass Gravesite *

Rochester was the home of the famous nineteenth-century abolitionist Frederick Douglass (1817–1895). Born a slave in Maryland, he learned to read and write as a young boy. He was first taught to read by a mistress in Baltimore who later stopped the lessons because of her husband's anger at the instruction. This led to an unquenchable desire to learn to read, and Douglass traded bread for instruction from young white boys who lived nearby. When he was returned to the plantation where he had already experienced cruel treatment, Douglass became imbued with a strong desire to escape. As his master in Baltimore suspected, Douglass's new ability to read and learn had destroyed any possibility that he would remain a docile slave. In 1838 he escaped to the North and sent for his bride-to-be, Anna, to join him. Douglass's imposing presence and his riveting accounts of slavery, led to his becoming a sought-after antislavery speaker.

Even though he was in the North, Douglass feared being picked up as a runaway and returned to his owner in Maryland; therefore, he spent some time in England. There he made some friends who collected enough funds to purchase his freedom. The same friends gave him $2,500 to use in starting an antislavery newspaper. Upon his return to the United States, Douglass settled in Rochester.

Douglass and his associate Martin Delaney (1812–1885), a man proud of his African heritage, founded the *North Star* newspaper in 1847. Its name was changed a few years later to *Frederick Douglass's Paper*. Passage of the Fugitive Slave Law caused much uneasiness among Douglass's friends who warned him that he should go to Canada for safety's sake. Douglass refused to give up his newspaper, however, and decided to stay in Rochester. He was cautious enough to move to a house on the outskirts of the city that could be reached only by a private road. His home (no longer standing) became a major station on the underground railroad. When he went each day to the paper's office at 25 East Main Street, Douglass would often find fugitive slaves sitting on the stairway. That night he would arrange for them to find refuge in other nearby cities.

Frederick and Anna had five children. They sent their daughter, Rosetta, to a fashionable girls school but was dismayed when he discovered that she was not allowed to mingle with the white students. He was also dissatisfied with the segregated colored school and

hired a tutor to teach his children at home. As a result of Douglass's proddings, the board of education of Rochester finally opened all the city's schools to Black children in 1857.

Although Douglass was on friendly terms with John Brown, they differed on the means to adopt in fighting slavery. Brown believed violence would be needed to end slavery, but Douglass favored political work within the framework of the law. During the Civil War Douglass helped recruit Black men to serve in two regiments organized in Massachusetts. Two of his sons, Charles and Lewis, were the first men from New York to enlist. After the war Douglass and his sons moved to Washington, D.C., where they published a newspaper, the *New National Era*. (Two of the Douglass homes in Washington, D.C., are open to the public and are described in that section.)

When Frederick Douglass died in 1895, his body was returned from Washington to Rochester to be laid to rest in Rochester's Mt. Hope Cemetery. The city united to honor one of its most illustrious citizens. His body lay in state at City Hall, and thousands of schoolchildren filed past to pay their final respects. A military escort and band accompanied mourners to the cemetery.

Today three monuments commemorate the great abolitionist. These include a bust at the University of Rochester's Frederick Douglass Building, placed there in June 1879, a bust at the Colgate Rochester Divinity School Library, and a bronze statue of Douglass in Highland Park. Four years after Douglass died, Gertrude Thompson, his great-granddaughter, unveiled the life-sized bronze statue of Douglass. Theodore Roosevelt, then governor of New York, made the principal address at the ceremony.

DATE OF SIGNIFICANCE:	1895
ADDRESSES:	Mt. Hope Cemetery, south of downtown Rochester via Mt. Hope Avenue (NY 15), Highland Park; Colgate Rochester Divinity School Library, University of Rochester Frederick Douglass Building, Rochester
TELEPHONE:	Cemetery, (716) 473-2755
VISITING HOURS:	Cemetery, daily, dawn–dusk
FEES:	None

SOURCES: Ruth Rosenberg-Naparsteck, city historian. Elizabeth G. Holahan, president, Rochester Historical Society. Leatrice M. Kemo, Rochester Museum & Science Center. *Webster's New Biographical Dictionary*, 271, 294. "Two Episodes of Anti-Slavery Days," 213–22. "Anti-Slavery Days in Rochester," 113–55. *Frederick Douglass*, 160–1.

Memorial African Methodist Episcopal Zion Church

Memorial A.M.E. Zion Church is associated with an early pastor of the church, Reverend Thomas James. Reverend James was born in slavery in 1804 in Canajoharie, New York. When he was eight years old, his family was divided for sale. His mother was dragged from the attic where she was hiding and sold away from her children, who never saw her again. James had three masters but ran away from the third. Before coming to Rochester, he spent some time as a worker on the canals.

Reverend James later traveled to New Bedford, where he served as pastor of Zion Chapel. In his autobiography, published in 1866, he noted that Frederick Douglass, who had recently escaped from slavery, one day visited his church. He called on Douglass to speak, and the moving presentation led to Douglass's being sent on a lecture tour by the American Anti-Slavery Society. The Douglass family made Zion Chapel their religious home in New Bedford.

James returned to Rochester in 1856 and served as pastor of Zion Church. In his years there, he knew about many Black people who had tried to escape from slavery. In his autobiography he told about a runaway woman slave who had been recaptured in 1823. She was being taken to court to be returned to her master in West Virginia when fifteen or twenty African Americans overpowered the officers and took her away. They were intercepted later, and the woman was taken from them. She committed suicide rather than go back to being a slave. In 1832 another woman slave was recaptured by her owner. The rescuers, again a group of Black people, were not successful in freeing her in Rochester. However, they followed the woman and her owner east to Palmyra, New York, where they were finally able to liberate her.

Zion Church was built in the nineteenth century for a Black congregation. Today the Rochester landmark is called the Memorial A.M.E. Zion Church.

DATE ESTABLISHED: 19th century
ADDRESS: 549 Clarissa Street, Rochester
TELEPHONE: (716) 546-5997
VISITING HOURS: Church office, by appointment Tues.–Thurs. 9–4, Fri.–Sat. 10–2; Sun. school, 9:30; Sun. service, 11
FEES: None
SOURCES: Telephone conversation Aug. 8, 1995, Marjorie Anderson, secretary, Memorial A.M.E. Zion Church. Elizabeth G. Holahan, president, Rochester Historical Society. "Anti-Slavery Days in Rochester," 113–55. *A History of Negro Slavery in New York. Frederick Douglass*, 82.

Margaret Woodbury Strong Museum

The Strong Museum launched its initiative of collecting and interpreting African-American history in 1989. Museum exhibits incorporate the contributions of African Americans locally and throughout the United States. Some past exhibits (including traveling exhibits) at the Strong Museum have included *Freedom's Journals: The History of the Black Press in New York State; Field to Factory: Afro-American Migration; Black Printmakers and the WPA; The Real McCoy: Afro-American Invention and Innovation, 1619–1930; Stitching Memories: African-American Story Quilts;* and *Climbing Jacob's Ladder: The Rise of Black Churches in Eastern American Cities, 1740–1877.*

A Strong Museum conference in 1989 highlighted the Civil Rights Movement of the mid-twentieth century with a focus on the weekend of July 24–26, 1964, when Governor Nelson Rockefeller ordered 1,500 National Guard members to restore order to the streets of Rochester.

DATE ESTABLISHED: October 1982
ADDRESS: One Manhattan Square, Rochester
TELEPHONE: (716) 263-2700
VISITING HOURS: Mon.–Sat. 10–5, Sun. 1–5; closed Thanksgiving, Christmas, New Year's Day
FEES: Adults, $5; senior citizens and students, $4; children 3–16, $3; children under 3, free
SOURCES: Linda B. Tabit, lead educator for family programs, Strong Museum. Elizabeth G. Holahan, president, Rochester Historical Society. Strong Museum brochures. Telephone call to site, Aug. 8, 1995.

South Granville

Lemuel Haynes House

Lemuel Haynes, an outstanding African American minister, was born in Connecticut in 1753 of a Black father and a white mother. At the age of five months the child was taken to the household of Deacon David Rose, where he was bound out to be a servant for twenty-five years.

As a child, Lemuel received some advantages that were denied to most African Americans in the 1700s. He attended a common school in Massachusetts and had Bible studies in the Rose household. When he was young, he impressed adults with his ability to remember much of the material he had heard. He often read a sermon aloud on Saturday nights, the time of religious instruction in the Rose household. One evening when he had finished reading, the Deacon asked whose sermon he had read. He replied, "It's Lemuel's sermon." Word spread about the youth's ability, and the local parish, which lacked a minister, began calling on Lemuel frequently to conduct services.

At the age of twenty-one, Lemuel was free of his indenture. He left the Rose household and enlisted in the Minutemen, fighting with them in battles at Lexington. Following his military experience, he returned to farming and the study of theology. Encouraged by neighbors who recognized his talent, Haynes studied in Connecticut to prepare for the ministry. When he was invited to preach in Middle Granville, he may have been the first Black man in America to serve as pastor of a white church. In 1785

when Haynes was ordained as a minister of the Congregational Church, he became the first Black man to be ordained by any religious sect in North America.

Haynes encountered disrespectful attitudes from some members of a congregation in Torrington, Connecticut, and their behavior forced him to leave that church. In spite of that experience, respect grew over the years for his skill as a preacher and theologian. When Middlebury College awarded him the honorary Master of Arts degree in 1804, it was the first such degree bestowed on a Black person in America.

Haynes spent the final eleven years of his life as a pastor in South Granville, New York. He died in 1833, at the age of eighty, and his wife, Elizabeth, died three years later. Both are buried in the South Granville cemetery. Haynes was well respected in many churches in which he served and was held in high esteem in those communities for his accomplishments.

The Haynes House is the dwelling where the Reverend Haynes lived during the last eleven years of his life. The small frame house has two stories and a cellar. The interior still has a large fireplace with a Dutch oven; there are wide floorboards throughout the house.

DATE BUILT:	1793; Haynes residence, 1822–1833; restoration, 1967
ADDRESS:	Parker Hill Road off NY 149, South Granville (from NY 22 in Granville turn right onto NY 149; go approximately 2 1/2 miles to South Granville; turn left onto Parker Hill Road; the house is the second on the right on Parker Hill)
VISITING HOURS:	Private, visitors may drive by
SOURCES:	Telephone conversation June 15, 1994, Mitchell Van Guilder, Granville resident. NRHPINF.

Stillwater

Saratoga National Historical Park

In 1777 General John Burgoyne led a bold but unsuccessful British campaign to split the American colonies by coming south from Canada along the Lake Champlain-Hudson River Valley route. He left St. John's, Canada, on June 17 with a force of some 9,000 soldiers. Meanwhile, the Americans had brought together an army of nearly 20,000 men who surrounded the British at Saratoga about thirty miles north of Albany. Exhausted by the long march and faced with overwhelming numbers, the British were forced to surrender. Burgoyne ordered the 6,000 surviving members of his command to stack their weapons along the west bank of the Hudson. This was one of the colonists' most decisive victories. Because it so impressed the French that they agreed to recognize the rebellious Americans and aid them militarily, the Battle of Saratoga led ultimately to American independence.

The brigades that served in the Saratoga campaign were estimated to be about 4 percent Black. Black soldiers served in racially mixed units in both battles at Saratoga. Some African Americans who enlisted were free; some were slaves who remained slaves after their service; still others received their freedom after the war. For example, Peter Brewer of New Boston, New Hampshire, a Black soldier, enlisted as a private in the First New Hampshire Regiment, which fought in both battles of Saratoga. He was killed in the second battle on October 7, 1777. Another African American, Sampson Brown of the Fifteenth Massachusetts, also was killed at Saratoga. A third African American, Agrippa Hull, fought six years with the Continental army. Four years of his service were under the command of General Taddeus (Tadeusz) Kosciusko, a Polish patriot who had joined George Washington's armies. An unidentified artist painted a portrait of Hull that hangs in the historical room of the Stockbridge Library in Massachusetts.

Unfortunately, some American officers were unwilling to recognize the patriotism of the African Americans who served under them. A number of these officers were slaveowners who had grave concerns about arming Black men. In a letter General Philip Schuyler wrote to General Heath on July 28, 1777, he expressed contempt for his Black soldiers:

> ...of the few Continental Troops we have had... one-third part is composed of men too far advanced in years for field service; of boys, or rather children, and mortifying barely to mention, of Negroes.[2]

Facing the threat of invasion from Canada and a thrust against Philadelphia, the Americans needed as many men as possible for long-term service in the Continental Army. Some enlisted men were farmers who had to return home at harvest time; if they had not, their families would have starved. As a result, the army decided to accept African Americans. Some were offered freedom for enlisting in place of their owners. Black soldiers served as foot soldiers, orderlies, or drummers. This was the last U.S. armed force until the Korean conflict that was racially integrated.

Today Saratoga National Historical Park includes more than 2,700 acres of battlefield sites. An automobile tour starts with maps and exhibits in the Visitors' Center; it then begins at the parking area and covers nine miles and ten tour stops. The 155-foot Saratoga Monument, which overlooks the Hudson Valley and the flats where the surrender took place, commemorates the surrender of the British forces under General John Burgoyne to American General Horatio Gates on October 17, 1777. The surrender followed two battles of Saratoga in the present town of Stillwater, and the British retreat to what is now the Schuylerville area.

DATE OF SIGNIFICANCE:	Oct. 17, 1777; park established, 1948
ADDRESS:	Park entrances, 30 miles north of Albany on US 4 and NY 32; Visitors Center, at the main section of the Historical Park along US 4 just north of Stillwater; General Philip Schuyler House and Saratoga Monument, a few more miles north in Schuylerville
TELEPHONE:	(518) 664-9821
VISITING HOURS:	Park, daily Apr.–Nov. 30 9–5; Schuyler House, Memorial Day–Labor Day, daily 9–5; monument, mid-June–Labor Day daily 9–5; Visitors Center closed Thanksgiving, Christmas, New Year's 🏃🏃
FEES:	Adults, $3 for tour road only; children, free
SOURCES:	Paul Okey, park historian. *A Teacher's Guide to Saratoga National Historical Park*. National Park Service pamphlets and flier on the Saratoga park and on the Schuyler House.

Syracuse

Jerry Rescue Memorial

The most famous antislavery event in Syracuse was the rescue of a Black man, William Henry, who was also known as Jerry. He had escaped from slavery in Missouri and come to Syracuse via the underground railroad. He then worked for several years in Syracuse as a cabinetmaker and cooper. Jerry should have been able to live a peaceful life in freedom because the state of New York had abolished slavery in 1827; however, the federal government enacted the Fugitive Slave Law of 1850, which eliminated safe havens everywhere.

The law specified that if a white person claimed that a Black person was a fugitive, the Black person had no right to a jury trial. A white official could receive two times the usual fee if he ruled that the Black person was a fugitive rather than ruling the opposite. The law punished citizens who helped a fugitive escape. Many free Black people fled because they feared being kidnapped and sent into slavery. Reverend Samuel Ward, a Black abolitionist, spoke out against the law in an editorial in his newspaper, the *Impartial Citizen:*

> Now, this bill strips us of all manner of protection, by the writ of habeas corpus, by jury trial, or by any other process known to the laws of civilized nations, that are thrown as safeguards around personal liberty. But while it does this, it throws us back upon the natural and inalienable right of self-defense—self protection. It solemnly refers to each of us, individually, the question, whether we will submit to being enslaved by the hyenas which this law creates and encourages, or whether we will protect ourselves, even if, in so doing, we have to peril our lives, and more than peril the useless and devilish carcasses of Negro-catchers. It gives us the alternative of dying freemen, or living slaves.[3]

The Liberty Party of abolitionists called a meeting for October 1, 1851. On the day prior to the meeting, the county fair was in progress, and the city saw a bustle of activity: federal agents arrested Jerry on trumped-up charges of theft. Then they explained that he had been arrested as a fugitive slave.

Jerry slipped away from the officers and made a dash for freedom. Farmers had brought large loads of wood to the city and were standing waiting for purchasers. Jerry, handcuffed, began to dodge in and out among the loads of wood. A young boy, Horace McGuire, who was delivering newspapers, witnessed the flight. Years later he described the incident to the Rochester Historical Association:

> With my papers under my arm, I saw the colored man handcuffed, dodging his pursuers, among the loads of wood. Boy-like, neglectful I fear of our subscribers, I followed the crowd and witnessed the fight. Jerry fought with a determined effort to be free but was overpowered, his clothing badly torn, his face covered with blood and one of his ribs broken. A passing wagon was impressed into the service of the officers and Jerry thrown into it, one of the officers sitting on his breast and another on his legs and others leading the horses as they drove the prisoner back to the police station.[4]

The police took Jerry to the police station (today the site is known as the Jerry Rescue Site). News spread about the capture. Church bells rang, and crowds gathered. The abolitionists held a meeting that evening to plan a rescue. White abolitionist Gerrit Smith, with others, advocated using force to rescue Jerry. Authorities guarded the police station and all roads out of the city. At the same time abolitionists continued with their plans. They secured a light carriage and a pair of the fastest horses in the city.

Near midnight more than 2,000 abolitionists gathered. Proceeding to the hardware store of a sympathetic owner, they seized iron bars and axes, rushed to the prison, and overpowered the guards. Then they hurried Jerry into a carriage and scattered in all directions to confuse those on their trail. The men driving Jerry's carriage wove in and out among the streets, finally arriving at a safe house. Jerry remained there for several days, where he was given medical treatment and suitable clothing for the next part of his journey.

On October 5, 1851, Jerry's rescuers took him to Oswego, New York. The last moments before freedom had to be carefully planned. A schooner sailed out of Oswego's harbor as it normally would have, but returned after dark to meet a small boat pulled out by

Jerry's friends. At last, Jerry was on his way to freedom in Canada. Jerry lived there for two years until he died in 1853 of tuberculosis.

The Liberty Party members had their convention on October 1, 1850. They never could have known when planning their meeting that the night before the meeting, 2,000 people would help with the daring rescue of William "Jerry" Henry. They rejoiced that his liberty had won the day. This incident, and the courage of the citizens in rescuing Henry, made Syracuse known nationally as being in the forefront of abolitionist activities.

In the early 1990s a monument commemorating Jerry's rescue was installed on the west side of Clinton Square, facing the site at Clinton and Water Streets where the mob had stormed the Syracuse jail in 1851 and freed Jerry. The building, which became widely known as the "Jerry Rescue Building," was demolished in 1974.

DATE OF SIGNIFICANCE: 1851

ADDRESS: Clinton Street (between Erie Boulevard W and Water Street), Syracuse

SOURCES: Judy Haven, researcher, Onondaga Historical Association. "The Rescue: Monument to our Proudest Moment." "History Preserved." *Syracuse and the Underground Railroad.*

Tarrytown

Foster Memorial African Methodist Episcopal Zion Church

Foster Memorial African Methodist Episcopal Zion Church, built in 1865 by free Black people, is the oldest Black church in continuous use in Westchester County, and may be one of the oldest in New York State. The congregation played an important role in the underground railroad.

The present-day village of Tarrytown is located on land that once belonged to an Algonquin Indian tribe. In 1681, a Dutch merchant of New Amsterdam, Frederick Philipse, purchased this area as part of his extensive manor and developed the land under the tenant farm system. Because the Philipse family was loyal to the crown during the American Revolution, the land was confiscated and sold to the tenants. The village grew from the Hudson River docks up the hill to the Albany Post Road.

In 1790 there were 357 free Black people in Westchester County, many of whom worked as farmhands or house servants. All slaves in New York were freed by law in 1827. The A.M.E. Zion denomination originated in New York City in 1796. In 1860 a congregation of the church was organized to serve the growing Black population in Tarrytown. It helped freed people in the village and also assisted runaway slaves. In the 1850s such help was an important factor in guiding fugitives up the Hudson River into Canada.

Mrs. Amanda Foster (1806–1904) was instrumental in developing the church. She was born in the household of New York Governor George Clinton but was separated from her mother when she was six weeks old. She served in different households until about the age of fifteen. Then she began working as a stewardess on a steamer. Traveling in the South with her "free papers," she was deeply moved by the sight of slavery. Amanda gave her free papers to a slave girl to help the girl escape.

Amanda married and her husband settled in Tarrytown. He operated a barber business and she opened a small confectionary store. When her first husband died, she remarried to Henry Foster, who was also a barber and who operated a livery business as well. The deeply religious couple adopted two children. The Fosters were among the few individuals who established the Tarrytown congregation. Church members met at first in a number of temporary quarters, including Foster's store. She raised funds in the early 1860s from white families who patronized her candy store and her husband's barber shop. The brick church was constructed in 1864. Amanda Foster was honored as the mother of the church. In 1886 the congregation numbered forty members and thirty-five Sunday School students. Members rented pews for three dollars per year.

In the nineteenth and early twentieth century, many social activities in the town were separated by race. Social and religious activities for the Black community centered around the church. The church assisted Black people who migrated north and settled in the Tarrytown area prior to World War I. During financially lean years church members often supported their pastor by bringing him a pound of food.

Foster Memorial Church is situated among single- and multifamily houses. Although altered since its completion in 1865, much of the early building still remains. The two-story structure is built of red brick with an artificial stone veneer. The former Foster home is directly east of the church.

In October 1984 the cornerstone was replaced at Foster Memorial A.M.E. Zion Church, marking its 120th anniversary. Members found in it a time capsule containing a roster of its members, a Sunday Service program, and a dime dated 1910. These were all later replaced. In 1982 the church was placed on the State and National Register of Historic Places. The Amanda Foster gravesite at Sleepy Hollow Cemetery was one of four African American historic sites designated as a Westchester County Tricentennial Historic Site.

DATE BUILT: Church, 1864–1865

ADDRESS: Church, 90 Wildey Street; cemetery, 540 N. Broadway, Tarrytown

TELEPHONE: Church, (914) 631-2002, or (914) 761-4786; cemetery, (914) 631-0081

VISITING HOURS: Church, Sun. 11; Sleepy Hollow Cemetery, Mon.–Fri. 8:30 A.M.–9:30 P.M.; Sat. 9–noon

SOURCES: NRHPINF. Westchester County Historical Society Library. Telephone conversation Jan. 28, 1995, May Foley, secretary, Foster Memorial Church. *"The Hills" in the Mid-Nineteenth Century.* "Foster Memorial AME Zion to Mark 120th Anniversary."

Notes

1. William S. McFeely, *Frederick Douglass* (New York: Simon & Schuster, 1991), 269.
2. Exhibit sheets, Saratoga National Historical Park, Edward A. Hoyt, researcher (Stillwater, New York: National Park Service).
3. Samuel Ward, "Editorial," *Impartial Citizen,* quoted in *The Liberator* (11 Oct. 1850), quoted in Herbert Aptheker, ed., *A Documentary History of the Negro People in the United States,* vol. 1 (New York: Citadel, 1990), 306.
4. Horace McGuire, "Two Episodes of Anti-Slavery Days," *Rochester Historical Society Bulletin* 4 (1916), 213–17.

Works Consulted

Academic American Encyclopedia. Danbury, Conn.: Grolier, 1993.

"Adam Clayton Powell, Jr." Michael W. Williams, ed. In *The African American Encyclopedia,* vol. 5. New York: Marshall Cavendish, 1993.

The African American Encyclopedia. Michael W. Williams, ed. New York: Marshall Cavendish, 1993.

The African American Presence in New York State History: Four Regional History Surveys. Monroe Fordham, ed. New York: The New York African American Institute, State Univ. of New York, Albany, 1989.

And Why Not Every Man? Helene C. Phelan. Interlaken, N.Y.: Heart of the Lakes, 1987.

"Anti-Slavery Days in Rochester." Amy Hanmer-Croughton. *Rochester Historical Society Bulletin* 14 (1936): 113–55.

Black Arts New York 3, no. 6 (Feb. 1990), 1. [Newsletter of the Harlem Cultural Council]

The Black 100: A Ranking of the Most Influential African Americans, Past and Present. Columbus Salley. New York: Citadel, 1993.

"Foster Memorial AME Zion to Mark 120th Anniversary." Janis Tinsley. *(Tarrytown, New York) Gannett Westchester Newspapers,* 20 Oct. 1984.

Frederick Douglass. William S. McFeely. New York: Simon & Schuster, 1991.

"Griffing Papers." Joseph Borome. *The Journal of Negro History* 33 (1948): 469–70. Quoted in *A Documentary History of the Negro People in the United States,* vol. 2. Herbert Aptheker, ed. New York: Citadel, 1990.

"The Hills" in the Mid-Nineteenth Century: The History of a Rural Afro-American Community in Westchester County, New York. Edythe Quinn Caro. Westchester County Historical Society, 1988.

Historic Hurley in the Mid-Hudson Valley. Hurley, N.Y.: Town of Hurley. [brochure]

The Historical and Cultural Atlas of African Americans. Molefi K. Asante and Mark T. Mattson. New York: Macmillan, 1991.

The History of Bethel A.M.E. Church, Huntington, New York. Jeannette Johns. Huntington, N.Y.: The Author, 1993.

A History of Negro Slavery in New York. Edgar J. McManus. Syracuse, N.Y.: Syracuse, 1970.

"History Preserved, Woman Will Sculpt Monument to Honor 1851 Jerry Rescue." Mike Grogan. *(Syracuse, New York)* Post Standard, *1 Oct. 1988.*

Hurley in the Days of Slavery. *Olive M. Clearwater and John J. Hofler. Hurley, N.Y.: The Authors, 1986.*

"If We Must Die." Claude McKay. In I Am the Darker Brother. *Arnold Adoff, ed. New York: Macmillan, 1968, 63.*

International Library of Negro Life and History: Historical Negro Biographies. *Wilhelmena S. Robinson. New York: Publishers, 1970.*

Ithaca's Neighborhoods: The Rhine, the Hill, and the Goose Pasture. *Ithaca, N.Y.: DeWitt Historical Society of Tompkins County, 1988.*

John Brown Farm. *Lake Placid, N.Y.: New York State Office of Parks, Recreation and Historic Preservation and New York State Environmental Conservation, June 1985. [brochure]*

The Negro's Civil War: How American Blacks Felt and Acted During the War for the Union. *James M. McPherson. New York: Ballantine, 1991.*

Old House Museum. *Fort Edward, N.Y.: Fort Edward Historical Association.*

"The Rescue: Monument to Our Proudest Moment." (Syracuse, N.Y.) *Herald-American,* 30 Aug. 1987.

"Rocks `n' Rolling, Hurley's Stones Also Its Homes." Irene Gardner Keeney. *Albany (N.Y.)* Times Union, *25 June 1989.*

Syracuse and the Underground Railroad. *Evamaria Hardin. Syracuse, N.Y.: Erie Canal Museum, 1989. [pamphlet]*

A Teacher's Guide to Saratoga National Historical Park. *Rev. ed. Washington, D.C.: U.S. Department of the Interior, 1989.*

"Two Episodes of Anti-Slavery Days." Horace McGuire. Rochester Historical Society Bulletin *4 (1916): 213–22.*

Walk, Drive Around Historic Hurley. *Hurley Heritage Society. Hurley, N.Y.: The Society, 1981. [pamphlet]*

Webster's New Biographical Dictionary. *Springfield, Mass.: Merriam-Webster, 1988.*

Weeksville Then and Now. *Joan Maynard and Gwen Cottman. Brooklyn, N.Y.: Society for the Preservation of Weeksville & Bedford-Stuyvesant History, 1983, 1988.*

North Dakota

Washburn

Fort Mandan

A Black man named York was part of North Dakota's early history as a member of the famous Lewis and Clark expedition. Between 1804 and 1806, explorers Lewis and Clark recorded observations about North Dakota's Indian tribes, vegetation, and game. York, who accompanied the expedition as a servant, was valued for his strength and wilderness skills as well as for his ability to make friends with the Indians encountered along the way. York participated fully in the tasks needed to make the expedition a success and had a voice in the decision-making process.

The expedition arrived in October 1804 at a Mandan Indian village. There the explorers had to cut down cottonwood trees to build cabins. Then the men lived for five months on insufficient rations.

Today Fort Mandan, which is situated in a wooded area, has a replica of the original campsite, as well as a visitors center. The Fort Mandan museum displays Indian artifacts, including arrowheads and flints. The center offers no interpretation of York, the African American who traveled with the expedition; the reader, however, is aware from several passages in this book that there was an African American presence in the journey and is able to see the terrain that York traversed.

DATE BUILT: 1804

ADDRESS: 3 miles by County Road 17, in Fort Mandan Park, Washburn

TELEPHONE: (701) 462-8535

VISITING HOURS: Fort, open all year during daylight hours; Visitors Center, end of May–Oct. 1, Tues.–Sun. 1–5 🍴

FEES: None

SOURCE: Telephone call to site, June 18, 1994.

Williston

Fort Buford

Two companies of the Tenth Cavalry and Twenty-fifth Infantry, all-Black units, were among those stationed at the remote Fort Buford, a place so cold—winters often were 45|SD to 50|SD below zero—and so isolated that General Philip Henry Sheridan referred to it as "the American Siberia." The fort, built in 1866, protected railway crews from the Indians and served as a base for supplies. Soldiers stationed here, both Black and white, had more police action than the fighting action regarded as typical for soldiers. When the men arrived at Fort Buford late in the 1880s, they found a military reservation of thirty square miles with the barracks and its flagpole in the middle. Because of the large size of the village, they seldom encountered any settlers; therefore, they had few of the problems of prejudice from townspeople that other Black soldiers met. At the same time, the soldiers had few opportunities for social interaction outside their immediate setting. In addition to protecting the railway, the Black soldiers were involved in the Pullman strike.

After Fort Buford closed in 1895, the Black infantrymen were transferred to Fort Assiniboine in Montana. Today a museum at the old fort shows pictures and articles that describe the Indian wars of the 1870s. Included is a life-sized photograph of a Black soldier, who is also mentioned in the site brochure. The museum has a scale model of the fort, replicas of the soldiers' uniforms and other accoutrements, and information about barracks life. One can also examine the roller skates, balls, cards, and poker chips used by the soldiers in their leisure time. The museum provides information about such famous Indian leaders as Sitting Bull, Chief Joseph, and Chief Gall.

DATE BUILT:	1866
ADDRESS:	24 miles southwest of Williston on ND 1804
TELEPHONE:	(701) 572-9034
VISITING HOURS:	May 15–Sept. 15, daily 9–6; or by appointment; closed major holidays ♀♂
FEES:	Adults, $4; children 6–15, $2; children under 6, free
SOURCE:	Telephone conversation June 18, 1994, Charles Stalnaker, site supervisor.

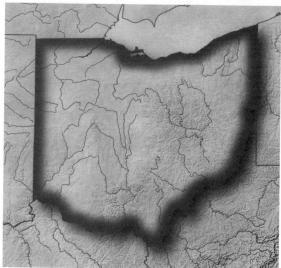

Akron

John Brown House

Famed white abolitionist John Brown (1800–1859) lived in this two-story house for two years in the 1840s. By the end of the next decade, he conceived his ill-fated plan to free the slaves after first seizing the arsenal at Harpers Ferry in West Virginia. Although the plan failed and John Brown was hanged, his ideas and the ideal of freedom continued to blaze across the country, intensifying sentiment both for and against slavery.

Brown's name was not soon forgotten. A few years after his death, Black men marched in the Civil War to the words and melody of the song "John Brown's Body," and today a memorial at Perkins Park in Akron honors him. The interpretation at this house, however, does not so much concentrate on Brown as an abolitionist but rather on Brown as a man who lived here for two years while working for Simon Perkins, the founder of Akron, Ohio. One of Brown's jobs was to care for Perkins' sheep. (For additional John Brown sites, see the Kansas City and Osawatomie, Kansas; Lake Placid, New York; Chambersburg, Pennsylvania; and Harpers Ferry, West Virginia, sections of this book.)

ADDRESS:	Brown House, 514 Diagonal Road; tours of both the Perkins Mansion and the Brown House begin at the Perkins Mansion, 550 Copley Road, Akron
TELEPHONE:	(330) 535-1120
VISITING HOURS:	Tues.–Sun. 1–5; closed some holidays, check in advance ♀♂
FEES:	Tours, adults, $3; senior citizens and children up to 16, $2
SOURCE:	Telephone conversation June 17, 1994, Sandy Pecimon, assistant to the director, Perkins Mansion and John Brown House.

Burlington

Macedonia Church
Promised Land Monument

Macedonia Church is one of the oldest Black church buildings still standing in America. The church was constructed on Macedonia Ridge, north of Burlington, Ohio, in the fall of 1849.

From 1799, Burlington, Ohio, had been a sanctuary for runaway and freed slaves. Additional freed people came to the area in 1849 after Virginia planter James Twyman emancipated thirty-seven slaves in his will and left them $10,000 to purchase land and homes in one of the free states. Thirty-two of the former slaves traveled 400 miles north to Ohio and settled in Burlington as free people. Farmland was deeded to them in 1849.

The freed African Americans joined with a Black congregation that had been established in the area since 1820. Before the arrival of the newcomers, church members had worshiped in individual members' cabins. When the former slaves arrived, they joined members of the existing congregation and their white neighbors in using row-boats to transport lumber across the Ohio River. They then carried the lumber up Macedonia Ridge and built the present church there.

Today the church remains much as it was when built, a one-story, twenty-by-thirty-foot, one-room frame building. The bell tower contains the original bell. The interior has the original pressed-tin ceiling. Outside and to the rear of the church is a one-story restroom structure built about 1955.

Although the congregation has dwindled to two or three African American families, they treasure the church and have a homecoming there each year, drawing families from other Ohio cities, from West Virginia, and from Kentucky. Owen Pleasant, nearly eighty-one years old in 1994, is a man with a sharp memory and a mind filled with stories of local history, as well as a descendant of one of the freed slaves who came to Ohio from Virginia. One of his ancestors bore the last name of her former owner, Twyman. Pleasant spearheaded a recent campaign to clean up the Thirty-Seventh Cemetery where the freed slaves were buried starting in 1849. Thanks to Pleasant's efforts, a monument was erected there and more than two hundred townspeople attended the ceremony. Seven and one-half feet in height, the granite monument depicts an ox cart of the type that brought the freed people from Virginia, a picture of guards with shotguns sent on the trip by the former slaveowner to protect the people as they traveled, the inscribed names of the thirty-seven former slaves, and the words "Promised Land." The cemetery, located in Burlington, is open to the public.

Macedonia Church, for many years a center of the community's activities and the mother church of many other Baptist churches, is listed in the *National Register of Historic Places.*

DATE BUILT:	1849
ADDRESS:	Church, 2.3 miles north from new U.S. 52 on Burlington-Macedonia Road; Thirty-Seventh Cemetery, from downtown Burlington go to the Wal-Mart and turn right, go to Sam's Garage and turn left onto Fifth Street to the cemetery
VISITING HOURS:	Interior not generally accessible; visitors may drive by 👥
FEES:	None
SOURCES:	NRHPINF. Telephone conversation June 20, 1994, Owen Pleasant, descendant of one of freed slave settlers.

Cincinnati

Harriet Beecher Stowe Cultural Resource Center

The Harriet Beecher Stowe Cultural Resource Center preserves the Black history of Cincinnati and Ohio through its periodic exhibits on African American themes such as slavery and the underground railroad, African American politicians and legislators in Ohio, art from Senegal and by local Black artists.

The Harriet Beecher Stowe House on Gilbert Avenue was the home of the Reverend Lyman Beecher, head of Lane Theological Seminary, and of his daughters, Catherine and Harriet. Harriet Beecher Stowe, who lived in Cincinnati between 1833 and 1850, learned firsthand about many aspects of slavery, including the story of a slave who had escaped with her children across the icy and dangerous waters of the Ohio River. (See the entry for Ripley, Ohio.) She used some of these stories in her book *Uncle Tom's Cabin,* a work that persuaded thousands of white Americans to become involved in the antislavery cause. (For additional information on Stowe, see the listings for Hartford, Connecticut; Brunswick, Maine; and Dresden, Ontario, in the section on Canada in the Michigan chapter.)

DATE BUILT:	1830
ADDRESS:	2950 Gilbert Avenue, Cincinnati
TELEPHONE:	(513) 632-5120
VISITING HOURS:	Tues.–Thurs. 10–4; closed federal and state holidays; tours offered to groups 👫
FEES:	None
SOURCES:	Telephone call to site, July 19, 1991. Nzingha Dahla, museum director. Dr. Sherlon P. Brown, University of Toledo. *National Register of Historic Places,* 581.

Cleveland

African American Museum

The African American Museum collects, houses, and displays information and artifacts associated with people of African descent. The displays show how African and African American contributions have been at the center of human progress from the beginning of history.

Exhibits include the inventions of Garrett A. Morgan, an inventor who lived in Cleveland. Morgan invented the first automatic traffic light, a belt fastener for sewing machines, and a smoke mask that has saved countless lives. The museum makes available a variety of self-esteem-building materials that are available for display in homes, schools, churches, and businesses.

Saturday School staff members teach African history and heritage courses. One exhibit, *To Color America,* included portraits from the Smithsonian National Portrait Gallery. Another exhibit, *Malcolm X—A National Hero,* was on loan from the California Afro-American Museum.

Programs include guided tours of the museum, special and traveling exhibits, a Saturday School, Friday night forums, and a gift and book shop.

DATE ESTABLISHED:	1953
ADDRESS:	Icabod Flewellen Building, 1765 Crawford Road, Cleveland
TELEPHONE:	(216) 791-1700
VISITING HOURS:	Mon.–Sat., 10:30–2:30; closed Christmas 👫
FEES:	Adults, $2.50; children under 12, $1.25
SOURCES:	African American Museum; Dr. Sherlon P. Brown, University of Toledo. Telephone conversation Aug. 9, 1995, Donald Lynch, secretary/tour guide, African American Museum.

Karamu House*

Karamu House, founded by Russell and Rowena Jelliffe, was the first professional Black theater outside New York. It opened in 1915 as a settlement house serving the area from East Fourteenth Street to East Fifty-fifth Street between Carnegie and Woodland Avenues. In 1940 the center adopted the name *Karamu,* a Swahili word meaning "a central place of group activities."

Karamu founders Russell and Rowena Jelliffe were white social workers from Illinois who had met in school. From time to time in the settlement house they listened to Charles Waddell Chesnutt, an African American writer from Cleveland (1858–1932), as he spoke of the variety of ethnic groups in the East Thirty-eighth Street area—including Italian, Polish, Black—and expressed his belief that the races should be brought together to share their experiences. As a result of Chesnutt's suggestion, the Jelliffes began to invite people of diverse cultural and racial backgrounds into the settlement house to share art, dances, and food. Needing more space, they began raising money; fund-raising activities included the buying of individual bricks. The Child Development Center, the first new building, soon housed all activities. As more funds came in work started on two theater buildings.

Today Karamu House is a metropolitan center that provides education and diverse experiences in the performing, visual, and cultural arts; it also serves as an arena where artists can practice and demonstrate their talents. Distinguished Karamu House alumni include Langston Hughes, Robert Guillaume, and Ron O'Neal.

DATE ESTABLISHED:	1915
ADDRESS:	2355 E. Eighty-ninth Street, Cleveland
TELEPHONE:	(216) 795-7070
VISITING HOURS:	Gallery, pre-theater by appointment ♟
FEES:	Charge for performances and classes, discounts for members
SOURCES:	Shraine L. Newman, public relations coordinator, Karamu House. Telephone conversation Jan. 7, 1995, Thelma McKinley, registrar and cultural arts and education coordinator, Karamu House. Paper from Karamu House. Karamu flier for 1989–1990 season.

Columbus

Martin Luther King Jr. Center for the Performing and Cultural Arts

From the quality of its architecture to the breadth of its programming, the Martin Luther King Jr. Center substantially enriches the surrounding community. It is housed in two renovated historic buildings—a former Knights of Pythias Temple and an elementary school whose large windows made it a wonder in its day. The Pythian Temple building (which originated as a vaudeville house before becoming the temple) was designed in 1926 by Black architect Samuel Plato, a graduate of Simmons College in Louisville, Kentucky. Plato took a correspondence course to learn the construction business; he later designed the Girls Dormitory (1909) and the Boys Dormitory (1924) at Simmons College in Louisville. He owned his own construction firm and became one of Kentucky's best-

known builders. (See the Louisville, Kentucky, section for additional examples of Plato's work.)

Many famous Black entertainers performed in the 1930s and 1940s in the first-floor theater of the building, which Plato designed. Therefore, the building's use as an arts center fits its cultural heritage. In 1987 the two buildings were renovated and joined, and a main gallery was added, creating one large facility of 60,000 square feet—an arts facility that encourages creative exploration for all ages. Programs include plays, performances by dance groups, and festivals. Musicians have available a computerized MIDI laboratory, and children participate in a Summer Cultural Camp. The center sponsors a Classic Jazz Fair, a Family Fair, and Great Performances. The art gallery sponsors a variety of exhibits from quilts to contemporary art. The small gallery recently has shown the work of five African American masters as well as the work of Mexican American artists.

DATE ESTABLISHED:	1986
ADDRESS:	867 Mt. Vernon Avenue, Columbus
TELEPHONE:	(614) 252-5464
VISITING HOURS:	Mon.–Sat. 9–5, Sun. and evenings for special events
FEES:	Donations welcomed
SOURCES:	NRHPINF. Telephone conversation June 20, 1994, Barbara Nicholson, executive director.

Dayton

Paul Laurence Dunbar State Memorial *

Paul Laurence Dunbar (1872–1906) was the first Black poet after Phillis Wheatley to attain a national reputation, and he was the first to concentrate on themes about Black people and their lives.

Dunbar was born to former slaves and grew up in poverty. His mother took in washing, and Paul and his two half-brothers worked at odd jobs to supplement her income. Although Matilda Dunbar worked hard, she also took time to share songs, stories, and poems with her sons. Young Paul attended public schools in Dayton and began writing poetry at the age of seven. His teachers recognized his talent and supported his efforts. When he entered the old Central High School, he was the only Black student there. He became president of the Philomathean Literary Society and served as editor of the *High School Times* in his senior year. Teachers at the high school introduced him to literature and honored him by presenting him at the 1892 meeting of the Western Association of Writers.

Newspapers around Dayton and in Chicago began carrying Dunbar's poems and short stories. He published his first book, *Oak and Ivy* (1893), with financial assistance from William Blocher of the United Brethren Printing House. Dunbar continued to write after graduating from high school. In spite of his talent, the only job he could find was that of an elevator operator.

As Dunbar's work became better known, benefactors sent him to New York and then to England, where he gave a recital with Samuel Coleridge-Taylor, noted English composer of African and English descent, who set some of Dunbar's poems to music. On his return, Dunbar worked for a period at the Library of Congress and produced poems, articles, short stories, and his first novel, *The Uncalled*.

Returning to Dayton in 1903, Dunbar purchased this house for his mother and himself. The young writer had been plagued with health problems throughout his life. In 1899 he had a serious bout of pneumonia and later suffered from tuberculosis. Although he lived only three years in this house before dying, he had never stopped writing because writing was the central meaning of his life.

The Dunbar house, a substantial brick, two-story house with a welcoming porch, contains many of Dunbar's personal belongings. His mother continued to live in the house after his death, keeping his books, manuscripts, and even his study as they were when he was alive. Matilda Dunbar died in 1936.

The state of Ohio purchased the Dunbar home that same year, commemorating it as a historic site. Today Dunbar House is devoted to the exhibition and care of artifacts belonging to the artist and to the study of his life. A restoration and renovation returned the residence to its turn-of-the-century condition. The house is listed in the *National Register of Historic Places*.

DATE ESTABLISHED:	c1890; Dunbar residence, 1903
ADDRESS:	219 N. Paul Laurence Dunbar Street, Dayton
TELEPHONE:	(513) 224-7061
VISITING HOURS:	Labor Day–Memorial Day, Mon.–Fri. by appointment only; Memorial Day–end of Sept., Wed.–Sat. 9–5:30, Sun. noon–5
FEES:	Adults, $2.50; children under 12, $1; school groups, $.50 per person or $10 per bus; special rates for groups
SOURCES:	Personal visit, summer 1990. LaVerne Sci, manager, Dunbar House. Telephone conversation Mar. 7, 1995, Ethel Oliver, tour guide, Dunbar House. *National Register of Historic Places*, 589. National Historic Landmark Status Report. "Paul Laurence Dunbar House."

Women's Christian Association No. 2

Although the building housing the former Women's Christian Association was vacant as of mid-1994, it is worth seeing because it represents the type of housing provided for young Black women in a segregated era.

In the late nineteenth century, white residents denied African Americans access to essential social services and forced them to live in restricted areas of the city. The Dayton Young Women's Christian Association restricted its facilities and programs to white females with the result that in 1889, a group of Black leaders decided to organize the Women's Christian Association. They incorporated in 1909 and purchased this building that same year. The housing, modest but graceful for its day, provided a wholesome environment for women's social activities and provided a facility where young working women could rent rooms at a reasonable cost. Services were also provided for the community from this setting. During World War I, when local Black troops were poorly housed and inadequately supplied, African American women used this site as a base for providing assistance to them.

Ironically the decline of this site began in 1918 when the white organization, the Dayton YWCA, began to provide services to the Black community. The Women's Christian Association, unaware perhaps that the group was hastening its own demise, approved of the new focus and, in cooperation, leased its building to the YWCA for a dollar per year. By 1924 the white YWCA had outgrown the leased quarters and had constructed its own building on Summit Street. At a time when the two organizations increasingly duplicated each other's efforts, the general neighborhood around this house began to decline, and the site was viewed as a less-desirable location for young women. The doors of the historic old building on Fifth Street closed in 1973.

The Women's Christian Association building, a rectangular frame building constructed in the late nineteenth century, has an entry on the right side of the facade; it is approached by a stoop with a wrought-iron railing.

The building, which is associated with the Black community's efforts to provide essential social services in an era of segregation, is listed in the *National Register of Historic Places*.

DATE BUILT:	c1900; purchased by the Women's Christian Association, 1909
ADDRESS:	800 W. Fifth Street, Dayton
VISITING HOURS:	Unoccupied, visitors may walk or drive by
SOURCES:	Personal visit to site, summer 1990. NRHPINF. Telephone conversation June 17, 1994, Nancy Horlacher, Dayton collection librarian, Dayton/Montgomery County Library.

Harveysburg

East End School

This historic building, commonly called the East End School, was built around 1829. It served both Black children and some Indian children living in the area.

William Harvey, a white Quaker, first purchased land in this area and established the settlement of Harveysburg. He and his wife were sympathetic to antislavery ideas. Harvey's brother, Dr. Jesse Harvey, and his wife, Elizabeth, founded the East End School. Elizabeth was one of the school's first instructors. The East End School operated until the turn of the century when its enrollment began to decline. The remaining students were integrated into a nearby formerly all-white school, and the schoolhouse was closed. Later it was converted into a private dwelling.

Many years later, in 1976, the Harveysburg Community Historical Society began to write a history of the village. Recognizing the historical significance of the school, its members made plans to restore it. To raise funds, they sold cornmeal pies and sauerkraut pies at festivals and held ice cream socials. The Ohio Department of the Interior and private donors gave supplemental funds.

The school is a brick, rectangular one-story structure with six-over-six windows. Restorers provided the school with electricity and a new belfry. They repaired windows and the chimney, repaired floors and walks, and removed the partitions that had been added when the school became a residence. The schoolhouse originally had no street number, so the committee bestowed the number 1776 as an address.

Although the building was known locally as the East End School, the *National Register of Historic Places* lists it as the Elizabeth Harvey Free Black School, honoring the school's founder. Built in a Quaker town, it may have been the first free school for Black children in the Northwest Territory. It definitely was the first free school for them in Ohio. The historic building is used as a meeting place for the Harveysburg Community Historical Society, and it provides a site for the display of historical items.

DATE BUILT: 1829–1831

ADDRESS: 1776 North Street, Harveysburg

TELEPHONE: Mrs. Walter McCarren, (513) 897-6195

VISITING HOURS: By appointment

SOURCES: Wiley Smith III, acting chairperson, Department of Pan-African Studies, Kent State University. Telephone conversation May 10, 1994, Mrs. Walter McCarren, Harveysburg Community Historical Society. "First Black School in Ohio being Restored in Harveysburg."

Mount Pleasant

Village of Mount Pleasant Historic District

During the first half of the nineteenth century, Mount Pleasant was both an up-and-coming industrial center and a leading center of the abolitionist movement in Ohio. Although Mount Pleasant was primarily a Quaker community, people of other views lived here, too. Underground railroad routes from Wheeling, West Virginia, passed through southern Jefferson County and through Mount Pleasant, and tradition indicates that no slave who arrived at this community was ever taken back into captivity.

Today Mount Pleasant is a community of less than 500 individuals—it is small in size but large in pride in its antislavery heritage. Some descendants of slaves still live in this former stop on the underground railroad. Many nineteenth-century buildings remain from the abolitionist period, and volunteers give tours of six of them—the Quaker Meeting House; the Benjamin Lundy Home; the 1804 log cabin of P. L. Bone, a former drummer in the Civil War; a general store; the tin shop; and the Elizabeth House Mansion Museum. The museum has a map of the local underground railroad route and the original free-labor store sign. Although most of the structures are private, visitors can walk by to view the exteriors in this two-block area.

The Quaker Meeting House is one of the most important buildings in the historic district. From the early nineteenth century it housed an association whose members worked against slavery. The brick, two and one-half–story structure has two interesting features—the separate entrances for men and women and the movable partition that could be lowered to separate the sexes.

The Benjamin Lundy House was another important antislavery site. In 1815 Lundy, a white man dedicated to the abolitionist movement, founded one of the first antislavery societies, the Union Humane Society, in St. Clairsville, Ohio. In 1821 he established his influential journal, the *Genius of Universal Emancipation*, at this site in Mount Pleasant. The Lundy House includes two attached brick dwellings that are accessible to each other through an interior door. The wing housed a free-labor store where Lundy chose to fight against slavery by selling only products not made with slave labor.

DATE BUILT: Nineteenth century; Meeting House, 1814

ADDRESS: Roughly bounded by Third, North, High, and South Streets, Mount Pleasant

TELEPHONE: (614) 769-2893 or (614) 769-2020

VISITING HOURS: Most sites private, visitors may drive or walk by; tours by appointment 👥

FEES: Tour, $6 per person; students 5–18, $3; children under 6, free

SOURCES: Telephone conversation June 17, 1994, Sherry Sawchuk, president, Historical Society of Mount Pleasant. Reverend Lloyd G. Smith, Historical Society of Mount Pleasant. Mount Pleasant Historical Society Museum. *Webster's New Biographical Dictionary,* 627. *National Register of Historic Places,* 583.

Oberlin

John Mercer Langston House

John Langston, the son of Ralph Quarles, a white plantation owner, and Lucy Langston, a slave of African and Indian ancestry, was born in Virginia in 1829. When John was a child, both his parents died, and he was sent to Ohio in accordance with his father's wishes to live under the guardianship of the Gooch family. When he was ten years old, the Gooches decided to move to Missouri. This created a danger for John because Missouri was a slave state. It was feared that he might be forced to live as a slave. Fortunately, his half-brother intervened and sought the help of an Ohio court. As a result of this intervention, John was placed in the care of an abolitionist minister.

Langston attended a private school in Cincinnati for three years. In 1844 he entered the preparatory department of Oberlin College. After graduating from the college, he continued postgraduate studies in theology at Oberlin. His real interest, however, was in law. Rejected by law schools because of his race, Langston studied privately with attorney Philemon Bliss. Langston passed the bar in 1854 and was admitted to the practice of law.

That same year Langston married Carolina Wall, and he and his bride set up housekeeping on a farm he owned in the township of Brownhelm. He built up a professional law practice there and became a well-known figure in the town. In March 1855 the community elected him as its town clerk—perhaps the first time that an African American had won an elective office in the United States.

In 1856 Langston moved back to Oberlin, thinking that he could expand his practice in that larger community. Before long voters elected him to serve on the city council and the local board of education. When the Civil War broke out, Langston helped recruit Black soldiers for service in the Forty-fourth and Forty-fifth Massachusetts Black regiments. During the Reconstruction period Langston moved to Washington, D.C., where he worked for a time for the Freedmen's Bureau. Later he was asked by Howard University to organize a new law department. He served the university in a number of capacities— as dean of the law school, vice president, and later acting president of the university.

Next, Langston entered the U.S. diplomatic service and was stationed at posts in Haiti and Santo Domingo. Returning to the United States, he became the president of a college now known as Virginia State University at Petersburg. Turning his attention next to politics, he was elected as the first Black Congressman from Virginia in 1890. He was not reelected, however, and retired to private life in Washington, D.C. There he wrote his autobiography, *From the Virginia Plantation to the National Capital*. He died in Washington in November 1897.

The Langston House in Oberlin is the only existing house associated with this outstanding American. He lived in the home during the twelve years when he was active in politics and in his law practice in Oberlin.

DATE BUILT:	House, 1855; Langston residence, 1856–1867
ADDRESS:	207 E. College Street, Oberlin
VISITING HOURS:	Private, visitors may drive or walk by
SOURCE:	NRHPINF.

Oberlin College

Oberlin College, like Berea College in Kentucky, was one of the first accredited colleges in America to enroll Black students in the 1800s. Established in 1833, Oberlin had an official policy of nondiscrimination in its admissions. When Lucy Sessions graduated from Oberlin in 1850, she was the first Black woman in the United States to earn a college degree.

An important center of the abolitionist movement in the Midwest, Oberlin also was involved in the underground railroad. In 1859 John Copeland Jr., a student at Oberlin College, was one of three Black men to die with John Brown in the famous raid at Harpers Ferry, West Virginia. A monument in the city park honors the three Black men who died at Harpers Ferry: John Copeland Jr., Shields Green, and Lewis Leary.

DATE ESTABLISHED: 1833

ADDRESS: Tappan Square, Oberlin

TELEPHONE: Admissions, (216) 775-8411; Campus Visit Program, (800) 622-6243

VISITING HOURS: Guided tours during school year, Mon.–Fri. 10–noon, 2:30, 4:30, Sat. 10–noon; summers, by appointment; closed last week of Mar.

SOURCES: Telephone call to site, June 17, 1994. Telephone conversation Mar. 7, 1995, Leslie Curtis, assistant, Campus Visit Program. *National Register of Historic Places,* 586.

Put-in-Bay

Perry's Victory and International Peace Memorial

Perry's Victory and International Peace Memorial is a 352-foot-high granite column that commemorates the Battle of Lake Erie during the War of 1812. This is one of the few national parks with a Black theme. Approximately one in four sailors, or 130 of the men serving on the nine vessels in the American fleet, was Black. When Oliver Hazard Perry assembled his fleet in 1813, United States armed forces were segregated. (In fact, they were not to be officially integrated until more than a century later after World War II.) Perry was dissatisfied with the men sent to him, referring to them as "a motley set—Blacks, soldiers, and boys."

His superior, Commodore Chauncey, replied, "I have yet to learn that the color of a man's skin or the cut and trimmings of the coat, can affect a man's qualifications or usefulness. I have nearly fifty Blacks on board of this ship and many of them are among my best men."[1] Thereupon, Perry tendered his resignation to the Secretary of the Navy, stating that he had not been speaking about the men's color but of

their lack of training and experience. In the end Perry was persuaded to retain his command and began a rigorous training program that paid off. On September 10, 1813, the American fleet met and destroyed a British fleet of six vessels in the Battle of Lake Erie, the only instance in history when an entire British fleet was sunk or captured.

Other than their names, little is known of the men who won the historic Battle of Lake Erie in the War of 1812 and secured the old Northwest. According to the National Park Service, only three of the more than one hundred Black men who fought aboard the fleet have been positively identified. Anthony Williams fought on board the schooner *Somers.* Jesse Williams, a seaman, was wounded in the battle. Cyrus Tiffany, a Black man from Massachusetts, returned to Rhode Island with Perry and continued to serve with him until Perry's death in 1819.

Visitors to the peace monument walk up two flights (thirty-seven steps) and then take an elevator the rest of the way. There is no handicap access to the monument.

DATE ESTABLISHED: 1912–1915

ADDRESS: South Bass Island in Lake Erie, Put-in-Bay (about 3 miles from the mainland, accessible by car ferry daily from Catawba Point and Port Clinton, Apr.–Nov.)

TELEPHONE: (419) 285-2184

VISITING HOURS: Third Sun. in June–Labor Day, Sun.–Thurs. 10–7, Fri.–Sat. 10–10; closing hour varies in Sept.; winter months, by appointment 👥

FEES: Adults, $2; children 16 and under, free; ferries $4–$8 each way for adults, depending on the speed and luxury of the boat

SOURCES: Gerard T. Altoff, supervising park ranger. Telephone conversation June 21, 1994, Marty O'Toole, lead park ranger. "Blacks in the Battle of Lake Erie."

Ripley

John Rankin House State Memorial

Rankin House may have sheltered more than two thousand runaway slaves who were on their way to freedom. The home of the Reverend John Rankin and his wife, Jean, is situated high on a hill overlooking the village of Ripley, the Ohio River, and the Kentucky shoreline. From 1825 to 1865 the Rankins and their neighbors, including free African Americans in Brown County, took in escaping slaves and helped them on their way. At night the Rankins kept a beacon burning in the upper window of their home to show the way.

The passage of the Fugitive Slave Act of 1850, however, made the underground railroad activities of the Rankins and their friends more difficult and more dangerous. Under the terms of the law, ex-slaves located in free territory were subject to capture and return to their place of bondage if their masters could prove ownership. Anyone known to shelter runaways was subject to a heavy fine. As a result, owners, informers, and the infamous bounty hunters were quick to pursue escapees. The financial rewards for such actions were large and tempting.

Despite these difficulties, the abolitionists at Ripley persisted in their courageous work — hiding runaways, feeding and clothing them, and helping them move on to safety in Canada. Although as many as twelve persons at a time were sheltered in the Rankin home, not one was ever recaptured.

Harriet Beecher Stowe (1811–1896), the famous novelist, at one time sat here and listened to John Rankin tell the story of Eliza, a slave, who had carried her children across the Ohio River's thawing ice. Stowe modified the story a bit and used it as one of the most dramatic episodes in *Uncle Tom's Cabin.*

> The huge green fragment of ice on which she alighted pitched and creaked as her weight came on it, but she stayed there not a moment. With wild cries and desperate energy she leaped to another and still another cake;—stumbling—leaping—slipping—springing upwards again! Her shoes are gone—her stockings cut from her feet—while blood marked every step; but she saw nothing, felt nothing, till dimly, as in a dream, she saw the Ohio side, and a man helping her up the bank.[2]

The full account of this episode is, if anything, even more remarkable than the fictional version. Eliza and her husband first reached the Rankins in the middle of the night. The man had fallen into the river while leaving a boat and was covered with ice. Although

the husband continued on his way to Canada, Eliza stayed behind, determined to free her six children still in Kentucky.

Returning to Kentucky, Eliza came back again to the Rankins' home; one of her children was strapped to her back in a shawl. Using a board attached to a rope, she had made her way from one treacherous ice floe to another. Eliza soon led that child to safety in Canada but resolved to make yet another trip back to Kentucky to rescue the other five youngsters. The next spring she did so. Upon reaching the home of her old master, Eliza concealed herself beneath the floor of her cabin. The next time her master and his wife left the plantation to visit friends, Eliza and the five remaining children set out, carrying bundles of clothing and other household goods. The weight of these bundles slowed them down on the eleven-mile trip to the river. Since the ferry that was to have taken them north had already left, Eliza and the children hid in a thicket along the river bank. John Rankin sent her a message that she should stay concealed until nighttime.

Disguised as a woman, Rankin then crossed into Kentucky with a group of young men as his helpers. From his home he had noted a group of thirty-one men with dogs and hunting rifles in search of the runaways. Rankin and his friends led the bounty hunters on a chase away from the river while Eliza and her children were rescued by a trusted ferryman. The story ended happily; Eliza and her children finally made their way to Canada.

Jean Lowry Rankin, the abolitionist's wife and mother of thirteen, died in 1878. She had been an integral part of efforts to help in the underground railroad. Reverend Rankin himself died in 1886 at the age of 93. Four Black men served with his sons and sons-in-law as his pallbearers. Both Reverend Rankin and his wife are buried in the Ripley cemetery.

Rankin House was purchased by the state of Ohio in 1938. The house was restored and today is used to interpret the work of the Rankin family and Ohio's contribution to the antislavery movement. Visitors may retrace the route of escaping slaves by climbing a replica of the stairway used by slaves to reach safety at the Rankin home. A book about Rankin House, *The Freedom Light,* is available at the site.

DATE BUILT:	1828
ADDRESS:	Take US 62 to the west side of Ripley, entrance road runs north off US 62
TELEPHONE:	(937) 392-1627
VISITING HOURS:	Memorial Day–Labor Day, daily noon–5; Labor Day–Oct. 31, Sat.–Sun. noon–5; closed Nov.–Memorial Day 👥
FEES:	Adults, $2; children, $.50
SOURCES:	Telephone call to site, June 17, 1994. Telephone conversation Jan. 7, 1995, Lobena Frost, Rankin House. L `Vera Seipelt, hostess, Ripley museum. *National Register of Historic Places*, 568. *Ripley, Ohio. Historical Collections of Brown County, Ohio. Uncle Tom's Cabin.*

Salem

Freedom Hall Museum

The Salem Historical Society's Freedom Hall Museum is a replica of a carpentry shop once used by abolitionists. The original building was constructed on Ellsworth Street in 1838. During the antislavery period, a group of antislavery activists held secret meetings in an upstairs room over the shop.

Salem was the western headquarters of Ohio's antislavery movement. Abolitionists in the town arranged to hear speakers—often at secret meetings for members of the movement. They also hid slaves in homes and barns and helped the freedom seekers escape to Canada. Many well- known opponents of slavery spoke in Salem's old Town Hall (no longer standing), including Frederick Douglass, Sojourner Truth, Parker Pillsbury, and William Lloyd Garrison. Parker Pillsbury (1809–1898) was an abolitionist born in Hamilton, Massachusetts. He traveled widely to lecture on antislavery topics.

The replica of the old carpentry shop with its meeting hall upstairs was completed in 1988, using 1845 flooring from an old Virginia courthouse. Most of the museum's memorabilia are ephemera, including baskets made by a former slave, pictures relating to slavery, some antislavery artifacts, and a bill of sale documenting the sale of Ada Carter for $400.

DATE BUILT:	1838; replica, 1988
ADDRESS:	208 S. Broadway, Salem
TELEPHONE:	(216) 332-4959
VISITING HOURS:	May 1–Dec. 1, Sun. 2–4; closed legal holidays and from the second week of Dec.–Apr. except by appointment 👥
FEES:	Adults, $2; children 11–16, $1; children 10 or under with parents, free; third graders from Salem, Ohio, free
SOURCES:	Mrs. C. J. Lehwald, museum curator and director. Telephone conversation June 17, 1994, Ms. Josephine Rupe, director. *Webster's Biographical Dictionary*, 1185.

Sandusky

Underground Railroad Sites

Sandusky, Ohio, was noted as an abolitionist center and an important stop on the underground railroad. Its location on the southern shore of Lake Erie was highly suitable because of Sandusky's closeness to the islands in the lake and Canada. Erie County was reported to be most active in helping slaves to escape. Between forty and one hundred free Black residents lived in the town before the Civil War. As a result, the sight of escaping Black slaves did not arouse suspicion.

Most of the runaways passing through Sandusky came from Kentucky. Other Ohio communities along the underground railroad were Cincinnati, Toledo, Oberlin, and Cleveland. Some fugitives came alone, but most arrived in families or groups. One man arrived in Sandusky in a coffin with breathing holes. Although he was near death on arrival, a doctor revived him, and in a few days he was on his way to freedom in Canada.

Another group used a loophole in the law to escape. One Sunday a group of slaves with their owner boarded a ship bound for Detroit. By law, slaves were safe from arrest on Sunday. As the ship approached Canada, the captain let a small boat down and the slaves rowed to freedom. The owner could do nothing to prevent their escape.

Several Sandusky sites are associated with the city's underground railroad system. Although the interiors are not open, visitors may enjoy taking a driving tour to see the exteriors. The houses are varied and interesting architecturally as well as for the antislavery history of their former occupants.

The ORAN FOLLETT HOUSE (now a museum operated by the Sandusky Library) is rumored to have a room in which slaves were kept, although museum director Helen Hansen has found no solid evidence to substantiate this belief. The house is located at 404 Wayne Street at East Adams and is open to visitors. A reference room contains local history, but the exhibits do not focus on Black history.

SECOND BAPTIST CHURCH, at 315 Decatur Street, is built around another church that sheltered fugitive slaves before the Civil War. The enclosed structure is often referred to as the "Antislavery Baptist Church." This African American congregation organized in 1849, at first coming together for the purpose of helping other Black people who were arriving from the South. They worshiped for a period in an old frame house formerly used as a church by a white congregation that had split over the issue of slavery. The Black congregation paid for the church by 1859; later they added a basement. Second Baptist was Sandusky's first Black church and was, according to member Elaine Lawson, the only church in Sandusky associated with the underground railroad. Some of its young founders were free; others were fugitive slaves. They all boldly assisted other runaways who came by way of Sandusky because from that point they could easily "island hop" to Canada. Shipping, a major industry in Sandusky, provided opportunities to smuggle slaves across to freedom.

In 1975 the congregation remodeled the church, and the old walls are no longer visible. The members, however, retain an awareness of their history. To visit the church, call in advance and make an appointment with the pastor.

The RUSH SLOANE HOUSE, 403 East Adams, was home to the best-known of Sandusky's abolitionists. Under the Fugitive Slave Act two slave owners brought suits against Sloane for helping their slaves escape to Canada. One owner lost his case on a technicality, but the other won. In 1854 a judge ordered Sloane to pay a $4,300 fine. Sloane's incensed neighbors organized a committee and raised $393. Sloane had to pay the rest himself. Sloane House is a large, beautiful structure capped with a completely enclosed widow's walk.

Other homes still existing in Sandusky were recorded by early historians as underground railroad sites. They are

Thomas C. McGee House,
536 East Washington Street.

George Barney House,
422 East Washington Street.
This huge house, now painted white,
still has behind it another original house from
the early period.

Henry F. Merry House,
330 East Adams Street.

Joseph M. Root House,
231 East Adams Street.

Lucas S. Beecher House,
West Washington Row. This limestone house,
smaller than the Sloane House,
has been restored inside and out.

DATE OF SIGNIFICANCE:	The decades before the Civil War
ADDRESS:	See individual sites
TELEPHONE:	Follett House Museum, (419) 627-9608; Second Baptist Church, (419) 625-1411
VISITING HOURS:	Most sites private, visitors may walk or drive by 🚶🚶
SOURCES:	Telephone conversation June 19, 1994, Jean Gardner, guide, Follett House Museum. Telephone conversation June 19, 1994, Elaine Lawson of Second Baptist Church. Helen M. Hansen, curator, Follett House Museum. "Route to Freedom." *From the Widow's Walk.*

Westerville

Benjamin Hanby House

The Hanby House in Westerville was a station on the underground railway, as was the former Hanby House in Rushville, Ohio. William Hanby was a bishop who edited the *Religious Telescope* for the United Brethren Church. He was also a founder of Otterbein College in Westerville.

Benjamin Hanby, William's son, was the most famous of the eight Hanby children. He wrote "My Darling Nellie Gray" and "Ole Shady" (also known as the "Song of the Contraband"). "My Darling Nellie Gray" told of Joe Selby, a fugitive slave who had escaped on the underground railroad and had to leave behind the woman he loved. Both songs had a strong influence on persons who believed in the antislavery movement.

Hanby House, the pre-Civil War home of the William Hanby family, has been restored and furnished as in the 1850s period. Visitors see *Gift of Song*, a seventeen-minute film that describes Hanby's life; then they can take a tour of the house. Originally Hanby House was a four-room structure with a barn behind it. Family members who were returning home knew how many slaves were hidden in the house by the number of flowers in a white vase in the window. Fugitive slaves stayed in the barn and came into the house to eat, sing, and pray. When it was safe to leave for the next stop, Mount Vernon, they departed, carefully hidden under hay and tools in a wagon. Today Hanby House still has a white vase with flowers in the window.

DATE BUILT:	1854
ADDRESS:	160 W. Main Street, Westerville
TELEPHONE:	(614) 891-6289
VISITING HOURS:	May 1–Oct. 31, Sat. 10–4, Sun. 1–5; by appointment other days ♛♛
FEES:	Adults, $1.50; seniors and AAA members, $1.20; groups of 5 or more, $1.25 each; children 6–12, $.50; children under 6, free
SOURCE:	Telephone conversation June 17, 1994, Carol R. Krumm, curator.

Wilberforce

National Afro-American Museum and Cultural Center *

The National Afro-American Museum is a federal museum dedicated to the study of African American history and culture. It is located on the original eighty-eight-acre campus of Wilberforce University, the oldest Black college operated by a Black organization prior to the Civil War. The college also was a site on the underground railroad.

The National Afro-American Museum and Cultural Center is housed in a modern, one-story, 35,000-square-foot granite structure on a site overlooking a natural ravine. It was originally organized in 1972 as a joint project of the state of Ohio and the federal government. The first phase of the complex, including the newly constructed museum and the renovated Carnegie Library, opened in 1988. The museum includes exhibition space, a center for historical research, an art gallery, a children's mini museum, a theater, and an amphitheater as well as a cafeteria and picnic areas.

The museum creates a wide range of special exhibits. For example, *From Victory to Freedom: Afro-American Life in the Fifties* displayed artifacts typical of homes, businesses, clothing styles, and entertainment in the fifties. The museum also sponsored the *Holiday Festival of Black Dolls* and *Rhythm and Blues: Black American Popular Music, 1945–1955.*

DATE ESTABLISHED:	Museum, 1972; this site, 1988
ADDRESS:	1350 Brush Row Road, Wilberforce
TELEPHONE:	(937) 376-4944
VISITING HOURS:	Tues.–Sat. 9–5, Sun. 1–5; closed Mon., all holidays except Martin Luther King Jr. Day ♛♛
FEES:	Adults, $3.50; students with I.D. and children, $1.50; scheduled school tours, free
SOURCES:	John E. Fleming, director National Afro-American Museum. Linda S. Buckwalter, administrative assistant National Afro-American Museum. *The National Afro-American Museum and Cultural Center. From Victory to Freedom. Holiday Festival of Black Dolls. Your Donor's Guide to Preserving Afro-American History and Culture.*

Wilberforce University
Central State University

Wilberforce University and Central State University once were housed on the same campus. Wilberforce, the older of the two universities, is the oldest college in America established and operated by African Americans before the end of the Civil War. (See the Cheyney State University listing in Cheyney, Pennsylvania, and the Lincoln University listing in Oxford, Pennsylvania, for information on other Black universities established before the Civil War.) Wilberforce University traces its history back to the time before the Civil War when the underground railroad provided safe havens and a way to freedom. Many of the free Black men and women and escaped slaves in Ohio needed an institution of higher learning. Wilberforce was established to meet this need.

The origins of Wilberforce University are intertwined with the development of an earlier school, Union Seminary. In 1844 the Ohio Conference of the African Methodist Episcopal Church selected a tract of land twelve miles west of Columbus, Ohio; there the church leaders established Union Seminary to educate young men in academic subjects, agriculture, and the mechanical arts and to provide instruction for those who wished to enter the ministry. At the same time, leaders of the Methodist Episcopal Church were starting a movement to educate African Americans from Ohio and neighboring free states; they approved the establishment of an institution called Ohio African University. The church leaders selected a site in Wilberforce (then known as Tawawa Springs), a small community with a history of underground railroad activity, and the school, the forerunner of Wilberforce University, opened in 1856.

Although enrollment at Ohio African University exceeded two hundred at the high school and college levels by 1860, the progression of the Civil War, a drop in financial support, and a $10,000 debt burden caused the school to close in 1862. School officials made plans to sell the property. Then Bishop Daniel Payne of the A.M.E. Church made an alternate suggestion—Union Seminary would move to the more-desirable location in Wilberforce. The A.M.E. Church purchased the college in 1863, and Reverend Payne was selected as president, becoming the first Black college administrator in the United States. The newly incorporated school was named in honor of the eighteenth-century British abolitionist William Wilberforce (1759–1833), who helped to end the slave trade in England.

In 1888 the Ohio legislature established Central State University, a normal and industrial school for Black students. The school had its own trustee board but educated students on the Wilberforce campus. In 1947 Central State University, the newer college,

became a separate university. The historic campus where the two colleges once operated together became a part of the conference center of the National Afro-American Museum. Today, Wilberforce University, Central State University, and the National Afro-American Museum are located within a short distance of one another.

The old Wilberforce University campus has been transformed over the years. The original Shorter Hall burned to the ground on the same night that President Abraham Lincoln was assassinated, but it was soon rebuilt. The present Shorter Hall, constructed on the old campus in 1922, was the main administration center. Carnegie Library, constructed in 1909 and remodeled in 1938, was a brick structure with a full basement. The library was a gift of philanthropist Andrew Carnegie. In the spring of 1974, a massive tornado damaged many of the older buildings that were still in use on the old campus. Repairs were made to buildings on a temporary basis. Then the old campus was sold, and the Ohio General Assembly and U.S. Congress designated the campus as the location for the National Afro-American Museum and Cultural Center. The Carnegie Library structure now houses museum administrative staff as well as historical items relating to Black history and Black culture.

Wilberforce University moved to a new campus on a gently rising slope located approximately one mile from the site of the original campus. In 1974 the Old Fountain was transferred and reconstructed on the new site.

DATE ESTABLISHED:	Central State University, 1947 (as an independent university); Wilberforce University, 1844; Ohio African University, 1856 (1863, as Wilberforce University)
ADDRESS:	Central State, 1055 N. Bickett Road; Wilberforce University, Brush Row Road, Wilberforce
TELEPHONE:	Central State University, (937) 376-6011; Wilberforce University, (513) 376-2911
VISITING HOURS:	By appointment during school sessions
SOURCES:	Jacqueline Y. Brown, librarian, Archives, Wilberforce University. Joan Baxter, executive secretary, Greene County Historical Society. *Wilberforce University Bulletin. International Library of Negro Life and History*, 139.

Colonel Charles Young House

Colonel Charles Young (1864–1922) was the third Black man to graduate from West Point. He was the highest ranking Black officer in World War I after serving under President Theodore Roosevelt as America's first Black military attaché. After graduating from West Point, Colonel Young was assigned to the Tenth Infantry. Later he served with both the Twenty-fifth Infantry and Ninth Cavalry.

In 1894 Young received a federal appointment as professor of science and military tactics at Wilberforce University in Ohio. He also taught French and mathematics and coached the drama and glee clubs. Young was talented in languages, including German, Italian, Spanish, Latin, and Greek. He played several musical instruments and composed music.

At the outbreak of the Spanish-American War in 1898, Colonel Young briefly was given command of the Ninth Ohio Volunteer Infantry (Colored). At their first encampment, Camp Alger in Virginia, a group of white soldiers refused to salute Young because of his color. Since they had refused to respect him, he took off his coat and made them salute the coat for its rank.

Young had several other appointments. Following service in the West, he was appointed as United States military attaché to Haiti by Theodore Roosevelt, the first African American to receive this type of appointment. When Young died in 1922, a memorial service was held in the great hall of New York College. Following the service, his body was taken to Washington, D.C., and interred in Arlington's marble amphitheater.

Colonel Young lived in this brick, nineteenth-century residence from 1894 to 1898. The house is located in Green County, approximately two-thirds of the way from Xenia to Wilberforce.

The Young House has served as the Omega Psi Phi Fraternity House, home to a national Black fraternity. Beautifully restored, the house is open to visitors by appointment.

DATE OF SIGNIFICANCE: Young residence, 1894–1898
ADDRESS: Columbus Pike between Clifton and Stevenson Roads, Wilberforce
TELEPHONE: National Afro-American Museum and Cultural Center, (513) 376-4944

VISITING HOURS: By appointment
SOURCES: Telephone call June 17, 1994, National Afro-American Museum and Cultural Center. Telephone conversation June 17, 1994, Mrs. Joan Baxter, director, Greene County Historical Society Museum. *National Register of Historic Places,* 578.

Notes

1. "Blacks in the Battle of Lake Erie," Washington, D.C.: National Park Service, 1.
2. Harriet Beecher Stowe, *Uncle Tom's Cabin* (New York: Bantam, 1981), 58.

Works Consulted

"Blacks in the Battle of Lake Erie." Washington, D.C.: National Park Service. [manuscript]

"First Black School in Ohio Being Restored in Harveysburg." Lorraine Wise. (Wilmington, Ohio) *News Journal,* 2 Feb. 1990.

From the Widow's Walk: A View of Sandusky. Helen Hansen. Sandusky, Ohio: Follett House Museum, Branch of Sandusky Library, 1991.

From Victory to Freedom: Afro-American Life in the Fifties. Wilberforce, Ohio: National Afro-American Museum and Cultural Center. [flier]

Historical Collections of Brown County, Ohio. Carl N. Thompson, comp. Piqua, Ohio: Hammer Graphics, 1969.

Holiday Festival of Black Dolls. Wilberforce, Ohio: National Afro-American Museum and Cultural Center, 27–29 Oct. 1989. [flier]

International Library of Negro Life and History: Negro Americans in the Civil War. Charles H. Wesley and Patricia W. Romero. New York: Publishers, 1970.

The National Afro-American Museum and Cultural Center. Wilberforce, Ohio: National Afro-American Museum and Cultural Center. [flier]

National Historic Landmark Status Report. Washington, D.C.: Department of the Interior, 1979.

National Register of Historic Places. Washington, D.C.: National Park Service, 1976.

"Paul Laurence Dunbar House." Columbus, Ohio: The Ohio Historical Society. [brochure]

Perry's Victory and International Peace Memorial. Washington, D.C.: National Park Service, 1989. [brochure]

Ripley, Ohio: Its History and Families. Eliese Bambach Stivers. Georgetown, Ohio: The Brown County Genealogical Society, 1965.

"Route to Freedom: Slaves Found Sanctuary in Sandusky." Mark Davidson. *Sandusky Register,* 21 Feb. 1988.

Uncle Tom's Cabin. Harriet Beecher Stowe. New York: Bantam, 1981.

Webster's Biographical Dictionary. 1st ed. Springfield, Mass.: G. & C. Merriam, 1964.

Webster's New Biographical Dictionary. Springfield, Mass.: Merriam-Webster, 1988.

Wilberforce University Bulletin. Wilberforce, Ohio: Wilberforce University, 1987.

Astoria Vicinity

Fort Clatsop National Memorial

Members of the adventure-filled Lewis and Clark Expedition were sent to explore the virtually unknown and vast territory of the Louisiana Purchase that the United States had bought from France in 1803. President Thomas Jefferson placed his personal secretary, Captain Meriwether Lewis, in charge of the expedition. Lewis chose William Clark as his second in command. The bold group set out from St. Louis in 1803 and returned there in 1806 after encountering many hazards and learning much about the new lands and their inhabitants during the voyage.

Among the members of the group there was a Black slave and servant named York. He became a valued member of the expedition, highly respected for his physical strength and his prowess in exploring the wilderness. His ability to communicate with the Indians proved of considerable help to Lewis and Clark. York was also a skilled hunter who knew how to live off the land. In November 1805 York, along with other members of the exhausted group, agreed with their leaders' decision to spend the winter at what is now Astoria. Together with others, York helped build Fort Clatsop on the Columbia River, where the group spent the winter of 1805–1806. When the expedition returned to St. Louis in September 1806, it was greeted with jubilation. Although York was included in the celebrations, many years passed before he received his freedom.

The Fort Clatsop National Memorial has a replica of the log fort the expedition members built in the winter of 1805. The large exhibit hall includes a modest amount of information about York's role in the expedition, but information presented about him depends on the interpreter and the questions asked by visitors. Museum features also include a seventeen-minute slide show, a thirty-minute film about the Lewis and Clark Expedition, and a canoe-landing trail. The Fort Clatsop Historic Association bookstore carries books about the famous expedition.

DATE BUILT:	1805
ADDRESS:	5 miles southwest of Astoria off US 101
TELEPHONE:	(503) 861-2471
VISITING HOURS:	Mid-June–Labor Day, daily 8–6; Labor Day–Apr. 1, daily 8–5; closed Christmas 👫
FEES:	Adults 17 and older, $2; families, $4; U.S. citizens 65 or older Golden Lifetime Pass, $10; youths under 17, free; free Labor Day–Apr. 1
SOURCES:	Telephone conversation June 21, 1994, Alice Morton, office automation assistant, and Sandra Reinebach, business manager, Fort Clatsop Historical Association. Jeffrey Uecker, museum educator, Oregon Historical Society. *Northwest Black Heritage: The Pioneers.*

Portland

Oregon Historical Society Library
Sovereign Hotel Murals

York, a Black man who traveled with the Lewis and Clark Expedition, is represented among the figures that decorate the west wall of Portland's Sovereign Hotel. Other explorers represented are Captain Robert Gray, Captain Meriwether Lewis and William Clark, and Sacajawea. The mural is huge—six or seven stories high—and is completed in a trompe-l'oeil style that incorporates the hotel windows into the design in such a way that they seem to disappear.

The Oregon Historical Society has owned the Sovereign Hotel since 1982. The library of the society has documents about Black people who homesteaded in the Pacific Northwest in the late 1800s. The collection, appropriate for adult researchers, includes a vertical file with pamphlets, clippings, books, public manuscript materials, records of African American organizations, Black-owned Oregon newspapers, oral history recordings, and personal papers of individuals.

DATE ESTABLISHED:	Murals, c1988
ADDRESS:	1230 S.W. Park Avenue, Portland
TELEPHONE:	(503) 222-1741
VISITING HOURS:	Mural, dawn–dusk; Oregon Historical Society library, Tues.–Sat. noon–4:45
FEES:	Mural, free; library, nonmembers, $4.50

SOURCES:	Telephone conversation June 21, 1994, Stephen Hallberg, catalogue librarian. "Spellbinding Historic Murals on Sides of Sovereign Hotel Will Be Among Stunning Accomplishments Foreseen for 1988."

Tour of Black History through Art

Although there are few identified Black historic sites remaining in Oregon, the story of African Americans who settled the West is portrayed in a series of murals in Portland executed by Isaac Shamsud-Din. One of the leading artists of the Northwest, Shamsud-Din has created contemporary art that shows the vitality, adventure, and achievement of Black pioneers. Prudence Roberts, Senior Curator at the Portland Art Museum, described Shamsud-Din's art as "very, very colorful, densely packed with information and incidents, with vibrant color and sense of motion—murals that a family would enjoy seeing."[1]

Shamsud-Din grew up in Portland, Oregon, in the 1950s and studied art at Portland State University. During the late 1960s he served as a college lecturer in Black studies and was later selected to be Portland's visual-arts ombudsman.

As a child, Shamsud-Din wanted to learn more about his Black heritage. He eventually spent twenty years in a search that culminated in the desire to use art to preserve and share the knowledge he had gained. He was commissioned to paint a variety of murals at several Oregon sites. Some of his works in Portland are described in the following sections.

ADDRESS:	See individual listings
VISITING HOURS:	Contact each center to arrange visit and to be sure that the mural is currently displayed
SOURCES:	Jeffrey Uecker, museum educator, Oregon Historical Society. Telephone conversation June 21, 1994, Prudence Roberts, senior curator, Portland Art Museum. Telephone conversation June 21, 1994, Sandra Tate, assistant director, Littman and White Art Galleries, Portland State University. *Northwest Black Heritage. Perspectives.*

Harriet Tubman Mural

Located at the Harriet Tubman Middle School, the 1983 work is acrylic on plaster wall. It shows the accomplishments of Harriet Tubman, an African

American famed for her escape from slavery and her repeated returns to the South to lead others to freedom. The Artists in the Schools Program of the Oregon Arts Commission commissioned the work. Children enjoy seeing the mural.

ADDRESS: 2231 N. Flint, Portland
TELEPHONE: (503) 916-5630

Kwazulu

The Children's Museum in Portland commissioned this 8-foot-by-24-foot acrylic-on-panel mural by Isaac Shamsud-Din in 1984. It is on display intermittently.

ADDRESS: 3037 S.W. Second Avenue, Portland
TELEPHONE: (503) 823-2227

Pioneers—Agents of Change

The Cascade Division of the Salvation Army commissioned this 10-foot-by-8-foot acrylic mural in 1979.

ADDRESS: Moore Street Center, Portland
TELEPHONE: (503) 239-1224

Three Untitled Works in Progress

Benson High School in Portland commissioned this mural in 1985.

ADDRESS: 546 N.E. Twelfth Street, Portland
TELEPHONE: (503) 916-5100

Untitled

The Artists in the Schools Program of the Oregon Arts Commission commissioned this work in 1982.

The painting, located at the Woodlawn Elementary School, is 10 feet by 11 feet in acrylic on plaster wall.

ADDRESS: 7200 N.E. Eleventh Street, Portland
TELEPHONE: (503) 280-6282

Vanport

This oil-on-canvas mural, located in the Smith Student Center at Portland State University, is one of Shamsud-Din's earlier works. The Art Department of Portland State University commissioned the 14 1/2-foot-by-9 1/2-foot mural.

ADDRESS: Portland State University, stairwell of the Smith Student Center, Portland
TELEPHONE: (503) 725-4522
VISITING HOURS: Mon.–Fri. 7 A.M.–10 P.M., Sat. 8 A.M.–10 P.M., Sun. 10–5; closed holidays

Note

1. Telephone conversation June 21, 1994, Prudence Roberts, senior curator, Portland Art Museum.

Works Consulted

The Oregon Historical Society Presents Northwest Black Heritage: The Pioneers. Karen Broenneke. Portland, Ore.: Oregon Historical Society. [classroom packet]

Perspectives. Portland Art Museum, Dec. 10–Jan. 26, 1985–1986.

"Spellbinding Historic Murals on Sides of Sovereign Hotel Will Be Among Stunning Accomplishments Foreseen for 1988." Thomas Vaughan. *Oregon Historical Society News* 32, no. 1 (Feb. 1988).

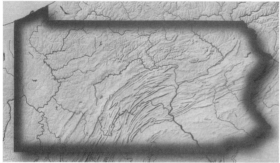

Buckingham

Mount Gilead African Methodist Episcopal Church

Mount Gilead African Methodist Episcopal Church, a small, one-room stone church, has a proud history as a part of the underground railroad. Slaves making their way north passed through this section of southeastern Pennsylvania. Mount Gilead Church was the last stop before the fugitives were smuggled into New Jersey to continue on their way to freedom. The original church was built of logs in 1832; it was rebuilt in stone in 1852.

DATE CONSTRUCTED:	1852
ADDRESS:	Holicong Road, Buckingham
TELEPHONE:	(215) 794-7307
VISITING HOURS:	Congregation meets approximately 3 times per year; by appointment with Mr. or Mrs. William Hopkins, church caretakers
FEES:	Donations appreciated
SOURCES:	Telephone conversation June 16, 1994, Mrs. Mildred Hopkins, church caretaker. "Forming an Identity through the Church."

Chambersburg

John Brown House

This site is associated with John Brown, a white abolitionist who passionately advocated emancipation for Black people even if it could be obtained only through violent means. Brown led a raid at Harpers Ferry, West Virginia, in October 1859. He and his followers planned to seize the federal arsenal, free large numbers of slaves, and establish a stronghold where the freed people could live in peace. Although the rebellion was not successful, the effort aroused the country and caused many people to question the institution of slavery. The raid at Harpers Ferry and the ensuing uproar were among the factors that led to the Civil War. (See the listings for Kansas City and Osawatomie, Kansas; West Des Moines, Iowa; Akron, Ohio; Harpers Ferry, West Virginia; and Lake Placid, New York, for additional information on John Brown.)

In June 1859 John Brown rented an upstairs bedroom in this house from Abram Ritner, the owner, and lived here until mid-October. To conceal his identity, Brown called himself Dr. Isaac Smith and told people he was in the area to develop iron mines. He was quietly purchasing tools and weapons needed for the raid and storing them in a warehouse on Chambersburg's North Main Street. While living here, Brown became a part of the local community. He taught Sunday School at a church on the campus of Pennsylvania State University and preached at the Falling Spring Presbyterian Church in Chambersburg.

Abolitionist leaders, including the African American leader Frederick Douglass, visited John Brown at this site. Although they discussed plans for the capture of Harpers Ferry, Douglass did not participate in the raid. After the failure of the planned uprising, four of Brown's followers escaped and returned to this house, asking for asylum. Ritner hid them for a while in a nearby grove and gave them other assistance.

This house is Pennsylvania's only existing landmark associated with John Brown. In 1864, years after Brown's death, rebel soldiers burned the downtown section of Chambersburg to the ground. Ritner's home was located outside the center of town, however, and was not harmed.

The John Brown House is a two and one-half-story structure constructed of logs with clapboarding. The earliest section of the building probably dates from 1820 to 1840. It is listed in the *National Register of Historic Places*. The Pennsylvania Historical and Museum Commission operates the restored house, which is used today as offices of the American Heart Association.

DATE BUILT: c1820–1840

ADDRESS: 225 E. King Street, Chambersburg

TELEPHONE: (717) 263-2870

VISITING HOURS: Mon.–Fri. by appointment

SOURCES: NRHPINF. Telephone conversation June 15, 1994, Sharon Strike, division director, American Heart Association. *The John Brown House.*

Cheyney

Cheyney State University
Melrose

The Melrose residence at Cheyney University is significant in Black history for its association with Cheyney State University and with Dr. Leslie Pinckney Hill, an outstanding educator and leader from Cheyney State. The university had its start in 1828 when a Quaker philanthropist, Richard Humphrey, left a bequest of $10,000 to establish a school that would prepare teachers to instruct African American children in academics, agriculture, and the mechanical arts and trades. The training farm was established in 1837, and by 1842 the school, known as the Institute for Colored Youth, was one of the first of its kind in the nation devoted solely to the instruction of Black students.

The Institute for Colored Youth moved from Lombard Street in Philadelphia to Bainbridge Street, then to York Road. Fanny M. Jackson Coppin was one of the school's outstanding teachers. Born in slavery in Washington, D.C., in 1836, she was freed when her aunt, who earned only $6 a month, purchased Coppin for $125. Coppin attended a number of schools including Oberlin College in Ohio, where she

studied Greek, mathematics, and French. She taught former slaves who came to Ohio after the Civil War. She came to the Institute for Colored Youth in 1865 and four years later was appointed principal.

Needing more space than was reasonably available in Philadelphia for the agricultural curriculum, in 1902 the school bought the Cheyney farm, a site that had belonged to Quaker farmers John and Thomas Cheyney and that had a house, Melrose, built about 1785. The school moved to the farm in 1903 and used the former farmhouse as the president's house until 1968.

Dr. Leslie Pinckney Hill (1880–1960) led the college during a period of growth. He had graduated from Harvard University with high distinction—cum laude and Phi Beta Kappa—and served as class orator. After graduation, he headed the English Department at Tuskegee University from 1904 to 1907. While there, he married the dean of women, Jane Ethel Clark. When the position opened as principal of the Institute for Colored Youth in Philadelphia, Hill's mentor, Booker T. Washington, recommended him for the position.

As principal of the Institute, Hill transformed the school into a respected liberal arts college. Although the agricultural program continued, Hill steered the program away from the emphasis on preparing students for sharecropping and menial labor. He introduced a variety of promising agricultural practices and advanced craft skills. As the father of six daughters, Hill always advocated women's rights. Hill was active in community activities, organizing a variety of programs and encouraging Black people to remain aware of their cultural roots and heritage. He was a gifted speaker, and was often requested to address predominantly white audiences.

The Institute for Colored Youth was recognized as a teachers' college in 1902 and became a state normal school, at which time it changed its name to Cheyney State College (later University). The state began to support the college in 1922, and in 1942 it was accredited by the American Association of Teachers' Colleges. Graduates were successful not only in teaching but also in many other fields, including business, public service, and medicine.

Melrose, the house where the Hill family lived, was built in three sections, one prior to 1785, one in 1807, and one about 1850. The two and one-half–story residence originally was a single-family farmhouse with a cooking fireplace and with corner fireplaces in some rooms. The exterior remains much as it appeared when built. The 122-acre farm now forms the university campus. Melrose is listed in the *National Register of Historic Places.*

DATE BUILT: Central section, c1785

ADDRESS: Hill Drive, northwest corner of Creek and Cheyney Roads, Cheyney

TELEPHONE: (610) 399-2000

VISITING HOURS: Private; campus accessible during regular academic hours; closed summer

SOURCES: NRHPINF. *International Library of Negro Life and History,* 67.

Cornwall

Cornwall Iron Furnace

Although large numbers of slaves were brought to America to work in agriculture in the South, significant numbers were also used in both the South and the North in manufacturing operations, including the iron-making industry. In the eighteenth and nineteenth centuries iron furnaces dotted the Pennsylvania countryside, and villages with schools, churches, and shops grew around them. This industry used slave labor as early as 1766.

In 1742 Peter Grubb established the Cornwall Iron Furnace, which became the heart of a vast industrial plantation. The furnace was ideally situated for iron making because the surrounding area contained enormous quantities of iron ore, limestone, and timber. Workers continued day and night to make iron for domestic and military products.

Black workers were an important part of the operation. At the time of the American Revolution, approximately 6,000 slaves lived in Pennsylvania, ten of them in Lebanon Township in 1779. As early as April 1766, eleven Black people, slave and free, were listed in the journal at Cornwall. They worked among people of different nationalities, including a

few indentured servants, most of whom came from Germany or Great Britain. In 1780 thirteen of the thirty-seven workers were Black. In that same year, however, a law passed in Pennsylvania called for the gradual emancipation of slaves; by 1792 only one Black person was listed as still working at Cornwall Furnace.

At least one slave who worked at the furnace emancipated himself. A hill in nearby Mt. Gretna is named "Governor Dick" after a slave who took on legendary fame by running away from Cornwall Furnace on April 17, 1796. On July 8 the following appeal for his capture appeared in a Pennsylvania newspaper:

> Twenty Dollars Reward.
> RAN away from Cornwall Furnace, Dauphin County, on Sunday the 17th of April last, a Negro man, called Dick, alias Governor Dick: he is an elderly man, bald headed, about five feet ten inches high, stout made, has a down look, is slightly marked on each of his temples with the small scores usual to some of the natives of Africa, has large feet, and a remarkable scar on the great toe of his right foot, occasioned by its being split with an axe. He is by trade a rough carpenter, and values himself greatly on his dexterity in that occupation. Had on when he went away, a new drab-coloured coatee, with metal buttons, jackets and overalls of the same, a new wool hat, and took with him some old clothes. As he lived in the early part of his life in Hartford County, State of Maryland, it is probable he has shaped his course to that quarter. Whoever secures the said Negro so that the owners may get him again, shall receive the above reward, and reasonable charges, if brought home.
> July 8th, 1796. Rudolph Kelker, jun.[1]

The records do not indicate whether Dick was ever recaptured.

The furnace remained in operation until 1883 when anthracite coal replaced charcoal as a fuel and made the furnace obsolete. The mines, however, continued in operation until 1974, and a surviving community nearby still reflects the period from 1857 to 1883.

Today Cornwall Furnace is one of the world's best-preserved iron-making facilities. The furnace, air blast machinery, and related buildings are still intact. The complex has a sandstone foundry with large stone furnace; Cornwall mine, the oldest continuously used iron mine in America; and a village of two-family houses constructed in the 1860s. The site also includes a Visitors Center in the Eighteenth Century charcoal house, a roasting oven, coal bins, and several other buildings. Guided tours are provided, and the Visitors Center contains exhibits.

DATE ESTABLISHED: 1742

ADDRESS: Rexmont Road at Boyd Street, Cornwall

TELEPHONE: (717) 272-9711

VISITING HOURS: Tues.–Sat. 9–5; Sun. noon–5; open on Memorial Day, July 4, Labor Day; closed Mon., New Year's, Easter, Thanksgiving, Christmas 👫

FEES: Adults, $3.50; senior citizens over 60, $2.50; children 6–17, $1.50; children under 6, free

SOURCES: Richard B. Stratton, Cornwall Iron Furnace. Telephone conversation Aug. 8, 1995, Karen Viozzi, guide, Cornwall Iron Furnace. *National Register of Historic Places*, 641. *Cornwall Iron Furnace.* "The Rise of an Iron Community," 15, 16, 92, 93.

Cornwells Heights

Bensalem African Methodist Episcopal Church

Bensalem A.M.E. Church, also known as Little Jerusalem, was built in 1830. It is one of the oldest African American churches in America that is still standing. The congregation dates back to 1820 when the Reverend James Miller founded it. The first members of the congregation included the Briggs, Bosley, Fraizer, and Mounts families. All of them were African Americans, who were among the original settlers in Bucks County. Most of the early church members were interred on a burial ground connected with the church.

Bensalem A.M.E. Church is a frame, one and one-half–story, one-room building. Constructed in 1830 with shiplap wooden siding, it was renovated in 1860 and 1896. In one renovation the structure was covered with shingles. In the 1960s the front was stuccoed. Reverend Ellsworth Collins, pastor of the church since 1988, notes that Bensalem Church had no indoor plumbing, including running water, until the early 1990s.

The interior features the original woodwork, including random-width floorboards, waist-level wainscoting, hand-painted board pews, and a pulpit and altar rail assembled by joinery and without nails. The church still serves the community of Bridgewater in Bucks County, Pennsylvania. Eight direct descendants of the original members are in the congregation. The building is listed in the *National Register of Historic Places*.

DATE BUILT: 1830

ADDRESS: 1200 Bridgewater Road, Cornwells Heights

TELEPHONE: Disconnected

VISITING HOURS: Information on access to interior not available; visitors can walk or drive by

SOURCES: NRHPINF. Telephone conversation Aug. 20, 1995, Reverend Ellsworth S. Collins, pastor, Bensalem A.M.E. Church.

Elverson

Hopewell Furnace National Historic Site

Most people are aware of the role Black slaves played in America's agriculture, but few realize that Black people also worked as slaves, apprentices, and free laborers in America's early industries. In Pennsylvania African Americans made a significant contribution to the iron furnace industry, most often as unskilled laborers but sometimes as highly qualified workers who received pay equal to that of white workers.

Ironmasters owned Black slaves and also guided Black apprentices who worked for them for a specified number of years. In addition, they at times hired free Black people. Sometimes runaway slaves were employed for a period of time, after which they would move on to other localities.

In Elverson, Pennsylvania, Mark Bird built Hopewell Furnace on the headwaters of French Creek in 1771. Black slaves were employed there in the iron-making process, which required heavy labor. Raw materials—iron ore, limestone, and hardwood forests for charcoal—all were available in the area. Miners would dig the ore from mines or wash it from nearby streams; teamsters would then haul it to the furnace. Colliers would stack the wood and ignite it, watching the pit to ensure a slow, even burning. Finally the charcoal would be taken out, cooled, and taken by wagon to the furnace.

At the furnace the founder and workers added charcoal, limestone, and ore and periodically drained off the molten iron. Molders ladled the hot liquid into sand molds; skilled workers then cast intricate designs. Hopewell manufactured a variety of cookware and other iron products including stoves.

Laborers were scarce in the rural areas where the furnaces were situated. The furnaces had to be close to forests, the source of their fuel, and few people lived in those remote regions. To remedy this, owners used Black slaves, free Black workers who were paid, and indentured workers, both Black and white. Some poor Black parents apprenticed their children to ironmasters so that their children could learn a trade. Once the trade was learned, the ironmaster could profit by selling the unexpired time of the indenture.

Slaves were listed in furnace records by their first names as Negro Robin, Negro Samuel, Black Majer, or Black York. Some had been taken from their mothers at an early age and sold to a succession of owners before coming to the furnace. A boy named Davy, for example, was sold at the age of four for $100. He was sold again as a servant at twelve years. Within three months he went to work for an ironmaster. At the age of eighteen he became the property of a firm at the Birdsboro forge.

As the furnaces and their products became more important in the half-century after 1780, Black workers became more valuable. In the counties where iron was produced, ironmasters were the largest holders of slaves. In 1779 the Hopewell firm owned twelve slaves. Some free Black workers lived under the same conditions as white workers. They ate in the same company dining rooms and lived in homes on the iron plantation. In the early 1800s several Black men had relatively high-paying jobs as fillers, colliers,

and miners. They were not admitted to the top jobs of molders and founders.

A Black community founded by escaped slaves grew up in the wooded valley of the Six Penny Creek, not far from the Hopewell Furnace, Joanna Furnace, and Birdsboro Forge. Many of the residents worked in the iron industries and founded the A.M.E. Mount Frisby Church in 1856. Two Black men who fought in the Union army during the Civil War were buried in the cemetery at the rear of the church.

Other Black people employed at the furnaces worshiped in predominantly white local churches. The records of these churches often listed their Black members. A Black man, Bill Jacobs, was buried in the cemetery of the Bethesda Baptist Church that numbered many Black and white Hopewell employees among its members. Originally Bill Jacobs had been an indentured servant who worked as a teamster before attaining the higher status of a coachman and gardener for Clement Brooks, the ironmaster of Hopewell Furnace. Because Black and white families lived near each other and sometimes worshiped in the same churches, a certain antislavery feeling developed in this area. Some white community members may have assisted escaping slaves.

By the mid-1830s Hopewell's prosperity was beginning to wane. Other companies that had developed better methods of producing high-quality iron at less expense were located closer to the urban markets. As a result, the furnace closed down in 1883, and its workers had to look for employment in towns or cities.

Hopewell Furnace, now a national historic site, has been restored as closely as possible to its appearance in the 1820–1840 period by the National Park Service. This is the finest example of an early American "iron plantation," which was the forerunner of today's iron and steel giants. Hopewell was one of Pennsylvania's most important furnace operations, producing pig iron and finished castings from 1771 until 1883. Today's visitors to Hopewell can see what a nineteenth-century iron community was like, including the restored waterwheel, blast machinery, the ironmaster's mansion, and numerous other structures. They can see a place where more than 100 Black people were employed in various capacities.

DATE ESTABLISHED:	1771
ADDRESS:	About 6 miles south of Birdsboro on PA 345; 10 miles from the Morgantown interchange on the PA Turnpike via PA 23 E. and PA 345 N.; French Creek State Park adjoins the Hopewell Furnace site; Elverson
TELEPHONE:	(610) 582-8773
VISITING HOURS:	Daily 9–5; demonstrations of molding and casting, June–Labor Day; village trades and activities, July–Aug.; closed Thanksgiving, Christmas, New Year's
FEES:	Adults, $2; children under 17, free; seniors 62 and over, free; Dec.–Feb., free
SOURCES:	Telephone call to site Sept. 8, 1991. Survey form completed by Richard N. Pawling, Hopewell Furnace National Historic Site. Derrick M. Cook, superintendent, Hopewell Furnace National Historic Site. Telephone conversation Aug. 8, 1995, Becky Ross, park ranger, Hopewell Furnace National Historic Site. *Hopewell Furnace.* "Negro Labor in the Charcoal Iron Industry of Southeastern Pennsylvania," 466–86. *Black Iron—Black Laborers at Hopewell Furnace (1771–1883).* "A Comparison of Negro and White Labor in a Charcoal Iron Community," 487–97.

Gettysburg

Intercultural Resource Center

The Intercultural Resource Center is located on the campus of Gettysburg College. The center's Historical Portrait Collection includes portraits of Daniel Payne, bishop of the A.M.E. Church; Major Martin Delany, the first African American field officer in the Civil War; Catherine Delany, wife of Martin Delany and an agent on the underground railroad; and Congressman Thaddeus Stevens, a white abolitionist and civil rights champion. The collection also includes a portrait of Mrs. Lydia Smith, a native of Gettysburg, who was housekeeper to Congressman Stevens. Many of the personalities featured in the Historical Portrait Collection are not widely known.

The center's records indicate that from the 1840s on, African Americans in Gettysburg met on North Washington Street for religious instruction. Daniel Alexander Payne, later bishop of the A.M.E. Church,

arrived at Gettysburg in 1835 to enroll at the Lutheran Theological Seminary. On April 19, 1837, the college's board of trustees gave Payne permission to use one of the college classrooms to offer his Bible class to African Americans. Payne later became the first president of Wilberforce University. (See the entry for Ohio.)

A booklet put out by the center notes that Gettysburg is the only liberal arts college in America that provides genealogical research on African American families. The center houses census records, immigration records, Freedmen's Bureau Savings Bank records, and information about U.S. Colored Troops who served in the Civil War. Other documents include cohabitation records of former slaves in Mississippi as well as emancipation records of former slaves in Washington, D.C. The documents provide a wealth of information for African Americans in search of information about their roots. The center also houses a library of books by African and African American writers.

DATE ESTABLISHED:	1989
ADDRESS:	239 N. Washington Street, Gettysburg
TELEPHONE:	(717) 337-6311
VISITING HOURS:	Mon.–Fri. 9–5; closed major holidays except Labor Day 🎎
FEES:	Maximum $20 per search
SOURCES:	Harry Bradshaw Matthews, dean, Gettysburg College. *Gettysburg: The Intercultural Resource Center. Gettysburg Intercultural Advancement News.* "Reception Room Portrait Collection, Intercultural Resource Center." "Gettysburg College and the Intercultural Resource Center."

Kennett Square

Longwood Friends Meeting House

The community of Kennett Square, located near the Maryland border, was a crucial part of the underground railroad. The Longwood Friends Meeting House in Chester County was both a refuge for fugitive slaves and a center at which abolitionists gathered to further the cause of freedom. The meeting house, now restored, is located at the entrance to Longwood Gardens in Kennett Square.

In addition to free Black people who were active in conducting slaves on their way to freedom, white people also helped, including the Quakers who formed this meeting house in 1854. This group had been disowned by other Quakers who considered its abolitionist views too radical. Sojourner Truth, William Lloyd Garrison, Lucretia Mott, and poet John Greenleaf Whittier were abolitionists who spoke at this site.

The Longwood Friends Meeting House, an important underground railroad station, is owned today by Longwood Gardens, a public display garden that draws 800,000 visitors each year. The historic structure houses the Chester County Tourist Bureau, which has a permanent exhibit about the local underground railroad.

DATE ESTABLISHED:	1854
ADDRESS:	Chester County Tourist Bureau, Kennett Square
TELEPHONE:	(610) 388-0281
VISITING HOURS:	Apr.–Oct., daily 10–6; Nov.–Mar., daily 10–5; closed Thanksgiving, Christmas
FEES:	None
SOURCES:	Telephone conversation June 15, 1994, Pam Carter, publicity and functions coordinator, Longwood Gardens. "How the Friends and Other Friends Helped the Slaves."

La Mott

Camptown Federal District

The town of La Mott, in Cheltenham Township, is situated on part of the site of Camp William Penn, the first training camp for Black troops during the Civil War. From 1863 to 1865 Camp William Penn in Cheltenham Township was the primary recruitment and training station for the Third Regiment of the U.S. Colored Troops. Approximately 16,000 soldiers were cycled through the camp.

The town of La Mott, located about eight miles outside Philadelphia, was named for Lucretia C. Mott (1793–1880), a Quaker who worked in the antislavery, women's rights, temperance, and peace movements. Lucretia Mott and her husband, James, retired to an old farmhouse (called the "Roadside") in Cheltenham

in the late 1850s. There they established a refuge for runaway slaves traveling north to safety.

Lucretia Mott, an ordained minister in the Quaker Society of Friends, traveled about with her husband to preach against slavery. She organized the Philadelphia Female Anti-Slavery Society and expressed her opposition to slavery in her writings. In 1840 she represented the United States as president of the World's Anti-Slavery Convention.

During the Civil War the Motts strongly supported the Union cause. Although Black soldiers had served in the U.S. armed forces ever since the Revolutionary War, the Military Act of 1862 was the first federal law enabling the President to call Black men into military service. When Black troops were allowed to serve, they trained at first with white troops in Philadelphia. However, race riots broke out, ending that arrangement. Mott's son-in-law, Edward Davis, was a real estate developer, a major landholder in the area, and an advocate of the abolitionist cause. In 1863 he donated a portion of his property as a training camp for Black soldiers. The site was beyond the city limits and away from the strong anti-Black sentiments of some Philadelphians. More than 10,000 Black soldiers were housed at Camp William Penn.

The Quaker and abolitionist community in Cheltenham Township welcomed the recruits, providing friendship and a positive atmosphere. Lucretia Mott served as a spiritual leader in the community. She worked for the right of Black people to use public transportation in visits to their relatives at Camp William Penn. At the age of seventy, Mott gave inspirational sermons and speeches to the soldiers.

When the Civil War ended, Davis resumed his real estate activities. In that period integrated residential settings, even in northern cities, were rare. Davis, however, developed La Mott for both Black and white residents. He sold some of his land to wealthy white Philadelphians. In addition, he set aside thirty acres with small building lots to be sold for $150 to $250 each to Black and white purchasers. This land on the site of the former Camp William Penn was at first known as "Camptown." Davis donated land for the first school in the village; Black and white children attended it together.

The first residence in La Mott is still standing. The stone house located at Willow and Butcher Streets was built in 1854 for a tenant farmer, William Butcher, who was La Mott's first Black resident. Some of the early houses, including six houses on Keenan Street, were built with lumber salvaged from the army barracks. The house at 7310 Keenan Street, one of the original houses, has been in the same family since 1884. The house at the end of Keenan Street, a Gothic-revival cottage with an ornamental scalloped bargeboard, was constructed about 1882. La Mott's first school, which is located at Willow and Sycamore Streets, was built of local stone in 1878. The building now houses both the La Mott Free Library and the community center. The firehouse, built in 1915, also was constructed of local stone.

Davis also donated a parcel of land for the first church; it was constructed in 1888 at Cheltenham Avenue and Schoolhouse Lane. After it burned down, it was replaced by the African Methodist Episcopal Church, a brick-and-stone structure built in 1911. A state historic marker stands next to it.

Many Black people were leaders in the community. William Watson operated a brickyard from his property. Edward Davis in 1879 became La Mott's first Black real estate investor. George Elkins helped to organize the La Mott Building and Loan Association, which encouraged Black ownership by subdividing larger lots into more affordable ones. William Anderson in 1915 became Cheltenham Township's first Black police officer. Aubrey Bowser, a descendant of one of La Mott's earliest Black landowners, won a scholarship to Harvard University. He later gained prominence as a

judge and was one of the founders of the National Association for the Advancement of Colored People.

Today the community has almost 4,000 residents, 80 percent of whom are Black. A national historic site, Camptown Federal District, La Mott was a major stop on the underground railroad, the first federal training camp for Black soldiers, and one of America's first planned integrated communities founded after the Civil War. In addition to the state historical marker at the A.M.E. Church, it has another one near the entrance to Latham Park. A state plaque honoring Lucretia Mott stands near the site of her home "Roadside." A granite monument honoring Camp William Penn is located outside the La Mott Community Center.

The original tradition of social and racial harmony remains a feature of La Mott today. Many descendants of the original families, including the Butchers, Bowsers, Tripletts, MacLeers, Schusters, and Millers, still reside in the community, providing a strong, positive link to the past.

DATE BUILT:	First residence, 1854; first schoolhouse, 1878; current A.M.E. Church, 1911
ADDRESS:	District, roughly bounded by Penrose Avenue, Graham Lane, Dennis Street, and Cheltenham Avenue; community center, in the old schoolhouse, Willow Avenue at Sycamore; library, 7420 Sycamore; church, 1505 W. Cheltenham Avenue, La Mott
TELEPHONE:	Community center, (215) 635-3255; library, (215) 635-4419; church, (215) 782-1165
VISITING HOURS:	Community center, Mon.–Fri. 8:30–4:30; contact other sites for visiting hours 👥
SOURCES:	NRHPINF. *Fighting for Freedom.* "Keeping up the Fight for Recognition." "Tracking the Underground Railroad." *La Mott, An Historic Community.* "A Community Seeks Its Place in History."

Oxford

Lincoln University

Lincoln University, a historically Black college, was founded in 1854 and is one of America's oldest liberal arts colleges established for students of African descent. John Miller Dickey founded the university, which was originally chartered as "Ashmun Institute" to commemorate Liberia's first president, Jehudi Ashmun (1794–1828). In 1866 the school was renamed Lincoln University in honor of Abraham Lincoln. Black professors first taught at Lincoln University in 1932.

The campus, located in a region of rolling farmlands in southern Chester County, Pennsylvania, includes twenty-seven main buildings and twenty-one faculty residences. Lincoln Hall (Ashmun Hall), built in 1866 and the oldest building on the campus, once housed all the school's facilities. Amos and Vail Halls are also two of the original buildings on the campus. The Langston Hughes Memorial Library, a newer building, houses one of the most extensive collections of African art and artifacts in the United States. It also contains personal papers of the poet Langston Hughes.

Lincoln University enrolled approximately 1,251 students in 1988–1989, 90 percent of whom were African American. From 1854 to 1954 the university's graduates accounted for approximately 20 percent of Black physicians and 10 percent of Black attorneys in the United States. Some outstanding Lincoln graduates include the late Thurgood Marshall, Supreme Court justice; Benjamin Azikiwe, president of Nigeria; Langston Hughes, poet; Kwame Nkrumah, president of Ghana; and Roscoe Lee Browne, stage and screen actor.

DATE ESTABLISHED:	1854
ADDRESS:	On US 131, 45 miles southwest of Philadelphia between Oxford and West Grove
TELEPHONE:	(610) 932-8300; visitor's information, ext. 289
VISITING HOURS:	By arrangement with campus visitors information bureau ♟
SOURCE:	Lisa M. Collins, Lincoln University.

Philadelphia

Afro-American Historical and Cultural Museum

The Afro-American Historical and Cultural Museum, a three-story concrete, steel, and glass structure, houses an archive, a 280-seat auditorium, a gift shop, and four exhibition spaces. Stanley Arnold, museum archivist, notes that the museum was the first institution specifically built by a major city to house and interpret collections of African American culture. Its primary mission is to feature contributions of African Americans in the Philadelphia region and the state of Pennsylvania. Within the museum, visitors have viewed a variety of important exhibits, including *Climbing Jacob's Ladder: The Rise of Black Churches in Eastern American Cities, 1740–1977.*

Reaching beyond the museum walls, the staff offers visitors an African American heritage tour that reviews twenty-two sites in Philadelphia.

DATE ESTABLISHED:	1976
ADDRESS:	701 Arch Street, Philadelphia
TELEPHONE:	(215) 574-0380
VISITING HOURS:	Tues.–Sat. 10–5, Sun. noon–6; closed Mon., all major public holidays ♟
FEES:	Adults, $4; students, seniors 55 and over, and children 5–12, $2; group rates available
SOURCES:	Telephone call to site, June 15, 1994. Stanley Arnold, archivist; Carl R. Nold, director; The State Museum of Pennsylvania. Robert Weible, chief, division of history, Pennsylvania Historical and Museum Commission, Harrisburg.

All-Wars Memorial to Black Soldiers

Pennsylvania erected the All-Wars Memorial in 1934 to honor Black Pennsylvanians who have fought in the nation's wars. The memorial's design includes an eighteen-foot column. Columbia is depicted offering laurel wreaths to twelve life-sized figures encircling the column.

DATE BUILT:	1934
ADDRESS:	Lansdowne Drive, West Fairmount Park, Philadelphia
VISITING HOURS:	Daily, dawn–dusk
FEES:	None

Balch Institute for Ethnic Studies

Balch Institute is one of America's premier institutions that focuses on immigration and multiculturalism in the United States. Museum, library, and educational programs cover all ethnic groups. For persons involved in research, the Balch Institute Library offers a wide variety of literature on Philadelphia's African Americans, covering the period from 1865 to the present. The collection also includes photographs of some African American families and organizations in Philadelphia.

DATE ESTABLISHED: 1971

ADDRESS: 18 S. Seventh Street, Philadelphia

TELEPHONE: (215) 925-8090

VISITING HOURS: Mon.–Sat. 9–5; closed Sun., all legal holidays 🏃🏃

SOURCE: James F. Turk, director of education, Balch Institute.

Frances Ellen Watkins Harper House

Frances Ellen Watkins Harper was well known as a reformer who worked in antislavery, women's, and temperance movements. When the Civil War ended, Harper continued her efforts to improve the civil rights of Black people. She also wrote poetry and essays on topics related to the life of African Americans.

Frances Ellen Watkins was born in Baltimore in 1825 to free Black parents. Her parents died when she was very young, and an aunt and uncle raised her. Her uncle, William Watkins, was an outstanding abolitionist and a minister in the African Methodist Episcopal Church. He operated his own school, the Watkins Academy, in Baltimore and wrote for the abolitionist paper *The Liberator.*

Even though this was a family of free Black people, opportunities were not equal for Baltimore's African Americans. Although Frances was educated, her first job at the age of fourteen was as a seamstress and nursemaid for a white family. Frances began writing during her teen years and published her first poetry book during that period. At the age of twenty-six she moved to Columbus, Ohio, where she began to teach domestic science at Union Seminary. Because she soon realized that she was more interested in working for the antislavery cause than in teaching, she directed her efforts increasingly to the abolitionist movement. One of the factors influencing her decision was that Maryland about this time passed a law

prohibiting free Black people from moving to Maryland to live there; this meant that she could no longer go back to visit her family.

In the next years Frances joined her cousin, William Watkins Jr., in giving antislavery lectures in New England. She married Fenton Harper, and they had one child. After her husband's death, the administrator of the estate seized the farm she had purchased with her own savings to pay her husband's debts, leaving her almost nothing. This experience influenced her to become active in the women's movement, not only to earn a living once more but also because she began to realize the inequality of women before the law.

Harper sympathized with John Brown as he prepared for the raid on Harpers Ferry in 1859. Later, she spent two weeks with Brown's wife prior to Brown's execution. In her lectures Harper spoke about those who had participated in the raid.

After the Civil War Harper returned to lecturing, appearing at suffrage conventions and serving on committees of women's organizations. Although these groups were made up primarily of white women, many of whom accepted some types of racism, there was no other place for her to turn at that time. By the end of the nineteenth century Black feminists began organizing clubs for Black women.

Harper also continued her writing. Her book *Poems on Miscellaneous Subjects* was reprinted several times, and her poems and essays were printed in Black newspapers and journals. Her novel *Iola LeRoy or Shadows Uplifted,* published in 1892, was the first published by an African American woman.

In her travels Harper saw the poverty of the freed Black people and the abuses they suffered. She joined the struggle to attain the vote for Black people and was pleased to see the passage of the Fifteenth Amendment.

Harper moved to 1006 Bainbridge in 1870, sharing the house with her daughter. She died after a brief illness in 1911. She had spent her life working to better conditions for Black people and for women, and her writing and humanitarian efforts made her one of the nineteenth century's outstanding women.

The Harper house is a brick, three-story corner row house. Although the high, narrow house has had numerous alterations over the years, its basic structure remains intact.

DATE OF SIGNIFICANCE: Harper residence, 1870–1911

ADDRESS: 1006 Bainbridge Street, corner of Adler Street, Philadelphia

VISITING HOURS: Private, visitors may drive or walk by

SOURCES: NRHPINF. "One Great Bundle of Humanity," 21–43.

Mother Bethel African Methodist Episcopal Church *

Mother Bethel African Methodist Episcopal Church, the mother church of the A.M.E. denomination, was built on the site of the original 1793 church. The congregation began in 1793, and shortly after that Richard Allen established the A.M.E. Church.

Richard Allen was born a slave in 1760 in Delaware. A Quaker lawyer owned him, but a man named Stockley later bought him and his family. Allen was allowed to join in religious activities and became a convert to the Methodist faith. He joined the Methodist Society at age seventeen and was allowed to conduct services. His owner, Stockley, eventually came to believe that he could not reconcile his religious faith with the ownership of slaves. Although

Stockley did not free his slaves, he allowed Allen and his brothers to buy their freedom for $2,000 each.

Allen received his license to preach in 1784 and became a circuit preacher, moving about to preach in three states. In 1786 Allen was asked to minister to Black people at St. George's Methodist Episcopal Church in Philadelphia. This assignment made him the first Black person to serve as pastor in a Methodist church. As increasing numbers of Black people came to the church to hear Allen preach, tensions increased, and white parishioners became irate. Black church members had a 5:00 A.M. service and were tolerated at services if they sat in "Negro pews" reserved for them, but they were not allowed to use the church for their own social meetings.

Richard Allen and Absalom Jones, another Black member of the church, responded to the discrimination by forming the Free African Society, which provided religious and social activities for African Americans. However, bigotry increased in the church, making separation inevitable. In November 1787 church members Absalom Jones and William White attempted to kneel in prayer during a church service in a section of the newly built gallery that they did not know was closed to them. The white church elders caused a commotion by directing them to move and roughly attempting to remove Jones from the church. In protest, Allen and Jones led the Black parishioners out of St. George's.

The African Americans who left St. George's Church held their worship services at the Free African Society. When the society later voted to establish an Episcopal church, Allen declined to be the pastor because he wanted to remain a Methodist, so Absalom Jones became pastor of the new Episcopal church. Allen then bought a frame blacksmith shop and had it moved to a lot he owned at Sixth and Lombard Streets (the present site of the church). In July 1794 the congregation dedicated the converted structure and named it Bethel, to make it clear that the congregation was not under the leadership of St. George's. In November 1794 Allen issued a declaration of independence, using for the first time the name African Methodist Episcopal Church.

The congregation erected a new building in 1805 and used it until 1841. Its third church building, used from 1841 to 1889, was said to have had a tunnel for escaping slaves. The present church, a three-story granite building with stained-glass windows and a tower, was built in 1889 and dedicated in 1890.

Mother Bethel Church served not only the spiritual needs but also the social and physical needs of Black people in the community. When a yellow fever epidemic struck Philadelphia in 1793, physician Benjamin Rush asked the Free African Society of Philadelphia to assist in nursing sick people and carrying the dead. Richard Allen, Absalom Jones, and William Gray took the lead in helping. Mother Bethel Church formed a paramedical staff that saved more than 200 lives during the epidemic. About 10 percent of Black people in the city died in this epidemic; 300 Black people died while helping others in the epidemic. They are believed to be buried in Washington Square or in unmarked graves at the Friends Meeting House at Fourth and Arch Streets.

In 1814 Allen together with James Forten, a Revolutionary War veteran and a wealthy Black leader in Philadelphia, organized a force of 2,500 free Black volunteers to defend Philadelphia against the British during the War of 1812. Forten, who was born of free Black parents, made a fortune in the sailmaking business and was an abolitionist leader in the city.

The church provided other services that the white city government did not extend to Black people. It also provided a forum where African Americans could discuss issues of the day. When the American Colonization Society formulated a plan to send Black people to Africa, Allen, Forten, and many others opposed the idea. In 1817 Forten chaired a meeting at Bethel Church to protest plans to send Black people to Africa by members of the American Colonization Society and those who sympathized with them. Those present at the meeting unanimously adopted a resolution that stated in part:

> Whereas our ancestors (not of choice) were the first successful cultivators of the wilds of America, we their descendants feel ourselves entitled to participate in the blessings of her luxuriant soil, which their blood and sweat manured; and that any measure or system of measures, having a tendency to banish us from her bosom, would not only be cruel, but in direct violation of those principles, which have been the boast of this republic.[2]

The congregation of Mother Bethel Church fought the racist laws known as the Black codes and opposed laws that would have prevented Black people from entering free states in the North. Church members also worked for the abolition of slavery. Today Mother Bethel Church is a memorial to Bishop Richard Allen, the outstanding American religious leader whose sense of justice and dignity led him to establish a new denomination. Allen died in 1831. Today a basement crypt houses a museum and Allen's tomb. Mother Bethel Church, one of America's earliest Black churches, is listed in the *National Register of Historic Places*.

DATE ESTABLISHED: 1794; present church, 1889

ADDRESS: 419 S. Sixth Street, Philadelphia

TELEPHONE: (215) 925-0616

VISITING HOURS: Mon.–Sat. 10–3

SOURCES: NRHPINF. *National Register of Historic Places*, 648. *The Negro Almanac*, 5th ed., 224. *Webster's New Biographical Dictionary*, 363. *Thoughts on African Colonization*, 62–63. *African Americans. Voices of Triumph*, vol. 2, *Leadership*, 124–6.

Henry O. Tanner House

Tanner House was at one time the home of one of America's best-known Black artists. Henry O. Tanner was born at Pittsburgh in 1859, the son of Bishop Benjamin Tucker Tanner and Sarah Miller Tanner. The family moved into this residence in Philadelphia about 1872.

At the age of twelve or thirteen, young Henry watched an artist paint a landscape of a hillside. This inspired in him a strong desire to become a painter, too. He was further impressed by the work of two Black artists, Edmonia Lewis and Edward Bannister, whose works were exhibited at the Philadelphia Centennial Exposition of 1876.

With his father's encouragement, Henry enrolled at the Pennsylvania Academy of Fine Arts in 1880. His teacher, the well-known painter Thomas Eakins, instructed Tanner in draftsmanship and other aspects of the artistic tradition. Tanner soon began to sell some of his paintings. Moving to Atlanta in 1888, he opened a photography studio and taught at Clark College in that city. Later he spent some time among the Black people of the Blue Ridge Mountains in North Carolina. One of his admired works titled *The Banjo Lesson* was perhaps begun at this time. (It was later completed after Turner settled in France.)

The racial discrimination in the United States was a source of depression for Tanner, who moved to Paris in 1891. Because the welcoming attitude of France appealed to him, he spent the rest of his life there. His works were accepted and exhibited in Paris salons. At the Paris Exposition of 1900 he was honored with the Medal of Honor. He died in France in 1937.

The Tanner homesite in Philadelphia is a three-story building. The interior has been altered, and the exterior wood-framed bay has been covered with aluminum siding. The Tanner residence is listed in the *National Register of Historic Places*.

DATE OF SIGNIFICANCE: Tanner residence, c1872
ADDRESS: 2908 W. Diamond Street, Philadelphia
VISITING HOURS: Private, visitors may walk or drive by
SOURCES: NRHPINF. *The Negro Almanac*, 5th ed., 225.

Temple University – Charles L. Blockson Afro-American Collection

More than one million items—rare books, photographs, slave narratives, recordings, private papers of prominent African Americans, and broadsides— make up this collection about Black Americans. The collection originated in the 1940s when its curator, Charles L. Blockson, then a ten-year-old boy in Norristown, Pennsylvania, began a search for Black heroes. The great-grandson of a man who escaped on the underground railroad, Blockson knew there had to be Black achievers other than George Washington Carver and Booker T. Washington, the men who were presented each year on "Colored History Day" in his school. When Blockson (who says that he never had a Black teacher in his life) asked one of his teachers about Black heroes other than Washington and Carver, the teacher responded that "Negroes were born to serve white people."

Stung by the statement, Blockson began his lifelong quest for information about his own heritage. He purchased books about Black people whenever he could and found many rare books whose worth had not been recognized. At Pennsylvania State, where he was a member of the football team, Blockson searched for more books whenever the team traveled. The earliest book that he found was a 1557 book on the history of Africa. The collection became extensive over the years, and in 1983 Blockson donated it to Temple University.

Today the Afro-American Collection, one of the tour sites listed by the Philadelphia Convention and Tours Bureau, is visited by scholars and lay people from many parts of the world. Blockson, the curator, is an important resource in his own right. In 1994–1995 he served as chairperson of a National Park Service committee charged with identifying underground railroad sites in the United States. His 1977 book, *Black Genealogy*, is widely used by African Americans who are searching for their roots. Blockson wrote an article on the underground railroad for the *National Geographic* in July 1984 and wrote "Sea Change in the Sea Islands" for the December 1987 *National Geographic*. In 1994 he wrote the *Hippocrene Guide to the Underground Railroad*.

DATE ESTABLISHED: Collection, 1940; donated, 1983
ADDRESS: Sullivan Hall, Temple University, Thirteenth and Berks Mall, Philadelphia
TELEPHONE: (215) 204-6632
VISITING HOURS: By appointment Mon.–Fri. 9–5; closed weekends, holidays 🏃🏃
SOURCES: Telephone conversation Jan. 25, 1995, Charles L. Blockson, curator. *Black Genealogy. Philadelphia's Guide: African-American State Historical Markers.*

University of Pennsylvania–The University Museum of Archaeology/Anthropology

The University of Pennsylvania museum's African collection consists of more than 10,000 objects from nearly every major cultural area of the African continent, with the richest material from the West African and former Belgian Congo areas.

Most items in the collection were gathered between 1897 and 1930. Although much of the collection dates from the early twentieth century to the present, some Benin brasses and ivories date from the sixteenth to the nineteenth centuries.

Some of the objects include a mankala (an Ethiopian wooden board game with counters), a beautifully carved wooden door from the Ivory Coast, a xylophone made of wood and gourds, and a finely detailed ostrich-egg water container geometrically incised and inlaid with pigment.

DATE ESTABLISHED:	1887
ADDRESS:	Thirty-third and Spruce Streets, Philadelphia
TELEPHONE:	(215) 898-4000
VISITING HOURS:	Tues.–Sat. 10–4:30, Sun. 1–5; closed Mon., holidays, Sun. June–Aug. 👥
FEES:	Adults, $3; children, students, and senior citizens, $1.50
SOURCE.	Pam Kosty, public information officer

Wesley African Methodist Episcopal Zion Church

Wesley A.M.E. Zion Church is a two-story stone church in the Gothic style. The church has a huge stained-glass window and a stone belltower. There are three red doors under Gothic arches on the street level. Inside, the large sanctuary with a U-shaped balcony seats approximately 2,000 people.

In 1784 there were over 15,000 Methodists in America, and Black people were joining this denomination in increasing numbers. To escape the uneasy racial atmosphere encountered in the white-dominated Methodist Church at Philadelphia, Richard Allen and other African Americans formed their own congregation, which was known as Mother Bethel. Allen became in time a bishop of the A.M.E. Church. Four years after the establishment of Mother Bethel, some members of the congregation became dissatisfied and decided to found their own church in 1820. This congregation is known today as the Wesley A.M.E. Zion Church and is known familiarly as "Big Wesley."

For many years the Wesley A.M.E. congregation occupied a church at 1500 Lombard Street in Philadelphia. In 1925–1926 the present-day church was built on this site, just prior to the Great Depression. Because of high construction costs, the congregation was for many years burdened with a huge debt load. Despite this handicap, its charitable members continued their outreach to the poor and hungry in the community. In one winter they fed more than 34,000 people of different races and creeds. During the Depression years they also provided clothing, paid insurance policies so as to keep some people's policies from lapsing, and operated a rent-free apartment house. In a Tuesday night service called "Joy Night," they combined prayer, music, and devotional services and collected money for the poor. By 1950 Big Wesley was out of debt. Today the church is listed in the *National Register of Historic Places.*

DATE ESTABLISHED:	Congregation, 1820; present church, 1925–1926
ADDRESS:	1500 Lombard Street (corner of Fifteenth Street), Philadelphia
TELEPHONE:	(215) 735-8961
VISITING HOURS:	Mon.–Fri. 10–2; Sun. service 11
SOURCES:	NRHPINF. Telephone conversation Jan. 29, 1995, Reverend Doctor Joseph W. Walton, pastor, Wesley A.M.E. Church.

Valley Forge

Valley Forge National Park

In 1777 Black soldiers were among those who struggled through the hard winter at Valley Forge with George Washington's Continental Army. Phillip Field, a Black man from New York, was among those who died. Another Black man, Salem Poor, survived the hardships of that winter. Salem Poor already had fought with the Massachusetts Regiment at Bunker Hill and had been cited for his bravery as a soldier. (See the entry on the Battle of Bunker Hill in the Massachusetts section.)

DATE OF SIGNIFICANCE: 1777–1778
ADDRESS: Valley Forge
TELEPHONE: Visitors center, (610) 783-1077
VISITING HOURS: Park, daily dawn–dusk; Visitors Center and Washington's Headquarters, daily 9–5; closed Christmas ♟
FEES: Washington's Headquarters, adults, $2; youth 16 and under, free
SOURCES: Telephone call to site, June 15, 1994. *The Negro Almanac*, 5th ed., 225.

Notes

1. Gary T. Hawbaker, ed., *Runaways, Rascals, and Rogues, Missing Spouses, Servants and Slaves: Abstracts from Lancaster County, Pennsylvania Newspapers [and] Lancaster Journal, 1794–1810*, vol. 1 (Hershey, Pa.: The Author, 1987), 12.
2. From meeting of Black people in Philadelphia, Jan. 1817, in William Lloyd Garrison, *Thoughts on African Colonization, or an Impartial Exhibition of the Doctrines, Principles, & Purposes of the American Colonization Society, Together with the Resolutions, Addresses, & Remonstrances of the Free People of Color*, pt. 2 (Boston, 1832), 9–10, quoted in Herbert Aptheker, *A Documentary History of the Negro People of the United States*, vol. 1 (New York: Citadel, 1990), 71.

Works Consulted

African Americans: Voices of Triumph. Vol. 2, *Leadership.* Alexander, Va.: Time-Life, 1993.

Black Genealogy. Charles L. Blockson with Ron Fry. Englewood Cliffs, N.J.: Prentice-Hall, 1977.

Black Iron: Black Laborers at Hopewell Furnace (1771–1883). National Park Service. [flier]

"A Community Seeks Its Place in History." Will Thompson. *Philadelphia Inquirer,* n.d.

"A Comparison of Negro and White Labor in a Charcoal Iron Community." Joseph E. Walker. *Labor History* 10, no. 3 (summer 1969): 487–97.

Cornwall Iron Furnace. Cornwall, Pa.: Pennsylvania Historical and Museum Commission. [brochure]

Fighting for Freedom. Philadelphia: Civil War Library and Museum. [brochure]

"Forming an Identity through the Church: Philadelphia Places of Pride," *Philadelphia Inquirer,* 28 Feb. 1989.

Gettysburg: The Intercultural Resource Center. [booklet]

"Gettysburg College and the Intercultural Resource Center." Harry Bradshaw Matthews. *Journal of the Afro-American Historical and Genealogical Society* 8, no. 3 (fall 1987).

Gettysburg Intercultural Advancement News 4, no. 2 (Feb. 1990). [newsletter]

Hopewell Furnace. National Park Service, U.S. Dept. of the Interior. [brochure]

"How the Friends and Other Friends Helped the Slaves: Philadelphia Places of Pride." John Corr. *Philadelphia Inquirer,* 2 Feb. 1989.

International Library of Negro Life and History: Historical Negro Biographies. Wilhelmena S. Robinson. New York: Publishers, 1970.

The John Brown House. Robert N. Sieber. Harrisburg, Pa.: Bureau of Historic Sites and Properties, Pennsylvania Historical and Museum Commission, 1978.

"Keeping up the Fight for Recognition." Daniel Rubin. *Philadelphia Inquirer,* 8 Feb. 1989.

La Mott, An Historic Community. Prepared by Wallace Roberts & Todd, Planners, Urban Designers, Landscape Architects, and Architects, Philadelphia. [poster]

National Register of Historic Places. Washington, D.C.: National Park Service, 1976.

The Negro Almanac: A Reference Work on the Afro-American. 5th ed. Harry A. Ploski and James Williams, eds. Detroit, Mich.: Gale Research, 1989.

"Negro Labor in the Charcoal Iron Industry of Southeastern Pennsylvania." Joseph E. Walker. *Pennsylvania Magazine of History and Biography* 93, no. 4 (Oct. 1969): 466–86.

"One Great Bundle of Humanity: Frances Ellen Watkins Harper." Margaret Hope Bacon. *Pennsylvania Magazine of History and Biography* 113, no. 1 (Jan. 1989): 21–43.

Philadelphia's Guide: African-American State Historical Markers. Philadelphia: Charles L. Blockson Afro-American Collection/William Penn Foundation, 1992.

"Reception Room Portrait Collection, Intercultural Resource Center." Gettysburg College, 16 July 1990. [paper]

"The Rise of the Iron Community." Frederic K. Miller. *Lebanon County Historical Society* 12, no. 3a (1950): 15, 16, 92, 93.

Thoughts on African Colonization, or an Impartial Exhibition of the Doctrines, Principles, & Purposes of the American Colonization Society, Together with the Resolutions, Addresses, & Remonstrances of the Free People of Color. Part 2. William Lloyd Garrison. (Boston, 1832), 62–63. Quoted in *A Documentary History of the Negro People in the United States,* vol. 1, Herbert Aptheker (New York: Citadel, 1990), 71.

"Tracking the Underground Railroad." Sandra Long. *Philadelphia Inquirer,* 4 Feb. 1985.

Webster's New Biographical Dictionary. Springfield, Mass.: Merriam-Webster, 1988.

Rhode Island

Kingston

George and Sarah Fayerweather House

George Fayerweather, a slave owned by the Reverend Samuel Fayerweather, pastor of St. Paul's Episcopal Church in North Kingston, Rhode Island, was the founder of a leading African American family in Kingston. His son, George II, was born in slavery in 1774 and learned the blacksmith trade. When freed from slavery, George II married a Native American princess, and they built this cottage in 1820. George set up a blacksmith's shop to the right of the house; there members of this family practiced the blacksmith trade for more than one hundred years, passing the business down through the generations. The smith's shop was the heart of the town, a place where many boys watched with fascination as the smiths went about their work.

George Fayerweather II and his wife had twelve children. When he died in 1841, his son, Solomon, continued the business, serving for the next sixty years as the village blacksmith. He died in 1901 at age eighty-three. Solomon's brother, George III, also a blacksmith, married Sarah Harris, who was born in Norwich, Connecticut, in 1812, one of twelve children.

Sarah Harris's family had moved from Norwich to Canterbury, Connecticut, and as a young woman, Sarah worked there as a servant. However, she wanted to become a schoolteacher and applied for admission to the Prudence Crandall School for Girls in Canterbury. (See the listing for Connecticut.) Although Sarah was the first Black student to be admitted to the school, extreme racial hostility in the town and violent opposition to school integration finally forced Crandall to close the school.

During this period of turbulence in Canterbury, Sarah had been preparing to marry George Fayerweather III of Kingston. After their marriage George III and Sarah lived in the Helme house (no longer extant) that stood next door to the Fayerweather house in Kingston. Sarah kept in touch with Prudence Crandall; the Fayerweathers even named their first baby Prudence Crandall Fayerweather. Their residence became a center of antislavery activity in the community. Frederick Douglass and William Lloyd Garrison, famous abolitionists, were entertained in their house. Sarah lived in the Helme house until her death in 1878 at the age of 63. She was highly respected in the community, and a residence hall on the campus of the University of Rhode Island was named Fayerweather Hall in her honor.

The Fayerweather house on Moorsfield Road was restored in 1965 by the Kingston Improvement Association and today houses the Fayerweather Craft Guild.

DATE OF SIGNIFICANCE: 19th century

ADDRESS: Moorsfield Road, corner of RI 138 and RI 108, Kingston

TELEPHONE: (401) 789-9072

VISITING HOURS: 3rd Sat. in May–Dec. 10, Tues., Thurs., Sat. 10–4 or by appointment 👫

SOURCES: Telephone conversation June 15, 1994, Ms. Steffanie Windus, local resident. Telephone conversation June 15, 1994, Mr. Ward Abusamra, Kingston Improvement Association. Telephone conversation Jan. 27, 1995, Claire Sweet, librarian, South Kingston Public Library. *Rhode Island's Freedom Trail. Kingston: A Forgotten History.* "A Profile in Dedication: Sarah Harris and the Fayerweather Family." *The New England Galaxy.*

Newport

Colonial Burial Ground, God's Acre

From the early days of the colony, Rhode Island slaves were often buried at the side or foot of their owners' graves. In Newport an African American section was developed in the Colonial Burial Ground and named "God's Acre." In the early part of the nineteenth century, the African Union Society developed procedures and regulations to ensure that deceased members would receive a decent funeral procession and a decent burial at this site. There is conjecture that a Black slave and mason named Zingo Stevens was the official stonecutter for the African Union Society, but this has not been substantiated. There are, however, two stones that were cut and signed in the 1760s by a Black man named Pompe Stevens. Some of the more-ornate stones in God's Acre may have been paid for by slave owners.

The Colonial Burying Ground, a national historic site, is well worth seeing. Ringed with lovely cherry trees, the grounds contain approximately 4,000 tombstones that date from as early as 1660. The God's Acre section is one of the best-preserved of such early burial grounds of Black Americans. Although the earliest stone in God's Acre dates from the 1700s, the majority of the four hundred African American burials at this site were for free Black residents of Newport.

DATE ESTABLISHED:	1600s
ADDRESS:	Cemetery, Farewell Street, Newport (from the Newport Bridge take the exit to downtown Newport; turn right and go 1/4 mile to the entrance)
VISITING HOURS:	Dawn–dusk
SOURCES:	Telephone conversation June 15, 1994, Jeanne Desrosiers, Covell Guest House. Telephone conversation June 16, 1994, John Canham, chairman, Advisory Commission on the Common Burying Ground. Telephone conversation Jan. 26, 1995, Ronald Onorato, professor of art and architectural history, University of Rhode Island. *Rhode Island's Freedom Trail.*

Quaker Meeting House

The restored building at 30 Marlborough Street is the oldest surviving Quaker meeting house in America. At this site in 1717, John Farmer, a Quaker, made an early, positive antislavery statement. Although he did not have permission to do so, Farmer tried to read his *Epistle concerning Negroes* to those attending the yearly meeting. As a result of this bold act, the Society of Friends disowned him.

Some of the Quakers owned slaves at that time, and the issue of slave ownership was a matter of contention. In 1733 the quarterly meeting of Friends approved Elihu Coleman's tract against slavery and gave Coleman permission to print his work. By 1773 the yearly meeting opposed slavery and disowned those who went against this decision. John Farmer's earlier stand had not been taken in vain.

DATE BUILT:	1699; restored, 1807
ADDRESS:	30 Marlborough Street, Newport
TELEPHONE:	(401) 846-0813
VISITING HOURS:	By appointment with one-week advance notice
SOURCES:	Telephone conversation June 16, 1994, and Jan. 26, 1995, Ron Potvin, curator of manuscripts, Newport Historical Society. *Rhode Island's Freedom Trail.*

Isaac Rice House

Both escaping slaves and abolitionists found shelter at the home of Isaac Rice, a Black man who had been born free in 1792 at Narragansett, Rhode Island, and who had moved to Newport at an early age. Rice worked as a gardener for Governor Gibbs of Rhode Island; during this assignment Rice planted the trees in Touro Park in Newport.

In the course of his work, Rice overheard the conversations of African American servants who had accompanied their masters on their summer sojourns in Newport. As a result, Rice grew to hate the institution that bound human beings as slaves and began to work to help free the slaves.

The house on the corner of William and Thomas Streets became an underground railroad shelter. Frederick Douglass, a friend to Rice, stayed here when he came to Newport. Rice also served his church faithfully, giving generously to the Colored Union Church and Society and serving as the Society's clerk. He died in 1866.

PERIOD OF SIGNIFICANCE:	19th century
ADDRESS:	54 William Street, Newport
VISITING HOURS:	Private, visitors may walk or drive by
SOURCES:	*The Underground Railroad in New England. Rhode Island's Freedom Trail.*

Wanton-Lyman-Hazard House

The Wanton-Lyman-Hazard House, 17 Broadway, was once the governor's mansion and was nearly destroyed in the 1765 Stamp Act Riots. The house, a typical middle-class merchant dwelling of the 1675–1750 period, is an example of the type of dwelling in which slaves lived and worked in the North. The colonial, three-story residence was owned by patriots, merchants, and governors, most of whom owned slaves who also lived here.

One room in the house is reported to have been the slave quarters. Partial evidence for this is the back stairway leading from the kitchen to the second-story room; this stairway would not have been used by the white family members. The room is simply furnished but not in an authentic manner as a slave's living quarters.

DATE BUILT:	1675
ADDRESS:	17 Broadway, Newport
TELEPHONE:	(401) 846-0813

VISITING HOURS: June 15–Aug. 31, Tues.–Sat. 9–5; closed
Sun., Mon., holidays, Sept.–June 14 👫

FEES: $3

SOURCES: Bert Lippincott, Newport Historical
Society. Telephone conversation June 16,
1994, and Jan. 26, 1995, Ron Potvin,
Newport Historical Society.

Portsmouth

Battle of Rhode Island Historic District

Although Black soldiers served in regular army units
in most of the American colonies during the
Revolutionary War, Rhode Island was an exception.
Here, between 1778 and 1781, Black men were
enrolled in a separate, predominantly Black unit
known as the First Rhode Island Regiment. They had
an extra incentive because the Rhode Island legislature had declared that every slave in the state who volunteered to serve would be declared free and would
be paid a regular soldier's wages.

Between 1776 and 1779 British troops, including
mercenary soldiers from Hesse in Germany, were stationed in Rhode Island. In August 1778 the Americans
started an offensive against the British entrenched
troops, hoping for help from the French fleet. When
the French failed to give support at that time, the
American forces were trapped in a difficult situation.
The Black soldiers were asked to hold the line against
a British assault. The British had occupied Newport
and had driven the American forces from the island
on which the town is located. Following up their
advantage, the British troops, including their Hessian
contingents, made three charges against the
Americans. The Black regiment beat the aggressors
back three times. This brave action enabled the
American commander to organize an orderly retreat
that saved the regiment from destruction. The 200
freedmen of the First Rhode Island Regiment showed
great courage in repulsing veteran European soldiers.

This is the only Revolutionary War battle in
which Black Americans fought as a distinct racial unit.
The site today consists primarily of private houses
that were not standing at the time of the battle. State
route 24 is the only major road that goes into the
battlefield site; the route terminates near Barker Brook
and merges into West Main Road nearby. The
National Association for the Advancement of Colored
People has erected a marker and flagpole on a high
grassy site at this interchange. The symbols commemorate the courage of the First Rhode Island Regiment
in the Battle of Rhode Island.

DATE OF SIGNIFICANCE: 1778

ADDRESS: Historic District, Lehigh Hill and
both sides of RI 21 between Medley
and Dexter Streets; Rhode Island
Black Regiment Park, left of northbound junction of RI 114 and RI 24,
Portsmouth

VISITING HOURS: Private, visitors may drive by

SOURCES: NRHPINF. *National Register of Historic
Places*, 668. *Before the Mayflower*, 67.
*Rhode Island's Freedom Trail. Black Heroes
of the American Revolution.*

Prescott Farm Historic District

Tack Sisson (various sources give his name as
Jack Sisson and even as Quarco Honeyman) was a
Black man from Newport who served as a commando
during the Revolutionary War. He became known
when, in a July 1777 raid against the British, he
helped to capture British General Richard Prescott.
Prior to this incident the British had captured
Major General Charles Lee of the Continental
Army. In order to persuade the British to exchange
prisoners, the Americans first had to capture a
British officer. Six officers and thirty-eight men,
including Sisson, set out in small boats to an area
near Prescott's headquarters in a farmhouse near
Portsmouth. Although guards protected the farmhouse, the darkness of midnight enabled three of the
American soldiers to creep up, stealthily evading the
guards. Sisson stepped forward and smashed down
the doors of the general's bedroom. General Prescott
surrendered, and the Americans took him away, as a
newspaper later noted, "without his breeches."
Prescott later was exchanged for General Lee, and
Sisson later joined the First Rhode Island Regiment.
The restored farmhouse where the bold capture took
place stands along West Main Road at the
Middleton-Portsmouth town line.

DATE OF SIGNIFICANCE: 1777

ADDRESS: Tour origin, 2009 W. Main Road, Middleton; farmhouse, Portsmouth

TELEPHONE: (401) 847-6230

VISITING HOURS: Tours (including the country store, windmill, and herb garden, but not the farmhouse, which is private) Apr.–Oct., Mon.–Fri. 10–4 🍴

FEES: Farm, free; museum and windmill, adults, $2; children, $1.50

SOURCES: Telephone conversation June 16, 1994, John Lingley, herb farmer and tour guide. *Rhode Island's Freedom Trail. International Library of Negro Life and History*, 32. *The African American Encyclopedia*, 1460.

Providence

Bannister House

The Bannister residence once was home to an outstanding African American painter, Edward Mitchell Bannister, and his wife, Christina. Christina Bannister was well known in her own right as a prominent person in civic and community work.

Edward Bannister was born in 1828 in New Brunswick, Canada. Orphaned at early age and poor, he moved to Boston and began working at odd jobs. He loved to draw, and by the age of ten was showing strong interest in sketching many kinds of scenes.

In 1867 Bannister read an article in the *Boston Herald* that maintained that Black people were incapable of producing art. He was determined to prove that the writer's idea was wrong. Bannister's paintings during this period were of New England landscapes. In 1870 he moved to Rhode Island and established the Providence Art Club, a group that is still active.

In spite of Bannister's talent, he encountered much racial prejudice. For example, in 1876 he was awarded a medal at Philadelphia's Centennial Exposition for his painting *Under the Oaks*. When the judges discovered that they had awarded the honor to a Black man, however, they selected another work of art for the honor. Only the demands of other competitors prevented the judges from depriving Bannister of the award. Yet he persisted in his work and, by the time of his death in 1901, Bannister

had gained national recognition as a painter. Some of Bannister's work can be viewed at the Museum of Art in the Rhode Island School of Design. Several of his works are in the museum's permanent collection, but they are not always on display at any given time.

Christina Bannister, Bannister's wife, spent her years in Providence working to improve the lives of African Americans. She worked for years to raise money for a home in Providence for elderly Black people. She succeeded when, in 1890, the Rhode Island State Assembly enacted legislation incorporating a Home for Aged Colored Women. Donations from local families provided land, money to build the home, and furnishings. Mrs. Bannister saw her dream come true when the home for aged women was ready for occupancy that same year.

In 1977 the home moved to 35 Dodge Street in East Providence; it was then renamed the Bannister House in honor of Christina Bannister.

The Bannister residence on Benevolent Street, before remodeling, was a simple wood cottage.

DATE OF SIGNIFICANCE: Bannister residence, 1883–1898

ADDRESS: House, 93 Benevolent Street; Museum of Art, 224 Benefit Street, Providence

TELEPHONE: Museum, (401) 454-6507

VISITING HOURS: House, private, visitors may walk or drive by; museum, Tue.–Wed., Fri.–Sat. 10:30–5, Thurs. noon–5, Sun. and holidays 2–5, closed Mon.

FEES: Museum: Adults, $2; seniors, $1; youth 5–18 and college, $.50

SOURCES: Telephone conversation Jan. 28, 1995, Judith Davidson, reception supervisor, Museum of Art, Rhode Island School of Design. *International Library of Negro Life and History*, 47.

Brick Schoolhouse

The Brick Schoolhouse on Meeting Street was constructed in 1769 on land acquired by the town proprietors. At first the town maintained a school on the first floor, while Brown University used classroom space on the upper floor. During the Revolution, however, the building was used as a storage house for munitions and as a cartridge-manufacturing facility.

When public education was permanently established in Providence in 1800, this structure became one of the district schools. The statewide Public Schools Law in 1828 provided for public primary education for Black children under the age of ten and authorized a segregated public grammar school at this site on Meeting Street. In the 1850s, the Meeting Street School began to offer the African American students a high school education in addition to grammar school instruction. All African American children in Providence attended either the Meeting Street School or a grammar school that opened in 1837 on Pond Street.

Around 1908 the Meeting Street School became a school for tubercular children. It later served as a school for disabled children and adults. In 1987 the Brick Schoolhouse was recycled as the headquarters of the Providence Preservation Society.

DATE BUILT:	1769; Black children's school, 1828–1908
ADDRESS:	24 Meeting Street, Providence
TELEPHONE:	(401) 831-7440
VISITING HOURS:	By appointment 👥
SOURCES:	Amy Jordan, director of education and tourism, Providence Preservation Society. *Rhode Island's Freedom Trail.*

Civil War Monument

African American soldiers served during the Civil War in the Fourteenth Regiment Rhode Island Heavy Artillery (Colored). Their acceptance as members of the Union Army did not come easily, for public opinion at first ran heavily against the idea of arming Black men as soldiers. As the war progressed, however, Union officials realized that they needed Black recruits and encouraged them to enlist. With the exception of a few emergency situations, Black men were not used as soldiers by the Confederate army. The Confederates were fighting to maintain slavery and had good reason to believe the loyalty of African American soldiers would not be on their side.

The Civil War monument honors, among other Civil War veterans, the proud African American men from the Fourteenth Regiment Rhode Island Heavy Artillery (Colored), which was organized in 1863 and stationed for duty in 1864–1865 in New Orleans.

DATE ESTABLISHED:	Design submitted, 1866; monument dedicated, 1871
ADDRESS:	Kennedy Plaza, Washington and Exchange Streets, Providence
VISITING HOURS:	Daily dawn–dusk
FEES:	None
SOURCES:	Telephone call June 16, 1994, Providence Preservation Society. *Rhode Island's Freedom Trail.*

Congdon Street Baptist Church

The frame building at 17 Congdon Street was the second meeting house built for the Black community in Providence. The First Meeting House and School stood at Meeting and Congdon Streets between 1820 and 1863 and served both as a church and as a school for Black children. Black people of all denominations met at the earlier site, and many of Providence's Black churches originated from the First Meeting House.

The church had its origins when, in 1819, African Americans and some of their white friends met to make plans for establishing a house of worship for the Black people of Providence. The group selected a lot on Meeting Street, and assisted by the Society of Friends and others, erected their house of worship and dedicated it in 1820. The original church no longer stands; the current church was built in 1874–1875.

DATE ESTABLISHED:	1820; second meeting house, 1874–1875
ADDRESS:	17 Congdon Street, Providence
TELEPHONE:	(401) 421-4032
VISITING HOURS:	By appointment only; contact church for information
SOURCES:	Telephone call to site, June 16, 1994. Providence Preservation Society. *National Register of Historic Places,* 670. *Rhode Island's Freedom Trail.*

Fox Point

Fox Point was a neighborhood of African Americans and newcomers who arrived here from the Cape Verde Islands, a former Portuguese colony off the west coast of Africa. They settled in Providence, seeking new opportunities. In the Fox Point area they met people who were slaves or former slaves. Many were sailors or persons engaged in the maritime industry.

This community of African Americans can trace its roots back to the eighteenth and nineteenth centuries.

DATE ESTABLISHED: 18th century

ADDRESS: Wickenden Street, Benefit Street, parts of N. Main Street, and Indian Point, Point Street Bridge, Providence

SOURCES: Linda A'vant, Rhode Island Black Heritage Society. Telephone information June 16, 1994, Providence Preservation Society. *Rhode Island's Freedom Trail.*

India Point

India Point was the port of entry for Cape Verdean windjammers transporting passengers and cargo between the Cape Verde Islands and New England. The African immigrants came here in search of a new life in America. A few of the older houses still are standing in this area, which is near another Black historic area, Fox Point.

DATE ESTABLISHED: 18th century

ADDRESS: Gano Street, exit 3, I-195 West, Providence

SOURCE: *Rhode Island's Freedom Trail.*

Rhode Island Black Heritage Society

The Rhode Island Black Heritage Society—the state's largest facility for preserving and documenting local and national Black historical information—is located on the main floor of the Opportunities Industrialization Center building. The society includes a library with a reading area and a large wall area for exhibits. Library and archive collections include photographs, slides, taped interviews, and artifacts from local Black homes and organizations.

The society collects, preserves, and exhibits informative materials on the lifestyle and institutions of Black citizens and makes this information available through lectures, school curricula, exhibits, and other activities. Each month it features local Black artists in the gallery space. Collections range from materials on Africans in Rhode Island in the early seventeenth century to information on recent Black migrants to the state.

DATE ESTABLISHED: 1974

ADDRESS: 46 Aborn Street, Providence

TELEPHONE: (401) 751-3490

VISITING HOURS: Mon.–Fri. 9–4:30; closed weekends, major state holidays ♟♟

FEES: None

SOURCES: Alma J. Smith, library staff, Rhode Island Black Heritage Society. Linda A'Vant Coleman, executive director, Rhode Island Black Heritage Society. Telephone conversation June 16, 1994, James Clements, museum assistant. *Creative Survival.*

Works Consulted

The African American Encyclopedia. Vol. 5. Michael W. Williams, ed. New York: Marshall Cavendish, 1993.

Before the Mayflower: A History of Black America. 5th ed. Lerone Bennett, Jr. New York: Penguin, 1988.

Black Heroes of the American Revolution. Burke Davis. New York: Odyssey/Harcourt Brace Jovanovich, 1976.

Creative Survival: The Providence Black Community in the 19th Century. Providence: The Rhode Island Black Heritage Society, n.d.

International Library of Negro Life and History: Historical Negro Biographies. Wilhelmena S. Robinson. New York: Publishers, 1970.

Kingston: A Forgotten History. Christian M. McBurney. Kingston, R.I.: Pettaquamscutt Historical Society, 1975.

National Register of Historic Places. Washington, D.C.: National Park Service, 1976.

"A Profile in Dedication: Sarah Harris and the Fayerweather Family." Carl R. Woodward. Reprint from *The New England Galaxy* 15, no. 1 (Summer 1973), 3–14.

Rhode Island's Freedom Trail. Carl Senna, ed. Warwick, R.I.: Rhode Island Black Heritage Society, 1986.

The Underground Railroad in New England. Richard R. Kuns and John Sabino, eds. Boston: American Revolution Bicentennial Administration, Region I, with Boston 200, the Bicentennial and Historical Commissions of the Six New England States and the Underground Railroad Task Force, 1976.

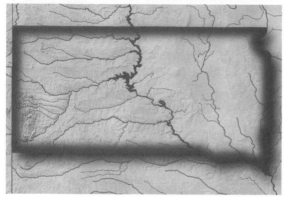

South Dakota

Fort Meade

Old Fort Meade Cavalry Museum

Fort Meade was built in 1878 as a command post during the conflict with the Sioux Indians. From 1880 to 1888 Companies A, D, H, and K of the Twenty-fifth Infantry were stationed here. Although the soldiers were assigned to protect white settlers and Black Hills miners from the Sioux, they themselves encountered, as did the Indians, prejudice and hostility from nearby white settlers in the town of Sturgis. One such incident involved a Black soldier, Corporal Ross Hallon of Company A, who was being held in the jail on a murder charge. Townspeople from Sturgis forcibly took him from the jail and hanged him from a tree. He was buried in the nearby cemetery where the bodies of twelve other Buffalo Soldiers also lie.

Today Fort Meade is inactive as a military base, but the grounds still contain some of the original buildings. A Veterans Administration hospital operates the base, and a military academy provides training for the National Guard. The museum, which is operated by a nonprofit, nongovernment association, features a video on fort life as well as exhibits on Native American life and the experiences of the cavalry soldiers. In response to the increasing number of requests for information about the Buffalo Soldiers, the museum plans to expand that aspect of its interpretation. The current exhibit on the Buffalo Soldiers at Fort Meade includes written materials, pictures, and a coat made of buffalo skin.

DATE BUILT:	1878
ADDRESS:	1 mile east of Sturgis on SD 34 (at Sturgis, leave the interstate but continue on the same road to a four-way stop; turn right and continue one mile to the Fort)
TELEPHONE:	(605) 347-9822
VISITING HOURS:	Memorial Day–Labor Day, daily 8–7; May and Sept., daily 9–5; tours on request during winter months 👫
FEES:	Adults, $2; children under 12, free
SOURCES:	Carrie Lavarnway, curator, South Dakota Historical Society, State Agricultural Heritage Museum. Telephone conversation June 18, 1994, Logan Lamphere, guide.

Lake City Vicinity

Fort Sisseton Historic Park

Fort Sisseton, which was originally known as Fort Wadsworth, was established during the last half of the nineteenth century to protect settlers from the Indians. It was founded in 1864 near Lake City, South Dakota. Not far away, along the bank of the Minnesota River, lived some of the Santee Sioux. Two years before the opening of the fort the Sioux under Chief Little Crow had rebelled in an uprising that lasted for five months. Their rebellion was not without cause; the Indians could rightfully complain of unfair trading practices and broken treaties. They especially resented the white settlers who were beginning to homestead on Indian lands. The uprising was bloody. There were more than a thousand casualties, and many homes of the white settlers were destroyed. Eventually the

Indian leaders were convicted. Some of them were executed, and a great many Indians fled to the west.

At this point Fort Sisseton and other forts were set up to protect the white settlers. The Indians respected the Black soldiers stationed at Fort Sisseton—men of the Twenty-fourth and Twenty-fifth Colored Infantry Regiments—whom the Indians named the "Buffalo Soldiers."

The Buffalo Soldiers of the above-named regiments as well as those of the Twenty-fifth U.S. Infantry were made up of Black men who served at Fort Sisseton from May 1884 until April 1888. The company had 92 men in 1886, 104 in 1887, and 100 in 1888.

During the 1870s the railroad began to move into the Dakota Territory, the Indians were moved from the area, and many new settlers began to arrive. In time gold was discovered in the Black Hills farther to the west. The facility at Fort Sisseton no longer seemed to be essential, and it was closed down in 1889.

Even though the fort is no longer an active military post, it is still maintained by the government. During the first weekend of June a celebration is staged to celebrate its contribution to the history of the region. A tour highlights Fort Sisseton's past; it includes visits to the barracks, guardhouse, officers quarters, post infirmary, library-schoolhouse, and trading post. Visitors can view the stone buildings and breastworks put up during the 1860s. The guardhouse has bricks carved with names of soldiers from the Twenty-fifth Infantry Regiment.

DATE ESTABLISHED. 1864–1888

ADDRESS· Near Lake City (from Lake City go 28 miles west on ND 10, then 6 miles south)

TELEPHONE: (605) 448-5701, or main office, (605) 448-5474

VISITING HOURS: Memorial Day–Labor Day, daily 10–6; to request a tour after Labor Day, call the main office 👫

FEES: Historical Festival, adults, $2; children under 12, free; or SD park sticker (admission to any state park for the year), adult annual rate, $15; daily $2; children under 12, free; subject to change in 1996

SOURCES: Wendy L. Lewis, visitor services specialist, Fort Sisseton State Historic Park. Telephone conversation June 18, 1994, Norma Johnson, tour services. Telephone conversation Aug. 10, 1995,

SOURCES: Dave Daberkow, park manager, Fort Sisseton. Joanita Kant Monteith, Codington County Historical Society, Inc. Information sheet from Fort Sisseton State Historic Park. *Ft. Sisseton Historical Festival. Fort Sisseton State Park.*

Yankton

Allen African Methodist Episcopal Church

After the Civil War, several Black families, many from Alabama and other parts of the South, migrated to South Dakota. Some of them found work on the docks along the Missouri River; others worked as plasterers, barbers, domestics, or janitors. One African American, Tom Douglass, owned a restaurant. He traveled to Missouri to encourage others to migrate to Yankton. Among others, Douglass persuaded Henry and Isaac Blakey to move to Yankton, where they arrived in 1905.

In 1885 people from the African American community had built the Allen African Methodist Episcopal Church, South Dakota's oldest African American church. Other churches were soon organized. Reverend George Tillman was pastor of the Christian Methodist Episcopal Church, and the congregation of Second Baptist built its church in Yankton in 1916.

By 1920 Yankton had a population of 144 African Americans. Unfortunately, they began to face growing racial animosity. Klan cross burnings and activities were directed primarily against Catholics, but these activities also alarmed the Black community. These hostilities led to the organization of a Yankton chapter of the National Association for the Advancement of Colored People.

During the difficult years of the Great Depression, Allen Chapel and other Black churches provided leadership and places where people could share their resources and find a sense of community. Today services are led by a minister from Sioux City. The chapel is Yankton's only Black historic site.

DATE BUILT: 1885

ADDRESS: 508 Cedar Street, Yankton

TELEPHONE: (605) 665-1449

VISITING HOURS: Sun. service, 11

SOURCES: Telephone conversation June 20, 1994, Mr. Nate Blakey, community resident. "Black People in South Dakota History."

Works Consulted

"Black People in South Dakota History." Sara L. Bernson and Robert J. Eggers. *South Dakota History* 73, no. 3 (summer 1977), 241–70.

Fort Sisseton Historical Festival. South Dakota Department of Game, Fish, and Parks, Division of Parks and Recreation. [brochure]

Fort Sisseton State Park. South Dakota Department of Game, Fish, and Parks, Division of Parks and Recreation. [brochure]

Bennington

Old First Church

Members of the Old First Church (First Congregational Church) in Bennington were noted in the early nineteenth century for their opposition to slavery. They demonstrated these views by welcoming to their midst a Black minister, the Reverend Lemuel Haynes (1753–1833). Haynes was born in West Hartford, Connecticut. His mother was white, his father was African. Haynes served as a Minuteman April 19, 1775, in the battles of Lexington and Concord. Later he was one of three Black soldiers to participate with Ethan Allen and his Green Mountain Boys from Vermont in the Battle of Ticonderoga. The other two Black volunteers served with him on May 10, 1775, as the men stormed the British fort and captured cannons from the enemy forces. After fighting in the northern campaigns of the Revolutionary War, Haynes returned to farming. In 1778 he married a white woman, Elizabeth Babbitt. Of their nine children, one became a lawyer and another a physician.

In 1780 Haynes obtained a license to preach in the Congregational Church. He was one of the first Black ministers certified to preach by a predominantly white denomination, and he was the first African American pastor of a white church. Haynes was the first Black man to be awarded an honorary degree from an American college when Middlebury College awarded him an honorary M.A. in 1804. (The first Black college graduate probably was Alexander Twilight, who received a bachelor's degree from Middlebury College in 1823. See the next listing.)

The Bennington Museum on West Main Street in Bennington has a painting of Reverend Haynes preaching at Old First Church. (For further information on Haynes, see the section on South Granville, New York.)

DATE ESTABLISHED:	1805
ADDRESS:	Monument Avenue, Old Bennington Village
TELEPHONE:	(802) 447-1223
VISITING HOURS:	Sun. service, 11; Memorial Day–July 1, Sat. 10–noon, Sun. 1–4; July 2–Oct. 16, daily 10–noon, 1–4; other times by appointment
FEES:	Donations welcome
SOURCES:	Telephone conversation Apr. 9, 1994, Nancy Andrews, secretary, Old First Church. *Before the Mayflower*, 64, 305, 444, 629, 633.

Brownington

Brownington Village Historic District

The Old Stone House in the Brownington Village Historic District is one of Vermont's most interesting sites related to Black history. The Reverend Alexander Lucius Twilight (1795–1857), who designed and erected the building, probably was one of the first Black college graduates in America and was the first Black person to serve in a state legislature. He graduated from Middlebury College in 1823 and served in the Vermont House of Representatives from 1836 to 1838.

Twilight served as headmaster of Brownington Academy (also known as the Orleans County Grammar School). Twilight may have had an office on the second floor. The school closed in 1859 and the building later was moved from its original location. The structure now houses Brownington's Grange Hall.

In the 1830s, Twilight wanted to construct a new building for the school, but the board of trustees advised against the idea and would not help.

Undaunted, Twilight proceeded with help from his neighbors. For two years, between 1834 and 1836, they quarried stone from nearby fields, split and hauled the granite, and erected a four-story, thirty-room building. Many Vermonters later marveled that Twilight had accomplished this feat on his small salary as minister and headmaster.

Twilight named the dormitory/classroom building Athenian Hall. The structure, which had no indoor plumbing or central heating, may have depended on the huge kitchen fireplace and fifteen small charcoal-burning fireplaces for heat. The residents had to obtain their drinking water by draining rainwater from the roof down through pipes into the kitchen area.

Athenian Hall served the school for almost a quarter of a century. Twilight instructed local schoolchildren either in the stone building or the Orleans County Grammar School. His desk and Bible are still on view—visible symbols of a man of accomplishment.

The school closed two years after Twilight's death in 1857. A few years later his wife sold the residence, which later became a boarding house. In 1918 the Orleans County Historical Society purchased the fine old building and restored it. Today the Old Stone House contains twenty-five rooms with historical exhibits about the county. It is one of the best preserved school buildings from this era in America.

This site also contains the Alexander Twilight House, which dates from about 1820. Located next to the Old Stone House, it is perhaps the first dwelling owned by the Twilights in Brownington. The renovated homestead has farm tools and machinery on display. Across the road from the Old Stone House is the Twilight farm, which was built soon after Alexander and Mercy Twilight arrived in Brownington in 1829. The house was large enough to board several students.

The graves of Alexander and Mercy Twilight are located in the graveyard of the Brownington Congregational Church.

The Brownington Village Historic District, with the Old Stone House so closely associated with Alexander Twilight, is listed in the *National Register of Historic Places*.

DATE BUILT:	Homestead, c1820; Old Stone House, 1834–1836
ADDRESS:	Brownington Village, about 30 miles north of Saint Johnsbury (on I-91, take the Irasburg-Orleans exit, go east through Orleans, then take a sharp right onto VT 58; at the fork in the road turn to the left and go about 2 miles)
TELEPHONE:	(802) 754-2022
VISITING HOURS:	May 15–June 30, Sept. 1–Oct. 15, Fri.–Tues. 11–5; July–Aug., daily 11–5 ⅋⅋
FEES:	Adults, $3; children under 12, $1; Orleans County residents, $2; special rates for student groups
SOURCES:	Telephone conversation Jan. 27, 1995, Tracy Martin, site manager. *A Walking Tour of Brownington Village Historic District.*

Burlington

John Wheeler House

Vermont, the first state added to the thirteen original colonies, in 1777 also passed the first state constitution to forbid slavery. (Technically, Vermont did not become a state until 1791; it had existed for fourteen years as an independent republic.) By 1837 there were nearly one hundred antislavery societies in Vermont, and many citizens who were active in antislavery societies also were active in the underground railroad. Residents of Burlington, Vermont, and surrounding areas were very active in the abolition movement, and there were a number of underground railroad stops in this area.

Oral tradition maintains that John Wheeler, a minister and sixth president of the University of Vermont, assisted fugitive slaves who were fleeing to Canada, but there is no written documentation of the extent of involvement. He had lived in South Carolina in 1819 and had held religious services for slaves in South Carolina cities. When Wheeler returned to Vermont, he remained involved in antislavery activities.

Today the history department of the University of Vermont is housed in the Wheeler House, a brick, two-story house with basement. In the past the house served as an infirmary. The front of the house is intact, but the rear kitchen and servant wings were converted first to infirmary rooms and then to offices. The parlor and bedrooms are intact, although they are used now for university purposes.

DATE BUILT:	1840
ADDRESS:	442 Main Street, Burlington
TELEPHONE:	(802) 656-3180
VISITING HOURS:	By appointment Mon.–Fri. 8:30–4:30
SOURCES:	Telephone conversation Apr. 8, 1994, Thomas Visser, research assistant professor of history, University of Vermont. Letter from Bridget M. Butler, administrative assistant, Department of History, The University of Vermont, 9 Jan. 1992. *The Underground Railroad in New England.*

Ferrisburgh

Rokeby Museum

In 1791 Thomas R. Robinson (1761–1851) and his wife, Jemima, moved from Rhode Island to Vermont and purchased a farm known as "Rokeby." The Robinsons were Quakers. Their homestead at the time consisted of more than 1,000 acres and encompassed a hill overlooking the Champlain Valley.

Prior to the Civil War, their son, Rowland Thomas Robinson (1791–1879), inherited the farm. Together with his wife, Rachel, he founded the Vermont Anti-Slavery Society, the first statewide antislavery organization in the nation. A leader in the local underground railroad, Robinson was also a friend of abolitionists Frederick Douglass, Lucretia Mott, and William Lloyd Garrison.

The Robinsons concealed runaway slaves in an east chamber of their house called the hidden room, which adjoined a bedroom; its entry door was not readily seen. When the fugitives left at night they were taken to their next stop at North Ferrisburgh, Charlotte, or East Montpelier. Moving north from those locations, they were helped to cross the border into Canada.

In addition to being an underground railway station, Rokeby also served as an early school, a Quaker meeting house, and the town's first library. Today the house is a museum, Vermont's only underground railway station open to the public. It displays two centuries of furnishings as well as records of the Vermont Anti-Slavery Society and items that belonged to the Robinson family. Visitors may see the room in which the fugitives hid.

DATE BUILT:	House, 1780s and 1814; museum, 1962
ADDRESS:	US 7 (north of Ferrisburgh off US 7), Ferrisburgh vicinity (from the south: approximately 3 miles north of Vergennes on US 7, historic site marker and front entrance sign on the right; from the north: approximately 2 miles south of the village center of North Ferrisburgh on US 7, historic site marker and museum entrance on your left)
TELEPHONE:	(802) 877-3406
VISITING HOURS:	May 15–Oct. 1, Thurs.–Sun. with 45-minute guided tours of the main house at 11, 12:30, and 2; tours of the outbuildings self-guided; closed Mon.–Wed., Oct. 2–May 14; office hours Wed.–Fri. 9–5 🍴
FEES:	Adults, $4; senior citizens and students, $3; children under 12, $1
SOURCES:	Telephone conversation Apr. 9, 1994, Jim Mullin, caretaker, Rokeby Museum. Karen E. Petersen, director, Rokeby Museum. *The Underground Railroad in New England. National Register of Historic Places*, 767.

Woodstock

Titus Hutchinson House

The Titus Hutchinson House was the home of an active stationmaster for the underground railroad. Hutchinson was a former State Supreme Court Chief Justice. He assisted slaves when they arrived from South Woodstock, then helped to move them on to Royalton or Stafford.

Hutchinson House is a large, white, frame residence on the Woodstock village square. During construction for a bridge, a tunnel was discovered that ran from the Hutchinson home to the Kedron River. (The tunnel is closed now.)

Since the early 1980s the Woodstock Historical Association (located around the corner from the Hutchinson House at 26 Elm Street) has owned Hutchinson House. Before they purchased it, the residence served for many years as an inn and a restaurant. Now the first floor houses a retail art gallery and the rest of the house contains private office space. The exterior has retained its original appearance, but some remodeling was done inside.

The house is easily accessible, as it is in the center of town. Visitors who wish to see the interior (there are no signs of the tunnel today) should refer requests to the Woodstock Historical Association.

DATE BUILT:	Late 18th century
ADDRESS:	One, The Green, Woodstock
TELEPHONE:	Woodstock Historical Association, (802) 457-1822
VISITING HOURS:	Enterprises private; make appointment to see interior by contacting the Woodstock Historical Association
SOURCES:	Telephone conversation Apr. 11, 1994, Kit Nichols, assistant to the director, Woodstock Historical Association. *The Underground Railroad in New England.*

Works Consulted

Before the Mayflower: A History of Black America. 5th ed. Lerone Bennett Jr. New York: Penguin, 1988.

National Register of Historic Places. Washington, D.C.: National Park Service, 1976.

The Underground Railroad in New England. Richard R. Kuns and John Sabino, eds. Boston: American Revolution Bicentennial Administration, Region I, with Boston 200, the Bicentennial and Historical Commissions of the Six New England States and the Underground Railroad Task Force, 1976.

A Walking Tour of Brownington Village Historic District. Elaine Magalis. Brownington, Vt.: Orleans County Historical Society. [brochure]

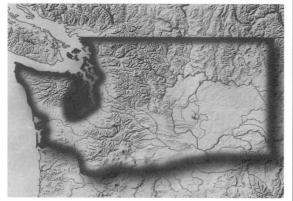

Centralia

George Washington Park

George Washington, an African American pioneer in the West, was the founder of Centralia, Washington, and Centralia's city park is named in his honor. Born in Virginia in 1817 to a slave father and a white mother, George was adopted and raised by a white family who later moved to frontier settlements in Ohio and Missouri. As the years passed, George grew to be a six-foot-tall young man known for his strength and for his expert skill in marksmanship. He also was a talented miller, tanner, cook, and weaver. In 1850 Washington and his foster parents joined other families in a train of fifteen wagons and traveled to the Oregon Territory. Washington, who married at age 50, successfully homesteaded in an undeveloped region. In 1872, on a site between the Columbia River and Puget Sound, he established the town that

would become Centralia. As the town's founder, George Washington not only encouraged growth by selling lots, he also donated funds for churches and a cemetery. His generosity was especially evident in the 1893 panic when he literally saved many Centralians from starvation by bringing in wagonloads of food and by providing his fellow citizens with relief funds. When he died in an accident in 1905, the mayor of Centralia proclaimed a day of mourning.

Washington is honored with a beautiful park in Centralia that bears his name and by a plaque in the park. Visitors will enjoy strolling there and looking at the display of flowers. The only building in the park, the Centralia Timberland Library, contains a book, *The Man Who Founded a Town*, that tells George Washington's story.

ADDRESS: Main Street at Gold Street, Centralia

TELEPHONE: Centralia Timberland Library, (360) 736-0183

VISITING HOURS: Park, 24 hours; library, Mon.–Thurs. 10–9, Fri.–Sat. 9–5

SOURCES: Telephone conversation May 14, 1994, Mike Dinkins, reference librarian, Centralia Timberland Public Library. *The Black West.*

Ilwaco

Lewis and Clark Interpretive Center

The Lewis and Clark Interpretive Center incorporates into its self-guided tour a modest amount of information about York, the Black man who accompanied Lewis and Clark on their expedition from St. Louis to the Pacific Ocean between 1803 and 1806. A notebook at the front desk that tells about members of the expedition includes a paragraph on York. A large mural that includes both pictures and written information about the journey contains York's picture. He is represented, too, among some small-sized dolls downstairs.

ADDRESS: Fort Canby State Park, 3 miles southwest off US 101 at the tip of Cape Disappointment (from Portland take US 30 to Astoria, then US 101 north to Ilwaco, then follow signs 3 miles south and west to the park)

TELEPHONE:	(360) 642-3029
VISITING HOURS:	Daily 10–5
FEES:	None
SOURCE:	Telephone conversation Apr. 30, 1994, Ken Weichel, volunteer, Lewis and Clark Interpretive Center.

Seattle

Douglass–Truth Library

Funded by the city's library system and by gifts from community organizations, the Douglass–Truth Library documents the Black experience in the United States with emphasis on the Pacific Northwest. The marvelous collection, named for outstanding Black Americans Frederick Douglass and Sojourner Truth, contains 6,500 volumes, including 500 children's books, adult books, catalogues of other collections, magazines, an index of articles from local newspapers, and 1,000 files of information about local African American individuals and institutions.

The unique reference collection of children's books shows how Black characters were portrayed between 1863 and the present. They illustrate the pre-vailing views—from stereotypical to realistic—that existed when they were written; this provides an invaluable record for research and teaching.

The collection began in 1965 when the changing ethnic makeup of the community drew attention to the need for more books about African Americans. The Alpha Kappa Alpha sorority donated more than 300 relevant books, a gift that was supplemented by the Black friends of Yesler Branch Library and later by a 1984 library-services grant.

ADDRESS:	Library, 2300 E. Yesler Way, Seattle
TELEPHONE:	(206) 684-4704
VISITING HOURS:	Mon.–Wed. 1–9, Thurs. 10–9, Sat. 10–6, winter Sun. 10–5 in addition to Mon.–Sat. hours; closed holidays 👫
FEES:	None
SOURCE:	Telephone conversation Apr. 30, 1994, John Sheets, branch librarian, Douglass–Truth Library.

East Madison Avenue Black Heritage Sites*

Three structures related to the history of Seattle's African American community are located in the East Madison Avenue area, Seattle's oldest settlement of Black Americans. They are the First African Methodist Episcopal Church, the Mt. Zion Church, and the William and Sarah Grose House.

SOURCE:	Telephone conversation Apr. 7, 1994, Esther Mumford, local Black history sites author.

First A.M.E. Church

The First African Methodist Episcopal Church has a sanctuary constructed from about 1910 to 1912 on land purchased by the congregation in 1890. An education wing was constructed next to the church about 1985. The main structure and the education wing both are two-story buildings. The sanctuary, which has a fellowship hall on the lower level, is con-structed of rust-colored brick and has a tower with beige trim. First A.M.E. Church has been designated as a historic landmark by the city of Seattle.

DATE ESTABLISHED:	1912
ADDRESS:	1522 Fourteenth Avenue at E. Pine Street, Seattle
TELEPHONE:	(206) 324-3664
VISITING HOURS:	Office hours, Tues.–Fri. 10–4; Sun. ser-vices, 8, 11; Sun. school, 9
SOURCE:	Telephone conversation June 11, 1995, Dorothy Johnson, office volunteer, First A.M.E. Church.

Mt. Zion Baptist Church

Located at the southeast corner of Nineteenth Avenue and East Madison Street, Mt. Zion Baptist Church contains a sanctuary that is a work of art in itself. The strikingly beautiful, contemporary church features motifs from the African and African American heritage. The two-level structure has a library, Sunday School office, choir room, a fellow-ship hall, commercial kitchen, and three large classrooms on the lower level. The upper level contains the sanctuary, administrative offices, and an educational wing. Eighteen large stained-glass windows in the sanctuary depict Black historical figures, including, among others, Prince Hall, Sojourner Truth, and Dr. Martin Luther King Jr. The windows, with their vivid shapes and colors, were created for Mt. Zion Baptist Church by a company in Cleveland, Ohio. The stained glass circles the sanctuary with portraits near the choir stand and pulpit, in the rear, and on the side of the chapel that adjoins the sanctuary. Symbolism also is contained in twelve wooden beams in the sanctuary that represent the twelve tribes of Israel and the Twelve Apostles. Created from wood from the Pacific Northwest, the beams were left unfinished to represent the unfinished status of Christians. Red and purple colors in the church represent royalty, divinity, and the blood of Christ, while skylights re-create the four gospels of the New Testament of the Bible. Symbolism is extended through the colors of ten flags that include, among others, the flag of the United States, the Christianity flag, and flags of the state of Washington, the Black Liberation Movement, the National Baptist Convention, and the National Council of Churches.

Founded by a small group of men from Tennessee, the congregation of Mt. Zion Baptist Church dates back to 1890. For most of the years from the founding date, members have worshiped at this site on Nineteenth Avenue. An earlier church structure was torn down in the early 1970s, and the present church soon was constructed on the same site.

DATE ESTABLISHED: Congregation, 1890; present building, early 1970s

ADDRESS: 1634 Nineteenth Avenue, Seattle

TELEPHONE: (206) 322-6500

VISITING HOURS: Office hours, Mon.–Fri. 9–5; Sun. services, 8, 10:45

SOURCE: Telephone conversation June 10, 1995, Reverend LaVerne C. Hall, church administrator, Mt. Zion Baptist Church.

William and Sarah Grose House

The Grose House at Twenty-fourth and Howell in East Madison stands as a symbol of the early community of Black settlers. William Grose came to Seattle in the 1860s, and in 1882 he and Sarah purchased a twelve-acre tract for use as a ranch. They operated a hotel, but it was destroyed by fire in 1889. Retiring from the hotel business, they moved into their newly built house in 1890. The large bungalow just north of the Grose House was built in the 1920s by a Grose granddaughter and her husband. The old farmhouse has been little modified since its construction, although new condominiums have consumed much of the land.

DATE ESTABLISHED: 1890

ADDRESS: 1733 Twenty-fourth Avenue at Howell Street, Seattle

VISITING HOURS: Private, visitors may walk or drive by

Dr. Martin Luther King Jr. Memorial *

A thirty-foot-tall Zimbabwean granite memorial is surrounded by a verdant four-acre park in Seattle. Designed with a wide base and gracefully narrowing to the apex, the monument symbolizes Dr. Martin Luther King Jr.'s moving statement, "I've been to the mountaintop."

Dedicated on November 16, 1991, the monument, located in an African American community in Seattle, grew out of the dream of Charlie James, a Seattle citizen who announced in 1983 that he would see that the city had a monument to the slain civil rights leader. Over a period of years other individuals joined the effort and a committee was formed. The county and state legislatures also contributed significant funds. The monument, possibly the largest such structure honoring King outside the South, is located in a lovely setting with a hill sloping down to it. It rests in a reflecting pool; a waterfall, gently with a soft musical sound, cascades from the top of the monument to the pool. Plaques embedded in the surrounding walls describe significant incidents in King's life. Children can pause here to play in the park, or they can take a moment to reflect with their families on the meaning of King's life and philosophy and his sacrifice for peace.

DATE ESTABLISHED: 1991

ADDRESS: Southeast corner of Martin Luther King Jr. Way and S. Walker Street, Seattle

VISITING HOURS:	24 hours 👫
FEES:	None
SOURCES:	Telephone conversation Apr. 7, 1994, Esther Mumford, local Black heritage sites author. *A Guide to the History, Culture, and Art of African Americans in Seattle and King County, Washington.*

Tumwater

Simmons Party Memorial

George Washington Bush, an African American, led the first American settlers to the Puget Sound area in 1843, bringing his own family and seven white companions over the Old Oregon Trail. Bush was born free in Pennsylvania but moved to Missouri, where he worked as a servant for a French family. He prospered in Missouri as a cattle trader. Because he had earlier explored the wilderness as far as the Pacific Coast, he was welcomed as a guide when families wanted to go west in a wagon train. One factor in his decision to leave Missouri may have been a law that banned free Black people from settling in the state.

The group came to Oregon, and Bush settled in Oregon's Willamette Valley in 1844. He became one of the wealthiest men in the region. Oregon, however, had restrictive laws prohibiting Black people, slave or free, from entering. The group was supportive of Bush, who apparently had helped two members of the traveling party on their way to Oregon, and its members voted to go north. Bush and his son, Owen, established a farm in the Tumwater area and prospered there. By the 1850s he was one of the most successful farmers in Thurston County, Washington

Territory. A generous man, he assisted his neighbors who were less prosperous. In 1854, when the validity of the land claim to his farm was threatened, his neighbors showed their respect by petitioning Congress to confirm the claim.

One of Bush's sons, William Owen Bush, was elected to Washington's first State Legislature about 1889.

George Bush's name is among those inscribed on a monument in the beautiful Tumwater Falls Historical Park. Here visitors may walk a mile-long trail that winds around the Deschutes River, with its bridges and tumbling waterfalls. A granite monument in the park, approximately twelve feet in height, contains a brass plaque with the city seal and the names of about two dozen pioneers who braved the Oregon Trail to come West and settle near Puget Sound.

ADDRESS:	Foot of Grant Street, Tumwater Falls Historical Park, Tumwater
TELEPHONE:	(206) 943-2550
VISITING HOURS:	Winter, 8–4:30; summer, 8–dusk
SOURCES:	Telephone conversation April 30, 1994, Derrick Jordan, caretaker, Tumwater Falls Historical Park. *International Library of Negro Life and History,* 58–59. *The Black West*

Works Consulted

The Black West: A Documentary and Pictorial History. 3d ed., rev. William Loren Katz. Seattle: Open Hand Publishing, 1987.

International Library of Negro Life and History: Historical Negro Biographies. Wilhelmena S. Robinson. New York: Publishers, 1970.

Beloit

Fairbanks Flats

During most of the 1800s, the Black population of Beloit was small. In 1881 some families joined together in organizing the first Black church society. The picture changed, however, during World War I when the Fairbanks-Morse Corporation—an engine-manufacturing company and the city's largest employer—recruited hundreds of Black workers from the South to work in the defense industry. Most of these workers lived in Fairbanks Flats—a development built on company land—or they lived on the west or southeast sides of Beloit.

There was some controversy about the location of Fairbanks Flats. The city of Beloit had originally intended to develop an extensive park system, a part of which would have been on the west side of the Rock River where Fairbanks Flats was built. The company disregarded the wishes of the city by buying up the land. A subsidiary of Fairbanks-Morse, Eclipse Home Makers, built twenty-four units of housing in 1917 on the land and rented the units to Black employees of Fairbanks-Morse.

Fairbanks Flats is a rare example in Wisconsin of planned segregated housing. The company deliberately set out to keep its Black workers in a segregated area on the outskirts of town. It is worth noting, too, that the company practiced discrimination not only in the location of its imported Black and white workers but also in the quality of their housing. White workers were for the most part located close to the plant in one-story cottages on curved streets in a landscaped setting. The white area was called Eclipse Park. By way of contrast, the Black workers were housed in four identical concrete-block apartment buildings. Each building consisted of six two-story units; the design was plain and undistinguished. Housed in the Fairbanks Flats were both skilled and unskilled laborers, including blacksmiths, molders, and other workers. The flats became the nucleus of the Black community. Nearby a Black YMCA was founded.

After World War II ownership of the Fairbanks Flats changed hands. People who were not employed by Fairbanks-Morse began to move into the apartments. Still those renting and living in the development were predominantly Black.

DATE BUILT: 1917

ADDRESS: 205, 215 Birch Avenue; 206, 216 Carpenter
                  Street, Beloit

VISITING HOURS: Private, visitors may drive by

SOURCES: Cultural Resource Management in
                  Wisconsin, study unit on Black history, State
                  Historical Society of Wisconsin. Survey
                  form, Historic Preservation Division, State
                  Historical Society of Wisconsin.

Fond du Lac

Octagon House *

Octagon House, which was used as a hiding place on the underground railroad, has all the mystery and intrigue a person could want with its nine secret passageways within its octagonal shape. Research by the daughter of the present owners of the house indicates that it was not built for altruistic purposes; instead, it was designed for security reasons by a crafty and suspicious fur trader. Isaac Brown, a leading citizen in the town of Fond du Lac, built Octagon House. He traded furs and other goods with Indians but for some reason appeared to fear an attack. Therefore, he wanted a residence where he could hide both his family members and trading goods. The octagonal house was perfect; leftover spaces in the corners of the rooms made it difficult to calculate where the true ends of the walls should be, and into these nooks and crannies Brown managed to tuck nine hiding spaces. A walk-through closet hid a secret room. One fireplace was a fake. The house also had a hidden room in a wall, a fake wall in a broom closet, and a corner cupboard that a person in the know could walk behind and find a hiding place. A crawl space in the basement led two ways to the attic—by stairway and by ladder. Octagon House even had an underground tunnel leading to an adjacent woodshed.

At some point during the Civil War, Brown, who at one time was mayor of Fond du Lac, took an interest in the underground railroad and began using his highly suitable house to hide runaway slaves.

In 1975 Octagon House was slated for demolition; fortunately it was saved. Other underground railroad houses in the area have been demolished or have

been kept strictly secret by owners who desire privacy. For those who want to enlarge their understanding of the underground railroad, Octagon House is an opportunity. The one and one-half–story frame and concrete house is located on a site that once was the shoreline of the Fond du Lac River. Its secrets are now open to visitors.

DATE BUILT: c1856

ADDRESS: 276 Linden Street, Fond du Lac

TELEPHONE: (920) 922-1608;
                  special events recording, (414) 924-9393

VISITING HOURS: Call for times and tours 👥

FEES: Adults, $6.50; children 12 and younger, $4

SOURCES: Telephone conversation June 24, 1994, Julia
                  Hansen, The Historic Octagon House. Mr.
                  Bob Kuhnz, Fond du Lac County Historical
                  Society. *National Register of Historic Places*, 853.

Madison

East Dayton Street Historic District

The first Black resident reached Madison in 1847; others began arriving before the Civil War. They lived scattered around the city in rented houses, rooming houses, or apartments, and most of them worked as laborers, teamsters, or cooks or had small businesses. George and Carrie Williams came to Madison in 1850. They operated a barbershop and hairdressing salon and cleaned clothing. Carrie William's brother, William Noland, operated a grocery, a bakery, and a saloon; he also manufactured a health tonic and worked as a veterinarian and chiropodist. Although the governor of the state appointed him a notary public in 1857, racial prejudice apparently prevented Noland from taking the position. The June 25, 1876, *Capital Times* noted that David Jones, the secretary of state, declaring that "this man is a n——r," had refused to file the required bond.

Benjamin Butts was another early Black resident. After mustering out of the Union Army at Camp Randall in Madison, he remained in the city. For twenty-eight years he operated a barber- shop in the basement of the First National Bank. He later worked as a porter and messenger for the State Historical

Society. In 1900 the Butts family was one of nineteen Black families in Madison.

By 1930 Madison's Black population numbered 348. The households were concentrated in south Madison around Mills, Regent, and Erin Streets and in another smaller area along East Dayton and North Blair Streets. Houses in the East Dayton Historic District are valuable because they are all that remain from the early Madison Black community. The district consists of three frame buildings that were built around the 1850s and moved from downtown early in the twentieth century. They are located in the Old Market neighborhood six blocks east of the Capitol Square in an area that originally was a cattail swamp.

The East Dayton Street area began to decline in the 1960s as new housing opportunities opened in the suburbs. Parking lots and storage yards began to claim the old area, and most of the old houses have been demolished. Those that remain are described in the listings that follow.

DATE BUILT:	1850s
ADDRESS:	Old Market neighborhood, 6 blocks east of the Capitol Square, Madison
VISITING HOURS:	Private, visitors may walk or drive by
SOURCES:	NRHPRF. NRHPINF. State Historical Society of Wisconsin. Telephone conversation June 24, 1994, Mrs. Charlyne Hill, member of the pioneering Hill family.

Miller House

The Miller House on 647 East Dayton Street is a two-story, frame building with two units. The structure, built in 1853, was moved from downtown Madison to this site in 1908. It is associated with the William and Anna Mae Miller family, a prominent Madison family that operated a rooming house and also sought to improve conditions for Madison's Black community.

William Miller was born in Richmond, Kentucky, in 1872. He attended Berea College in Kentucky and a law school in Chicago. He was attending law school and waiting on tables at a hotel in Milwaukee as a summer job in 1901 when he accepted an invitation from Governor Robert M. LaFollette to come to Madison to work as a messenger in the governor's office.

Miller arrived in Madison during a period when many African Americans were leaving the South to escape racial tensions and discrimination. He actively participated in organizations that sought to better conditions for Black people, including the NAACP. W. E. B. Du Bois, a scholar, a leader, and an editor of the NAACP's *Crisis Magazine*, on several occasions was a guest in the Miller home.

Miller served nineteen years until his death in 1929, as messenger to Governor LaFollette. When Miller died, LaFollette, then a U.S. Senator, returned from Washington for Miller's funeral.

Anna Miller also was well educated. Born in Stanford, Kentucky, in 1877, she attended Knoxville College and Kentucky State Normal School. Anna and William Miller married in 1903. Emphasizing the importance of education for their children, they sent them to the Lincoln School in Madison, which served many families of higher income. The Millers declined to accompany Senator-elect LaFollette to Washington, D.C., because Washington's schools were segregated.

In spite of her qualifications, Mrs. Miller's career was limited to cooking for sororities and fraternities. She was an active community leader, however, and organized a literary society. She became a charter member of the local chapter of the Order of the Eastern Star.

Lucile Miller, the Miller's first child, was born in 1904. Like her parents, she was active in community affairs. She and others sought to open dormitories at the University of Wisconsin to Black students; they campaigned against segregation of the USO at Truax Air Force Base; and they helped to reorganize the NAACP in 1943. Lucile Miller lived in the family house on Dayton Street until 1978.

The building then became vacant and fell into poor condition. Fortunately, in 1986 a developer restored the house, returning the exterior to its 1908 appearance. Using old photographs and descriptions from Lucile Miller, the restorer removed asbestos shingles to reveal the original clapboards and brought back the old porches. The interior has the original wide-plank pine floors and a spindled stair rail; the garden, landscaped again, has the original lilac bush. The completed Miller House restoration received a City-County Preservation Award.

DATE BUILT: 1893; moved to this site, 1908
ADDRESS: 647 E. Dayton Street, Madison
VISITING HOURS: Private, visitors may walk or drive by

649–653 East Dayton Street
114 North Blount Street

The three buildings at 649–653 East Dayton and 114 North Blount Streets are significant as being among the few remaining buildings from Madison's turn-of-the-century African American community. The two buildings on East Dayton were moved to this site in 1901 and 1912 and joined together with a wing. The house on North Blount Street was moved here in 1923.

John and Martha Turner and their adopted son, Alfred, came to Madison from Kentucky in 1898. John Turner, who was middle-aged when he arrived, worked in Madison as a day laborer. In 1901 the Turners moved the two-story, clapboard, commercial building to the 649 East Dayton address. They housed inside it the Douglas Beneficial Society, a self-help organization they had earlier established for Madison's Black families.

The house at 653 East Dayton Street, corner of Blount Street, was moved to the site in 1912 and a wing was added to connect the two buildings. The clapboard house has a large porch; the first-floor windows have six panes over six. The house, with one side facing Blount Street and the other facing Dayton Street, was the residence of Reverend C. H. Thomas, minister of the African Methodist Episcopal Church, and his wife, Caroline Thomas. John and Amanda Hill bought the building in 1917. Hill, a trustee of the A.M.E. Church, operated a shoe-shining parlor downtown; he and his wife also owned a grocery store in the former Douglas Beneficial Hall building. In 1923 they moved the small, clapboard-sided house to this area on Blount Street. The one and one-half–story house had a front porch with Victorian-style turned posts, a one-story wing, and a shed-roofed addition. Although the grocery store closed after John Hill's death, members of the Hill family have continued to occupy the historic properties and have kept them in good condition.

DATE BUILT: 649 E. Dayton, 1850s, moved to this site, 1901; 653 E. Dayton, moved to this site, 1912; 114 N. Blount Street, built c1850s, moved to this site, 1923
ADDRESS: 649–653 E. Dayton Street, and 114 N. Blount Street, Madison

Milton

Milton House Museum *

This site served as a hostelry on a stagecoach road; later it was an active station on the underground railroad. The hexagonal main block is of stuccoed concrete. Nearby is a one and one-half–story log cabin constructed around 1838.

Joseph Goodrich, a former New Yorker, built the main structure in 1839 as a stage stop, post office, and inn. He was a community leader who helped lay the foundation of the village. Among other contributions, he donated land for a public square and erected several buildings.

A letter written in 1955 by Mabel Davis Van De Mark, mentions the tunnel that led from the hexagonal inn to the log cabin behind the main structure. She noted, "About 1890 I visited Uncle Ezra and Aunt

Libby—they managed the Milton House—and he showed me the narrow tunnel which was about five feet high and told me it was used to help slaves escape from the southern plantations north toward Canada." Van De Mark's Uncle Ezra was Joseph Goodrich's son, and he ran the Milton House Inn following Joseph Goodrich's death.

Although Wisconsin was not a heavily traveled underground railroad route, there was some antislavery activity in the state. James Clark of the State Historical Society of Wisconsin has noted that by 1840 abolitionists were active in southeastern Wisconsin; the underground railroad existed in that area. Such assistance to fugitives, if discovered, would have carried heavy penalties according to the Fugitive Slave Act of 1850. Joseph Goodrich and his friends, however, were abolitionists who did not hesitate to engage in antislavery work. An entry in a biographical dictionary about him gave the following description: "He was for many years a decided anti-slavery man, a member of the old Whig Party, and, after it, a consistent member of the Republican Party. His home was a refuge for the fugitive slave."[1]

Older people in the area passed down stories of people who were hidden at this house before being helped on their way to Canada. The tunnel, now full-height and of cement, originally was a crooked, dirt crawl space with a small room mid-way. Both ends of the tunnel were well concealed. Regular visitors to the inn would have had no reason to have used such an inconvenient passage from the inn to the cabin, but the tunnel did make sense as a hiding place for fleeing slaves.

Notes by Dr. Salisbury of the Milton Historical Society Archives indicate that Goodrich cared for fugitives in the basement of the inn, where they could eat and rest. If there was danger, they would crawl through the tunnel, move up through a trap door in the floor of the log cabin, and hurry on through Storrs Lake to Bowers Lake, the Otter Creek area, and Lake Koshkonong. They would not have gone through the inn itself because Goodrich did not know if all his patrons were in favor of the abolitionist program.

The site also is believed to have been associated with Sojourner Truth. Sojourner Truth, born a slave as Isabella Baumfree, later traveled across the country preaching against slavery. She may have been a guest at the Milton House, a friend of Goodrich, and possibly a speaker at the academy in Milton. The late Mrs. Nellie Daland, a local artist, painted a portrait of Sojourner Truth, using a picture in a book as a model. This portrait hangs on the wall of the Milton House Museum.

The tunnel at this site is believed to be unique as the only underground railroad segment that actually was underground and that is intact and open to the public. At the museum today, the story of the inn's role in the underground railroad is interpreted for visitors.

DATE BUILT:	1839 or 1844
ADDRESS:	18 S. Janesville Street, Milton
TELEPHONE:	(608) 868-7772
VISITING HOURS:	Memorial Day–Labor Day, daily 11–4; May, Labor Day–Oct. 15, weekends 👫
FEES:	Adults, $3; children 5–18, $1.75; children under 5, free
SOURCES:	Doris Hoag, Milton Historical Society. "Wisconsin Defies the Fugitive Slave Law." "Underground Railroad." *National Register of Historic Places*, 858. Letter from Mabel Davis Van DeMark, 1955, from the Milton Historical Society.

Milwaukee

America's Black Holocaust Museum *

Through books, paintings, photographs, and artifacts, America's Black Holocaust Museum shows how African Americans experienced their own holocaust, similar to that experienced by the Jewish people during World War II. The story moves from slavery's beginnings in Africa to the post-Civil War Reconstruction period.

The museum, founded by James Cameron with his own privately obtained funding, opened June 19, 1988. It moved to larger quarters on North Fourth Street on November 9, 1944; there artifacts and photographs are arranged in twelve rooms and 12,000 square feet of space. Cameron, the museum's director, recommends that visitors be eight years and older because the stark quality of some of the exhibits, including realistic wax effigies of lynchings, might frighten younger children. Those who see the exhibits usually are deeply moved on seeing the atrocities that Black Americans endured.

ADDRESS: 2233 N. Fourth Street, Milwaukee

TELEPHONE: (414) 264-2500

VISITING HOURS: Mon.–Sat. 9–6; by appointment Sun., holidays

FEES: Adults, $5; children under 12, $2.50

SOURCES: Telephone conversation Jan. 7, 1995, James Cameron, founder and director. *Hippocrene U.S.A. Guide to Black America*, 373.

Milwaukee County Historical Society Museum

The Milwaukee County Historical Society Museum includes an exhibit on Blacks in Milwaukee history as well as a growing archival collection on the history of African Americans in Milwaukee. It is well adapted for use by researchers. The Milwaukee Historical Society's quarterly magazine has published several articles relating to contributions by African Americans to the growth of Milwaukee.

ADDRESS: 910 N. Old World Third Street, Milwaukee

TELEPHONE: (414) 273-8288

VISITING HOURS: Society, Mon.–Fri. 9:30–5, Sat. 10–5, Sun. 1–5; library, Mon.–Fri. 9:30–noon, 1–4:30, Sat. 10–noon, 1–4:30; closed major holidays 👫

FEES: Exhibits, free; library, user fee $1 per day

SOURCE: Telephone conversation June 24, 1994, Kathleen O'Hara, assistant for public relations, Milwaukee County Historical Society.

Wisconsin Black Historical Society Museum

One area of the Wisconsin Black Historical Society Museum exhibits thirteen dramatic four-foot-by-eight-foot murals depicting the history of the Black people from Africa through to the present day. Artifacts are in a separate area called the Bronzeville Room. Here, the visitor sees living quarters from the 1930s and 1940s—rooms representative of typical Milwaukee Black families of that era. The living quarters, a living room and a smaller room, are small because they actually were "tight" for the immigrants who came to Milwaukee to

work as laborers. The smaller room, perhaps a bedroom or combination-use room, illustrates the crowded living conditions of the era. The exhibits, along with the tour guide's explanations, promote a feeling for the sweep and scope of African American history.

DATE ESTABLISHED: 1988

ADDRESS: 2620 W. Center Street, Milwaukee

TELEPHONE: (414) 372-7677; fax, (414) 372-4882

VISITING HOURS: Mon.–Thurs. 2–6, Sat. 9–2; hours may vary, call in advance; closed Fri., Sun., major holidays 👫

FEES: Adults, $3; children, $1.50

SOURCES: Nancy M. Moser, marketing/communications, Milwaukee Public Museum. Kathleen O'Hara, assistant for public relations, Milwaukee County Historical Society. Professor William L. Van Deburg, University of Wisconsin–Madison. Telephone conversation June 25, 1994, Clayborn Benson, director, Milwaukee Black Historical Museum.

Viroqua

Vernon County Historical Museum

Vernon County—an area located east of Wildcat Mountain—was settled as an integrated community during the nineteenth century by people of varying ethnic origins, including Norwegian, Irish, and Czech backgrounds along with a sizable number of African Americans. Black farms were interspersed with white-owned farms. Churches and schools were established and built jointly. Integration included social activities, mutual assistance on the farms, and even occasional intermarriages.

The first Black settlers in the county were Walden Stewart and Wesley Barton, both of whom came from Illinois. Stewart arrived in May 1855. He was a free Black man who had been born in North Carolina. He and his wife, Hettie, lived about twenty years in Illinois before pulling up stakes and pioneering in Vernon County. Stewart was sixty years of age when he settled at the town of Forest.

Wesley Barton founded the community of Barton Corners and became its first postmaster in 1859. Since then, Barton Corners has changed its name and is now known as Burr Corners.

Revels Valley in Vernon County is named for another early Black settler, Mycajah Revels, who came from Indiana. In 1856 six Black families migrated here from North Carolina. Some of them bought land and farmed it; others lumberjacked; still others manufactured barrels and shingles. Some of the farmers set up a mill at which they ground sorghum, wheat, and corn. After children shucked and shelled the corn, the miller ground the kernels into cornmeal and corn flour. The wheat also was ground into flour. The juice from the ground sorghum was turned into syrup and molasses.

The 1870 census listed sixty-two Black settlers among eleven families. Fifty years later the 1920 census reported one hundred African Americans in the area. The numbers afterward declined as more and more young people left the farms for better employment opportunities elsewhere. Exhibits in the Vernon County Historical Museum depict the contributions of all ethnic groups to the growth of the county.

DATE BUILT: 1989

ADDRESS: 410 Center Street, Viroqua

TELEPHONE: (608) 637-7396

VISITING HOURS: May 15–Sept. 15, Tues.–Sun. 1–5;
                     Sept. 15–Nov. 1, Thurs.–Fri. 1–4

FEES: None; donations accepted

SOURCES: Judy Gates, curator, Vernon County
                     Historical Museum. *Our Heritage,
                     Discover It. Black Settlers in Rural Wisconsin.*

Note

1. Files of the Milton Historical Society, Milton, Wisconsin.

Works Consulted

Black Settlers in Rural Wisconsin. Zachary Cooper. Madison, Wis.: The State Historical Society of Wisconsin, 1977.

Hippocrene U.S.A. Guide to Black America: A Directory of Historic and Cultural Sites Relating to Black America. Marcella Thum. New York: Hippocrene, 1992.

National Register of Historic Places. Washington, D.C.: National Park Service, 1976.

Our Heritage, Discover It. Viroqua, Wis.: Volunteers from the Vernon County Historical Society and the

Wisconsin Humanities Committee and National Endowment for the Humanities. [brochure]

"Underground Railroad." Dr. Rachel Salisbury. Transcript of tape on the program for the Milton Historical Society, 1976.

"Wisconsin Defies the Fugitive Slave Law." James I. Clark. Madison, Wis.: State Historical Society of Wisconsin, 1955. [paper]

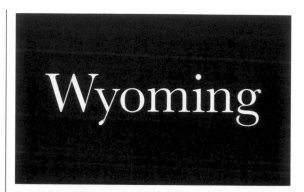

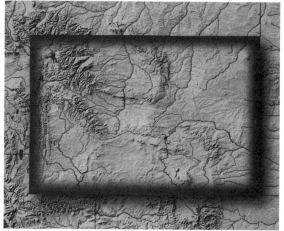

Buffalo

Fort McKinney

In the nineteenth century Black men came to Wyoming with the United States Army. An 1866 act was the impetus for organizing two Black cavalry regiments, the Ninth and Tenth, and four Black infantry regiments, the Thirty-eighth, Thirty-ninth, Fortieth, and Forty-first. Three years later the Thirty-eighth and Forty-first merged to create the Twenty-fourth Regiment and the Thirty-ninth and Fortieth became the Twenty-fifth Regiment. Of the Black units that fought continuously on the frontier through the 1890s, some were stationed in Wyoming. They kept the peace in areas where civilians had settled. They were assigned to fight Native Americans, and they provided protection for stagecoaches and mail stations.

The Ninth Cavalry arrived at Fort McKinney in August 1885. Previously its men had had eighteen years of distinguished service in the Southwest. When they were first stationed here, there were only twelve Black people living in all of Johnson County, and the soldiers encountered some negative racial stereotypes.

Most of the tour of duty for the Ninth Cavalry was routine, even monotonous. Tasks included guard details, stable duty, and serving as kitchen police. The final days, however, for D troop of the Ninth were spectacular ones: four troops of the Ninth departed for South Dakota in a rush to rescue Colonel James Forsyth and his men who were surrounded by Indians in a valley. Ninth Cavalry troops posted at Fort McKinney also spent time on the Shoshone-Arapaho Wind River Indian Reservation at Fort Washakie near here.

Today the exteriors of the remaining buildings at Fort McKinney can be viewed. However, the buildings serve a different purpose today, and interpretation of the Black history of the site is not a priority. The Veterans Home of Wyoming now occupies the site; its staff will give a tour by appointment. Before coming to visit, families may wish to go to the Johnson County Library, which has a wealth of information on Fort McKinney—books, photographs, pamphlets, and newspaper clippings—including material about the Black troops stationed here.

DATE OF SIGNIFICANCE: Ninth Cavalry arrived, 1885

ADDRESS: 700 Veterans Lane (from Buffalo, take US 16 west [the Scenic Byway through the Big Horn Mountains] approximately 2 miles to Fort McKinney); Johnson County Library, 117 N. Adams Street, Buffalo

TELEPHONE: Veterans Home of Wyoming, (307) 684-5511; Johnson County Library, (307) 684-5546

VISITING HOURS: Veterans Home of Wyoming, by appointment Mon.–Fri. 7:30–4:30; Johnson County Library research collection, Mon.–Thurs. 10–8, Fri.–Sat. 10–5

FEES: None

SOURCES: Telephone conversation June 21, 1994, Petty Myers, history librarian, and Nancy Jennings, librarian, Johnson County Library. Telephone conversation June 21, 1994, staff at the Veterans' Home of Wyoming. Todd Guenther, curator, South Pass City State Historic Site. Frances Seely Webb Collection, Casper College. Hayward Schrock, curator Fort Caspar Museum. Helen Larsen, director, Anna Miller Museum, Newcastle, Wyoming. "The Black Regular Army Regiments in Wyoming."

Cheyenne

F. E. Warren Base Museum

In 1898 units of the Twenty-fourth Regiment arrived at Fort D. A. Russell outside Cheyenne and at Camp Pilot Butte near Rock Springs. Those who came to garrison Fort Russell arrived straight from duty in Cuba. Four companies remained in Cheyenne, while six companies continued west to Fort Douglas.

The base museum, one of the original brick structures on the present-day Warren Air Force Base, was originally named Fort D. A. Russell. The last Wednesday in July is Heritage Day and the base opens other buildings for this special event.

DATE ESTABLISHED: Fort, 1867

ADDRESS: Warren Heritage Museum, Building 210, Francis E. Warren Air Force Base, Cheyenne

TELEPHONE: (307) 775-2980

VISITING HOURS: Memorial Day–Labor Day, Wed.–Sat. 1–4; rest of year, Wed., Fri., Sat. 1–4; closed holidays 👥

FEES: None

SOURCES: Patsy Burgess, secretary, Warren Historical Association. Telephone call to site, June 21, 1994.

South Pass City

South Pass City State Historic Site *

The discovery of gold at Sutters Mill in California in 1848 sent many people west hoping to make a fortune. By the 1860s new mother lodes had been discovered in Colorado, Nevada, Idaho, and Montana, and boom towns sprang up to accommodate the thousands of immigrants. In 1867 the Carissa mine began producing gold, and South Pass City was built to accommodate those who had joined the rush to this area.

South Pass is located five miles south of this site. At an altitude of 7,550 feet, South Pass was the lowest and easiest route across the Continental Divide. It also was the halfway point on the Oregon–California Trail, a route of approximately 2,000 miles that led from Missouri to Oregon and California. Thousands of slaves and free Black individuals traversed the trail between 1840 and 1867, and many stayed to work in the historic mining town of South Pass City. In 1868, during a presidential election, the United States marshal from Cheyenne had to escort African Americans to the polls through a mob. Black men inadvertently, because they were allowed to vote, paved the way for making Wyoming the first place in the nation to enfranchise women. William Bright, who was elected to the Territorial Legislature in 1869, introduced the first successful women's suffrage bill in the country. Wyoming then received the nickname "the Equality State."

Today South Pass City is a ghost town maintained by the state. Visitors can see the old buildings and their contents. These silent sentinals of the past belonged to African Americans, too, because Black people were a significant part of the town's heritage. Arriving primarily for mining opportunities, Black men and women worked in various businesses as well as in mining; they also experienced a race riot while here. Although only one photograph and one exhibit panel in South Pass City tell the story of the African American pioneers, their presence was large in this city, today a picturesque ghost town.

DATE ESTABLISHED: 1867

ADDRESS: 36 miles southeast of Lander (turn off at milepost 43, continue for 2 miles on a gravel road to the ghost town); or US 287 southeast from Lander to WY 28 to South Pass City Road

TELEPHONE: (307) 332-3684

VISITING HOURS: May 15–Sept. 30, daily 9–5 🏃

FEES: Adults, 18 or older, $1; children, free

SOURCES: Telephone conversation May 2, 1994, Todd Guenther, curator South Pass City State Historical Site. *Atlas of United States History.* The Academic American Encyclopedia.

Works Consulted

The Academic American Encyclopedia. Danbury, Conn.: Grolier, 1993. [electronic version]

Atlas of United States History. Maplewood, N.J.: Hammond, 1989.

"The Black Regular Army Regiments in Wyoming, 1885–1912." Frank N. Schubert. Master's thesis, University of Wyoming, Laramie, May 1970.

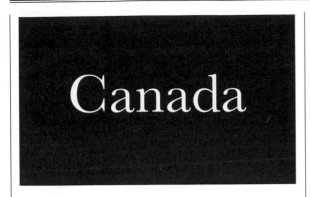

Canada

Across the Detroit River to Freedom

Runaway slaves fled to many areas in Canada in the nineteenth century. Today the province of Ontario, near Detroit, still has several historic sites related to Black Canadians that visitors are able to see by going to Windsor, Ontario, from Detroit by way of a tunnel or by way of the Ambassador Bridge. From Windsor, visitors can travel to several of the sites in a day's round-trip drive.

To fugitive slaves, few places were more symbolic of freedom than Canada. Thousands of slaves who escaped from the South stayed on in northern states of the United States. Many, however, especially after passage of the 1850 Fugitive Slave Law, did not feel safe anywhere in the United States. The law made it possible for a master to pursue "his" escaped slaves all the way into northern states and to take them back into slavery. Some free Black people felt an intense fear that they, too, might be kidnapped and sold into slavery. The northern states no longer were the promised land. Segregation and racism were rampant in politics, employment, education, public accommodations, and social affairs. For all of these reasons, many saw Canada as the true promised land. Although immigrants to Canada had to struggle for their livelihood, they were free from added burdens of legalized slavery and discrimination.

African American immigrants to Canada sometimes met Black people whose families had arrived in Canada in the 1700s. Some of those families had been among the Loyalists who founded Ontario in the 1700s. Other Black people had fought with the British during the American Revolutionary War. When the American Revolution ended in 1783, the area that would become Ontario was a vast wilderness inhabited by Native Americans and fur traders. Many white people who had been loyal to Britain during the revolution were forced into exile. Some came to Canada, taking their slaves with them. Together they cleared the land and established farms.

By 1791 opposition to slavery grew in Canada, culminating in the Anti-Slavery Act of 1793. The act prevented the further importation of slaves and limited the term of bondage of slaves already in Canada. Freed from slavery, Black Canadians began to participate in business, education, and social life. Some fought to defend the British cause during the War of 1812 and the Rebellion of 1837, in part to protect against the possibility of a return to slavery.

By the beginning of the 1800s, Canada had become a haven for slaves escaping from oppression in the United States. From the beginning of the nineteenth century until slaves were emancipated in the United States, 30,000 to 40,000 fugitive slaves made their way to Canada by means of the underground railroad. They arrived by barge, steamer, wagon, or other means.

Several well-known leaders worked directly or indirectly for the underground railroad. The most noted underground railroad leader was Harriet Tubman. Born in slavery about 1820 on a Maryland plantation, she made nineteen trips into the South, guiding hundreds of slaves to freedom in Canada. In 1851 she settled in St. Catherines, Ontario, a primary end point of her rescue efforts. Later she moved to New York. (See the listing in Auburn, New York.)

The white abolitionist John Brown chose Chatham, Ontario, as a setting for planning his raid on the federal arsenal at Harpers Ferry. In 1858, he held a series of meetings in Chatham to plan the strategy for the raid. Many Black people felt the plan would fail and stayed away. Osborne Anderson was one who did attend the meetings in Chatham. Anderson was born free in 1830 in Pennsylvania and attended Oberlin College in Ohio. In 1850 he moved to Canada, where he learned the printing trade. He met John Brown in the spring of 1850 at a convention in Chatham, Ontario. Anderson began serving as recording secretary at some of Brown's secret meetings. He later participated in the raid on the federal arsenal. John Brown and other participants in the raid either were killed or were executed; only Anderson was able to escape. As the sole survivor of the raid, he later wrote an account of the event called *A Voice From Harpers Ferry*. Although the raid was unsuccessful, it had an electrifying effect in awakening the United States to a realization that the question of slavery could not be ignored. The raid was one of the factors leading to the Civil War. (See the Harpers Ferry, West Virginia, listing.)

Black Canadians, often with support from white communities, began to develop thriving communities. The Reverend Josiah Henson, a slave who escaped from Kentucky, started a Black community where the town of Dresden is now located. His Dawn Settlement was established thirteen years before Dresden was established; thus, Henson can be considered the town's founder.

Henry Bibb, a man who escaped from slavery in Kentucky, worked with Josiah Henson to purchase land for settlement. Bibb was born into slavery in 1815 in Shelby County, Kentucky. His mother was a slave; his father was a white man whom Bibb never knew. Bibb was hired out many times to work for others; his earnings were used to pay for the education of his master's son. After enduring years of cruel treatment, he escaped, fleeing to Ohio, then to Detroit in 1842. The Fugitive Slave Law was passed in 1851, making it easier for owners to find and capture slaves who had fled to the North. Bibb fled with his wife to Canada in 1851; there, he established Canada's first Black newspaper, *The Voice of the Fugitive*. Bibb, Josiah Henson, and some white philanthropists developed a plan to purchase thousands of acres of land that would be divided for sale to individual families. Some of the revenues were to be used for educational purposes. Henry Bibb died in 1854.

In 1853 Samuel Ringgold Ward founded another newspaper for Black readers, *The Provincial Freeman*, in Windsor and later published it in Toronto and Chatham. Ward was born in slavery in 1817 in Maryland. When he was about three years old, his family escaped, moving first to New Jersey, then to New York. In 1851 he aided a fugitive slave in a well-known case, and fearing that he might be apprehended for his help, Ward fled to Canada. There he assisted fleeing slaves. He hired Mary Ann Shadd as a subscription agent for his newspaper. By 1854 Shadd was chief editor and writer for the paper, serving as editor between 1854 and 1856. The paper ceased publication by 1857 or 1858 because few of the refugees could read or afford a subscription. Shadd met John Brown when he held his meetings in Chatham; he held one meeting in the house of her brother, Isaac Shadd. Mary Shadd, who later married and settled in Washington, D.C., has been called North America's first Black newspaper woman. (See the listing for Mary Ann Shadd Cary in the Washington, D.C., section.)

Some Black families in Canada chose to live in newly established Black communities. Just outside Chatham, Reverend William King, an Irish-born Presbyterian, established the Elgin Settlement that grew into Canada's most successful self-supporting all-Black community. Some of the schools that Black families established for their own children, including the Buxton Mission School, were popular with white families because they provided an education considered superior to that in the local white schools.

When the Civil War ended and slaves had been legally emancipated in the United States, some former fugitive slaves and expatriated free Black people returned from Canada to the United States because they now felt a measure of safety. Others remained in Canada, which now had become their chosen home.

SOURCES: *An Enduring Heritage. A Salute to Historic Black Abolitionists. Kentucky's Black Heritage. The Education of the Negro Prior to 1861.*

Amherstburg, Ontario

North American Black Historical Museum and Cultural Centre

Melvin Simpson, a resident of Amherstburg, Ontario, originated the idea of founding a museum that would create pride in Black history. He was a member of the Nazrey African Methodist Church, which was built in 1848 by former slaves who had fled from slavery in the United States to freedom in Canada. The underground railroad station in Amherstburg, one of Canada's earliest Black settlements, sheltered them.

Membership at Nazrey Church numbered seventy-five at one time, but it dwindled in the 1970s until only four faithful members remained. Watching the deterioration of the church structure, Simpson realized that it could survive only as part of a museum where visitors could learn about its heritage.

The remaining church members, along with other community residents, gathered resources and started the museum in a restored log house that dated back to the 1840s. They dedicated the North American Black Historical Museum and Cultural Centre in September 1981. The museum complex consists of a restored house and the Nazrey A.M.E. Church. Inside the museum, exhibits and video programs highlight the underground railroad and the history and culture of Canada's Black citizens. The museum has maps of underground railroad routes, slave bills of sale, old newspaper stories, and the old log cabin itself in which is displayed early African American furniture.

Visitors may see other related attractions nearby in the town. In 1841 a group of African American residents met at the John Liberty Home (built about 1830) on George Street and established the Amherstburg Baptist Association. Their goal was to promote unity and spiritual growth among Black Baptists. The congregation at First Baptist Church (built in 1848) on George Street played a part in establishing the Amherstburg Baptist Association.

Across the street from the museum is the Old King Street School, constructed about 1875. The limestone building on the site of the original log schoolhouse later housed the Mount Beulah Church of God in Christ.

DATE ESTABLISHED: Museum, 1981; other structures, 1840s

ADDRESS: 277 King Street, Amherstburg, Ontario

TELEPHONE: (519) 736-5433 or (519) 736-7353

VISITING HOURS: Apr. 18–Nov. 30, Wed.–Fri. 10–5; weekends 1–5 👫

FEES: (Canadian funds) adults, $3; senior citizens and students, $1; families, $7

SOURCES: Personal visit, summer 1990. *Black Historic Sites in Detroit. An Enduring Heritage. The North American Black Historical Museum Celebrates the 150th Anniversary of the Abolition of Slavery Act, 1834–1984 and Ontario's Bicentennial.*

Chatham, Ontario

First Baptist Church

The First Baptist Church, a meeting house constructed in 1853 by former slaves, was the religious and social focal point in Chatham's Black community and a natural gathering place for local abolitionists. On May 10, 1858, a white abolitionist from the United States named John Brown led a meeting in this building to develop final plans for his famous but unsuccessful raid at Harpers Ferry (West Virginia). Thirty-five white and twelve Black antislavery activists were present, including Reverend William C. Monroe from Detroit, who was elected chairman at the meeting. Monroe was the first minister of Detroit's Second Baptist Church, a Black church heavily involved in underground railroad activities. Also present were two of Brown's sons, Owen and John, as well as John Kagi, a white man who was elected Brown's secretary of war; Martin Delaney, a well-known Black activist and co-editor with Frederick Douglass of the *North Star;* and the brother and the husband of Mary Ann Shadd, America's first Black female newspaper editor. (For further information on John Brown, see entries for Kansas City and Osawatomie, Kansas; Chambersburg, Pennsylvania; West Des Moines, Iowa; Akron, Ohio; Lake Placid, New York; and Harpers Ferry, West Virginia. For further information on Reverend William Monroe, see the Detroit, Michigan, section on Second Baptist Church. For further information on John Kagi's house and secret cave, see the listing for John Brown's Cave and Museum in the Nebraska City, Nebraska, section. For further information on Mary Ann Shadd Cary, see the Washington, D.C., section.)

John Brown's plans were for him and his followers to seize the arsenal at Harpers Ferry, call for an uprising of slaves in the South, and then move to a stronghold in the mountains. (Harpers Ferry was at that time in Virginia; it is now in West Virginia, which became a separate state under northern control in 1863.) The bold plan pitted a handful of abolitionists against the armed power of the U.S. government and was bound to fail. Although the October 1859 raid did not attain its goal, it aroused both proslavery and antislavery adherents across the nation and was considered one of the factors that precipitated the Civil War.

Chatham has two other early Black churches—Campbell Chapel African Methodist Episcopal Church on King Street and Victoria Chapel British Methodist Episcopal Church on Wellington Street. Victoria Chapel's congregation hosted the 1856 convention where delegates withdrew from the African Methodist Episcopal Church. The delegates formed the British Methodist Episcopal Church, thus becoming the mother church of that denomination. Fire destroyed the original 1859 Victoria Chapel in 1907, and the congregation erected the present building in 1908.

DATE ESTABLISHED:	First Baptist, 1853; Campbell Chapel, c1887
ADDRESS:	135 King Street E, Chatham, Ontario
TELEPHONE:	Kent–Chatham Tourist Bureau, (519) 354-6125
VISITING HOURS:	Historical marker, daily dawn–dusk; church, at services or by appointment
FEES:	None
SOURCE:	*An Enduring Heritage.*

Dresden, Ontario

Uncle Tom's Cabin and Museum

When the Reverend Josiah Henson and other abolitionists purchased two hundred acres of Dresden land in 1841, their intent was to establish a settlement for refugees from slavery. A previous all-Black settlement, Wilberforce, Ohio, had failed, and the new community, given the optimistic name of Dawn Settlement, was formed as a place that would offer education, work, and security.

Henson was born in Maryland in 1789, and he and his mother were sold twice before he reached adulthood. He married and in 1825 was sent with other slaves to Kentucky. Although he became an ordained minister in 1828, his owners still traded him.

Promises made to a slave meant little if a master chose not to honor those promises. Henson's master gave him permission to earn his freedom for $400. Henson patiently raised the money only to be told that the new price of freedom was $1,000. Until that point of betrayal, Josiah Henson had been a loyal and trusted slave. He even had acknowledged the institution of slavery by tacitly granting that it was reasonable to ask a man to buy his freedom. When his master went back on his word, however, and Henson learned that his master was planning to sell him again, he reassessed the situation and decided to take freedom for himself and his family by escaping.

Reaching Canada, Henson was active in founding Dawn Settlement, which established a church, a brickyard, a sawmill and a gristmill, and Canada's first vocational school. The vocational school's curriculum was designed to provide the kind of education that would help the settlement become self-supporting.

When Henson wrote a pamphlet describing his life story, the Anti-Slavery Society of Boston published it as *The Life of Josiah Henson, Formerly a Slave, Now an Inhabitant of Canada.* One of its readers was Harriet Beecher Stowe, who was moved by the account. She later used some of the incidents described by Henson in her 1852 novel *Uncle Tom's Cabin.* (Unfortunately the name Uncle Tom later became synonymous with a docile, servile personality.) (See the entries for Stowe in the Hartford, Connecticut; Brunswick, Maine; and Cincinnati, Ohio, sections.)

Today the six buildings in the museum complex include the Reverend Henson's house and the British American Institute cemetery where he and his family are buried. The complex also includes the original Dawn Settlement church, a one-story building with arched windows and wooden siding. Henson preached in this church, which was built around 1859. The site also includes a smokehouse made from the trunk of a giant sycamore tree and a cabin that housed newly arrived fugitives. The museum contains artifacts used to punish slaves as well as items and farm implements used by the early settlers.

DATE ESTABLISHED:	1841
ADDRESS:	Kent County Road 40, Dresden, Ontario
TELEPHONE:	(519) 683-2978
VISITING HOURS:	Third weekend in May–last Sun. in Sept., Mon.–Sat. 11–5, Sun. 1–5; closed Oct.–third weekend in May 👫
FEES:	(Canadian funds) Adults, $3; senior citizens and students 12–18, $2.50; children 6–11, $2; children under 6, free; families, $10
SOURCES:	Shelia E. Heflin, Owensboro, Kentucky Public Library. Larry Z. Scott, director, The Kentucky Museum. Park City Daily News, Aug. 21, 1989, Bowling Green, Kentucky. *An Enduring Heritage.*

North Buxton, Ontario

Raleigh Township Centennial Museum

Reverend William King, an Irish-born Presbyterian, was the primary force in establishing the Elgin Settlement in 1849. The settlement just outside Chatham in Raleigh Township was incorporated in 1850; in spite of initial resistance by some members of the whole community, it grew into a thriving all-Black settlement that provided a haven for escaping slaves who wanted to remain in Canada.

Isaac Riley, his wife, and four children were the first settlers in the Elgin Settlement. They arrived in 1849 and were the first to buy land here. Riley's son, Jerome, was a doctor who served in the Civil War and who helped establish the Freedmen's Hospital in Washington, D.C. Most of North Buxton's present residents are descendants of former slaves who came to Canada before the end of the Civil War.

The Raleigh Township Centennial Museum opened in 1961 as a memorial to the Elgin Settlement. It features the history and accomplishments of the settlers and displays artifacts of them and their descendants. The museum complex includes the old school, S.S. No. 13, constructed in 1863. Located next to the school are the Bethel

British Methodist Episcopal Church and Burial Ground, dating from about 1870. First Baptist Church, built in 1883, is located near the B.M.E. Church. St. Andrew's Presbyterian Church, which King established in 1868, is located at the heart of this settlement in Kent County. William King is buried in Maple Leaf Cemetery in Chatham.

The George Hatter House, built about 1863, was home to a former slave from West Virginia who came to Buxton during the 1850s.

DATE ESTABLISHED:	Buildings, c1863; museum, 1961
ADDRESS:	(10 miles south of Chatham) County Road 6, North Buxton, Ontario
TELEPHONE:	(519) 352-4799 or (519) 354-8693
VISITING HOURS:	May–Sept., Wed.–Sun. 1–4:30; other times by appointment; closed Mon., Tues., Oct.–Apr. 👫
SOURCES:	*Black Historic Sites in Detroit. An Enduring Heritage.*

Works Consulted

Black Historic Sites in Detroit. Detroit: Black Historic Site Committee, Detroit Historical Department, 1989.

The Education of the Negro Prior to 1861: A History of the Education of the Colored People of the United States from the Beginning of Slavery to the Civil War. C. G. Woodson. Washington, D.C.: The Associated Publishers, 1919.

An Enduring Heritage: Black Contributions to Early Ontario. Roger Riendeau and the staff of the Ontario Ministry of Citizenship and Culture. Toronto: Durdurn, 1984.

Kentucky's Black Heritage. Frankfort, Ky.: Kentucky Commission on Human Rights, 1971.

The North American Black Historical Museum Celebrates the 150th Anniversary of the Abolition of Slavery Act, 1834–1984 and Ontario's Bicentennial. Amherstburg, Ont.: The North American Black Historical Museum, 1984.

A Salute to Historic Black Abolitionists. Richard L. Green, ed. Chicago: Empak Enterprises, 1988.

Index

NANCY C. CURTIS, PH.D.,
was an assistant professor of early childhood education
at Boston University and, since 1989,
has been coordinator of
Black Student Achievement Programs
for the Anchorage Alaska School District,
in which she lives.

AN AMERICAN LOVE STORY: THIRTY YEARS
IN THE LIFE OF AN INTERRACIAL FAMILY:
BASED ON THE NINE-PART PBS SERIES
Zelda Stern, edited by Penelope Falk and Jennifer Fox
with the staff of *An American Love Story*
PB, $15.95, 1-56584-467-X, 224 pp.
with 40 black-and-white photographs
*The moving love story of a black man and a white woman,
published to coincide with the PBS broadcast of the
nine-part television series.*

BLACK FIRE: THE MAKING OF AN AMERICAN
REVOLUTIONARY
Nelson Peery
PB, $11.95, 1-56584-159-X, 352 pp.
*"A portrait of a fascinating life and a history of
twentieth-century black radicalism."*
—Kirkus Reviews

BLACK HERITAGE SITES: THE NORTH, VOLUME I
Nancy C. Curtis, Ph.D.
PB, $19.95, 1-56584-432-7, 256 pp.
*An award-winning travel guide to major landmarks of
African American history across the North.*

BLACK HERITAGE SITES: THE SOUTH, VOLUME II
Nancy C. Curtis, Ph.D.
PB, $19.95, 1-56584-433-5, 352 pp.
*An award-winning travel guide to major landmarks
of African American history across the South.*

BLACK JUDGES ON JUSTICE
Linn Washington
PB, $16.95, 1-56584-437-8, 288 pp.
*"Searingly candid interviews" (Derrick Bell) with
America's leading African American jurists.*

BLACK POPULAR CULTURE:
DISCUSSIONS IN CONTEMPORARY CULTURE #8
Michele Wallace et al., edited by Gina Dent,
copublished with Dia Center for the Arts
and the Studio Museum of Harlem
PB, $18.95, 1-56584-459-9, 384 pp.
with 58 black-and-white photographs
A Village Voice *Best Book—"spirited debate among
African American artists and cultural critics about issues
from essentialism to sexuality"* (Publishers Weekly).

BLACK TEACHERS ON TEACHING
Michele Foster, foreword by Lisa D. Delpit
HC, $23.00, 1-56584-320-7;
PB, $14.95, 1-56584-453-X; 192 pp.
*An oral history of black teachers that gives "valuable
insight into a profession that for African Americans was
second only to preaching"* (Booklist).

CARIBBEAN SLAVE SOCIETY AND ECONOMY:
A STUDENT READER
Hilary Beckles and Verene Shepherd, editors
HC, $40.00, 1-56584-085-2;
PB, $20.00, 1-56584-086-0; 496 pp.
*A fascinating comparison of slavery in the different
societies of the Caribbean.*

CLASS NOTES
Adolph Reed, Jr.
HC, $25.00, 1-56584-482-3, 320 pp.
*Essays on labor and race from one of America's most
provocative and insightful intellectuals.*

CRITICAL RACE THEORY: THE KEY WRITINGS
THAT FORMED THE MOVEMENT
Kimberly Crenshaw, Neil Gotanda, Gary Peller, and
Kendall Thomas; foreword by Cornel West
HC, $60.00, 1-56584-270-7;
PB, $30.00, 1-56584-271-5; 528 pp.
*The seminal texts on the interplay between law and
race in America.*

DAUGHTERS OF THE DUST: THE MAKING
OF AN AFRICAN AMERICAN WOMAN'S FILM
Julie Dash with Toni Cade Bambara and bell hooks
HC, $27.95, 1-56584-029-1;
PB, $18.95, 1-56584-030-5, 192 pp.
*The making of the film featuring the screenplay,
essays, interviews, Dash's story and production notes,
and brilliant full-color images.*

DISMANTLING DESEGREGATION: THE QUIET
REVERSAL OF BROWN V. BOARD OF EDUCATION
Gary Orfield, Susan E. Eaton, and the Harvard Project
on School Desegregation; foreword by Elaine R. Jones
HC, $30.00, 1-56584-305-3;
PB, $17.95, 1-56584-401-7; 496 pp.
*"A wise...authoritative book" (Jonathan Kozol) on
America's return to segregation.*

DRYLONGSO: A SELF PORTRAIT
OF BLACK AMERICA
John Langston Gwaltney
PB, $12.95, 1-56584-080-1, 320 pp.
*A classic on the ideas, values, and attitudes that inform
ordinary black life in America.*

FAMILIES AND FREEDOM: A DOCUMENTARY
HISTORY OF AFRICAN-AMERICAN KINSHIP
IN THE CIVIL WAR ERA
Ira Berlin and Leslie S Rowland, editors
HC, $25.00, 1-56584-026-9;
PB, $16.95, 1-56584-440-8, 304 pp.
*A sequel to the award-winning Free At Last, moving letters
from freed slaves to their families.*

FREE AT LAST: A DOCUMENTARY HISTORY
OF SLAVERY, FREEDOM, AND THE CIVIL WAR
Ira Berlin and Barbara J. Fields, et al.
HC, $27.50, 1-56584-015-1;
PB, $15.95, 1-56584-120-4, 608 pp.
*Winner of the 1994 Lincoln Prize, some of the most
remarkable and moving letters ever written by Americans,
depicting the drama of Emancipation in the midst of the
nation's bloodiest conflict.*

FREEDOM S UNFINISHED REVOLUTION:
AN INQUIRY INTO THE CIVIL WAR
AND RECONSTRUCTION
American Social History Project
PB, $17.95, 1-56584-198-0, 320 pp.
From the award-winning authors of Who Built America?,
*a ground-breaking high school-level presentation of the
Civil War and Reconstruction.*

HARLEM ON MY MIND: CULTURAL CAPITAL OF
BLACK AMERICA, 1900-1968
Allon Schoener, editor
PB, $19.95, 1-56584-266-9, 272 pp.
*A reissue of the first and most controversial book
to document Harlem life.*

MINING THE MUSEUM: AN INSTALLATION
BY FRED WILSON
Lisa G. Corrin, editor
HC, $45.00, 1-56584-108-5, 148 pp.
*A unique illustrated exploration of how African
and Native American history is methodically omitted
from the institutional record.*

THE MONKEY SUIT: AND OTHER SHORT FICTION
ON AFRICAN AMERICANS AND JUSTICE
David Dante Troutt
HC, $24.00, 1-56584-326-6, 240 pp.
*A genre-bending collection of short stories based on ten
classic legal cases involving African American struggles
for civil and human rights.*

PAUL ROBESON: A BIOGRAPHY
Martin Duberman
PB, $19.95, 1-56584-288-X, 816 pp.
*The critically acclaimed biography of one of this century's
most notable actors, singers, political radicals, and
champions of racial equality.*

PICTURING US: AFRICAN AMERICAN IDENTITY
IN PHOTOGRAPHY
Deborah Willis, editor
HC, $23.00, 1-56584-107-7;
PB, $14.00, 1-56584-106-9; 208 pp.
Winner of the International Center of Photography's
Award for Writing on Photography. Writers, filmmakers,
poets, and cultural critics use photographs to analyze
the modern African American experience.

RACE: HOW BLACKS AND WHITES THINK
AND FEEL ABOUT THE AMERICAN OBSESSION
Studs Terkel
HC, $24.95, 1-56584-000-3, 400 pp.
A candid and riveting chronicle of Americans'
attitude toward race.

REMEMBERING SLAVERY: AFRICAN AMERICANS
TALK ABOUT THEIR PERSONAL EXPERIENCES
OF SLAVERY AND EMANCIPATION:
A BOOK-AND-AUDIOTAPE SET
Edited by Ira Berlin, Marc Favreau, and Steven F. Miller;
published in conjunction with the Library of Congress
and the Smithsonian Institution
Boxed set: HC with 2 60-minute audiocassettes,
$49.95, 1-56584-425-4, 352 pp.
with 50 black-and-white photographs
A book-and-tape set featuring the only known original
recordings of interviews with former slaves, to be aired
on public radio simultaneous with publication.

SLAVES WITHOUT MASTERS: THE FREE NEGRO
IN THE ANTEBELLUM SOUTH
Ira Berlin
PB, $14.95, 1-56584-028-3, 448, pp.
A vivid and moving history of the quarter of a million free
blacks who lived in the South before the Civil War.

UP SOUTH: STORIES, STUDIES, AND LETTERS
OF THIS CENTURY S AFRICAN AMERICAN
MIGRATION
Malaika Adero
PB, $12.95, 1-56584-168-9, 238 pp.
Primary sources from the greatest migration
in American history.

WORDS OF FIRE: AN ANTHOLOGY OF AFRICAN
AMERICAN FEMINIST THOUGHT
Beverly Guy-Sheftall, editor; epilogue by Johnnetta B. Cole
PB, $20.00. 1-56584-256-1, 608 pp.
The first comprehensive collection to trace the development
of African American feminist thought.